Time Out Group Limited
Universal House
251 Tottenham Court Road
London W1T 7AB
Tel + 44 (0)20 7813 3000
Fax + 44 (0)20 7813 6001
Email guides@timeout.com
www.timeout.com

Editorial
Editor Lisa Ritchie
Additional editorial Ros Sales,
Yolanda Zappaterra
Editorial Director Sarah Guy
Management Accountant Margaret Wright

Design
Art Director Anthony Huggins
Designer Thomas Havell
Senior Designer (Commercial) Jason Tansley

Picture desk
Picture Editor Jael Marschner
Deputy Picture Editor Ben Rowe
Freelance Picture Researcher Lizzy Owen

Advertising
Sales Director St John Betteridge
Advertising (New York) Toccara Labady,
Christy Stewart

Marketing
Head of Circulation Dan Collins

Production
Production Controller Katie Mulhern-Bhudia

Time Out Group
Chairman & Founder Tony Elliott
Chief Executive Officer Tim Arthur
Chief Commercial Officer Kim O'Hara
Publisher Alex Batho
Group IT Director Simon Chappell
Group Marketing Director Carolyn Sims

Contributors
**Sections in this guide were written and
researched by** Kevin Aeh, Adam Feldman,
Alexandra Kadlec, Lee Magill, Amy Plitt,
Lisa Ritchie, Jonathan Shannon, Raven
Snook, Mari Uyehara, Jennifer M Wood.

The editor would like to thank the Time Out
New York team and all contributors to the *Time
Out New York* guide, whose work forms the
basis for parts of this magazine.

Cover photography Paolo Giocoso/
SIME/4Corners.

Printed and bound by Wyndeham (Roche) Ltd.

Contents

GW00601063

Times Square

NEW YORK FOR VISITORS 2014/15

New York in Focus

World class

With the opening of the
9/11 Memorial Museum
and – soon – shops,
restaurants and the
city's highest viewpoint,
the World Trade Center
is back in business.

In a city known for its sky-high
aspirations, Ground Zero was
a potent symbol of grief, and
for most of the decade following
9/11, it felt as if the gaping wound in
the middle of downtown Manhattan
would never be healed. Those who
made the pilgrimage to the site
were confronted by an impenetrable
fence, and although redevelopment
plans were announced in 2003,
years went by without much evidence
of progress. More than a decade
on, however, the new World Trade
Center has taken shape. The
National September 11 Memorial
opened on the tenth anniversary
of the attacks and the centrepiece
tower – one of three completed
skyscrapers on the site – is now
America's tallest building (take that,
Chicago!). This spring, on 21 May,
the long-awaited 9/11 Memorial
Museum opens to the public.

Together with the surrounding
tree-shaded plaza, the memorial
and museum occupy half of the WTC
site's 16 acres. The memorial itself,
Reflecting Absence, created by
architects Michael Arad and Peter
Walker, comprises two one-acre
'footprints' of the destroyed towers,
with 30-foot man-made waterfalls –
the country's largest – cascading
down their sides. Bronze parapets
around the edges are inscribed with
the names of the 2,983 victims of
the 2001 attacks at the World Trade
Center, the Pentagon and the
passengers of United Flight 93 as
well as those who lost their lives in
the bombing on 26 February 1993.

The museum pavilion, designed
by Snøhetta – the Oslo-based
firm behind its home city's New
Norwegian National Opera & Ballet
building – rises between the pools.
Its web-like glass atrium houses
two steel trident-shaped columns
salvaged from the base of the Twin
Towers. Visitors will be able to
descend to the vast spaces of
the WTC's original foundations
alongside a remnant of the Vesey
Street staircase known as the

'Survivors' Stairs', which was used
by hundreds of people escaping the
carnage. Foundation Hall contains
a preserved portion of the original
slurry wall, which was built to keep
the Hudson River from flooding
the buildings and withstood their
collapse. Also here is the 'Last
Column', a 36-foot-tall beam
covered in mementos, inscriptions,
and missing-person posters that
became a symbol of the recovery
efforts at Ground Zero.

The museum maintains a
permanent collection of nearly
40,000 artefacts (many of which
were donated by survivors or victims'
families), still and moving images,
archival documents, and oral
histories, which chronicle the
events leading up to the attacks,
commemorate the victims and
document how the world changed
after 9/11. One gallery is devoted
to artists' responses to the incident,
and the In Memoriam exhibition
contains nearly 3,000 portraits, bios
and audio remembrances. Objects
such as the East Village's Ladder
Company 3 fire truck, which was
dispatched to the towers with 11
firefighters who died during the
rescue, will be on display.

'Every artefact in the museum
has a story to tell,' says National
September 11 Memorial Museum
Director Alice Greenwald. 'Whether
monumental pieces of steel
structure from the Twin Towers that
convey both the scale of the site
before 9/11 and the scale of the
disaster on that day, or intimate
objects like a watch worn by a
passenger aboard one of the
hijacked planes that was recovered
at the crash site, they have the
power to connect us to history
with an unmatched immediacy.'

Admission to the museum is $24
($15-$18 reductions, free under-7s,
9/11 family members and rescue
and recovery workers).

In addition to memorialising the
tragedy, the rebuilt World Trade
Center has more impressive visitor
attractions than its previous
incarnation. In spring 2015, One
World Observatory opens on floors
100 to 102 of the 1,776-foot-high
1 World Trade Center, offering far-
reaching vistas that will give the
Empire State Building some serious
competition. Also on the horizon is
a multilevel shopping and dining
complex – larger than six football
fields – operated by shopping-mall
giant Westfield and spread across
the towers and starchitect Santiago
Calatrava's bird-like transit hub.
Lisa Ritchie and Jennifer M Wood

The Met's fashion makeover

The Costume Institute gets a new look – and a new name.

The Metropolitan Museum of Art (*see p37*) may be known for its paintings and ancient treasures, but fashion is increasingly what brings crowds to the institution. Nearly 700,000 people came to the stunning 'Alexander McQueen: Savage Beauty' retrospective in 2011, making it one of the most-visited exhibitions in the museum's history. Last year's 'Punk: Chaos to Couture' was a more modest success, as 450,000 people clamoured to see a replica of iconic NYC club CBGB's grotty bathroom. With more fashion-focused visitors than ever, the timing is perfect for the museum to open its revamped Costume Institute on 8 May. It'll be bigger and better, and – thanks to a particularly helpful benefactor – it'll be known by a new moniker: the Anna Wintour Costume Center. Yes, that Anna Wintour. Condé Nast's artistic director is one of the Met's biggest champions, having raised nearly $125 million for the

institute and frequently organising its annual celeb-studded Costume Institute Gala. And while it's unlikely that the famously tough editor will get as involved with the museum's exhibits as she does with the pages of *Vogue*, the first show in the new space (8 May-10 Aug) feels particularly fitting: it's devoted to 20th-century American designer Charles James, whose pieces were regularly featured in the mag (often in spreads shot by his friend, photographer Cecil Beaton). In addition to showcasing James's exquisite evening gowns and tailored clothing, the retrospective will look at his creative process: the designer was a perfectionist who took inspiration from architecture and used mathematics to create his game-changing pieces. We're guessing Wintour herself approves. *Amy Plitt*

Full steam ahead

It's all change at NYC's railway-line-turned park.

Already among the city's most popular attractions, the High Line (*see p26*) drew more than 4.5 million visitors in 2013. And its appeal is set to grow further in the coming year, as big additions at both ends come to fruition.

Once a gritty zone characterised by wholesale butchers, abandoned industrial spaces and gay nightspots with evocative names like the Mineshaft and the Ramrod, the Meatpacking District became a hub of fashionable boutiques and chic nightspots in the 1990s and early noughties before giving way to more mainstream popularity. What the neighbourhood has lacked, however, is culture. In spring 2015, the Whitney Museum of American Art (*see p36*) will take up residence at the southern foot of the High Line. The museum broke ground on its new home in 2011. Designed by Renzo Piano, the nine-storey, steel-clad building is a dramatic, asymmetrical structure with a series of outdoor terraces that rise like steps above the elevated

> ## Casual strollers can drop in for a taste of culture

park. A dramatic, cantilevered glass entrance leads off from a 8,500-square-foot public plaza below the High Line. The ground floor will have a restaurant helmed by Danny Meyer (the dining guru behind the Shake Shack franchise, among other high-profile eateries), a gift shop and an admission-free lobby gallery and project space – so even casual park strollers can drop in for a taste of culture. At 200,000 square feet, the new space is roughly three times the size of the Whitney's old uptown premises. For the first time, there will be space for a comprehensive display of the collection.

Meanwhile, at the other end of the line, the park hopes to debut the first phase of its final stretch by the end of this year. Eventually extending from 30th Street north to 34th Street and west to Twelfth Avenue, skirting around the under-construction mixed-used Hudson Yards development, it will feature a path through existing wild plant life, benches and picnic tables, plus a kids' play area incorporating the original sleepers. *Lisa Ritchie*

The Whitney's new downtown digs

On the waterfront

New paths and piers are creating an East River oasis.

While waterfront spaces such as lower Manhattan's Battery Park and the Upper West Side's Riverside Park have long been mainstays, in recent years the city has truly begun to harness its unique island topography for the pleasure of its citizens. Over the past decade, large swathes of the shoreline, mostly along the Hudson River, have been transformed into parkland, complete with user-friendly cycling and pedestrian paths. Yet much of the East River-hugging strip, especially in lower Manhattan, has been neglected. Between the ferry terminals east of Battery Park and the Manhattan Bridge, most of the riverfront alongside the traffic-choked FDR Drive was inaccessible, industrial or, in the case of Pier 17, a run-down tourist trap. Now the ambitious East River Esplanade and Piers Project, long championed by former mayor Michael Bloomberg, is filling in some of the gaps of the Manhattan Waterfront Greenway, an evolving network of paths that will eventually circumnavigate the island.

A two-mile esplanade with greenery and reimagined piers will connect Battery Park and the Lower East Side's Pier 35. Already, you can stroll from the Battery Maritime

Building (home of the Governors Island ferry) to Fulton Street, and stop for beer and a bite at the Watermark on the recently constructed bi-level Pier 15. The contemporary glass-fronted bar offers a harbour panorama and outside seating, but you can also admire the view without springing for a drink from the pier's upper deck, which has lounge chairs and grassy patches for chilling. Starting in early May, charter company Hornblower (www.hornblowernew york.com) will offer several daily sightseeing cruises from the pier throughout the summer.

This spring, the latest stretch of the esplanade's riverside paths, plus bocce and basketball courts, is scheduled to open between Pike Street and Rutgers Slip, and ground will break this summer on Pier 35; when it opens in 2015, the site will be a lawned oasis with seating, swings and an inter-tidal habitat for aquatic life. Looking further ahead, South Street Seaport's shuttered Pier 17 is slated to be transformed from a down-at-heel mall to a gleaming mixed-use complex including a marina and global food market – fitting, given that the area was once home to the Fulton Fish Market. *Lee Magill*

From top: renderings of Pier 35 and the esplanade; Watermark on Pier 15.

Theatre royal

Meet the Queen at a lavish supper-club spectacle.

The audience, dressed for a fanciful gala, files down a marble staircase. A nearly naked woman is splayed on a table. Exotic cocktails crowd a bar that resembles a mad scientist's laboratory, and waiters in outré black-tie outfits take you aside for one-on-one encounters. Acrobats get themselves in a twist as patrons stare on at close range.

This is just a sample of the divine decadence at *Queen of the Night*, the almost absurdly deluxe dinner-circus-nightlife experience by immersive-theatre king Randy Weiner. (He's also among the producers of *Sleep No More*, *see p107*, and the downtown fetish-burlesque club the Box.) Set in the Paramount Hotel's fabulous Diamond Horseshoe nightclub – shuttered since 1951, and recently refurbished at a cost of more than $20 million – the show takes the form of a 'dark debutante ball' held for her daughter by an elegant, somewhat sinister dancer known as the Marchesa. Designed and directed by Christine Jones, it borrows vague motifs from *The Magic Flute*; there is also a

continual flurry of circus elements overseen by Shana Carroll, of the neocirque troupe Les 7 Doigts de la Main (several alums of which are in the ensemble).

Like *Sleep No More*, *Queen of the Night* encourages participants to explore the glamorous space at their leisure. But the approach is more interactive: comely performers send you on mix-and-mingle adventures, and when the meal arrives – theatrical presentations of lobster, short ribs and suckling pig, created by chef Jason Kallert and 'food performance' expert Jennifer Rubell – it is served family-style at communal tables. Since the lavish cuisine and wine are included, tickets ($150-$175, or $275-$500 premium) are actually a pretty good deal.

The whole experience is not unlike a cruise-ship version of Stanley Kubrick's 1999 film *Eyes Wide Shut*, but in a pleasantly indulgent way. If it rarely seems quite like theatre, it is certainly immersive – this is how it might feel to be a strawberry dipped in chocolate. *Adam Feldman Diamond Horseshoe at the Paramount Hotel, 235 W 46th Street, between Seventh & Eighth Avenues (1-877 692 0803, www.queenofthenightnyc.com).*

Clash of the concept stores

We compare NYC's lastest fashion emporiums.

THE BASICS

Dover Street Market
160 Lexington Avenue, at 30th Street (1-646 837 7750, www.newyork.doverstreetmarket.com). Subway 6 to 28th or 33rd Street. Open 11am-7pm Mon-Sat; noon-6pm Sun.

Space Ninety 8
98 North 6th Street, between Berry Street & Wythe Avenue, Williamsburg, Brooklyn (www.spaceninety8.com). Subway L to Bedford Avenue. Open 10am-10pm Mon-Sat; 11am-9pm Sun.

NAME SIGNIFICANCE

The market is named after the store's original location on Dover Street in London.

Urban Outfitters opened Space 15 Twenty in LA a couple of years ago, so the Brooklyn outpost is an address-as-name brand extension.

NEIGHBOURHOOD

Murray Hill isn't exactly a fashion destination, so Dover Street gets points for being a high-fashion pioneer in the 'hood.

Ultra-trendy Williamsburg had been a prioriy for Urban Outfitters for a while, and when the company found this warehouse, it decided to open as a bigger concept.

SIZE

With seven small floors, it often feels like a contemporary-art gallery set in a tree house.

Space has five floors, including a rooftop lounge.

DESIGNERS/ MERCHANDISE

Rei Kawakubo of Comme des Garçons carefully curated the merch, including new names (on the fourth floor) mixed in with established brands like Prada, Saint Laurent and Nike.

Most of the goods are products you'd find at any Urban Outfitters (moderately priced men's and women's clothing, jewellery, home-decor goods), plus there's also an expanded record shop.

EXCLUSIVES

Dover Street offers loads of exclusive items and labels in the store, including the Mastermind x Black Comme des Garçons x DSMNY special tee and the Prada at Dover Street Market line.

The first-floor Market Space features handcrafted, one-of-a-kind-pieces – many created in New York. Think everything from 'zines to custom handmade bikes.

ARTWORK

The space is filled with cool art and displays, but a standout is the 60-foot sleeve of yarn by street knitter Magda Sayeg that covers one of the shop's columns.

Brooklyn-based artist Jason Woodside created pieces for the Adidas pop-up. Other original installations and fixtures are featured throughout the store.

FOOD/DRINK

On the first floor, you'll find Rose Bakery, the Parisian patisserie that sells tea, thin-crust pizzette, scones and other organic baked goods.

The Gorbals, the restaurant and bar by chef Ilan Hall (*Top Chef, Knife Fight*), occupies part of the third floor and the rooftop. *Kevin Aeh*

Coney Island thrills again

The seaside destination speeds into the 21st century.

For nearly 90 years, Coney Island's iconic wooden roller coaster the Cyclone has stood as both a literal and metaphoric symbol of its up-and-down history as an amusement hub. Since 2010, it's been part of Luna Park (www.lunaparknyc.com), a pleasure zone named after the original destroyed by fire in 1944 that features more than 40 attractions. This summer, the teeth-rattling ride is getting a state-of-the-art sibling.

Making its debut in late May, the Thunderbolt is the first custom roller coaster to be built alongside the Brooklyn boardwalk since the Cyclone. It's also the first in more than a century to turn riders upside down (in a 100-foot vertical loop). Kicking off with a dramatic 90-degree drop, in the span of two minutes, the stomach-flipping attraction zips passengers over turns, dives, corkscrews and hills at speeds of up to 55 miles per hour.

The Thunderbolt takes its name from the 1920s coaster that occupied the same spot for nearly 60 years. The original made a cameo appearance in Woody Allen's 1977 film *Annie Hall*, providing a shaky foundation for Alvy Singer's childhood home. The new incarnation is just one element of the ongoing revitalisation of the area. Now largely owned by Manhattan-based development firm Thor Equities, Coney Island is in the early stages of a development project, which is slated to include a 27-acre amusement district plus up to 5,000 new housing units. And for the first time in a long while, the seaside spot is finding its way on to the itineraries of tourists and residents alike. But Coney Island's future will always be inexorably linked to its past, with a boardwalk full of nostalgic carnival games, recently resurrected Circus Sideshows courtesy of the Coney Island Museum, and a 115-foot reminder that some thrills never get old. *Jennifer M Wood*

Clouds by Olaf Breuning.
Below: *Common Crossings* by Marianne Vitale

A breath of fresh art

NYC is seeing an explosion of creativity, encouraged by the creation of new green spaces.
Lee Magill previews five amazing – and free – outdoor works.

Skyscraper construction may be rampant in the city, but in recent years, the creation of green spaces is changing the very nature of the 21st-century urban experience. Thanks in no small part to the pro-parks policy of former mayor Michael Bloomberg, the past decade has seen dramatic developments and expansions, including the High Line, Brooklyn Bridge Park and Hudson River Park. While public art has long been a feature of the metropolis, these new open spaces – some of which, like the High Line, have a dedicated curator – are providing fertile ground for even more outdoor installations. And 2014 debuts a bumper crop.

Archeo, High Line
Art has been an important element of the converted rail line since it opened, and projects are commissioned by Cecilia Alemani, the Donald R Mullen, Jr curator & director of High Line Art. The year-long, site-specific group show Archeo (until March 2015), displayed along the High Line (Gansevoort Street to W 30th Street,

between Ninth & Tenth Avenues), features the work of seven international artists who employ outmoded machinery and other industrial relics to explore technology's various pitfalls – forced obsolescence, waste, hubris – and triumphs, from its nostalgia-inspiring beauty to its potential to create a future utopia. Among the works on view is *Common Crossings* by Marianne Vitale, an installation of nine altered railroad crossings. The solid-steel, 1,000lb components, which previously functioned as switches to change the direction of trains, are welded to bases and positioned vertically, creating a kind of totemic gathering that imbues them with a new and surreal identity.

Folly, Madison Square Park
This spring, Madison Square Park (Fifth Avenue to Madison Avenue, between 23rd & 26th Streets), which presents an ongoing programme of high-profile public art, mounts *Folly*, a series of three architectural works

by Rachel Feinstein (7 May-7 Sept 2014). Known for her fairytale-style sculptures, Feinstein riffs on the decorative architectural structures, such as faux ruins and castles, that adorned the grounds of many English stately homes in the 18th and early 19th centuries. As you wander through the park, look out for a house set precariously atop a cliff, a ship stranded in a tree and a Rococo-style hut, each made from connected, thin metal sheets. Although they appear to be three-dimensional, it's an illusion: the pieces have a flat back, like elements of a stage set. As the artist explains: 'This setting… will be the perfect backdrop for my theatre, where the real people who occupy the park will stand in as commedia dell'arte performers.'

Clouds, Central Park
Each spring, the Public Art Fund commissions an installation at the south-east corner of Central Park (Fifth Avenue, at 60th Street), and this year's piece, *Clouds* by the Swiss-born, NYC-based artist Olaf Breuning (on display

Dahn Vo's *We the People*

SAURIEN, ALEXANDER CALDER
With upward-facing spikes and broad arches extending out to claim public space, Calder's bright red, mobile-like but static work holds its own despite sitting beneath the cantilevered corner of a skyscraper. The placement does nothing to diminish its striking monumentality and dramatic impact, which draws in passers-by to interact and explore. While you're here, check out other large-scale works in 590 Madison Avenue's indoor sculpture garden, located just behind *Saurien*.
Madison Avenue, at 57th Street.

CRACK IS WACK, KEITH HARING
The cartoon-like figures, bold letters and vibrating lines in this large mural are characteristic of Haring's punk graffiti aesthetic. Covering both sides of an outdoor handball court's wall, the work conveys the artist's urgent anti-drug sentiment and his belief in democratic art. The locale has become known as the Crack Is Wack Playground, and the piece is one of Haring's last public artworks still visible in New York City.
E 128th Street, at Second Avenue.

LOVE, ROBERT INDIANA
One of the world's most widely recognised and copiously replicated motifs began with three paintings in 1965. MoMA helped to popularise the design by commissioning it for use on its Christmas cards. The artist began creating these one-word poems in sculptural form in 1966, and a monumental, Corten-steel variation was displayed in Central Park for six weeks in 1972. New York's current version – a 12-foot-high, red-and-blue iteration made from polychrome aluminium – has stood proudly in Midtown since 2000.
Sixth Avenue, at 55th Street.

RED CUBE, ISAMU NOGUCHI
Painted a vivid shade and perched on one of its corners, this site-specific sculpture stretches vertically, in seeming competition with the towering buildings around it. Noguchi combines art and architecture, pointedly emphasising the setting: a grey cylindrical hole in the cube's centre offers a focused view into the building behind it.
140 Broadway, between Cedar and Liberty Streets.

until 24 August 2014), is probably the most whimsical to date. It is also the artist's largest public artwork. Six polished blue aluminium clouds, which resemble a child's drawing, appear to float in the sky with the help of a forest-like series of steel supports. Their colourful, cartoon-like presence will no doubt lighten the spirit of parkgoers this summer.

We the People, City Hall Park & Brooklyn Bridge Park
Among the most highly anticipated outdoor artworks this year is 2012 Hugo Boss Prize-winner Dahn Vo's *We the People* (17 May-5 Dec 2014). The installation is part of a work in progress, already more than three years in the making, in which the artist will replicate each and every piece of the Statue of Liberty to scale in copper (the same material as the original). Vo, who had a solo show at the Solomon R Guggenheim Museum last year, will place some of the components in City Hall Park (Broadway, between Chambers Street & Park Row) and Brooklyn Bridge Park (Pier 3 Greenway Terrace, between Clark & Pierrepont Streets, Brooklyn Heights), two public spaces from which the artist's source of inspiration, Lady Liberty, can be seen. According to Vo, he will never put the pieces – which will eventually number 250 – together to replicate the statue itself; the work draws attention to the arduous process that sculptor Frédéric Auguste Bartholdi and his workers undertook to bring his vision to monumental fruition. The largest showing of the work to date, the NYC installation,

> ## New open spaces are providing fertile ground for more installations

presented by the Public Art Fund, will feature more than 50 pieces, including the never-before-seen re-creation of the draped sleeve of the statue's right arm, which will be installed in Brooklyn Bridge Park alongside a replica of the ear.

FLOW.14, Randalls Island
The third annual group show commissioned by the Randalls Island Park Alliance, FLOW.14 (16 May-30 Nov 2014), features works by five participants of the Artist in the Marketplace programme at the Bronx Museum of the Arts. Each piece is meant to inspire an appreciation of the shoreline and invite the viewer to engage with the environment of the uniquely situated island, which is surrounded by the Bronx to the south, Queens to the east and upper Manhattan to the west. Although not residential, it's home to two psychiatric facilities, several homeless shelters, a fire academy and a state police station, and is the site of annual events including May's Frieze New York (*see p11*). Urban explorers can seek out Kant Smith's ghostly *Chain Link House*, situated on a bluff overlooking Ward's Meadow Fields, which, according to the artist, recalls the presence of mental institutions and reform schools on the island. On the island's southern shore, a modern-day shrine by Dean Monogenis explores the concept of genius loci, place-specific protective deities, and the city pillars of Southeast Asia. *Ground*, a series of ten 'sculpted earth chairs' covered in living grass by Jessica Sanders, is among the other contemplation-inspiring works.

Toques of the town

Around the world, chefs are achieving hip-hop-mogul-level stardom, with open kitchens doubling as stages and Twitter followings to rival a Kardashian. If you're hoping to secure one of the hottest tables in NYC, bone up on the culinary heavyweights who are defining the flavour of the rapidly changing dining scene. **Mari Uyehara** offers a taste. Illustrations **Anne Gerrish**

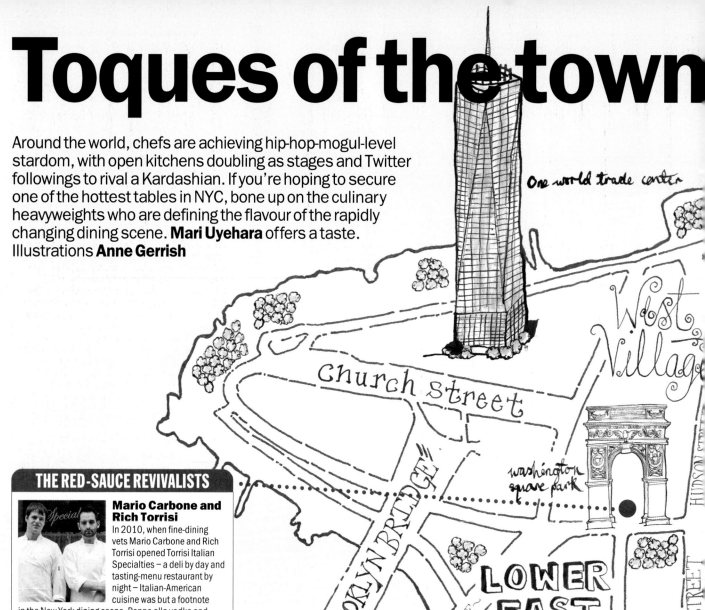

One world trade center

Church Street

West Village

washington square park

BROOKLYN BRIDGE

MANHATTAN BRIDGE

LOWER EAST SIDE

HUDSON STREET

THE RED-SAUCE REVIVALISTS

Mario Carbone and Rich Torrisi

In 2010, when fine-dining vets Mario Carbone and Rich Torrisi opened Torrisi Italian Specialties – a deli by day and tasting-menu restaurant by night – Italian-American cuisine was but a footnote in the New York dining scene. Penne alla vodka and chicken parm were as in vogue as a fat, gold pinky ring, but the pair set out to change the lowly status of these passé favourites with a novel conviction: the exclusive use of American products. Brandishing top-shelf domestic ingredients and pro techniques, the unique venture put an upmarket spin on both casual sandwich shop chow and traditional main dishes (eggplant rollatini filled with tuna belly confit). The updated genre proved wildly popular, drawing lines down the block and quickly outgrowing the space. So, in 2011, Carbone and Torrisi spun off their sandwich operations into a new restaurant, insta-hit **Parm**, and dedicated **Torrisi Italian Specialties** (for both, *see p52*) entirely to its chef's menu. The game-changing hot spots rejuvenated Italian-American cuisine, paving the way for the duo's next venture, **Carbone** (*see p55*), in 2013. A souped-up version of *Godfather*-esque restaurants, the ambitious ode to dusty red-sauce haunts boasted waiters in burgundy Zac Posen tuxes, artwork curated by Julian Schnabel and an expansive menu of luxe takes on tired classics including an antipasti sampler loaded with *crudos*, *uni* and foie gras. Earning heaps of praise from critics – including a five-star review from *Time Out New York* – Carbone and Torrisi pushed *nonna* cuisine from Bronx home kitchens into the spotlight.

THE MASH-UP ARTIST

Danny Bowien

It wasn't so long ago that the idea of cultural food mash-ups seemed dated, conjuring cheesy '90s dishes like wasabi mashed potatoes and that culinary four-letter word, fusion. But a new generation of chefs, like Momofuku's David Chang, laid that old aversion to waste, and one of the most exciting new practitioners is West Coast import Danny Bowien. The Korean-American blasted into town in 2012, with a spin-off of his wildly popular San Francisco eaterie Mission Chinese Food. The quirky downtown restaurant (currently shuttered while it moves locations) sported neon pink lights, a *Twin Peaks*-themed bathroom and exciting boundary-crossing plates, such as kung pao pastrami. For his sophomore venture, he pulled a surprising move, switching gears from Chinese to Mexican with **Mission Cantina** (*see p53*) in 2013. The Lower East Side hot spot turns out tasty, creative plates, including tacos with primo ingredients, such as skate and cumin lamb.

THE GASTROPUB CHAMPS

April Bloomfield

It's hard to imagine NYC without gastropubs, now found in nearly every neighbourhood, but in 2004, when British chef April Bloomfield and restaurateur Ken Friedman opened the **Spotted Pig** (*see p56*), there were none. Friedman (a music industry career changer) and Bloomfield (a vet of London's storied River Café) seemed an unlikely match-up, but they proved to be a powerhouse package. The Brit-Italian Spotted Pig – with its irreproachable comforts (a Roquefort-topped burger) and serious kitchen plates (ricotta gnudi) – was a slam dunk from the start, racking up two-hour waits midweek. Bloomfield's predilection for off cuts, in dishes like a crispy pig's ear salad, helped usher in the city's pork-and-offal era. Building on their success, the pair opened two ventures in cool-kid hotel the Ace. The **Breslin Bar & Dining Room** took the carnivorous excess of the Spotted Pig to improbable new levels, while the **John Dory Oyster Bar** (for both, *see p58*) showcased the meat maven's hand at seafood. Countless eateries have tried to mimic the formula, but have yet to surpass the duo's restaurants, where the food is as good as ever and the waits are just as long.

THE HAUTE EVANGELISTS

Daniel Humm

A few years back, certain food-scene prognosticators declared fine dining dead, battered by years of economic woes and the rise of casual restaurants offering innovative fare. But Daniel Humm and business partner Will Guidara put their money on big-ticket dining. In 2011, Humm and Guidara, then executive chef and GM, respectively, at the tony **Eleven Madison Park** (*see p58*), bought out owner Danny Meyer to reach for greater ambitions. They did away with the à la carte menu that had earned the restaurant four stars from the *New York Times*. Their 2012 revamp rolled out a tasting-menu tribute to New York City, showcasing flights of fancy such as tableside egg creams and a smoke-filled glass cloche of sturgeon representing the city's great delicatessen traditions. Humm and Guidara's high-stakes gamble paid off, injecting new energy in the city's haute cuisine. For their sequel project, the dapper pair teamed up with the opulent NoMad Hotel. Decked out in velvet curtains and mahogany wood, the eponymous dining room is matched by recherché fare, like a foie gras and truffle stuffed roasted chicken. With a recently published book (*I Love New York*) and new projects rumoured on the horizon, the duo have shaken up the world of high-end dining with a bit of New York verve.

THE SCI-CULINARY WIZARD

Wylie Dufresne

One of the world's most admired chefs, New York native Wylie Dufresne is renowned for his subversive creativity, but he started his career on a traditional path, boning up on classical cuisine with French empire-builder Jean-Georges Vongerichten. It was at his game-changing restaurant, **wd~50**, opened in 2003, that Dufresne developed his signature experimental cuisine, turning out witty, science-driven eats, like 'egg yolks' made of carrot juice and ice-cream fashioned in the uncanny likeness of an everything bagel. A decade later, Dufresne – now a James Beard Award winner and *Top Chef Masters* star – launched his follow-up, the highly anticipated **Alder** (*see p53*). While wd~50 evinces more formal dining with a tasting-menu-only format, hushed atmosphere and challenging composed plates, Alder is its casual analogue. The rollicking à la carte East Village spot highlights brainy dishes, such as clam chowder accompanied by 'oyster crackers' made with the actual bivalves, and pastrami on rye reimagined as a pasta dish, bringing Dufresne's conceptual cooking to the masses.

THE URBAN LOCAVORES

Carlo Mirarchi

It's now something of a cliché that young restaurants aspire to a seasonal, local ideal. But chef Carlo Mirarchi, along with partners Brandon Hoy and Chris Parachini, took Greenmarket aspirations to a new stratosphere with **Roberta's** (*see p64*). Opened in 2008 in the no-man's-land of Bushwick, Brooklyn, the ramshackle pizzeria debuted without gas or a liquor licence, just an oven and two hot plates, drawing post-shift chefs and hipsters for creative pies like a Paiges Breakfast Burrito (egg, potato, sausage, jalapeño). A DIY ethos pervades the spot, with plates incorporating pickings from the backyard garden and a food-centric radio station. But the menu evokes a focused simplicity, even as it evolved to encompass locally cured meats, thoughtful salads and handmade pastas. Playing the dual role of hipster clubhouse and required stop for visiting dignitaries in the food world (Alice Waters) and beyond (Bill and Hillary Clinton), the joint transformed Bushwick from desolate outer-borough 'hood into a legit dining destination. The team of young guns has since gone high-end, opening sleek on-site tasting-menu restaurant **Blanca**, which baits well-heeled gastronauts to a fringe locale for exceptional fare.

Flatiron building

east village

BROADWAY

MADISON AVENUE

PARK AVENUE

IN BROOKLYN

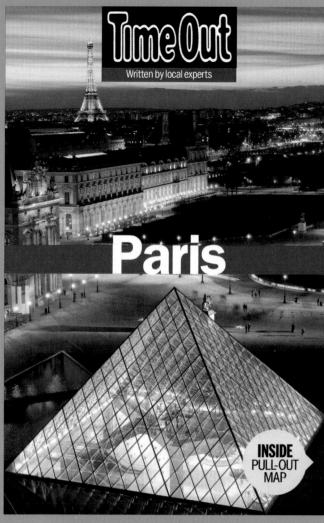

Written by local experts, rated 'Top Guidebook Brand' by Which?

Travel beyond the clichés

All new 2014 guidebook. Rewritten, redesigned and better than ever.

Keep up, join in Time Out

Diary

Mermaid Parade. *See p12.*

Plan your perfect trip

Time it right with our year-round guide to the best celebrations and shows.

New Yorkers hardly struggle to find something to celebrate. The venerable city-wide traditions are well known, but don't miss the neighbourhood shindigs: you can soak up the local vibe at quirky annual events such as Brooklyn's **Mermaid Parade** or East Village beatnik bash **Howl!**, and take advantage of free summer concerts and outdoor films in the city's green spaces, such as Bryant, Central and Madison Square Parks. We've given 2014 dates where possible, but before you set out or plan a trip around an event, it's wise to call or check online first as dates, times and locations are subject to change.

Spring

Armory Show
Though its name pays homage to the 1913 show that introduced avant-garde European art to an American audience, this contemporary international art mart debuted in 1999. It's now held on the Hudson River. *Piers 92 & 94, Twelfth Avenue, at 55th Street, Hell's Kitchen (1-212 645 6440, www.thearmoryshow. com). Subway C, E to 50th Street. Date early Mar.*

St Patrick's Day Parade
This massive march is even older than the United States – it was started by a group of homesick Irish conscripts from the British army in 1762. Today, thousands of green-clad merrymakers strut to the sounds of pipe bands. *Fifth Avenue, from 44th to 86th Streets, Midtown to Upper East Side (www.nycstpatricksparade.org). Date 17 Mar.*

Easter Parade
Starting at 10am on Easter Sunday, Fifth Avenue becomes a car-free promenade of gussied-up crowds milling around and showing off their extravagant bonnets. *Fifth Avenue, from 49th to 57th Streets, Midtown (1-212 484 1222). Subway E, M to Fifth Avenue-53rd Street. Date late Mar/early Apr.*

Tribeca Film Festival
See p90. Date Apr.

Sakura Matsuri (Cherry Blossom Festival)
The annual Sakura Matsuri celebrates both the blooms and Japanese culture with concerts, traditional dance, manga exhibitions, cosplay fashion shows and tea ceremonies. *For listings, see p43 Brooklyn Botanic Garden. Date late Apr.*

TD Five Boro Bike Tour
Thousands of cyclists take over the city for a 40-mile, car-free Tour de New York. The route begins near Battery Park, moves up through Manhattan and makes a circuit of the boroughs before winding up at Staten Island's Fort Wadsworth for a festival. *Lower Manhattan to Staten Island (1-212 870 2080, www.bikenewyork. org). Date 4 May.*

Frieze Art Fair New York
The New York edition of the tent-tastic London art fair first arrived on Randalls Island in 2011. A global array of around 190 galleries set up shop under a temporary structure overlooking the East River. *Randalls Island Park, (www.frieze newyork.com). Date 9-12 May.*

Lower East Side Festival of the Arts
Theater for the New City runs this annual celebration of artistic diversity. Over the course of three days, the venue's four theatres feature more than 70 theatrical troupes, poetry readings, aerial dance, films and family-friendly programming. Food and craft vendors set up outside. *Theater for the New City, 155 First Avenue, between 9th & 10th Streets, East Village (1-212 254 1109, www.theaterforthenewcity.net). Subway L to First Avenue; 6 to Astor Place. Date 23-25 May.*

Washington Square Outdoor Art Exhibit
In 1931, Jackson Pollock and Willem de Kooning propped up a few of their paintings on the sidewalk near Washington Square Park and called it a show. A lot has changed since then: now, more than 125 artists and artisans exhibit at the Washington Square Outdoor Art Exhibit. *Various streets surrounding Washington Square Park, from University Place, at 13th Street, to Schwartz Plaza, at 3rd Street, Greenwich Village (1-212 982 6255, www.wsoae.org). Subway A, B, C, D, E, F, M to W 4th Street; N, R to 8th Street-NYU. Date 24-26 May, 31 May, 1 June & 30 Aug-1 Sept, 6, 7 Sept.*

TOP TIP!
Cultural calendar
For more festivals and seasonal soirées, plus additional details about the annual events listed here, consult www.timeout.com/ newyork.

Summer

Howl! Festival
A reading of Allen Ginsberg's seminal poem kicks off this three-day arts fest – a grab bag of art events, film screenings, poetry readings, performance art and much more. *Various East Village locations (1-212 466 6666, www.howlfestival.com). Date 6-8 June.*

SummerStage
Now held in parks across the city, these concerts embody summer for many New Yorkers, and break down the boundaries between artistic mediums. Rockers, world music stars, orchestras and other performers take over the main stage in Central Park at this very popular, mostly free annual series. Show up early or plan to listen from outside the enclosure gates.
Rumsey Playfield, Central Park, entrance on Fifth Avenue, at 72nd Street, Upper East Side (1-212 360 2777, www.summerstage.org). Subway 6 to 68th Street-Hunter College. Date June-Aug.

Shakespeare in the Park
See p110. Date 3 June-17 Aug.

Celebrate Brooklyn!
Community arts organisation BRIC launched this series of outdoor performances to revitalise Prospect Park, and now the festival is Brooklyn's premier summer fête. It includes music, dance, film and spoken word acts.
Prospect Park Bandshell, Prospect Park West, at 9th Street, Park Slope, Brooklyn (1-718 855 7882, www.bricartsmedia.org). Subway F to Seventh Avenue. Date 3 June-24 Aug.

National Puerto Rican Day Parade
A whopping 80,000 Nuyoricans take part in the march, including *vejigantes* (carnival dancers). There are also colourful floats and live salsa and reggaetón bands at this freewheeling celebration of the city's largest Hispanic community and its culture.

Fifth Avenue, from 44th to 79th Streets, Midtown to Upper East Side (1-718 401 0404, www.nationalpuertorican dayparade.org). Date 8 June.

Governors Ball Music Festival
Catch big names in rock, pop and hip hop at this three-day outdoor festival. The 2014 lineup includes the Strokes, Jack White, TV on the Radio, local-boys-made-good Vampire Weekend, dubstep renegade Skrillex, UK house sensation Disclosure and soul fantasist Janelle Monáe.
Randalls Island Park (www.governors ballmusicfestival.com). Date 6-8 June.

Big Apple Barbecue Block Party
Get your fill of the best 'cue around as the country's top pit masters come together for this two-day outdoor carnivore's paradise. Bands, and chefs' demos and tips are also on the menu.
Madison Square Park, Flatiron District (www.bigapplebbq.org). Date 7, 8 June.

Museum Mile Festival
Eight of the city's most prestigious art institutions – including the Met, the Guggenheim and the Museum of the City of New York – open their doors to the public free of charge. Music, dance and children's activities turn this into a 23-block-long celebration, but you'll have to arrive early to stand a chance of getting into the museums themselves.
Fifth Avenue, from 82nd to 105th Streets, Upper East Side (1-212 606 2296, www.museummilefestival.org). Date 10 June.

River to River Festival
Lower Manhattan organisations present hundreds of free events – from walks to all manner of arts performances – at various waterside venues. Past performers have included Patti Smith, Laurie Anderson and Angélique Kidjo.
Various venues along the West Side & southern waterfronts of Manhattan (1-212 219 9401, www.rivertoriver nyc.com). Date 19-29 June.

SummerStage

Mermaid Parade
Glitter-covered semi-nude revellers, aquatically adorned floats and classic cruisers fill Surf Avenue for this annual art parade.
Coney Island, Brooklyn (1-718 372 5159, www.coneyisland.com). Subway D, F, N, Q to Coney Island-Stillwell Avenue. Date 21 June.

Midsummer Night Swing
Lincoln Center's Damrosch Park is turned into a giant dancefloor as bands play salsa, Cajun, swing and other music. For three weeks (Tue-Sat), each night's party is devoted to a different dance style, and is preceded by lessons. Beginners are, of course, welcome.
Damrosch Park at Lincoln Center Plaza, W 62nd Street, between Columbus and Amsterdam Avenues, Upper West Side (1-212 721 6500, www.midsummer nightswing.org). Subway 1 to 66th Street-Lincoln Center. Date 24 June-12 July.

Warm Up
Since 1997, PS1's courtyard has played host to one of the most anticipated, resolutely underground clubbing events in the city. Thousands of dance-music fanatics and alt-rock enthusiasts make the pilgrimage to Long Island City on summer Saturdays to drink and dance. The sounds range from spiritually inclined soul to full-bore techno.
MoMA PS1 (for listings, see p44). Date 28 June-6 Sept.

NYC LGBT Pride March
Downtown Manhattan becomes a sea of rainbow flags as lesbian, gay, bisexual and transgendered people from the city and beyond parade down Fifth Avenue in commemoration of the 1969 Stonewall Riots. After the march, there's a massive street fair and a dance on the West Side piers.
From Fifth Avenue, at 36th Street, to Christopher Street, Midtown to West Village (1-212 807 7433, www.nycpride.org). Date 29 June.

Macy's Fourth of July Fireworks
The city's star Independence Day attraction is also the nation's largest Fourth of July fireworks display. Traditionally launched from barges on the East River, the fireworks relocated to the Hudson in 2009, but new mayor Bill de Blasio has moved them back to the East Side this year so they're visible to more New Yorkers. The pyrotechnics start at around 9pm, but you'll need to scope out your vantage point much earlier. Spectactors are packed like sardines at prime spots.
1-212 494 4495, www.macys.com/ fireworks. Date 4 July.

Lincoln Center Out of Doors
Free dance, music, theatre, opera and more make up the programme over the course of three weeks at this family-friendly and ambitious festival.
For listings, see p102 Lincoln Center. Date 23 July-10 Aug.

Harlem Week
Get into the groove at this massive culture fest, which began in 1974 as a one-day event. Harlem Day is still the centrepiece of the event, but 'Week' is now a misnomer; besides the street fair serving up music, art and food along 135th Street, a wealth of concerts, films, dance performances, fashion and sports events are on tap for about a month.
Various Harlem locations (1-212 862 8477, www.harlemweek.com). Subway B, C, 2, 3 to 135th Street. Date 27 July-23 Aug.

Summer Restaurant Week
Twice a year, for two weeks or more at a stretch, some of the city's finest restaurants dish out three-course prix-fixe lunches for $25; some places also offer dinner for $38. For the full list of participating restaurants, visit the website. You'll need to make reservations well in advance.
www.nycgo.com/restaurantweek. Date late July/early Aug.

New York International Fringe Festival
Wacky and sometimes wonderful, downtown's Fringe Festival – inspired by the Edinburgh original – shoehorns hundreds of arts performances into 16 theatre-crammed days.
Various venues (1-212 279 4488, www.fringenyc.org). Date 8-24 Aug.

US Open
Flushing, Queens, becomes the centre of the tennis universe when it hosts the final Grand Slam event of the year.
USTA Billie Jean King National Tennis Center, Flushing Meadows Corona Park, Queens (1-718 760 6200, www.usopen.org). Date 24 Aug-8 Sept.

Autumn

West Indian-American Day Carnival Parade
This Caribbean celebration is never short on costumed stilt dancers, floats

blaring soca and calypso music, and plenty of flags from countries such as Barbados, Jamaica, and Trinidad and Tobago.
Eastern Parkway, from Schenectady Avenue to Flatbush Avenue, Crown Heights, Brooklyn (1-718 467 1797, www.wiadcacarnival.org). Subway 2, 3 to Grand Army Plaza; 3, 4 to Crown Heights-Utica Avenue. Date 1 Sept.

Feast of San Gennaro
Celebrate the martyred third-century bishop and patron saint of Naples at this 11-day festival that fills the streets of Little Italy every year. Come after dark, when sparkling lights arch over Mulberry Street and the smells of frying *zeppole* (custard- or jam-filled fritters) and sausages hang in the air. On the final Saturday in September, a statue of San Gennaro is carried in a Grand Procession outside the Most Precious Blood Church (109 Mulberry Street, between Canal & Hester Streets).
Mulberry Street, between Canal & Houston Streets; Grand Street, between Baxter & Mott Streets; Hester Street, between Baxter & Mott Streets, Little Italy (1-212 768 9320, www.sangennaro.org). Subway B, D, F, M to Broadway-Lafayette Street; J, N, Q, R, Z, 6 to Canal Street. Date 11-21 Sept.

Next Wave Festival
The festival is among the most highly anticipated of the city's autumn culture offerings, as it showcases only the very best in avant-garde music, dance, theatre and opera.
For listings, see p101 Brooklyn Academy of Music. Date Sept-Dec.

Dumbo Arts Festival
Dumbo has been an artists' enclave for decades, and this weekend of art appreciation is hugely popular. Expect gallery shows, installations, open studios, concerts and other arts events.
Various locations in Dumbo, Brooklyn (1-718 488 8588, www.dumboarts festival.com). Subway A, C to High Street; F to York Street. Date late Sept.

New York Film Festival
See p90. Date 26 Sept-12 Oct.

Open House New York Weekend
More than 150 architectural sites, private homes and landmarks open their doors during a weekend of urban exploration. Behind-the-scenes tours and educational programmes are also on offer.
1-212 991 6470, www.ohny.org. Date 11, 12 Oct.

CMJ Music Marathon & Film Festival
The annual *College Music Journal* schmooze-fest draws fans and music-industry types to one of the best showcases for new rock, indie, hip hop and electronica acts. The Film Festival, which runs in tandem, includes a wide range of feature and short films.
Various venues (1-212 235 7027, www.cmj.com). Date 21-25 Oct.

BARKING MAD
Check out the wackiest events on the NYC calendar.

Tompkins Square Park Halloween Dog Parade

Like an adult air-guitar tournament, the **Air Sex World Championships** (late June or July, www.airsexworld.com) lets punters display their skills playing an imaginary…um…instrument. Hosted by comedian Chris Trew, the young, virile and shameless take to the stage to show off their erotic technique. The rules are simple: no nudity, all orgasms must be simulated and there must be an imaginary partner or object involved in your act. A panel of judges (comics, sex professionals) adjudicate the first round, with the audience choosing the eventual winner. (New York is but one stop on the Air Sex World Championships' nationwide tour.)

To see a plethora of puppies in adorable outfits, head to late October's **Tompkins Square Park Halloween Dog Parade** (www.firstrunfriends.org), which has been an East Village institution for more than two decades. The getups are remarkably elaborate and conceptual; previous years have included Evita, ET and one of the sandworms from *Beetlejuice*. But one of our favourites was a spraypaint-toting pooch with a canvas bearing the signature 'Barksy'.

Improv Everywhere's annual barefaced, bare-legged mission, the **No Pants Subway Ride** (www.improveverywhere.com) began in January 2002 with a few people in one car on the downtown 6 train, but it's grown into a well-publicised mass event. Admittedly, it's not the mildly subversive, playful prank it was – it's now a chance for New Yorkers to perform a cheeky feat while supported by thousands of fellow residents. For unsuspecting visitors, it's a surreal spectacle.

New York City Wine & Food Festival
The Food Network's epicurean feast offers four belt-busting days of tasting events and celebrity-chef demos.
Various locations (www.nycwff.org). Date 16-19 Oct.

Village Halloween Parade
The sidewalks at this iconic Village shindig are always packed. For the best vantage point, don a costume and watch from inside the parade.
Sixth Avenue, from Spring to 16th Streets, Greenwich Village (www.halloween-nyc.com). Date 31 Oct.

Winter

New York Comedy Festival
This five-day laugh fest features both big names (Jerry Seinfeld, Louis CK and Ricky Gervais in recent years) and up-and-comers.
Various venues (www.nycomedy festival.com). Date early Nov.

New York City Marathon
Around 45,000 runners hotfoot it through all five boroughs over a 26.2-mile course.
Staten Island side of the Verrazano-Narrows Bridge to Tavern on the Green in Central Park (1-212 423 2249, www.tcsnycmarathon.org). Date 2 Nov.

Macy's Thanksgiving Day Parade & Balloon Inflation
At 9am on Thanksgiving Day, the stars of this nationally televised parade are the gigantic balloons, the elaborate floats and good ol' Santa Claus. The evening before, New Yorkers brave the cold night air to watch the rubbery colossi take shape at the inflation area around the Museum of Natural History (beginning at 79th Street & Columbus Avenue).
Central Park West, at 77th Street, to Macy's, Broadway, at 34th Street, Upper West Side to Midtown (1-212 494 4495, www.macys.com/parade). Date 27 Nov.

Rockefeller Center Tree-Lighting Ceremony
Proceedings start at 7pm, but this festive celebration is always mobbed, so get there early. Most of the two-hour event is devoted to celebrity performances, and then the 30,000 LEDs covering the massive evergreen are switched on.
Rockefeller Center, Fifth Avenue, Midtown (1-212 332 6868, www.rockefellercenter.com). Subway B, D, F, M to 47th-50th Streets-Rockefeller Center. Date late Nov/early Dec.

Unsilent Night
Downtown's arty, secular answer to Christmas carolling. Boom-box-toting participants gather under the Washington Square Arch, where they are given a cassette or CD of one of four different atmospheric tracks; you can also download the Unsilent Night app and sync up via smartphone. Everyone then presses play at the same time and marches through the streets of New York, filling the air with a beautiful, echoing 45-minute piece.
Washington Square Arch, Fifth Avenue, at Waverly Place, to Tompkins Square Park, Greenwich Village to East Village (www.unsilentnight.com). Subway A, B, C, D, E, F, M to W 4th Street. Date mid Dec.

New Year's Eve in Times Square
Get together with a million others and watch the giant illuminated Waterford Crystal ball descend amid a blizzard of confetti and cheering. Arrive by 3pm (earlier if the weather is nice) to stake out a spot in the Broadway-Seventh Avenue bowtie and be prepared to stay put. There are no public restrooms or food vendors, and leaving means giving up your spot. Endurance is rewarded with celebrity performances held across two stages, from 6pm.
Times Square, Theater District (1-212 768 1560, www.timessquarenyc.org). Subway N, Q, R, S, 1, 2, 3, 7 to 42nd Street-Times Square. Date 31 Dec.

New Year's Day Marathon Benefit Reading
Around 140 of the city's best poets, artists and performers gather at St Mark's Church in-the-Bowery and, one after another, recite their work to a hall full of listeners.
Poetry Project at St Mark's Church, 131 E 10th Street, at Second Avenue (1-212 674 0910, www.poetryproject.org). Date 1 Jan.

Winter Restaurant Week
Another opportunity to sample gourmet food at palatable prices.
For listings, see p12 Summer Restaurant Week. Date Jan/early Feb.

Chinese New Year
Gung hay fat choy!, the greeting goes. Chinatown is charged with energy during the two weeks of the Lunar New Year. The firecracker ceremony and parade are key events.
Around Mott Street, Chinatown (www.betterchinatown.com). Subway J, N, Q, R, Z, 6 to Canal Street. Date Feb.

Explore

Museums, attractions and great days out

Explore

Flatiron Building. *See p28*.

Discover New York

From iconic sights to offbeat curiosities, the metropolis never fails to fascinate.

First, accept that you can never see it all. The typical week's visit to the city will involve some tough choices. Similarly, it's self-defeating to attempt to hit all the major collections in one visit to an institution as large as the **Metropolitan Museum of Art** (*see p37*) or the **American Museum of Natural History** (*see p34*). So plan, pace yourself and take time to enjoy aimless wandering in picturesque areas like the West Village or Central Park. Because the city's museums are privately funded, and receive little or no government support, admission prices can be steep. However, these usually include entry to temporary shows as well as the permanent collections, and many institutions offer one day or evening a week when admission fees are either waived or switched to a

voluntary donation (and remember, 'suggested donation' prices are just that). Many museums are closed on Mondays – except on some public holidays, such as Columbus Day and Presidents' Day.

Charge up a MetroCard and you can travel seamlessly by subway and bus. The subway (*see p122*) is highly efficient and runs 24 hours a day. It is generally well populated, clean and relatively easy to navigate. Of course, you should keep your wits about you and take basic precautions, but New York these days is a pretty safe place. However, the very best way to get to know the city is by walking. Manhattan is a mere 13.4 miles long and 2.3 miles across at its widest point, and once you've mastered the grid, it's easy to find your way around (although it gets a little trickier downtown).

The Financial District

Commerce has been the backbone of New York's prosperity since its earliest days as a Dutch Colony. The southern tip of Manhattan quickly evolved into the Financial District because, in the days before telecommunications, banks established their headquarters near the port. The oldest part of the city, lower Manhattan is the city's financial, legal and political powerhouse, but as the arrival point for the 19th-century influx of immigrants, it played another vital role in the city's evolution.

This part of town is still in flux, as more than a decade of construction moves towards completion. The new

World Trade Center is finally taking shape and, in the wake of Hurricane Sandy's damage, the South Street Seaport is being transformed from a touristy eyesore into a waterfront destination where locals will want to stroll, shop and relax.

BATTERY PARK TO WALL STREET

It's easy to forget that Manhattan is an island – what with all those gargantuan skyscrapers obscuring your view of the water. Until, that is, you reach the southern point, where salty ocean breezes are reminders of the millions of immigrants who travelled on steamers in search of prosperity, liberty and a new home. This is where they landed, after passing through Ellis Island's immigration and quarantine centres.

On the edge of Battery Park, Castle Clinton was one of several forts built to defend New York Harbor against attacks by the British in the War of 1812 (others included Castle Williams on Governors Island, Fort Gibson on Ellis Island and Fort Wood, now the base of the Statue of Liberty). After serving as an aquarium, immigration centre and opera house, the sandstone fort is now a visitors' centre and ticket booth for **Statue of Liberty** and **Ellis Island** tours (*see p18*), as well as an intimate, open-air setting for concerts. The park is a key venue of the annual **River to River Festival** (*see p12*) – a summer celebration of downtown culture and the city's largest free arts festival.

Joining the throngs making their way to Lady Liberty, you'll head south-east along the shore, where several ferry terminals jut into the harbour. Among them is the **Whitehall Ferry Terminal**, the boarding place for the **Staten Island Ferry** (1-718 727 2508, www.nyc.gov/dot). Constructed in 1907, the terminal was severely damaged by fire in 1991, but was completely rebuilt in 2005. More than 75,000 passengers take the free, 25-minute journey to Staten Island each day; most are commuters but many are tourists, taking advantage of the views of the Manhattan skyline and the Statue of Liberty. Before the Brooklyn Bridge was completed in 1883, the Battery Maritime Building (11 South Street, between Broad & Whitehall Streets) served as a terminal for the ferry services between Manhattan and Brooklyn. Now, it's the launch point for a ferry to tranquil **Governors Island** (*see p19* **Island Getaway**). On the park's

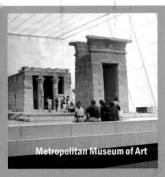

Metropolitan Museum of Art

Critic's choice

1 **National September 11 Memorial & Museum** A moving and monumental tribute. *See p19.*

2 **High Line** All aboard the former freight track-turned-park. *See p26.*

3 **Empire State Building** The world's most iconic skyscraper. *See p31.*

4 **Museum of Modern Art** Modern masterpieces and much more. *See p31.*

5 **Metropolitan Museum of Art** Dip into this massive era- and globe-spanning collection. *See p37.*

northern waterfront, the 1886 Pier A Harbor House, once the HQ for the harbour police, is reopening as a massive dining and drinking destination (www.piera.com).

Just north of Battery Park you'll find the triangular Bowling Green, the city's oldest park and a popular lunchtime spot for Financial District workers; it's also the front lawn of the Alexander Hamilton US Custom House, now home to the **National Museum of the American Indian**.

Dwarfed by the surrounding architecture, the Stone Street Historic District is a small pocket of restored 1830s buildings on the eponymous winding cobblestoned lane, also encompassing South William and Pearl Streets and Coenties Alley. Office workers and tourists frequent its restaurants and bars, including the boisterous **Ulysses' Folk House** (95 Pearl Street, between Broad Street & Hanover Square, 1-212 482 0400, www.ulyssesnyc.com) and **Stone Street Tavern** (52 Stone Street, between Broad Street & Hanover Square, 1-212 785 5658, www.stonestreettavernnyc.com).

Although the neighbourhood is bisected vertically by the ever-bustling Broadway, it's the east–west Wall Street that's synonymous with the world's greatest den of capitalism. The name derives from a defensive wooden wall built in 1653 to mark the northern limit of

New Amsterdam, and despite its huge significance, the thoroughfare is less than a mile long. At its western intersection with Broadway, you'll find the Gothic Revival spire of **Trinity Wall Street** (*see p18*). The original church burned down in 1776, and a second was demolished in 1839; the current version became the island's tallest structure when it was completed in 1846. **St Paul's Chapel** (*see p18*), the church's older satellite, is one of the finest Georgian structures in the US.

A block to the east of Trinity is the **Federal Hall National Memorial** (26 Wall Street, at Nassau Street, 1-212 825 6990, www.nps.gov/feha, closed Sat, Sun), an august Greek Revival building and – in a previous incarnation – the site of George Washington's first inauguration. It was along this stretch that corporate America made its first audacious architectural statements; a walk eastwards offers much evidence of what money can buy. Structures include the Bankers Trust Building at 14 Wall Street (at Broad Street), completed in 1912 and crowned by a seven-storey pyramid modelled on the Mausoleum of Halicarnassus; 40 Wall Street (between Nassau & William Streets), which battled the Chrysler Building in 1929 for the title of world's tallest building (the Empire State trounced them both in 1931); and the former Merchants' Exchange at 55 Wall Street (between Hanover & William Streets), with its stacked rows of Ionic and Corinthian columns, giant doors and a remarkable ballroom. Back around the corner is the Equitable Building (120 Broadway, between Cedar & Pine Streets), whose greedy use of vertical space helped to instigate the zoning laws that now govern skyscrapers; stand across the street from the building to get the best view. Nearby is the **Federal Reserve Bank**, with its huge gold vault.

The nerve centre of the US economy is the **New York Stock Exchange** (11 Wall Street, between Broad & New Streets, www.nyse.nyx.com). For security reasons, the Exchange is no longer open to the public, but the street outside offers an endless pageant of brokers, traders and their minions. For a lesson on Wall Street's influence over the years, visit the **Museum of American Finance**.

Alexander Hamilton US Custom House/National Museum of the American Indian

Cass Gilbert's magnificent Beaux Arts Custom House, completed in 1907, housed the Customs Service until 1973, when the federal government moved it to the newly built World Trade Center complex. Four monumental figures by Lincoln Memorial sculptor Daniel Chester French – representing America, Asia, Europe and Africa – flank the impressive entrance. The panels surrounding the elliptical rotunda dome were designed to feature murals, but this wasn't realised until the 1930s, when local artist Reginald Marsh was commissioned to decorate them under the New Deal's Works Progress Administration; the paintings depict a ship entering New York Harbor.

In 1994, the National Museum of the American Indian's George Gustav Heye Center, a branch of the Smithsonian, moved into the first two floors of the building. On the second level, the life and culture of Native Americans are illuminated in three galleries radiating out from the rotunda. The permanent exhibition, 'Infinity of Nations', displays 700 of the museum's wide-ranging collection of Native American art and objects, from decorated baskets to elaborate ceremonial headdresses, organised by geographical region. Changing exhibitions showcase contemporary artwork. On the ground floor, the Diker Pavilion for Native Arts & Culture is the city's only dedicated showcase for Native American performing arts.

1 Bowling Green, between State & Whitehall Streets (1-212 514 3700, www.nmai.si.edu). Subway R to Whitehall Street-South Ferry; 1 to South Ferry; 4, 5 to Bowling Green. Open 10am-5pm Mon-Wed, Fri-Sun; 10am-8pm Thur. Admission free.

Federal Reserve Bank

For security reasons, tours of this important financial institution must be booked well in advance – the easiest way to do this is online, as a calendar shows availability – and photo ID must be presented upon admission. Descend 50ft below street level and you'll find the world's largest known supply of monetary gold (over 12,000 tons, worth more than $300 billion), stored in a gigantic vault that rests on the solid bedrock of Manhattan Island. Visitors learn about the New York Fed's safeguarding of the precious metal, and the responsibilities and actions of the Federal Reserve. *Visitors' entrance: 44 Maiden Lane, between Nassau & William Streets (1-212 720 6130, www.ny.frb.org/aboutthefed/visiting.html). Subway 2, 3, 4, 5 to Wall Street. Tours (reservations required) 11.15am, noon, 12.45pm, 1.30pm, 2.15pm, 3pm Mon-Fri. Admission free.*

Fraunces Tavern Museum

True, George Washington slept here, but there's little left of the original 18th-century tavern he favoured during the Revolution. Fire-damaged and rebuilt in the 19th century, it was reconstructed in its current Colonial Revival style in 1907. The museum itself features period rooms, a collection of 800 reproduction regimental flags, paintings devoted to events of the Revolutionary War, and such Washington relics as a lock of his hair. It was here, after the British had finally been defeated, that Washington took tearful farewell of his troops and vowed to retire from public life. Luckily, he had a change of heart six years later and became the country's first president. You can still raise a pint in the bar, which is now run by Dublin's Porterhouse Brewing Company. *2nd & 3rd Floors, 54 Pearl Street, at Broad Street (1-212 425 1778, www.frauncestavern museum.org). Subway J, Z to Broad Street; 4, 5 to Bowling Green. Open noon-5pm daily. Admission $7; $4 reductions; free under-6s & active military.*

Governors Island

See p19 Island Getaway. *1-212 440 2202, www.govisland.com. Subway R to Whitehall Street-South Ferry; 1 to South Ferry; 4, 5 to Bowling Green. Then take ferry from*

Battery Maritime Building at Slip no.7. Open Late May-late Sept 10am-6pm Mon-Fri; 10am-7pm Sat, Sun (see website for hours and ferry schedule). Admission Ferry $2 round trip; free under-12s; free 10am-noon Sat, Sun.

Museum of American Finance

Situated in the old headquarters of the Bank of New York, the permanent collection traces the history of Wall Street and America's financial markets. Displays in the stately banking hall include a bearer bond made out to President George Washington and ticker tape from the morning of the stock market crash of 1929.
48 Wall Street, at William Street (1-212 908 4110, www.moaf.org). Subway R, 1 to Rector Street; 2, 3, 4, 5 to Wall Street. Open 10am-4pm Tue-Sat. Admission $8; $5 reductions; free under-7s; free Sat during 2014.

Statue of Liberty & Ellis Island Immigration Museum

The sole occupant of Liberty Island, *Liberty Enlightening the World* stands 305ft tall from the bottom of her base to the tip of her gold-leaf torch. Intended as a gift from France on America's 100th birthday, the statue was designed by Frédéric Auguste Bartholdi (1834-1904). Construction began in Paris in 1874, her skeletal iron framework crafted by Gustave Eiffel (the man behind the Tower), but only the arm with the torch was finished in time for the centennial in 1876. In 1884, the statue was finally completed – only to be taken apart to be shipped to New York, where it was unveiled in 1886. It served as a lighthouse until 1902, and as a welcoming beacon for millions of immigrants. These 'tired…poor…huddled masses' were evoked in Emma Lazarus's poem 'The New Colossus', written in 1883 to raise funds for the pedestal and engraved inside the statue in 1903. With a free Monument Pass, available only with ferry tickets reserved in advance, you can enter the pedestal and view the interior through a glass ceiling. Access to the crown costs an extra $3 and must be reserved in advance with your ferry tickets.

A half-mile across the harbour from Liberty Island is the 32-acre Ellis Island, gateway for over 12 million people who entered the country between 1892 and 1954. In the Immigration Museum (a former check-in depot), three floors of photos, interactive displays and exhibits pay tribute to the hopeful souls who made the voyage.
Liberty Island (1-212 363 3200, www.nps.gov/stli). Subway R to Whitehall Street-South Ferry; 1 to South Ferry; 4, 5 to Bowling Green; then take Statue of Liberty ferry (1-201 604 2800, 1-877 523 9849, www.statuecruises.com), departing roughly every 30mins from gangway 4 or 5 in southernmost Battery Park. Open ferry runs 9.30am-3.30pm daily. Purchase tickets online, by phone or at Castle Clinton *in Battery Park. Admission $17; free-$14 reductions.*

Trinity Wall Street & St Paul's Chapel

Trinity Church was the island's tallest structure when it was completed in 1846 (the original burned down in 1776; a second was demolished in 1839). A set of gates north of the church on Broadway allows access to the adjacent cemetery, where cracked and faded tombstones mark the final resting places of dozens of past city dwellers, including such notable New Yorkers as founding father Alexander Hamilton, business tycoon John Jacob Astor and steamboat inventor Robert Fulton. The church museum displays historic diaries, photographs, sermons and burial records.

Six blocks to the north, Trinity's satellite, St Paul's Chapel, is more important architecturally. The oldest building in New York still in continuous use (it dates from 1766), it is one of the nation's most valued Georgian structures.
Trinity Wall Street 89 Broadway, at Wall Street (1-212 602 0800, www.trinitywallstreet.org). Subway R, 1 to Rector Street; 2, 3, 4, 5 to Wall Street. Open 7am-6pm Mon-Fri; 8am-4pm Sat; 7am-4pm Sun. Admission free.
St Paul's Chapel 209 Broadway, between Fulton & Vesey Streets (1-212 602 0800, www.trinitywallstreet.org). Subway A, C, J, Z, 2, 3, 4, 5 to Fulton Street. Open 10am-6pm Mon-Sat; 7am-6pm Sun. Admission free.

WORLD TRADE CENTER & BATTERY PARK CITY

The streets around the site of the former World Trade Center have been drawing the bereaved and the curious since that harrowing day in September 2001. The worst attack on US soil took nearly 3,000 lives and left a gaping hole where the Twin Towers had once helped to define the New York skyline. After the site was fenced off, there wasn't much to see for almost a decade. Construction on the new World Trade Center complex, which will eventually include five office buildings, a performing arts centre and a transit hub designed by Santiago Calatrava, has been plagued by infighting, missed deadlines and budget overruns, but the National September 11 Memorial opened as planned on the tenth anniversary of the attacks. The **National September 11 Memorial Museum** opens its doors in late spring 2014, and the development's centrepiece skyscraper, 1 World Trade Center (the renamed Freedom Tower) – now the tallest building in America – counts media giant Condé Nast among its tenants. Santiago Calatrava's dramatic PATH/subway transport hub, scaled back due to budget constraints, is due for completion in 2015, but a Calatrava-designed 600-foot-long, marble-clad pedestrian corridor – soon to be lined with high-end stores – now links the PATH station and the

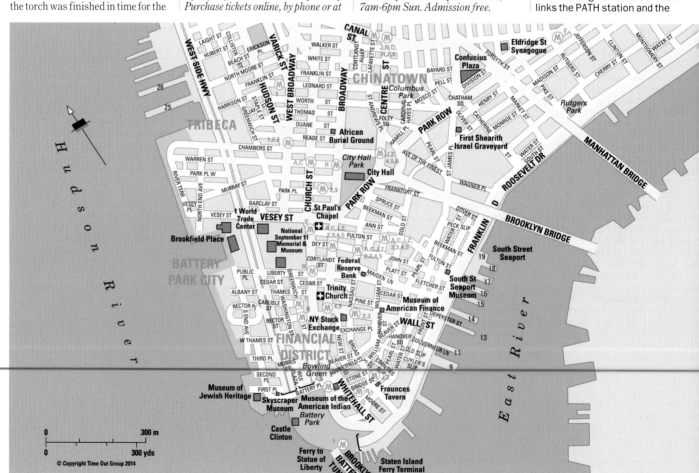

granite-and-glass corporate/retail/dining complex **Brookfield Place** (from Liberty to Vesey Streets, between the Hudson River & West Street, 1-212 417 7000, www.brookfieldplaceny.com). Overlooking a marina, the complex hosts numerous free arts events in its Winter Garden and is undergoing a major upgrade to its restaurant and retail offerings. A gallery above a food market due to open by publication of this guide includes outposts of popular NYC eateries such as East Village barbecue spot **Mighty Quinn's** (see p54) – good news given the scarcity of decent grub in the area.

Brookfield Place abuts **Battery Park City**, a 92-acre planned community devised in the 1950s to replace decaying shipping piers with new apartments, green spaces and schools. It's a man-made addition to the island, built on soil and rocks excavated from the original World Trade Center construction site and sediment dredged from New York Harbor. Home to roughly 10,000 people, the neighbourhood was devastated after 9/11, and nearly half of its residents moved away, although the area has been improved with new commercial development drawn by economic incentives. Visitors can enjoy its esplanade, a favoured route for bikers, skaters and joggers, and a string of parks that runs north along the Hudson River from Battery Park.

Providing expansive views of the Statue of Liberty and Ellis Island at its southernmost reaches, the stretch is dotted with monuments and sculptures. Close by the marina is the 1997 **Police Memorial** (Liberty Street, at South End Avenue), a granite pool and fountain that symbolically trace the lifespan of a police officer through the use of moving water, with names of the fallen etched into the wall. The **Irish Hunger Memorial** (Vesey Street, at North End Avenue) is here too, paying tribute to those who suffered during the famine from 1845 to 1852. Designed by artist Brian Tolle and landscape architect Gail Wittwer-Laird, the quarter-acre memorial incorporates vegetation, soil and stones from Ireland's 32 counties, and a reproduction of a 19th-century Irish cottage.

To the north, **Nelson A Rockefeller Park** (north end of Battery Park City, west of River Terrace) attracts sun worshippers, kite flyers and soccer players in the warm-weather months. Look out for Tom Otterness's whimsical sculpture installation, *The Real World*. Just east is Teardrop Park (between Warren & Murray Streets, east of River Terrace), a two-acre space designed to evoke the bucolic Hudson River Valley, and to the south are the inventively designed **South Cove** (on the Esplanade, between First & Third Place), with

its quays and island, and **Robert F Wagner Jr Park** (north of Historic Battery Park, off Battery Place), where an observation deck offers fabulous views of both the harbour and the Verrazano-Narrows Bridge; below it, Louise Bourgeois's *Eyes* gaze over the Hudson from the lawn. The **Museum of Jewish Heritage**, Gotham's memorial to the Holocaust, is on the edge of the green. Across the street at the **Skyscraper Museum**, you can learn about the buildings that have created the city's iconic skyline.

Museum of Jewish Heritage: A Living Memorial to the Holocaust
This museum explores Jewish life before, during and after the Nazi genocide. The permanent collection includes documentary films, thousands of photos and 30,000 artefacts, many donated by Holocaust

survivors and their families, which are displayed on rotation. The Keeping History Center brings the collection to life with interactive displays, including 'Voices of Liberty', a soundscape of émigrés' and refugees' reactions to arrival in the United States – the installation is made all the more poignant juxtaposed with the museum's panoramic views of Ellis Island and the Statue of Liberty. Special exhibitions tackle historical events or themes. The Memorial Garden features English artist Andy Goldsworthy's Garden of Stones, 18 fire-hollowed boulders embedded with dwarf oak saplings.
Edmond J Safra Plaza, 36 Battery Place, at First Place (1-646 437 4202, www.mjhnyc.org). Subway 4, 5 to Bowling Green. Open 10am-5.45pm Mon, Tue, Thur, Sun; 10am-8pm Wed; 10am-5pm Fri (until 3pm Nov-mid Mar); 10am-3pm eve of Jewish

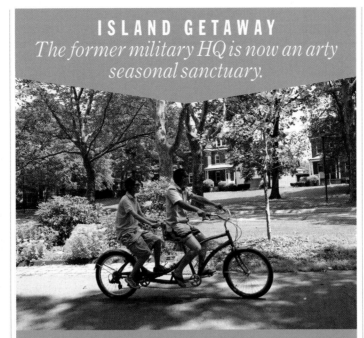

ISLAND GETAWAY
The former military HQ is now an arty seasonal sanctuary.

A 172-acre chunk of waterside real estate that can never be developed into luxury condos, **Governors Island** (see p17) is a secluded anomaly a scant 800 yards from lower Manhattan. The verdant commons and stately red-brick buildings evoke an Ivy League campus by way of a colonial New England village – oddly emptied of its inhabitants. The peaceful backwater has had a tumultuous history. Initially a seasonal fishing and gathering ground for the Lenape Indians, it had plentiful nut trees, earning it the name 'Noten Eylant' when the Dutch arrived in the 1620s. In 1674, the British secured it for 'the benefit and accommodation of His Majesty's Governors'.

The island's strategic position cemented its future as a military outpost, and it still retains a significant chunk of its military-era construction, including Fort Jay, started in 1776, and Castle Williams, completed in 1812. The modest patch has been the backdrop for some huge events. In 1909, it launched the first overwater flight, when Wilbur Wright circled the Statue of Liberty before flying back. Such legendary figures as Generals Ulysses S Grant and Douglas MacArthur had stints on the island.

Today, as well as providing a peaceful setting for cycling (bring a bike, or rent one on arrival), the island hosts a programme of events, and there are even plans for a day spa. In 2012, construction began on a new park, and 30 acres of green space are open to the public for the 2014 season. The Hammock Grove, with hammocks set among 1,500 trees, offers shady reclining, and 14 acres of lawn include two ball fields. Eventually, new hills constructed from the debris of demolished buildings will provide even more spectacular viewpoints for harbour panoramas.

holidays. Admission $12; $7-$10 reductions; free under-13s, members; free 4-8pm Wed.

National September 11 Memorial & Museum
Until construction is completed on the World Trade Center site, visitors must reserve timed entry passes to the memorial online or at the 9/11 Memorial Preview Site (20 Vesey Street, at Church Street), where you can learn about the development of the memorial and museum through models, renderings, films and artefacts. See also p2.
Enter on Albany Street, at Greenwich Street (1-212 266 5211, www.911memorial.org). Subway A, C, J, Z, 2, 3, 4, 5 to Fulton Street; E to World Trade Center; N, R, 1 to Rector Street. Open see website for information.

Skyscraper Museum
The only institution of its kind in the world, this modest space explores high-rise buildings as objects of design, products of technology, real-estate investments and places of work and residence. A large part of the single gallery (a mirrored ceiling gives the illusion of height) is devoted to temporary exhibitions. A substantial chunk of the permanent collection relates to the Word Trade Center, including original models of the Twin Towers and the new 1 World Trade Center. Other highlights of the display are large-scale photographs of lower Manhattan's skyscrapers from 1956, 1976 and 2004, and a 1931 silent film documenting the Empire State Building's construction.
39 Battery Place, between Little West Street & 1st Place (1-212 968 1961, www.skyscraper.org). Subway 4, 5 to Bowling Green. Open noon-6pm Wed-Sun. Admission $5; $2.50 reductions.

SOUTH STREET SEAPORT
New York's fortunes originally rolled in on the swells that crashed into its harbour. The city was perfectly situated for trade with Europe and, after 1825, goods from the Western Territories arrived via the Erie Canal and the Hudson River. By 1892, New York was also the point of entry for millions of immigrants. The South Street Seaport is the best place to appreciate this port heritage.

If you enter the Seaport area from Water Street, the first thing you're likely to spot is the whitewashed **Titanic Memorial Lighthouse**. It was originally erected on top of the Seaman's Church Institute (Coenties Slip & South Street) in 1913, the year after the great ship sank, but was moved to its current location at the intersection of Pearl and Fulton Streets in 1976. Check out the magnificent views of the Brooklyn Bridge from this part of the district.

When New York's role as a vital shipping hub diminished during the 20th century, the South Street Seaport area fell into disuse, but a massive redevelopment project in

Local New York, by New York Locals

New walking tours offer a rare insider's view into New York.

For first-time visitors to NYC, the to-do list often stops with big name sites like the Statue of Liberty. But what if you'd rather visit the regular, street level city?

Following their success as Walks of Italy, tour operator Walks of New York is focusing on these kinds of experiences. The aim is to encourage travelers to walk more, listen more and see more, finding their own version of NYC. The following are some of their top tips for finding yours.

Lower East Side, not Ellis Island.

Ellis Island houses a fantastic immigrant journeys to NYC but the the story of what happened when This is where you'll find the most synagogues and old tenement museum about Lower East Side tells they got here. traditional food, buildings.

Backstage at Broadway, better than first row.

It's great to see a show on Broadway but even better is hearing stories from behind the curtains.

One Met, Many Worlds.

The Met aims to open a world of art to every visitor. It's home to the 'Washington Crossing the Delaware' but there's also pre-Columbian gold! Take the time to see all of its worlds.

Times Square, better from above.

Visiting Times Square is a quintessential New York experience, better still is a nearby rooftop for a view above the chaos.

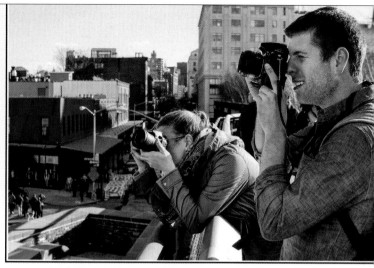

Want postcard-perfect pictures? Take them yourself.
Visit a souvenir shop, look through the postcard collection for the most iconic NYC shots and recreate them for yourself.

Among other exclusive tours, Walks of New York offers tours of the Lower East Side; Backstage Broadway Tours; Met Museum Tours; a midtown highlights walking tour including rooftop views of Times Square; and a High Line Photo Walk led by a professional photographer. All Walks of New York tours feature small groups of 12 people or fewer and expert local guides.

For information see **www.walksofnewyork.com**, phone us on **+1-888-683-8670** or follow us on social media using **#takewalks**.

WALKS OF
NEW YORK

the mid 1980s saw old buildings converted into restaurants, bars, chain stores and the **South Street Seaport Museum**.

Pier 17 once supported the famous Fulton Fish Market, a bustling, early-morning trading centre dating back to the mid 1800s. However, in 2006 the market relocated to a larger facility in the Hunts Point area of the Bronx. Interest in Pier 17 dwindled after redevelopment in the 1980s, but a plan by SHoP Architects will replace the now-shuttered mall with a mixed-use complex, including a marina and a global food market. The city's East River Esplanade and Piers Project has landscaped the stretch of waterfront between the Battery Maritime Building and Fulton Street; **Pier 15** has been transformed into a bi-level lounging space, comprising a lawned viewing deck above a maritime education centre and the **Watermark** (*see p65*), a stylish glass-enclosed bar.

South Street Seaport Museum
Founded in 1967, the South Street Seaport Museum celebrates the maritime history of New York City's 19th-century waterfront. However, at time of writing it was still closed due to damage from 2012's Hurricane Sandy and a reopening date had yet to be determined. The museum shop, comprising Bowne Printers and Bowne & Co Stationers (*see p72*), has remained open. The institution also has a fleet of historic vessels on Pier 16, including the 1607 lightship Ambrose and the 1885 schooner Pioneer, which offers excursions along the East River from May to October.
12 Fulton Street, between South & Water Streets (1-212 748 8600, www.southstreetseaportmuseum.org). Subway A, C, J, Z, 2, 3, 4, 5 to Fulton Street. Open Call or see website for information. Admission Call or see website for information.

CIVIC CENTER & CITY HALL PARK
The business of running New York takes place in the grand buildings in and around City Hall Park, an area that formed the budding city's northern boundary in the 1700s. The park itself was renovated just before the millennium, and pretty landscaping and abundant benches make it a popular lunching spot for office workers.

At the park's southern end, a granite 'time wheel' tracks its history. At the northern end of the park, **City Hall** houses the mayor's office and the chambers of the City Council. When City Hall was completed in 1812, its architects were so confident that the city would grow no further north that they didn't bother to put any marble on its northern side. Nevertheless, the building is a beautiful blend of Federalist form and French Renaissance detail. Overlooking the park from the west is Cass Gilbert's famous **Woolworth**

Building (233 Broadway, between Barclay Street & Park Place), which was the tallest building in the world when it was completed in 1913. The neo-Gothic skyscraper's grand spires, gargoyles, vaulted ceilings and church-like interior earned it the moniker 'the Cathedral of Commerce'.

Behind City Hall, on Chambers Street, is the 1872 **Old New York County Courthouse**; it's popularly known as the Tweed Courthouse, after William 'Boss' Tweed, leader of the political machine Tammany Hall, who pocketed some $10 million of the building's $14 million construction budget. What he didn't steal bought a beautiful edifice, with exquisite Italianate detailing. These days, it houses the city's Department of Education and a New York City public school, but it's also open for tours (1-212 788 2656, www.nyc.gov/designcommission). To the east, other civic offices and services occupy the one million square feet of office space in the 1914 **Manhattan Municipal Building** at 1 Centre Street. This landmark limestone structure, built by McKim, Mead & White, also houses New York City's official gift shop (www.nyc.gov/citystore, closed Sat, Sun).

The houses of crime and punishment are located in the **Civic Center**, near Foley Square, once the site of the city's most notorious 19th-century slum, Five Points. These days, you'll find the State Supreme Court in the New York County Courthouse (60 Centre Street, at Pearl Street), a hexagonal Roman Revival building; the rotunda is decorated with a mural called *Law Through the Ages*. The **Thurgood Marshall United States Courthouse** (40 Centre Street, between Duane & Pearl Streets) is a Corinthian temple crowned with a golden pyramid. The **Criminal Courts Building & Manhattan Detention Complex**

(100 Centre Street, between Leonard & White Streets) is still known as 'the Tombs', a nod to the original 1838 Egyptian Revival building – or, depending on who you ask, its current grimness. There's no denying that the hall's great granite slabs and looming towers are downright lugubrious.

Nearby, the **African Burial Ground** was officially designated a National Monument in 2006.

African Burial Ground National Monument
The African Burial Ground is a small remnant of a 6.6-acre unmarked gravesite where between 10,000 and 20,000 enslaved Africans were buried. The burial ground, which closed in 1794, was unearthed during the construction of a federal office building in 1991 and designated a National Monument 15 years later. In 2007, a stone memorial, designed by architect Rodney Leon, was erected; the tall, curved structure draws heavily on African architecture and contains a spiral path leading to an ancestral chamber.
Duane Street, between Broadway & Centre Streets, behind 290 Broadway (1-212 637 2019, www.nps.gov/afbg). Subway J, Z to Chambers Street; R to City Hall; 4, 5, 6 to Brooklyn Bridge-City Hall. Open Mar-Mid Nov 9am-5pm daily. Visitor centre 10am-4pm Tue-Sat. Admission free.

City Hall
Designed by French émigré Joseph François Mangin and John McComb Jr, the fine, Federal-style City Hall was completed in 1812. Tours take in the City Council Chamber and the Governor's Room, with its collection of American 19th-century political portraits and historic furnishings (including George Washington's desk). Individuals can book (at least two days in advance) for the Thursday morning tour;

City Hall

alternatively, sign up before 11.45am on Wednesday at the NYC tourism kiosk at the southern end of City Hall Park on the east side of Broadway, at Barclay Street for the first-come, first-served tour at noon that day.
City Hall Park, from Vesey to Chambers Streets, between Broadway & Park Row (1-212 788 2656, www.nyc.gov/designcommission). Subway J, Z to Chambers Street; R to City Hall; 2, 3 to Park Place; 4, 5, 6 to Brooklyn Bridge-City Hall. Open Tours (individuals) noon Wed, 10am Thur; (groups) 10.30am Mon. Reservations required. Admission free.

Soho & Tribeca

In the 1960s and '70s, artists colonised what had become a post-industrial wasteland South of Houston Street, squatting in abandoned warehouses. Eventually, they worked with the city to rezone and restore them. Others followed suit in the Triangle Below Canal Street, which was once the site of the city's main produce market. Today, many of the old factory buildings in Soho and Tribeca are occupied by designer stores and high-end restaurants, and those once-spartan loft spaces are among the most desirable real estate in the city. But you can still find pockets of experimental culture in this consumer paradise, in the form of scattered art galleries and Off and Off-Off Broadway theatres. Even if you're not shopping or dining, take a walk in the area to admire a well-preserved architectural legacy with a uniquely New York character.

SOHO
Now a retail mecca of the highest order, Soho was once a hardscrabble manufacturing zone with the derisive nickname Hell's Hundred Acres. In the 1960s, it was earmarked for destruction by over-zealous urban planner Robert Moses, but its signature cast-iron warehouses were saved by the artists who inhabited them as cheap live-work spaces. The **King & Queen of Greene Street** (respectively, 72-76 Greene Street, between Broome & Spring Streets, and 28-30 Greene Street, between Canal & Grand Streets) are both fine examples of the area's beloved architectural landmarks. The most celebrated of Soho's cast-iron edifices, however, is the five-storey **Haughwout Building**, at 488-492 Broadway, at Broome Street. Designed in 1857, it featured the world's first hydraulic lift (still in working condition).

After landlords sniffed the potential for profits in converting old loft buildings, Soho morphed into a playground for the young, beautiful and rich. It can still be a pleasure to stroll around the cobblestoned side streets on weekday mornings, and there are some standout shops in the area, but the large chain stores and sidewalk-encroaching street vendors along Broadway create a shopping-mall-at-Christmas crush on weekends. Although many of the galleries that made Soho an art capital in the 1970s and '80s decamped to Chelsea and, more recently, the Lower East Side, some excellent art spaces remain, including the recently expanded **Drawing Center**.

Drawing Center

This non-profit standout recently expanded its gallery space by 50%. Now comprising three galleries, the Drawing Center assembles shows of museum-calibre legends such as Philip Guston, James Ensor and Willem de Kooning, but also 'Selections' surveys of newcomers. Art stars such as Kara Walker and Chris Ofili received some of their earliest NYC exposure here.
35 Wooster Street, between Broome & Grand Streets (1-212 219 2166, www.drawingcenter.org). Subway A, C, E, 1 to Canal Street. Open noon-6pm Wed, Fri-Sun; noon-8pm Thur. Admission $5; $3 reductions; free under-12s; free 6-8pm Thur.

New York City Fire Museum

An active firehouse from 1905 to 1959, this museum is filled with all manner of life-saving gadgetry, from late 18th-century hand-pumped fire engines to present-day equipment.
278 Spring Street, between Hudson & Varick Streets (1-212 691 1303, www.nycfiremuseum.org). Subway C, E to Spring Street; 1 to Houston Street. Open 10am-5pm daily. Admission $8; $5 reductions.

TRIBECA

In just two decades, the Triangle Below Canal Street has morphed from an isolated, run-down corner to a wealthy enclave with a family- and celebrity-heavy demographic. Robert De Niro has been a key figure in the area's transformation, founding the **Tribeca Film Center** (375 Greenwich Street, at Franklin Street) with Jane Rosenthal in 1988, which contains industry magnet and neighbourhood stalwart **Tribeca Grill** (1-212 941 3900). A few blocks away, De Niro's **Tribeca Cinemas** (54 Varick Street, at Laight Street, 1-212 941 2001, www.tribecacinemas.com) hosts premières and glitzy parties, when it isn't serving as a venue for the **Tribeca Film Festival**.

The preponderance of hulking former industrial buildings gives Tribeca an imposing profile, but fine small-scale cast-iron architecture still stands along White Street and the parallel thoroughfares. Upscale eateries and, increasingly, retail cater to the well-heeled locals.

Museum

See above **Small Wonder**.
Cortlandt Alley, between Franklin & White Streets (no phone,

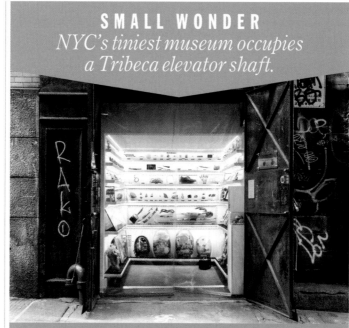

SMALL WONDER
NYC's tiniest museum occupies a Tribeca elevator shaft.

Institutions like the Metropolitan Museum of Art contain thousands of treasures. At the other end of the spectrum, there's **Museum** (*see below*), a 60-square-foot repository in an abandoned Tribeca freight elevator. The walk-in-closet-size space, founded by indie filmmakers Alex Kalman, Josh Safdie and Benny Safdie, showcases a mishmash of found objects and artefacts donated by hobbyists. Museum is only open at weekends, but viewers can also get a peek at the space when it's closed – look for small peepholes in a metal door on the narrow throughway between Franklin and White Streets. Exhibits for each season, lasting roughly six months, are acquired in various ways, including via a submissions email address. Season 3, on view for much of 2014, includes a selection of *Screw* magazine founder Al Goldstein's transcribed personal Dictaphone notes, memorabilia from one of Saddam Hussein's palaces, and part of a collection of 200 mosquitoes killed mid-bite amassed by a traveller in New Delhi. 'That works for us on a bunch of different levels,' says Alex Kalman of the latter, 'but on the simplest aesthetic level the almost-abstract forms they take are beautiful.'

Although Kalman acknowledges the humour inherent in the displays, he stresses that Museum is not merely an esoteric joke. 'We know that it's small, but its basically saying, these are not the things we're creating in society because we think they're important or valuable, these are the things we're creating because they are the things we want and need, and that tells us a lot about our psychology and who we are. It's trying to paint a very big portrait of humanity through the collection of our smallest things.'

www.mmuseumm.com). Subway J, N, Q, R, Z, 6 to Canal Street. Open noon-6pm Sat, Sun. Admission free.

Chinatown, Little Italy & Nolita

Take a walk in the area south of Broome Street and east of Broadway, and you'll feel as though you've entered not just a different country but a different continent. You won't hear much English spoken on the streets of Manhattan's Chinatown, which are packed with exotic-produce stands, herb emporiums, cheap jewellers, snack vendors and restaurants. As New York City's largest Asian community continues to grow, it merges with neighbouring Little Italy. Between Chinatown and fashionable Nolita (North of Little Italy), the historically Italian district has long been shrinking, but you can still get a taste of the old neighbourhood in its cafés and red-sauce eateries.

CHINATOWN

A steady flow of new arrivals keeps this neighbourhood – one of the largest Chinese communities outside Asia – full to bursting, with thousands of residents packed into the area surrounding East Canal Street. Some eventually decamp to one of NYC's three other Chinatowns in Sunset Park, Brooklyn, and Flushing and Elmhurst in Queens.

Mott and Grand Streets are lined with fish-, fruit- and vegetable-stocked stands selling some of the best and most affordable seafood and produce in the city – you'll see buckets of live eels and crabs, square watermelons and piles of hairy rambutans. Street vendors sell satisfying snacks such as pork buns and sweet egg pancakes by the bagful. Canal Street glitters with cheap jewellery and gift shops, but beware furtive vendors of (undoubtedly fake) designer goods. Between Kenmare and Worth Streets, Mott Street is lined with restaurants representing the cuisine of virtually every province of mainland China and Hong Kong; the Bowery, East Broadway and Division Street are just as diverse. Adding to the mix are myriad Indonesian, Malaysian, Thai and Vietnamese eateries and shops. The busy streets get even wilder during the **Chinese New Year** festivities (*see p13*).

Explore the Chinese experience on these shores at the elegantly conceived **Museum of Chinese in America**, which reopened in 2009 in much larger premises. The **Eastern States Buddhist Temple of America** (64 Mott Street, between Bayard & Canal Streets, 1-212 925 8787), founded in 1962, is one of the country's oldest Chinese Buddhist temples.

Museum of Chinese in America

Designed by prominent Chinese-American architect Maya Lin, MoCA reopened in an airy former machine shop in 2009. Its interior is loosely inspired by a traditional Chinese house, with rooms radiating off a central courtyard and areas defined by screens. The core exhibition traces the development of Chinese communities in the US from the 1850s to the present through objects, images and video. Innovative displays (drawers open to reveal artwork and documents, portraits are presented in a ceiling mobile) cover the development of industries such as laundries and restaurants in New York, Chinese stereotypes in pop culture, and the suspicion and humiliation Chinese-Americans endured during World War II and the McCarthy era. A mocked-up Chinese general store evokes the feel of these multi-purpose spaces, which served as vital community lifelines for men severed from their families under the 1882 Exclusion Act that restricted immigration. There's also a gallery for special exhibitions.
215 Centre Street, between Grand & Howard Streets (1-212 619 4785, www.mocanyc.org). Subway J, N, Q, R, Z, 6 to Canal Street. Open 11am-6pm Tue, Wed, Fri-Sun; 11am-9pm Thur. Admission $10; $5 reductions; free under-12s; free Thur.

LITTLE ITALY & NOLITA

Abandoning the dismal tenements of the Five Points district (in what is now the Civic Center and part of Chinatown), immigrants from Naples and Sicily began moving to Little Italy in the 1880s. The area once stretched from Canal Street to Houston Street, between Lafayette Street and the Bowery, but these days only the blocks immediately surrounding Mulberry Street exude a strong Italian presence. As families prospered in the 1950s, they moved to the outer boroughs and suburbs.

Another telling change in the district: St Patrick's Old Cathedral 260-264 Mulberry Street, between Houston & Prince Streets) no longer holds services in Italian, but in English and Spanish. Completed in 1809 and restored after a fire in 1868, this was the city's premier Catholic church until it was demoted upon consecration of the Fifth Avenue cathedral of the same name. But ethnic pride remains: Italian-Americans flood in from across the city during the 11-day Feast of San Gennaro (see p13).

Touristy cafés and restaurants line Mulberry Street between Broome and Canal Streets, but pockets of the past linger nearby. Long-time residents still buy fresh mozzarella from DiPalo's Fine Foods (200 Grand Street, at Mott Street, 1-212 226 1033). Legend has it that the first pizzeria in New York was opened by Gennaro Lombardi on Spring Street in 1905. Lombardi's moved down the block in 1994 (32 Spring Street, at Mott Street, 1-212 941 7994), but still serves its signature clam pies. Today the area's restaurants are largely undistinguished grills and pasta houses, but two reliable choices are Il Cortile (125 Mulberry Street, between Canal & Hester Streets, 1-212 226 6060) and La Mela (167 Mulberry Street, between Broome & Grand Streets, 1-212 431 9493). Drop in for dessert at Caffè Roma (385 Broome Street, at Mulberry Street, 1-212 226 8413), which opened in 1891.

Nolita became a magnet for pricey boutiques and trendy eateries in the 1990s. Elizabeth, Mott and Mulberry Streets, between Houston and Spring Streets, in particular, are home to hip shops.

Lower East Side

Once better known for bagels and bargains, the Lower East Side is now brimming with vintage and indie-designer boutiques, fashionable bars and contemporary art galleries. In fact, the former slum has been so radically altered by the forces of gentrification, it was placed on the National Trust for Historic Preservation's annual list of the 11 most endangered historic places in 2008. But new development hasn't yet destroyed the character of the erstwhile centre of immigrant life. You can still explore remnants of the old Jewish neighbourhood that the Marx Brothers and George Gershwin called home.

In the 19th century, tenement buildings were constructed on the Lower East Side, a roughly defined area south of Houston Street and west of the East River, to house the growing number of German, Irish, Jewish and Italian immigrants – by 1900 it was the most populous neighbourhood in the US. The appalling conditions of these overcrowded, unsanitary slums were captured by photographer and writer Jacob Riis in How the Other Half Lives in 1890; its publication spurred activists and prompted the introduction of more humane building codes. The dwellings have since been converted or demolished, but you can see how newcomers once lived by visiting the recreated apartments of the Lower East Side Tenement Museum (see p24).

The neighbourhood was also the focal point of Jewish culture in New York. Between 1870 and 1920, hundreds of synagogues and religious schools thrived alongside Yiddish newspapers, social-reform societies and kosher bakeries. Vaudeville and classic Yiddish theatre also prospered here. Today, most of these places are long gone, but vestiges of Jewish life can be found amid the Chinese businesses spilling over from sprawling Chinatown and the ever-multiplying fashionable boutiques, restaurants and bars. The Eldridge Street Synagogue (see p24), which has undergone extensive renovation, still has a small but vital congregation. Head east down Canal Street to admire the imposing façade of the Sender Jarmulowsky Bank (on the corner of Canal & Orchard Streets), which catered to Jewish immigrants until its collapse in 1914; note the seated classical figures flanking the clock above the doorway. Further down Canal, at the corner of Ludlow, you'll find he former home of the Kletzker Brotherly Aid Association, a lodge for immigrants from Belarus still marked by the Star of David and the year of its opening, 1892. The Forward Building (175 E Broadway, at Canal Street) was once the headquarters of the Jewish Daily Forward, a Yiddish-language paper that had a peak circulation of 275,000 in the 1920s; it's now home to multimillion-dollar condominiums.

Those looking for a literal taste of the old Jewish Lower East Side should grab a table at Katz's Delicatessen (see p53). Opened in 1888, this kosher deli continues to serve some of the best pastrami in New York (and was the site of Meg Ryan's famous 'fauxgasm' scene in When Harry Met Sally…). Essex Street Market (www.essexstreet market.com), which opened in 1940 as part of La Guardia's plan to get pushcarts off the streets, contains a mix of high-quality vendors selling cheese, coffee, sweets, produce, fish and meat.

By the 1980s, when young artists and musicians began moving into the area, it was a patchwork of

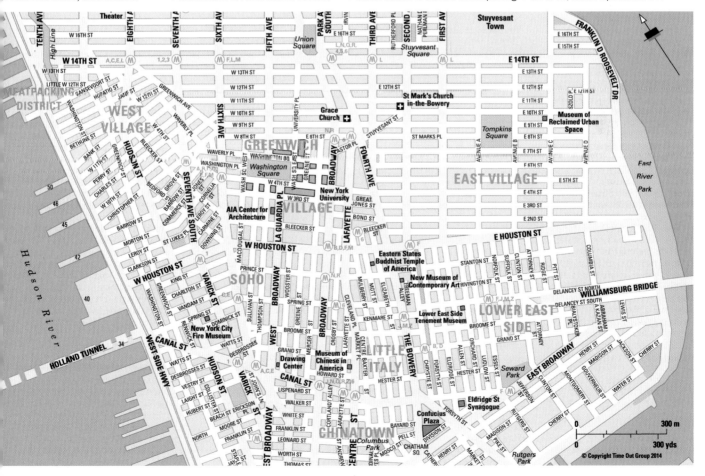

Asian, Latino and Jewish enclaves. Hipster bars and music venues sprang up on and around Ludlow Street, creating an annex to the East Village. That scene still survives, at spots like the **Bowery Ballroom** and **Cake Shop** (for both, *see p97*), but rents have risen dramatically and some stalwarts have closed.

These days, visual art is the Lower East Side's main cultural draw. Dozens of storefront galleries have opened in the vicinity over the past decade (for our picks, *see p82* **Gallery-Hopping Guide**). In 2007, the **New Museum of Contemporary Art** decamped here from Chelsea, opening a $50-million building on the Bowery. A narrow glass tower designed by Norman Foster, a block north, opened in 2010 as the HQ for high-profile dealers **Sperone Westwater** (257 Bowery, betwee E Houston & Stanton Streets, 1-212 999 7337, www.speronewestwater. com) whose stable includes Bruce Nauman and William Wegman.

Although the Orchard Street Bargain District – a row of shops selling utilitarian goods such as socks, sportswear and luggage, and beloved of hagglers – persists, the strip is at the centre of a proliferation of small indie shops. More mainstream commercial gloss is encroaching on the area in the form of high-rise hotels and apartment buildings, but as the area continues to change, groups such as the Lower East Side Conservancy are working to preserve its unique character.

Lower East Side Tenement Museum

This fascinating museum – actually a series of restored tenement apartments at 97 Orchard Street – is accessible only by guided tour, which start at the visitors' centre at 103 Orchard Street. Tours often sell out, so it's wise to book ahead. 'Hard Times' visits the homes of an Italian and a German-Jewish clan; 'Sweatshop Workers' explores the apartments of two Eastern European Jewish families as well as a garment shop where many of the locals would have found employment; and 'Irish Outsiders' unfurls the life of the Moore family, who are coping with the loss of their child. Visitors with kids may want to stop by quarters once occupied by a Sephardic Jewish Greek family and speak to an interpreter in period costume channelling the 14-year-old daughter of the house, Victoria Confino. The newest tour, 'Shop Life' explores the diverse retailers that occupied the building's storefronts, including a 19th-century German saloon. From mid March through December, the museum also conducts themed daily walking tours of the Lower East Side ($22-$45; $17-$40 reductions).
Visitors' centre, 103 Orchard Street, at Delancey Street (1-212 982 8420, www.tenement.org). Subway F to Delancey Street; J, M, Z to Delancey-

Museum at Eldridge Street (Eldridge Street Synagogue)

Essex Streets. Open Museum shop & ticketing 10am-6.30pm Mon-Wed, Fri-Sun; 10am-8.30pm Thur. Tours 10.30am-5pm Mon-Wed, Fri-Sun; 10am-8pm Thur (see website for schedule). Admission $22-$25; $17-$20 reductions.

Museum at Eldridge Street (Eldridge Street Synagogue)

With an impressive façade that combines Moorish, Gothic and Romanesque elements, the first grand synagogue on the Lower East Side is now surrounded by dumpling shops and Chinese herb stores, but rewind about a century and you would have found delicatessens and *mikvot* (ritual bathhouses). For its first 50 years, the 1887 synagogue had a congregation of thousands and doubled as a mutual-aid society for new arrivals in need of financial assistance, healthcare and employment. But as Jews left the area and the congregation dwindled, the building fell into disrepair.

A 20-year, $19.5-million facelift has restored its splendour; the soaring main sanctuary features hand-stencilled walls and a resplendent stained-glass rose window with Star of David motifs. The renovations were completed in autumn 2010, with the installation of a new stained-glass window designed by artist Kiki Smith and architect Deborah Gans. The admission price includes a guided tour (see website for schedule). In the new orientation centre, touch-screen displays highlight the synagogue's architecture, aspects of worship and local history, including other (extant and long-vanished) Jewish landmarks.
12 Eldridge Street, between Canal & Division Streets (1-212 219 0302, www.eldridgestreet.org). Subway F to

East Broadway. Open 10am-5pm Mon-Thur, Sun; 10am-3pm Fri. Admission $10; $6-$8 reductions; free under-5s; free Mon.

New Museum of Contemporary Art

Having occupied various sites for 30 years, New York City's only contemporary art museum finally got its own purpose-built space in late 2007. Dedicated to emerging media and under-recognised artists, the seven-floor space is worth a look for the architecture alone – a striking, off-centre stack of aluminium-mesh-clad boxes designed by the cutting-edge Tokyo architectural firm Sejima + Nishizawa/SANAA. Two ongoing exterior installations by Chris Burden add to the drama: the artist's 36ft-high *Twin Quasi Legal Skyscrapers* (2013) perch on the roof and his 30ft-long *Ghost Ship* (2005) hangs on the façade. The museum's café is run by the folks behind Hester Street Market, offering artisanal eats by a selection of local vendors. At weekends, don't miss the fabulous views from the minimalist seventh-floor Sky Room.
235 Bowery, between Prince & Stanton Streets (1-212 219 1222, www.newmuseum.org). Subway N, R to Prince Street; 6 to Spring Street. Open 11am-6pm Wed, Fri-Sun; 11am-9pm Thur. Admission $16; $10-$14 reductions; free under-18s (accompanied by an adult). Pay what you wish 7-9pm Thur.

East Village

Originally part of the Lower East Side, the East Village developed its distinct identity as a countercultural hotbed in the 1960s. By the dawning of the Age of Aquarius, rock clubs thrived on almost every corner. But in the '70s, the neighbourhood took a dive as drugs and crime prevailed – although that didn't stop the influx of artists and punk rockers. In the early '80s, East Village galleries were among the first to display the work of groundbreaking artists like Jean-Michel Basquiat and Keith Haring.

The blocks east of Broadway between Houston and 14th Streets may have lost some of their edge, and the neighbourhood's former tenements are increasingly occupied by young professionals and trust-fund kids, but humanity in all its guises converges in the parks, bargain restaurants, indie record stores and grungy watering holes on First and Second Avenues and St Mark's Place.

From the 1950s to the '70s, **St Marks Place** (E 8th Street, between Lafayette Street & Avenue A) was a hotbed of artists, writers, radicals and musicians, including WH Auden, Abbie Hoffman, Lenny Bruce, Joni Mitchell and GG Allin. The grungy strip still fizzes with energy well into the wee hours, but these days, it's packed with cheap eateries, tattoo parlours, and shops selling T-shirts, tourist junk and pot paraphernalia.

A short walk north brings you to **St Mark's Church in-the-Bowery** (131 E 10th Street, at Second Avenue, 1-212 674 6377, www.stmarksbowery.org). Built in 1799, the Federal-style church sits on the site of Peter Stuyvesant's farm; the old guy himself, one of New York's first governors, is buried in the adjacent cemetery. Regular services are still held, and the church is home to several cultural organisations, including the Poetry Project and Incubator Arts Project.

Cutting between Broadway and Fourth Avenue south of East 8th Street, Astor Place is the site of the **Cooper Union**. Comprising schools of art, architecture and engineering, it was the only free private college in the United States but the institution announced that it would have to start charging partial tuition fees in 2014. It was here, in February 1860, that Abraham Lincoln gave his celebrated Cooper Union Address, which argued for the regulation (though not abolition) of slavery and helped to propel him into the White House.

During the 19th century, Astor Place marked the boundary between the slums to the east and some of the city's most fashionable homes. **Colonnade Row** (428-434 Lafayette Street, between Astor Place & E 4th Street) faces the distinguished Astor Public Library building, which theatre legend Joseph Papp rescued from demolition in the 1960s. Today, the old library houses the **Public Theater** (see p109), a platform for first-run American plays, and cabaret venue **Joe's Pub** (see p97). Nearby, the **Merchant's House Museum** is a perfectly preserved specimen of upper-class domestic life in the 1800s.

Below Astor Place, Third Avenue (one block east of Lafayette Street) becomes the Bowery. For decades, the street languished as a seedy strip and the home of missionary organisations catering to the down and out. Although the sharp-eyed can find traces of the old flophouses, and the more obvious Gothic Revival headquarters of **Bowery Mission** at no.227 (between Rivington & Stanton Streets), the thoroughfare has been cleaned up and repopulated with high-rise condo buildings, restaurants, nightspots and hotels.

Elsewhere in the neighbourhood, East 7th Street is a stronghold of New York's Ukrainian community, of which the focal point is the **St George Ukrainian Catholic Church** at no.30. The **Ukrainian Museum** (222 E 6th Street, between Second & Third Avenues, 1-212 228 0110, www.ukrainianmuseum.org, closed Mon, Tue) houses folk and fine art and archival materials from that country. One block over, there's often a long line of loud fraternity types waiting at weekends to enter **McSorley's Old Ale House** (see p67). Festooned with aged photos, yellowed newspaper articles and dusty memorabilia, the 1854 Irish tavern is purportedly the oldest continually operating pub in New York and the spot where Lincoln repaired after giving his Cooper Union Address. Representing a different corner of the globe, **Curry Row** (East 6th Street, between First & Second Avenues) is lined with Indian restaurants that are popular with budget-minded diners.

Alphabet City (which gets its name from its key avenues: A, B, C and D) stretches towards the East River. It was once an edgy Puerto Rican neighbourhood with links to the drugs trade, but its demographic has dramatically shifted over the past 20 years. Avenue C is also known as Loisaida Avenue, a rough approximation of 'Lower East Side' when pronounced with a Hispanic accent. The **Nuyorican Poets Café** (236 E 3rd Street, between Avenues B & C, East Village, 1-212 505 8183, www.nuyorican.org), a clubhouse for espresso-drinking wordsmiths since 1974, is known for its Friday-night poetry slams, in which performers wage lyric battles before a score-keeping audience.

Dating from 1834, **Tompkins Square Park** (from 7th to 10th Streets, between Avenues A & B), honours Daniel D Tompkins, governor of New York from 1807 to 1817, and vice-president during the Monroe administration. Over the years, this 10.5-acre park has been a site for demonstrations and rioting. The last major uprising occurred in 1991, when the city evicted squatters from the park and renovated it to suit the influx of affluent residents. Along with dozens of 150-year-old elm trees (some of the oldest in the city), the landscaped green space has basketball courts, playgrounds and dog runs, and remains a place where bongo beaters, guitarists, multi-pierced teenagers, hipsters, local families and vagrants mingle.

North of Tompkins Square, around First Avenue and 11th Street, are remnants of earlier communities: discount fabric dealers, Italian cheese shops, Polish butchers and two great Italian coffee and cannoli houses: **De Robertis** (176 First Avenue, between 10th & 11th Streets, 1-212 674 7137, www.derobertiscaffe.com) and **Veniero's Pasticceria & Caffè** (342 E 11th Street, between First & Second Avenues, 1-212 674 7070, www.venierospastry.com).

Merchant's House Museum
Merchant's House Museum, the city's only fully preserved 19th-century family home, is an elegant, late Federal-Greek Revival property kitted out with the same furnishings and decorations it contained when it was inhabited from 1835 by hardware tycoon Seabury Tredwell and his family. Three years after Tredwell's eighth daughter died in 1933, it opened as a museum. You can peruse the house at your own pace, following along with the museum's printed guide, or opt for the 2pm guided tour. Be sure to ascend to the servants' quarters on the renovated fourth floor, and note the original bell that summoned the four Irish immigrant maids at the top of the stairs.
29 E 4th Street, between Lafayette Street & Bowery (1-212 777 1089, www.merchantshouse.org). Subway B, D, F, M to Broadway-Lafayette Street;

6 to Bleecker Street. Open noon-5pm Mon, Thur-Sun. Guided tour 2pm. Admission $10; $5 reductions; free under-12s.

Museum of Reclaimed Urban Space
While the word 'museum' tends to evoke a sense of permanence, the Museum of Reclaimed Urban Space resides in more ephemeral digs. Known as C-Squat, the five-floor walk-up has housed activists, down-on-their-luck artists and members of several punk bands (including Leftover Crack, Old Skull and Nausea) from the 1970s to the present. 'People can knock on the door and sleep there, and work there,' says co-founder Bill Di Paola, who is also the founding director of advocacy group Time's Up!. Zines from art and activist centre ABC No Rio, an Occupy Wall Street banner and a Time's Up! energy bike that helped power Zuccotti Park during its occupation in 2011 illustrate how city residents created, protected and took back community spaces. Volunteers also lead daily tours to places like La Plaza Cultural (www.laplazacultural. com), a once-illegal plot that is now an official community garden.
155 Avenue C, between 9th & 10th Streets (1-646 833 7764, www.morusnyc.org). Subway L to First Avenue. Open 11am-7pm Tue, Thur-Sun. Admission Suggested donation $5.

Greenwich Village & West Village

Anchored by New York University, Greenwich Village, along with its western adjunct the West Village, is one of the most picturesque parts of the city. The stomping ground of the Beat Generation is no longer a cheap-rent bohemian paradise, but it's still a pleasant place for idle wandering, dining in excellent restaurants and hopping between bars and cabaret venues. The Meatpacking District, which over the past two decades has evolved from gritty industrial zone to gay cruising spot to hedonistic consumer playground, has a flashier feel. But the arrival of the new Whitney Museum in spring 2015 will bring a welcome injection of culture to the neighbourhood.

GREENWICH VILLAGE

Stretching from Houston Street to 14th Street, between Broadway and Sixth Avenue, Greenwich Village has been inspiring bohemians for almost a century. Now that it has become one of the most expensive neighbourhoods in the city, you need a lot more than a struggling artist's or writer's income to inhabit its leafy streets. Great for people-watching, **Washington Square Park** attracts a disparate cast of characters that

takes in hippies, students and street musicians. Skateboarders clatter near the base of the Washington Arch, a modestly sized replica of Paris's Arc de Triomphe, built in 1895 to honour George Washington. The 9.75-acre Village landmark recently received a $16-million redesign.

In the 1830s, the wealthy began building handsome townhouses around the square. A few of those properties are still privately owned and occupied, but many others have become part of the ever-expanding NYU campus. The university also owns the Washington Mews, a row of charming 19th-century former stables that line a tiny cobblestoned alley just to the north of the park between Fifth Avenue and University Place. Several famed literary figures, including Henry James (author of the celebrated novel which took its title from the square), Herman Melville, Edith Wharton, Edgar Allan Poe and Eugene O'Neill, lived on or near the square. In 1871, the local creative community founded the **Salmagundi Club** (47 Fifth Avenue, between 11th & 12th Streets, 1-212 255 7740, www.salmagundi.org), America's oldest artists' club. Now situated north of Washington Square on Fifth Avenue, it has galleries that are open to the public.

Greenwich Village continues to change with the times, for the better and for the worse. In the 1960s, 8th Street was the closest New York got to San Francisco's hippie Haight Street; Jimi Hendrix's **Electric Lady Studios** is still at 52 West 8th Street, between Fifth & Sixth Avenues. Although the strip was until recently a procession of piercing parlours, punky boutiques and shoe stores, it has been smartened up with the arrival of popular purveyors like **Stumptown Coffee Roasters** (see p56) and a boutique hotel, the **Marlton** (see p118). Once the dingy but colourful domain of Beat poets and folk and jazz musicians, the well-trafficked section of Bleecker Street between La Guardia Place and Sixth Avenue is now an overcrowded stretch of poster shops, cheap restaurants and music venues for the college crowd. Renowned hangouts such as Le Figaro Café (184 Bleecker Street, at MacDougal Street), Kerouac's favourite, are no more, but a worthy alternative is **Caffe Reggio** (see p55), the oldest coffeehouse in the village. Nearby, a former literati favourite of the likes of Hemingway and Fitzgerald, **Minetta Tavern** (see p56), has been rehabilitated by renowned restaurateur Keith McNally.

Although 1960s hotspot **Cafe Wha?** (115 MacDougal Street, between Bleecker & W 3rd Streets, 1-212 254 3706, www.cafewha. com) is now running on the fumes of its illustrious past, it has a decent house band. Nearby, the **Bitter End** (147 Bleecker Street, between La Guardia Place & Thompson Street,

1-212 673 7030, www.bitterend.com) has proudly championed the singer-songwriter – including a young Bob Dylan – since 1961. The famed Village Gate jazz club at the corner of Bleecker and Thompson Streets – which staged performances by Miles Davis, Nina Simone and John Cage – closed in 1993. However, in 2008, **Le Poisson Rouge** (see p98) opened on the site with a similar mission to present diverse genres under one roof.

Not far from here, in the triangle formed by Sixth Avenue, Greenwich Avenue and 10th Street, you'll see the Gothic-style **Jefferson Market Library** (a branch of the New York Public Library). The lovely flower-filled garden facing Greenwich Avenue was once the site of the Women's House of Detention, which was torn down in 1974. Mae West did a little time there in 1926, on obscenity charges stemming from her Broadway show Sex.

Just behind the library, off 10th Street, lies **Patchin Place**, which was home to some of the luminaries of New York's literary pantheon. This cul-de-sac lined with brick houses built during the mid 19th century is off limits to the public, but through the gate you can make out no.4, where the poet and staunch foe of capitalisation ee cummings resided from 1923 to 1962; and no.5, where Djuna Barnes, author of Nightwood, lived from 1940 to 1982.

AIA Center for Architecture

Designed by architect Andrew Berman, this three-storey building is a fitting home for architectural debate: the sweeping, light-filled design is a physical manifestation of AIA's goal of promoting transparency in terms of both access and programming. Berman cut away large slabs of flooring at the street and basement levels, converting underground spaces into bright, museum-quality galleries. 536 La Guardia Place, between Bleecker & W 3rd Streets (1-212 683 0023, www.cfa.aiany.org). Subway A, B, C, D, E, F, M to W 4th Street. Open 9am-8pm Mon-Fri; 11am-5pm Sat. Admission free.

WEST VILLAGE

In the early 20th century, the West Village was largely a working-class Italian neighbourhood. These days, the highly desirable enclave is home to numerous celebrities (including Claire Danes, Hugh Jackman, and Sarah Jessica Parker and Matthew Broderick), but a low-key, everyone-knows-everyone feel remains. The area west of Sixth Avenue to the Hudson River, from 14th Street to Houston Street, possesses the quirky geographical features that moulded the Village's character. Only here could West 10th Street cross West 4th Street, and Waverly Place cross… Waverly Place. One of the oldest parts of the Village, it retains a street layout based on the original settlers' horse paths.

Locals and visitors crowd bistros along Seventh Avenue and Hudson Street, and patronise the high-rent shops on this stretch of Bleecker Street, including no fewer than three Marc Jacobs boutiques. Venture on to the side streets for interesting discoveries, such as sumptuous perfume parlour **Aedes de Venustas** (see p77) on Christopher Street. The area's bohemian population may have dwindled years ago, but a few old landmarks remain. Solemnly raise a glass in the **White Horse Tavern** (see p68), a favourite of such literary luminaries as Ezra Pound, James Baldwin, Norman Mailer and Dylan Thomas, who included it on his last drinking binge before his death in 1953. On and just off Seventh Avenue South are jazz and cabaret clubs, including the **Village Vanguard** (see p100).

The West Village is also a historic gay neighbourhood, although the current scene has mostly migrated north to Hell's Kitchen. The **Stonewall Inn** (see p92), on Christopher Street, was the site of the 1969 riots that marked the birth of the modern gay-liberation movement. In Christopher Park, which faces the bar, is George Segal's Gay Liberation, a piece composed of plaster sculptures of two same-sex couples that commemorates the street's pivotal role in gay history.

MEATPACKING DISTRICT

The north-west corner of the West Village has been known as the Meatpacking District since the area was dominated by the wholesale meat industry in the early 20th century. As business waned, gay fetish clubs took root in derelict buildings and, until the 1990s, the area was a haunt for transsexual prostitutes. In more recent years, however, hip eateries and designer boutiques have moved in. Frequent mentions on Sex and the City, along with the arrival of swanky hotel **Gansevoort Meatpacking NYC** (see p115) in the noughties cemented the area's reputation as a mainstream consumer playground. Nightclubs, including **Cielo** (see p94), continue to draw after-dark pleasure seekers.

The 2009 opening of freight-track-turned-park the **High Line** has brought even bigger crowds to the area. Slick style hotel the **Standard** (see p115) straddles the elevated park at West 13th Street, and its seasonal Biergarten, nestled beneath it, is a great spot for a pint.

High Line

Running from Gansevoort Street in the Meatpacking District through Chelsea's gallery district to 30th Street, this slender, sinuous green strip – formerly an elevated freight train track – has been designed by landscape architects James Corner Field Operations and architects Diller Scofidio + Renfro. In autumn 2012, construction began on the final section, which will open in three phases, starting in late 2014. Stretching from 30th to 34th Streets, it skirts the West Side Rail Yards, which are being developed into a long-planned residential and commercial complex, Hudson Yards. 1-212 500 6035, www.thehighline.org. Open usually 7am-10pm daily (hours vary seasonally; see website for updates).

Chelsea

Formerly a working-class Irish and Hispanic neighbourhood, the corridor between 14th and 29th Streets west of Sixth Avenue emerged as the nexus of New York's queer life in the 1990s. Due to rising housing costs and the protean nature of the city's cultural landscape, it's since been eclipsed by Hell's Kitchen to the north (just as Chelsea once overtook the West Village), but you'll still find bars, restaurants and shops catering to the once-ubiquitous 'Chelsea boys'. The cityscape shifts from leafy side streets lined with pristine 19th-century brownstones to an eclectic array of striking industrial and contemporary architecture on the far west side. In recent years, the local buzz has shifted to the previously neglected Hudson-hugging strip that has evolved into the city's main gallery district.

Internationally recognised spaces such as **Mary Boone Gallery**, **Gagosian Gallery** and **Gladstone Gallery**, as well as numerous less exalted names, attract swarms of art aficionados (for our picks, see p82 Gallery-Hopping Guide). The High Line has brought even more gallery-hoppers to the area as it provides a verdant pathway from the boutique- and restaurant-rich Meatpacking District to the art enclave. Traversing the elevated promenade, you'll pass through the old loading dock of the former Nabisco factory, where the first Oreo cookie was made in 1912. This conglomeration of 18 structures, built between the 1890s and the 1930s, now houses **Chelsea Market** (75 Ninth Avenue, between 15th & 16th Streets, www.chelseamarket.com). The ground-floor food arcade offers artisanal bread, wine, baked goods and freshly made ice-cream, among other treats.

Also among the area's notable industrial architecture is the **Starrett-Lehigh Building** (601 W 26th Street, at Eleventh Avenue). The stunning 1929 structure was left in disrepair until the dot-com boom of the late 1990s, when media companies, photographers and designers snatched up its loft-like spaces.

While some of the Hudson River piers, which were once terminals for the world's grand ocean liners, remain in a state of ruin, the four that lie between 17th and 23rd Streets have been transformed into mega sports centre **Chelsea Piers** (see p79).

To get a glimpse of how Chelsea looked back when it was first developed in the 1880s, stroll along **Cushman Row** (406-418 W 20th Street, between Ninth & Tenth Avenues) in the Chelsea Historic District. Just to the north is the block-long **General Theological Seminary of the Episcopal Church** (440 W 21st Street, between Ninth & Tenth Avenues). The seminary's land was part of the estate known as Chelsea, owned by poet Clement Clarke Moore, author of A Visit from St Nicholas (more commonly known as 'Twas the Night Before Christmas), and the guest wing has been converted into the **High Line Hotel** (see p116).

High Line

Explore

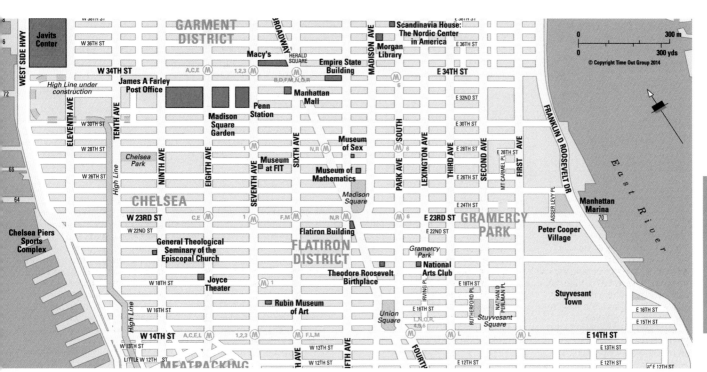

A hostelry with a more notorious history is nearby. The **Chelsea Hotel** on West 23rd Street has been a magnet for creative types since it first opened in 1884; Mark Twain was an early guest. The list of those who have stayed here reads like an international *Who's Who* of the artistic elite: Sarah Bernhardt (who slept in a coffin), William Burroughs (who wrote *Naked Lunch* here), Dylan Thomas, Janis Joplin and Jimi Hendrix, to name a few. In the 1960s, it was the stomping ground of Andy Warhol's coterie of superstars, and the location of his 1966 film *The Chelsea Girls*. The hotel gained punk-rock notoriety on 12 October 1978, when Sex Pistol Sid Vicious stabbed his girlfriend, Nancy Spungen, to death in Room 100. It's still home to about 80 permanent residents, working artists among them, but the Chelsea, recently acquired by fashionable boutique-hotel developer King & Grove (www.king andgrove.com), was undergoing renovations at the time of writing and not taking reservations for short-term guests.

The weekend flea markets tucked between buildings along 25th Street, between Seventh Avenue and Broadway, have shrunk in recent years (casualties of development), but you'll still find a heady assortment of clothes, furnishings, cameras and knick-knacks at the rummage-worthy **Antiques Garage** (see p79).

Not far from here, the Fashion Institute of Technology, on 27th Street, between Seventh and Eighth Avenues, counts Calvin Klein, Nanette Lepore and Michael Kors among its alumni. The school's **Museum at FIT** mounts excellent free exhibitions.

Museum at FIT

The Fashion Institute of Technology owns one of the largest and most impressive clothing collections in the world, including some 50,000 garments and accessories dating from the 18th century to the present. Under the directorship of fashion historian Dr Valerie Steele, the museum showcases a rotating selection from the permanent collection, as well as temporary exhibitions focusing on individual designers or spotlighting fashion from cultural angles. *Building E, Seventh Avenue, at 27th Street (1-212 217 4558, www. fitnyc.edu/museum). Subway 1 to 28th Street. Open noon-8pm Tue-Fri; 10am-5pm Sat. Admission free.*

Rubin Museum of Art

Dedicated to Himalayan art, the Rubin is a very stylish museum – a fact that falls into place when you learn that the six-storey space was once occupied by famed fashion store Barneys. The ground-floor café used to be the accessories department, and retail lives on in the colourful gift shop. A dramatic central spiral staircase ascends to the galleries, where rich-toned walls are classy foils for the serene statuary and intricate, multicoloured textiles. The second level is dedicated to 'Gateway to Himalayan Art', a yearly rotating display of selections from the permanent collection of more than 2,000 pieces from the second century to the present day. The upper floors are devoted to changing exhibitions. *150 W 17th Street, at Seventh Avenue (1-212 620 5000, www.rmanyc.org). Subway A, C, E to 14th Street; L to Eighth Avenue; 1 to 18th Street. Open 11am-5pm Mon, Thur; 11am-9pm Wed; 11am-10pm Fri; 11am-6pm Sat, Sun. Admission $15; $10 reductions; free under-13s; free 6-10pm Fri.*

Gramercy & Flatiron

Lying east of Chelsea, the Gramercy and Flatiron neighbourhoods contain some of the city's most distinctive architecture – including the famous wedge-shaped building that gave the Flatiron District its name – and several inviting green spaces. Unfortunately, you'll probably only get tantalising over-the-gate glimpses of pretty Gramercy Park, which remains the exclusive preserve of residents of the surrounding buildings. But in recent years, the attractions for visitors have multiplied in this part of town, with the arrival of new museums, restaurants and shops, including the country's first **Museum of Mathematics** (see p28) and Italian-food mecca **Eataly** (see p79).

FLATIRON DISTRICT & UNION SQUARE

The Flatiron District extends from 14th to 29th Streets, between Sixth and Lexington Avenues. However, as with many NYC neighbourhoods, the borders are disputed and evolving – NoMad is slowly catching on as the new name for the blocks north of Madison Square Park.

The area was once predominantly commercial, home to numerous toy manufacturers and photography studios – it's still not uncommon to see models and actors strolling to and from their shoots. However, in the 1980s, the neighbourhood became more residential, as buyers were drawn to its 19th-century brownstones and early 20th-century industrial architecture. Clusters of upscale restaurants and shops soon followed. By the turn of the millennium, many internet start-ups had moved to the area, earning it the nickname 'Silicon Alley'.

There are two major public spaces in the locale: Madison Square Park and Union Square. Opened in 1847, **Madison Square Park** (from 23rd to 26th Streets, between Fifth & Madison Avenues) is the more stately of the two. In the 19th century, the square was a highly desirable address. Winston Churchill's grandfather resided in a magnificent but since-demolished mansion at Madison Avenue and 26th Street; Edith Wharton also made her home in the neighbourhood and set many of her high-society novels here. By the 1990s, the park had become a decaying no-go zone given over to drug dealers and the homeless, but it got a much-needed makeover in 2001 thanks to the efforts of the Madison Square Park Conservancy (www.madisonsquarepark.org), which has created a programme of cultural events, including Mad Sq Art, a year-round 'gallery without walls', featuring sculptural, video and installation exhibitions from big-name artists. A further lure is restaurateur Danny Meyer's original **Shake Shack**, which attracts queues in all weathers for its burgers – considered by many New Yorkers to be top of the heap. (For a review of the larger Upper West Side location, see p60.)

The square is surrounded by illustrious buildings. Completed in 1909, the **Metropolitan Life Tower** (1 Madison Avenue, at 24th Street) was modelled on the Campanile in Venice's Piazza San Marco (an allusion as commercial as it was architectural, for Met Life Insurance wished to remind people that it had raised funds for the Campanile after its fall two years earlier).

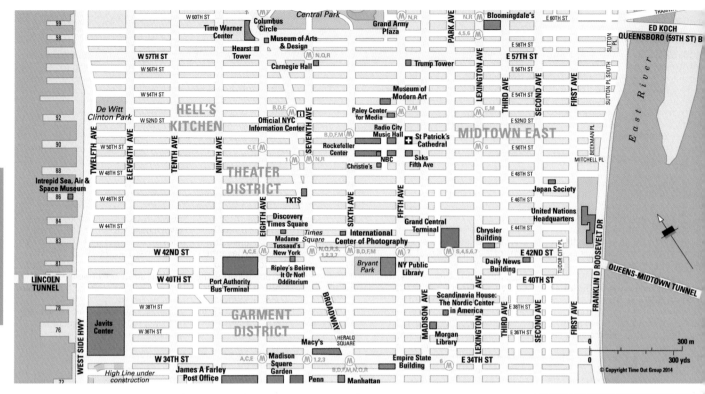

The **Appellate Division Courthouse** (35 E 25th Street, at Madison Avenue) features one of the most beautiful pediments in the city, while Cass Gilbert's **New York Life Insurance Company Building** (51 Madison Avenue, at 26th Street) is capped by a golden pyramid that's one of the Manhattan skyline's jewels.

The most famous of all Madison Square's edifices, however, lies at the southern end. The **Flatiron Building** (175 Fifth Avenue, between 22nd & 23rd Streets) was the world's first steel-frame skyscraper, a 22-storey Beaux Arts edifice clad conspicuously in white limestone and glazed terracotta. But it's the unique triangular shape (like an arrow pointing northward to indicate the city's progression uptown) that has drawn sightseers since it opened in 1902. Legend has it that a popular 1920s catchphrase originated at this corner of 23rd Street – police would give the '23 skidoo' to ne'er-do-wells trying to peek at ladies' petticoats as the unique wind currents that swirled around the building blew their dresses upward. Speaking of rampant libidos: the nearby **Museum of Sex** houses an impressive collection of salacious ephemera.

In the 19th century, the neighbourhood went by the moniker of Ladies' Mile, thanks to the ritzy department stores that lined Broadway and Sixth Avenue. These retail palaces attracted the 'carriage trade', wealthy women who bought the latest imported fashions and household goods. By 1914, most of the department stores had moved north, leaving their proud cast-iron

buildings behind. Today, the area is peppered with chain clothing stores, bookshops and tasteful home-furnishing retailers such as **ABC Carpet & Home** (*see p79*).

The Flatiron District's other major public space, Union Square (from 14th to 17th Streets, between Union Square East & Union Square West) is named after neither the Union of the Civil War nor the labour rallies that once took place here, but simply for the union of Broadway and Bowery Lane (now Fourth Avenue). Even so, it does have its radical roots: from the 1920s until the early '60s, it was a favourite spot for tub-thumping political oratory. Following 9/11, Union Square was the location of candlelit vigils and became a focal point for the city's grief. Formerly grungy, the park is fresh from a rolling renovation project started in the 1980s. These days, it's best known as the home of the **Union Square Greenmarket** (*see p80*).

Museum of Mathematics (MoMath)

The country's first Museum of Mathematics replaces lectures and textbooks with more than 30 eclectic exhibits covering topics such as algebra and geometry. Designed for visitors of all ages, MoMath aims to eliminate the intimidation factor. Think a ride on a square-wheeled trike could never be smooth? Find out just how bump-free it can be when you take said tricycle over a sunflower-shaped track, where the petals create strategically placed catenaries – curves used in geometry and physics – that make a level ride possible. Elsewhere, you can pass 3-D objects (or even your own body)

through the laser-light 'Wall of Fire', and the lasers will display the objects as two-dimensional cross-sections (a cone becomes a triangle and circle, for instance). Or collaborate with a pair of fellow visitors to pan, zoom and create your own video cameras to create a single composite image, which can be manipulated into a bevy of interesting 'Feedback Fractals' (or fragmented shapes).
11 E 26th Street, between Fifth & Madison Avenues (1-212 542 0566, www.momath.org). Subway N, R, 6 to 23rd Street. Open 10am-5pm daily (10am-2.30pm 1st Wed of each mth). Admission $16; free-$10 reductions.

Museum of Sex

Situated in the former Tenderloin district, which was bumping and grinding with dance halls and brothels in the 1800s, MoSex explores its subject within a cultural context. Highlights of the permanent collection of more than 15,000 objects range from the tastefully erotic to the outlandish: an 1890s anti-onanism device looks as uncomfortable as the BDSM gear donated by a local dominatrix, and there is kinky art courtesy of Picasso and Keith Haring. Rotating exhibitions in the three-level space include the likes of 'The Sex Lives of Animals'. The gift shop stocks books and arty sex toys, while the museum's bar dispenses aphrodisiac cocktails, stimulating soft drinks and light bites.
233 Fifth Avenue, at 27th Street (1-212 689 6337, www.museumofsex. com). Open 10am-8pm Mon-Thur, Sun; 10am-9pm Fri, Sat. Admission $17.50; $15.25 reductions. Under-18s not admitted.

GRAMERCY PARK

A key to **Gramercy Park**, the tranquil, gated square at the bottom of Lexington Avenue, between 20th and 21st Streets, is one of the most sought-after treasures in all the five boroughs. For the most part, only residents of the beautiful surrounding townhouses and apartment buildings have access to the park, which was developed in the 1830s to resemble a London square. The park is flanked by two private clubs; members of both also have access to the square. One is the **Players Club** (16 Gramercy Park South, between Park Avenue South & Irving Place, 1-212 475 6116, www.theplayersnyc.org), inspired by London's Garrick Club. It's housed in an 1847 brownstone formerly owned by Edwin Booth, the celebrated 19th-century actor and brother of John Wilkes Booth, Abraham Lincoln's assassin. Next door at no.15 is the Victorian Gothic Revival Samuel J Tilden House, which houses the **National Arts Club** (1-212 475 3424, www.nationalartsclub.org, closed Sat, Sun & July, Aug). The busts of famous writers (Shakespeare, Dante) along the façade were chosen to reflect Tilden's library, which, along with his fortune, helped to create the New York Public Library. The NAC's galleries are open to non-members, but call before visiting as they are sometimes closed for private events or between shows.

Leading south from the park to 14th Street, Irving Place is named after author Washington Irving (although he never actually lived here). Near the corner of 15th Street sits **Irving Plaza** (*see p97*), a music venue. At the corner of Park Avenue outh and 17th Street is the final ase of the once-omnipotent ammany Hall political machine. uilt in 1929, it now houses the New ork Film Academy. Popular local angout 71 **Irving Place Coffee & ea Bar** (*see p57*) is a good place o revive oneself with a cup of New ork State-roasted java. A few blocks way from here is the **Theodore oosevelt Birthplace**, a national istoric site.

The largely residential area ordered by 23rd and 30th Streets, ark Avenue and the East River is nown as **Kips Bay** after Jacobus ip, whose farm covered the area in he 17th century. Third Avenue is the istrict's main thoroughfare, and a ocus of restaurants representing a ariety of eastern cuisines, including fghan, Tibetan and Turkish.

heodore Roosevelt Birthplace ational Historic Site

he brownstone where the 26th resident of the United States was orn, and where he lived until he was 4 years old, was demolished in 1916. ut it was re-created after his death in 919, complete with authentic period urniture (some from the original ouse), personal effects and a trophy oom. The house can only be explored y guided tour.

8 E 20th Street, between Broadway & ark Avenue South (1-212 260 1616, ww.nps.gov/thrb). Subway 6 to 23rd treet. Tours hourly 10am-4pm Tue-at, except noon. Admission free.

Midtown

oaring office towers, crowded avements and taxi-choked streets that's the image most people ave of the busy midsection of Manhattan. This part of town draws isitors to some of the city's best-nown landmarks, including iconic kyscrapers like the Empire State uilding and the Chrysler Building, he dazzling electronic spectacle hat is Times Square and Rockefeller enter, with its picturesque easonal ice-skating rink. Fifth venue, the dividing line between Midtown West and Midtown East, s continuously clogged with hoppers from all over the world. ut there's more to midtown than onic architecture and commerce. n the far west side, the northern xtension of the High Line is ttracting galleries and shops, nd rapidly gentrifying Hell's itchen has emerged as the city's ottest gaybourhood.

HERALD SQUARE & THE GARMENT DISTRICT

eventh Avenue, aka Fashion venue, is the main drag of the arment District (roughly from 4th to 40th Streets, between roadway & Eighth Avenue) and here designers – and their staff – eed America's multi-billion-dollar lothing industry. Delivery trucks and workers pushing racks of clothes clog streets lined with wholesale trimming, button and fabric shops. Many designer showrooms hold sample sales (*see p72*).

Taking up an entire city block, from 34th Street to 35th Street, between Broadway and Seventh Avenue, is the legendary **Macy's** (*see p81*). With one million square feet of selling space spread across nine floors, it's the biggest and busiest department store in the world. Facing Macy's, at the intersection of Broadway, 34th Street and Sixth Avenue, is **Herald Square**, named after a long-gone newspaper, the *New York Herald*. The lower section is known as **Greeley Square** after editor and reformer Horace Greeley, owner of the Herald's rival, the *New York Tribune* (the two papers merged in 1924). Once seedy, the square now offers bistro chairs and tables that get crowded with shoppers and office lunchers in the warmer months. To the east, the many spas, restaurants and karaoke bars of small enclave **Koreatown** line 32nd Street, between Broadway and Fifth Avenue.

Located not in Madison Square but on Seventh Avenue, between 31st and 33rd Streets, **Madison Square Garden** (*see p96*) is home to the Knicks and Rangers, and has welcomed rock icons from Elvis to Lady Gaga as well as the Barnum & Bailey Circus and other big events. The massive arena is actually the fourth building to bear that name (the first two were appropriately located in the square after which they were named) and opened in 1968, replacing the grand old Pennsylvania Station razed four years earlier. This brutal act of architectural vandalism spurred the creation of the city's Landmarks Preservation Commission, which has saved many other edifices from a similar fate.

Beneath Madison Square Garden stands **Penn Station**, a claustrophobic catacomb serving 600,000 Amtrak, Long Island Rail Road and New Jersey Transit passengers daily and the busiest train station in America. A proposal to relocate the station across the street to the stately **James A Farley Post Office** (421 Eighth Avenue, between 31st & 33rd Streets) was championed by the late Senator Patrick Moynihan in the early 1990s. The project, which has stalled over the years, finally got the necessary funding and government approval, and Moynihan Station is expected to be completed in 2016.

THE THEATER DISTRICT & HELL'S KITCHEN

Times Square's evolution from a traffic-choked fleshpot to a tourist-friendly theme park has accelerated in the past few years. Not only has 'the Crossroads of the World' gained an elevated viewing platform atop the **TKTS** discount booth, from which visitors can admire the surrounding light show, but also stretches of Broadway, from 47th to 42nd Streets and from 35th to 33rd Streets, have been designated pedestrian zones, complete with seating, in an effort to streamline midtown traffic and create a more pleasant environment for both residents and visitors. Permanent plazas, designed by National September 11 Memorial Museum architects Snøhetta, are being developed in the 'Bowtie' from 42nd to 47th Streets, featuring continuous paved areas and granite benches. The first section should be completed by publication of this guide and the remainder by 2015.

Originally Longacre Square, the junction of Broadway and Seventh Avenue, stretching from 42nd to 47th Streets, was renamed after the *New York Times* moved here in the early 1900s. The first electrified billboard graced the district in 1904, on the side of a bank at 46th and Broadway. The same year, the inaugural New Year's Eve party in Times Square doubled as the *Times*'s housewarming party in its new HQ. Today, about a million people gather here to watch an illuminated Waterford Crystal ball descend every 31 December.

The paper left the building only a decade after it had arrived (it now occupies an $84-million tower on Eighth Avenue, between 40th and 41st Streets). However, it retained ownership of its old headquarters until the 1960s, and erected the world's first scrolling electric news 'zipper' in 1928. The readout, now sponsored by Dow Jones, still trumpets the latest breaking stories.

Times Square is also the gateway to the **Theater District**, the zone between 41st Street and 53rd Street, from Sixth Avenue to Ninth Avenue, where extravagant shows are put on six days a week (Monday is the traditional night off). While numerous showhouses stage first-rate productions in the area, only 39 are officially Broadway theatres (plus Lincoln Center's Vivian Beaumont uptown). The distinction is based on size rather than location or quality – Broadway theatres must have more than 500 seats. The Theater District's transformation from the cradle of New York's sex industry began in 1984, when the city condemned properties along 42nd Street ('Forty Deuce', or 'the Deuce' for short), between Seventh and Eighth Avenues. A change in zoning laws meant adult-oriented venues must now subsist on X-rated videos rather than live 'dance' shows; the square's sex trade is now relegated to short stretches of Seventh and Eighth Avenues, just north and south of 42nd Street.

Recording studios, record labels, theatrical agencies and media companies reside in the area's office buildings. The **Brill Building** (1619 Broadway, at 49th Street) was once a hive of music publishers and producers; such luminaries as Jerry Lieber, Mike Stoller and Carole King wrote and auditioned their hits here. Flashy attractions and huge retail stores strive to outdo one another in hopes of snaring the tourist throngs. The vast **Toys 'R' Us** (1514 Broadway, at 44th Street, 1-646 366 8800) boasts a 60-foot indoor Ferris wheel and a two-floor Barbie emporium.

The streets to the west of Eighth Avenue are filled with eateries catering to theatregoers, especially the predominantly pricey, tourist-oriented places along **Restaurant Row** (46th Street, between Eighth and Ninth Avenues). Locals tend to walk west to Ninth Avenue – in the

Times Square

40s and 50s, the Hell's Kitchen strip is tightly packed with inexpensive restaurants serving a variety of ethnic cuisines.

West of the Theater District lies **Hell's Kitchen**. The precise origins of the name are unclear, but are no doubt connected to its emergence as an Irish-mob-dominated neighbourhood in the 19th-century – the *New York Times* claims that the first known documented reference was in that very paper in 1881, to describe an unsavoury tenement in the locale. In the 1950s, clashes between Irish and recently arrived Puerto Rican factions were dramatised in the musical *West Side Story*. It was a particularly violent incident in 1959, in which two teenagers died, that led to an attempt by local businesses to erase the stigma associated with the area by renaming it Clinton (taken from a park named after one-time mayor DeWitt Clinton). The new name never really took, and gang culture survived until the 1980s.

Today, the area has emerged as New York's hottest queer neighbourhood, with numerous bars and the city's first gay-oriented luxury hotel, **The Out NYC** (*see p92*). As gentrification takes hold, new apartment blocks are also springing up in the former wasteland near the Hudson River. This area is dominated by the massive, black-glass **Jacob K Javits Convention Center** (Eleventh Avenue, between 34th & 39th Streets), which hosts a never-ending schedule of large-scale trade shows. A couple of major draws are also here: the **Circle Line Terminal**, at Pier 83, the departure point for the cruise company's three-hour circumnavigation of Manhattan Island (*see p123*), and the **Intrepid Sea, Air & Space Museum**, a retired aircraft carrier-cum-naval museum.

Discovery Times Square

This Discovery Channel-sponsored exhibition centre stages big shows on such crowd-pleasing subjects as King Tut, Pompeii, the *Titanic* and the Harry Potter franchise.
226 W 44th Street, between Seventh & Eighth Avenues (1-866 987 9692, www.discoverytsx.com). Subway A, C, E to 42nd Street-Port Authority; N, Q, R, S, 1, 2, 3, 7 to 42nd Street-Times Square. Open 10am-7pm Mon, Tue, Sun; 10am-8pm Wed, Thur; 10am-9pm Fri, Sat. Admission $27; $19.50-$23.50 reductions; free under-4s.

Intrepid Sea, Air & Space Museum

Commissioned in 1943, this 27,000-ton, 898ft aircraft carrier survived torpedoes and kamikaze attacks in World War II, served during the Vietnam War and the Cuban Missile Crisis, and recovered two space capsules for NASA. It was decommissioned in 1974, then resurrected as an educational institution. On its flight deck and portside aircraft elevator are top-notch examples of American military might, including the US Navy F-14 Tomcat (as featured in *Top Gun*), an A-12 Blackbird spy plane and a fully restored Army AH-1G Cobra gunship helicopter. In summer 2011, the museum became home to the Enterprise (OV-101), the prototype NASA Orbiter, which was recently retired (entry to the Space Shuttle Pavilion costs extra).
USS Intrepid, Pier 86, Twelfth Avenue & 46th Street (1-212 245 0072, www.intrepidmuseum.org). Subway A, C, E to 42nd Street-Port Authority, then M42 bus to Twelfth Avenue or 15min walk. Open Apr-Oct 10am-5pm Mon-Fri; 10am-6pm Sat, Sun. Nov-Mar 10am-5pm daily. Admission $24; $12-$20 reductions; free under-3s, active & retired US military.

Madame Tussauds New York

With roots in 18th-century Paris and founded in London in 1802, the world's most famous wax museum now draws celebrity-hungry crowds to more than a dozen locations worldwide. At the New York outpost, you can get a stalker's-eye view of paraffin doppelgangers of an array of political, sports, film and pop stars, from Barack Obama and Carmelo Anthony to Leonardo DiCaprio and Lady Gaga. A new crop of freshly waxed victims debuts every few months.
234 W 42nd Street, between Seventh & Eighth Avenues (1-866 841 3505, www.madametussauds.com/newyork). Subway A, C, E to 42nd Street-Port Authority; N, Q, R, S, 1, 2, 3, 7 to 42nd Street-Times Square. Open 10am-8pm Mon-Thur, Sun; 10am-10pm Fri, Sat. Admission $36; $29 reductions; free under-4s.

Ripley's Believe It or Not!

Times Square might be a little whitewashed these days, but you can get a feel for the old freak show at this repository of the eerie and uncanny. Marvel at such bizarre artefacts as a six-legged cow, the world's largest collection of shrunken heads and a cache of weird art that includes a portrait of President Obama composed of 12,600 gumballs. Carrying a torch for gritty bygone attractions, Ripley's provides a platform for a new generation of sideshow acts with free weekend performances by the likes of Albert Cadabra, the human blockhead, at the entrance (see website for schedule).
234 W 42nd Street, between Seventh & Eighth Avenues (1-212 398 3133, www.ripleysnewyork.com). Subway A, C, E to 42nd Street-Port Authority; N, Q, R, S, 1, 2, 3, 7 to 42nd Street-Times Square. Open 9am-1am daily (last entry midnight). Admission $33; $25 reductions; free under-4s.

FIFTH AVENUE & AROUND

The stretch of Fifth Avenue between Rockefeller Center and Central Park South showcases retail palaces bearing names that were famous long before the concept of branding was developed. Bracketed by **Saks Fifth Avenue** (49th to 50th Streets;

Intrepid Sea, Air & Space Museum

see p81) and **Bergdorf Goodman** (57th to 58th Streets; *see p80*), tenants include Gucci, Prada and Tiffany & Co (and the parade of big names continues east along 57th Street). Along with Madison Avenue uptown, this is the centre of high-end shopping in New York, and the window displays – particularly during the frenetic Christmas shopping season – are worth a look even if you're not buying.

Fifth Avenue is crowned by **Grand Army Plaza** at 59th Street, presided over by a gilded statue of General William Tecumseh Sherman. To the west stands the Plaza (*see p117*), the famous hotel that was home to fictional moppet Eloise. Stretching north above 59th Street (the parkside stretch is called Central Park South), is **Central Park** (*see pp34-35*).

Fifth Avenue is the main route for the city's many public processions: the **St Patrick's Day Parade** (*see p11*), the **LGBT Pride March** (*see p12*) and many others. Even without floats or marching bands, the sidewalks are generally teeming with shoppers and tourists. The most famous skyscraper in the world also has its entrance on Fifth Avenue: the **Empire State Building** (*see p31*), located smack-bang in the centre of midtown.

A pair of impassive stone lions, which were dubbed Patience and Fortitude by Mayor Fiorello La Guardia during the Great Depression, guard the steps of the beautiful Beaux Arts humanities and social sciences branch of the **New York Public Library** at 42nd Street, now officially named the Stephen A Schwarzman Building. Just behind the library is Bryant Park, a well-manicured lawn that hosts a popular outdoor film series in summer and an ice-skating rink in winter.

The luxury **Bryant Park Hotel** (*see p118*) occupies the former American Radiator Building on 40th Street. Designed by architect Raymond Hood in the mid 1920s, the structure is faced with near-black brick and trimmed in gold leaf. Alexander Woollcott, Dorothy Parker and her 'vicious circle' held court and traded barbs at the nearby **Algonquin** (*see p118*); the lobby is still a great place to meet for a drink. Just north of the park, on Sixth Avenue, is the always thought-provoking **International Center of Photography** (*see p31*).

Step off Fifth Avenue into **Rockefeller Center** (*see p31*) and you'll find yourself in a 'city within a city', an interlacing complex of 19 buildings housing corporate offices, retail space and Rockefeller Plaza. After plans for an expansion of the Metropolitan Opera on the site fell through in 1929, John D Rockefeller Jr set about creating the complex to house radio and television corporations. Designed by Raymond Hood and many other prominent architects, Rock Center grew over the decades, with each new building conforming to the original master plan and art deco design.

On weekday mornings, a crowd gathers at the NBC network's glass-walled, ground-level studio (where the *Today* show is shot), at the south-west corner of Rockefeller Plaza and 49th Street. The complex is also home to art auction house **Christie's** (20 Rockefeller Plaza, 49th Street, between Fifth & Sixth Avenues, 1-212 636 2000, www.christies.com, 9am-5.30pm Mon-Fri, usually closed Sat, Sun); pop into the lobby to admire a mural by conceptualist Sol LeWitt.

When it opened on Sixth Avenue (at 50th Street) in 1932, **Radio City Music Hall** (*see p98*) was designed as a showcase for high-end variety acts, but the death of vaudeville led to a quick transition into what was then the world's largest movie house. Today, the art deco jewel hosts concerts and a traditional Christmas Spectacular featuring renowned precision dance troupe e Rockettes. Visitors can get a eek backstage, and meet one of the gh-kicking dancers, on the Stage oor tour (every 30mins, 11am-3pm aily; $20, $15 reductions; see ww.radiocity.com for details).

Facing Rockefeller Center is the eautiful **St Patrick's Cathedral** (*see below*). Famous couples from Scott and Zelda Fitzgerald to Liza innelli and David Gest have tied e knot here; funeral services for uch notables as Andy Warhol and aseball legend Joe DiMaggio were eld in its confines. A few blocks orth is the **Museum of Modern Art MoMA**) and the **Paley Center for ledia** (for both, *see below*).

mpire State Building

inanced by General Motors executive ohn J Raskob at the height of New ork's skyscraper race, the Empire tate sprang up in a mere 14 months, eeks ahead of schedule and $5 iillion under budget. Since its opening 1931, it's been immortalised in ountless photos and films, from the riginal *King Kong* to *Sleepless in eattle*. Following the destruction of e World Trade Center in 2001, the ,250ft tower resumed its title as New ork's tallest building but has since een overtaken by the new 1 World rade Center. The nocturnal colour cheme of the tower lights – recently pgraded to flashy LEDs – often onours holidays, charities or special vents. The enclosed observatory on e 102nd floor is the city's highest ookout point, but the panoramic deck the 86th floor, 1,050ft above the treet, is roomier. From here, you can njoy views of all five boroughs and ve neighbouring states too (when e skies are clear).

50 Fifth Avenue, between 33rd 34th Streets (1-212 736 3100, ww.esbnyc.com). Subway B, D, F, M, , Q, R to 34th Street-Herald Square. pen 8am-2am daily (last elevator .15am). Admission 86th floor $27; 21-$24 reductions; free under-6s. 02nd floor $17 extra.

nternational Center f Photography

ince 1974, the ICP has served as a pre- minent library, school and museum evoted to the photographic image. hotojournalism remains a vital facet f the centre's programming, which lso includes contemporary photos nd video. Recent shows in the two- oor exhibition space have focused n the work of Elliott Erwitt, Richard vedon and Lewis Hine.

133 Sixth Avenue, at 43rd Street 1-212 857 0000, www.icp.org). ubway B, D, F, M to 42nd Street- ryant Park; N, Q, R, S, 1, 2, 3, 7 to 2nd Street-Times Square; 7 to Fifth venue. Open 10am-6pm Tue-Thur, at, Sun; 10am-8pm Fri. Admission 14; $10 reductions; free under-12s; ay what you wish 5-8pm Fri.

luseum of Modern Art (MoMA)

fter a two-year renovation based on a esign by Japanese architect Yoshio

Taniguchi, MoMA reopened in 2004 with almost double the space to display some of the most impressive artworks from the 19th, 20th and 21st centuries. The museum's permanent collection now encompasses seven curatorial departments: Architecture and Design, Drawings, Film, Media, Painting and Sculpture, Photography, and Prints and Illustrated Books. Highlights include Picasso's *Les Demoiselles d'Avignon*, Van Gogh's *The Starry Night* and Dali's *The Persistence of Memory* as well as masterpieces by Giacometti, Hopper, Matisse, Monet, O'Keeffe, Pollock, Rothko, Warhol and many others. Outside, the Philip Johnson-designed Abby Aldrich Rockefeller Sculpture Garden contains works by Calder, Rodin and Moore. The destination museum also contains a destination restaurant, the Modern, which overlooks the garden. If you find the prices too steep, dine in the bar, which shares the kitchen.

11 W 53rd Street, between Fifth & Sixth Avenues (1-212 708 9400, www.moma.org). Subway E, M to Fifth Avenue-53rd Street. Open 10.30am-5.30pm Mon-Thur, Sat, Sun; 10.30am-8pm Fri; 10.30am- 8.30pm 1st Thur of the mth & every Thur in July, Aug. Admission (incl admission to film programmes) $25; $14-$18 reductions; free under-17s; free 4-8pm Fri.

New York Public Library

Guarded by the marble lions Patience and Fortitude, this austere Beaux Arts edifice, designed by Carrère and Hastings, was completed in 1911. The building

Empire State Building

was actually renamed in honour of the philanthropist Stephen A Schwarzman in 2008, but Gothamites still know it as the New York Public Library, although the citywide library system consists of 91 locations. Free hour-long tours (11am, 2pm Mon-Sat; 2pm Sun, except July & Aug) take in the Rose Main Reading Room on the third floor, which at 297 feet long and 78 feet wide is almost the size of a football field. Specialist departments include the Map Division, which contains some 431,000 maps and 16,000 atlases, and the Rare Books Division, which boasts Walt Whitman's personal copies of the first (1855) and third (1860) editions of *Leaves of Grass*.

The library also stages major exhibitions and events, including the excellent 'Live from the NYPL' series of talks and lectures from big- name authors and thinkers (see website for schedule).

Fifth Avenue, at 42nd Street (1-917 275 6975, www.nypl.org). Subway B, D, F, M to 42nd Street-Bryant Park; 7 to Fifth Avenue. Open Sept-June 10am-6pm Mon, Thur-Sat; 10am- 8pm Tue, Wed; 1-5pm Sun. July, Aug 10am-6pm Mon, Thur-Sat; 10am- 8pm Tue, Wed (see website for gallery hours). Admission free.

Paley Center for Media

Nirvana for telly addicts and pop-culture junkies, the Paley Center (formerly the Museum of Television & Radio) houses an immense archive of almost 150,000 radio and TV shows. Head to the fourth-floor

TOP TIP!
Empire State express
Bypass one of three lines to the Empire State Building by buying tickets online. Alternatively, an express pass ($50) allows you to cut to the front.

library to search the system for your favourite episode of *Star Trek*, *Seinfeld*, or rarer fare, and watch it on your assigned console; radio shows are also available. A theatre on the concourse level is the location of frequent screenings, premières and high-profile panel discussions. There's also a small ground-floor gallery for themed exhibitions.

25 W 52nd Street, between Fifth & Sixth Avenues (1-212 621 6800, www.paleycenter.org). Subway B, D, F, M to 47-50th Streets-Rockefeller Center; E, M to Fifth Avenue-53rd Street. Open noon-6pm Wed, Fri-Sun; noon-8pm Thur. Admission $10; $5- $8 reductions. No credit cards.

Rockefeller Center

Constructed under the aegis of industrialist John D Rockefeller in the 1930s, this art deco city-within-a-city is inhabited by NBC, Simon & Schuster, McGraw-Hill and other media giants, as well as Radio City Music Hall, Christie's auction house, and an underground shopping arcade. Guided tours of the entire complex are available daily, and there's a separate NBC Studio tour (call the number above or see website for details).

The buildings and grounds are embellished with works by several well-known artists; look out for Isamu Noguchi's stainless-steel relief, *News*, above the entrance to 50 Rockefeller Plaza, and José Maria Sert's mural *American Progress* in the lobby of 30 Rockefeller Plaza (also known as the GE Building). But the most breathtaking sights are those seen from the 70th-floor Top of the Rock observation deck (combined tour/observation deck tickets are available). In the cold-weather months, the Plaza's sunken courtyard – eternally guarded by Paul Manship's bronze statue of Prometheus – transforms into a picturesque, if crowded, ice-skating rink.

From 48th to 51st Streets, between Fifth & Sixth Avenues (Tours & Top of the Rock 1-212 698 2000, NBC Studio Tours 1-212 664 3700, www.rockefellercenter.com). Subway B, D, F, M to 47-50th Streets- Rockefeller Center. Open Tours vary. Observation deck 8am-midnight daily (last elevator 11pm). Admission Rockefeller Center tours $17 (under-6s not admitted). Observation deck $27; $17-$25 reductions; free under-6s. NBC Studio tours $24; $21 reductions (under-6s not admitted).

St Patrick's Cathedral

The largest Catholic church in America, St Patrick's counts presidents and movie stars among its past and present parishioners. The Gothic-style façade features intricate white-marble spires, but equally impressive is the interior, including the Louis Tiffany-designed altar, solid bronze baldachin, and the rose window by stained-glass master Charles Connick. Note that due to crucial restoration work, part of the exterior may still be under scaffolding in 2014.

Fifth Avenue, between 50th & 51st Streets (1-212 753 2261, www.saint patrickscathedral. org). Subway B, D, F, M to 47-50th Streets-Rockefeller Center; E, M to Fifth Avenue-53rd Street. Open 6.30am-8.45pm daily. Admission free.

MIDTOWN EAST

Shopping, dining and entertainment options wane east of Fifth Avenue in the 40s and 50s. However, the area is home to many iconic landmarks and world-class architecture.

The 1913 **Grand Central Terminal** is the city's most spectacular point of arrival, although these days it welcomes only commuter trains from Connecticut and upstate New York. Looming behind the terminal, the **MetLife Building** (formerly the Pan Am Building) was the world's largest office tower when it opened in the 1960s. Other must-see buildings in the vicinity include **Lever House** (390 Park Avenue, between 53rd & 54th Streets), the **Seagram Building** (375 Park Avenue, between 52nd & 53rd Streets), the slanted-roofed **Citigroup Center** (from 53rd Street to 54th Street, between Lexington & Third Avenues) and the stunning art deco skyscraper that anchors the corner of Lexington Avenue and 51st Street, formerly the General Electric Building (and before that, the RCA Victor Building). A Chippendale crown tops the **Sony Building** (550 Madison Avenue, between 55th & 56th Streets), Philip Johnson's postmodern icon.

East 42nd Street has a wealth of architectural distinction, including the Romanesque Revival hall of the former **Bowery Savings Bank** (no.110) and the art deco details of the **Chanin Building** (no.122). Completed in 1930 by architect William Van Alen, the gleaming **Chrysler Building** (at Lexington Avenue) is a pinnacle of art deco architecture, paying homage to the automobile with vast radiator-cap eagles in lieu of traditional gargoyles and a brickwork relief sculpture of racing cars complete with chrome hubcaps. The **Daily News Building** (no.220), another art deco gem designed by Raymond Hood, was immortalised in the *Superman* films. Although the namesake tabloid no longer has its offices here, the lobby still houses its giant globe and weather instruments.

To the east lies the literally elevated **Tudor City** (between First & Second Avenues, from E 41st to E 43rd Streets), a pioneering 1925 residential development that resembles high-rise versions of England's Hampton Court Palace. At the end of 43rd Street is a terrace overlooking, and stairs leading down to, the **United Nations Headquarters**.

Grand Central Terminal
Each day, the world's largest rail terminal sees more than 750,000 people shuffle through its Beaux Arts threshold. Designed by Warren & Wetmore and Reed & Stern, the gorgeous transportation hub opened in 1913 with lashings of Botticino marble and staircases modelled after those of the Paris opera house. After midcentury decline, the terminal underwent extensive restoration between 1996 and 1998 and is now a destination in itself, with shopping and dining options, including the Campbell Apartment (1-212 953 0409), the Grand Central Oyster Bar & Restaurant (see p156), and a sprawling Apple Store (1-212 284 1800) on the East Balcony. Check the website for information about self-guided audio tours ($8; $6-$7 reductions). *From 42nd to 44th Streets, between Vanderbilt & Lexington Avenues (audio tours 1-917 566 0008, www.grandcentralterminal.com). Subway S, 4, 5, 6, 7 to 42nd Street-Grand Central.*

Japan Society
Founded in 1907, the Japan Society moved into its current home, complete with waterfall and bamboo garden, in 1971. Designed by Junzo Yoshimura, it was the first contemporary Japanese building in New York and is now the city's youngest official landmark. The gallery mounts temporary exhibitions on such diverse subjects as the art of anime, video games and textile design. *333 E 47th Street, between First & Second Avenues (1-212 832 1155, www.japansociety.org). Subway E, M to Lexington Avenue-53rd Street; 6 to 51st Street. Open varies. Gallery 11am-6pm Tue-Thur; 11am-9pm Fri; 11am-5pm Sat, Sun. Admission $12; $10 reductions; free under-16s; free 6-9pm Fri.*

United Nations Headquarters
The UN is undergoing extensive renovations that have left the Secretariat building, designed by Le Corbusier, gleaming – though that structure is off-limits to the public. The hour-long public tours discuss the history and role of the UN, and visit the Security Council Chamber (when not in session) in the newly renovated Conference Building. The General Assembly Hall is currently closed for building work until autumn 2014 or later. Although some artworks and objects given by member nations are not on public display during this period, you can now see other pieces for the first time in years, such as Norman Rockwell's mosaic *The Golden Rule*, on the third floor of the Conference Building. Note that until the renovations are complete, tours must be booked in advance online. *Temporary visitors' entrance: First Avenue, at 47th Street (tours 1-212 963 8687, http://visit.un.org). Subway S, 4, 5, 6, 7 to 42nd Street-Grand Central. Tours 10.15am-4.15pm Mon-Fri. Admission $18; $9-$11 reductions (under-5s not admitted).*

MURRAY HILL

Murray Hill spans 30th to 40th Streets, between Third and Fifth Avenues. Townhouses of the rich and powerful were once clustered around Madison and Park Avenues, including the home of Pierpont Morgan; his private library is now the **Morgan Library & Museum**, which houses some 500,000 rare books, prints, manuscripts, and objects. These days, the neighbourhood is populated mostly by upwardly mobiles fresh out of university, and only a few streets retain their former elegance. One is **Sniffen Court** (150-158 E 36th Street, between Lexington & Third Avenues), an unspoiled row of 1864 carriage houses. The neighbourhood got an injection of high fashion in late 2013 with the arrival of **Dover Street Market** (see p80).

Morgan Library & Museum
This Madison Avenue institution began as the private library of financier Pierpont Morgan, and is his critical gift to the city. Building on the collection Morgan amassed in his lifetime, the museum houses first-rate works on paper, including drawings by Michelangelo, Rembrandt and Picasso; three Gutenberg Bibles; a copy of *Frankenstein* annotated by Mary Shelley; manuscripts by Dickens, Poe, Twain, Steinbeck and Wilde; sheet music handwritten by Beethoven and Mozart; and an original edition of Dickens's *A Christmas Carol* that's displayed every Yuletide. A massive renovation and expansion orchestrated by Renzo Piano brought more natural light into the building and doubled the available exhibition space. The final phase restored the original 1906 building, designed by McKim, Mead & White. Visitors can now see Morgan's spectacular library (the East Room), with its 30ft-high book-lined walls and murals designed by Henry Siddons Mowbray (who also painted the ceiling of the restored Rotunda). *225 Madison Avenue, at 36th Street (1-212 685 0008, www.themorgan. org). Subway 6 to 33rd Street. Open 10.30am-5pm Tue-Thur; 10.30am-9pm Fri; 10am-6pm Sat; 11am-6pm Sun. Admission $18; $12 reductions; free under-13s; free 7-9pm Fri.*

Scandinavia House – The Nordic Center in America
One of the city's top cultural centres, Scandinavia House serves as a link between the US and the Scandinavian nations, and offers a full schedule of film screenings, lectures and art exhibitions. An outpost of Smörgås Chef (open 11am-10pm Mon-Sat, 11am-5pm Sun) serves tasty Swedish meatballs, and the shop is a showcase for chic Scandinavian design. *58 Park Avenue, at 38th Street (1-212 779 3587, www.scandinaviahouse. org). Subway S, 4, 5, 6, 7 to 42nd Street-Grand Central. Open varies. Gallery noon-6pm Tue, Thur-Sat; noon-7pm Wed; noon-5pm Sun (Dec only). Admission varies.*

Upper West Side & Central Park

The four-mile-long stretch west of Central Park is culturally rich and cosmopolitan. In the late 19th century, lavish apartment buildings sprang up alongside the newly completed green space. Then, in the 20th century, immigrants brought diverse shops and eateries to the avenues in between; some survive, but the arrival of new real estate and chain stores has had a homogenising effect. Although the neighbourhood is home to museums, including the American Museum of Natural History and the New-York Historical Society, its seat

Grand Central Terminal

of culture is largely concentrated on venerated performing-arts complex Lincoln Center.

UPPER WEST SIDE

The gateway to the Upper West Side is **Columbus Circle**, where Broadway meets 59th Street, Eighth Avenue, Central Park South and Central Park West – a rare rotary in a city of right angles. The architecture around it could make anyone's head spin. At the entrance to Central Park, a 700-ton statue of Christopher Columbus is dwarfed by the Time Warner Center across the street, which houses offices, apartments, hotel lodgings and **Jazz at Lincoln Center**'s stunning Frederick P Rose Hall. The first seven levels of the enormous glass complex are filled with high-end retailers and gourmet restaurants, such as **Per Se** (see p60). In 2008, the **Museum of Arts & Design** (see p34) opened in a landmark building on the south side of the circle, itself the subject of a controversial redesign.

A few blocks north, **Lincoln Center** (see p102), a complex of concert halls and auditoriums built in the early 1960s, is the home of the New York Philharmonic, the New York City Ballet, the Metropolitan Opera and a host of other notable arts organisations. The big circular fountain in the central plaza is a popular gathering spot – especially in summer, when amateur dancers converge on it to dance alfresco at Midsummer Night Swing (see p12).

The centre has completed a major overhaul that included a redesign of public spaces, refurbishment of the various halls and a new visitor centre, the **David Rubenstein Atrium** (Broadway, between W 62nd & W 63rd Streets). Conceived as a contemporary interior garden with lush planted walls, the Atrium stages free genre-spanning concerts on Thursday nights and sells week-of-show discounted tickets to performances at Lincoln Center, plus other Manhattan venues (see www.lincolncenter.org for details). It's also the starting point for guided tours of the complex (1-212 875 5350, $18, $15 reductions), which, in addition to the prestigious concert halls, contains several notable artworks, including Henry Moore's *Reclining Figure* in the plaza near Lincoln Center Theater, and two massive music-themed paintings by Marc Chagall in the lobby of the Metropolitan Opera House. Nearby is the **New York Public Library for the Performing Arts** (40 Lincoln Center Plaza, at 65th Street, 1-212 870 1630, www.nypl.org, closed Sun); alongside its extraordinary collection of films, letters, manuscripts, videos and sound recordings, it stages concerts and lectures.

Around Sherman and Verdi Squares (from 70th to 73rd Streets, where Broadway and Amsterdam Avenue intersect), classic early 20th-century buildings stand cheek-by-jowl with newer high-rises. The jewel is the 1904 **Ansonia Hotel** (2109 Broadway, between 73rd & 74th Streets). Over the years, residents of this Beaux Arts masterpiece have included Enrico Caruso, Babe Ruth and Igor Stravinsky; it was also the site of the Continental Baths, the gay bathhouse and cabaret where Bette Midler got her start, and Plato's Retreat, a swinging 1970s sex club.

After Central Park was completed, magnificently tall residential buildings rose up along Central Park West to take advantage of the views. The first of these great apartment blocks was the **Dakota** (at 72nd Street), so named because its location was considered remote when it was built in 1884. The fortress-like building is known as the setting for *Rosemary's Baby* and the site of John Lennon's murder in 1980 (Yoko Ono still lives there); other residents have included Judy Garland, Rudolph Nureyev, Lauren Bacall and Boris Karloff – but not Billy Joel, who was turned away by the co-op board when he tried to buy an apartment. You might recognise 55 Central Park West

TOP TIP!
Boats and beer
From late March to October, stop by Riverside Park's Boat Basin Café (www.boatbasincafe.com). The popular patio overlooks the marina.

(at 66th Street) from the movie *Ghostbusters*. Built in 1930, it was the first art deco building on the block. Heading north on Central Park West, you'll spy the massive twin-towered **San Remo Apartments** (at 74th Street), which also date from 1930. Rita Hayworth, Steven Spielberg, golfer Tiger Woods and U2's Bono have been among the building's many celebrity residents over the years.

A few blocks to the north, the **New-York Historical Society** (see p34) is the city's oldest museum. Across the street, the **American Museum of Natural History**'s dinosaur skeletons, dioramas and more lure visitors of all ages.

To see West Siders in their natural habitat, queue at the perpetually jammed smoked fish counter at gourmet market **Zabar's** (see p82). The legendary restaurant and delicatessen **Barney Greengrass**, the self-styled 'Sturgeon King' (see p60), has specialised in smoked fish, knishes and what may be the city's best chopped liver since 1908.

Riverside Park, a sinuous stretch of riverbank along the Hudson from 59th Street to 155th Street, was originally designed by Central Park's Frederick Law Olmsted, and subsequently extended. You'll probably see yachts, along with several houseboats, berthed at the **79th Street Boat Basin**. Several sites provide havens for quiet reflection. The **Soldiers' and Sailors' Monument** (89th Street, at Riverside Drive), built in 1902 by French sculptor Paul EM Duboy, honours Union soldiers who died in the Civil War; and a 1913 memorial (100th Street, at Riverside Drive) pays tribute to fallen firemen.

American Folk Art Museum
Following a budget crisis that forced the American Folk Art Museum to give up its midtown premises, the institution is still going strong in the small original space it had retained as a second location. Its unparalleled holdings of folk art include more than 5,000 works from the late 18th century to the present. Exhibitions explore the work of self-taught and outsider artists, as well as showing traditional folk art such as quilts and needlework, and other decorative objects. You can purchase original handmade pieces, among other items, in the large gift shop, and the museum regularly hosts free musical performances, inexpensive craft workshops and other events.
2 Lincoln Square, Columbus Avenue, at 66th Street (1-212 595 9533, www.folkartmuseum.org).

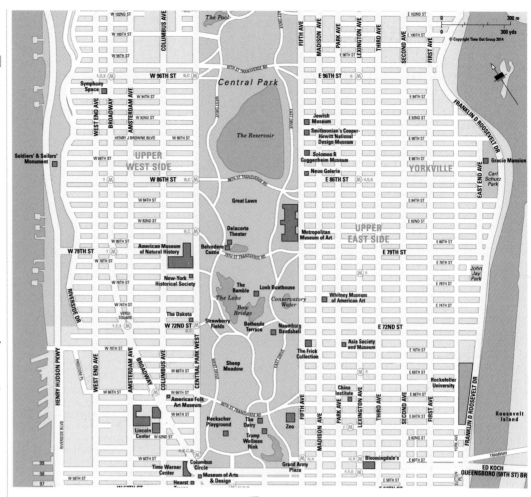

Subway 1 to 66th Street-Lincoln Center. Open noon-7.30pm Tue-Sat; noon-6pm Sun. Admission free.

American Museum of Natural History/Rose Center for Earth & Space

The American Museum of Natural History's fourth-floor dino halls are home to the largest and arguably most fabulous collection of dinosaur fossils in the world. Nearly 85% of the bones on display were dug out of the ground by Indiana Jones types, but during the museum's mid 1990s renovation, several specimens were remodelled to incorporate more recent discoveries. The tyrannosaurus rex, for instance, was once believed to have walked upright, Godzilla-style; it now stalks prey with its head lowered and tail raised parallel to the ground. A new exhibition devoted to the winged reptiles known as pterosaurs is on view until January 2015.

The Hall of North American Mammals, part of a two-storey memorial to Theodore Roosevelt, reopened in autumn 2012 after extensive restoration to its formerly faded 1940s dioramas. The Hall of Human Origins houses a fine display of our old cousins, the Neanderthals, and the Hall of Biodiversity examines world ecosystems and environmental preservation. A life-size model of a blue whale hangs from the cavernous ceiling of the Hall of Ocean Life, while in the Hall of Meteorites, the focal point is Ahnighito, the largest iron meteor on display in the world, weighing in at 34 tons.

The spectacular Rose Center for Earth & Space offers insight into recent cosmic discoveries via shows in the Hayden Planetarium and a simulation of the origins of the Universe in the Big Bang Theater. The museum also screens digital nature films in 3D, and the roster of temporary exhibitions is thought-provoking for all ages.

Central Park West, at 79th Street (1-212 769 5100, www.amnh.org). Subway B, C to 81st Street-Museum of Natural History. Open 10am-5.45pm daily. Admission Suggested donation $22; $12.50-$17 reductions.

Museum of Arts & Design

This institution explores the importance of the creative practice with a permanent collection of art, craft and design items dating back to 1950 through the present. MAD brings together contemporary objects created in a wide range of media – including clay, glass, wood, metal and cloth – with a strong focus on materials and process. And in 2008 the museum crafted itself a new home. Originally designed in 1964 by Radio City Music Hall architect Edward Durell Stone to house Huntington Hartford's Gallery of Modern Art, 2 Columbus Circle was a windowless monolith that had sat empty since 1998. The redesigned ten-storey building now has four floors of exhibition galleries, including the Tiffany & Co Foundation Jewelry

American Museum of Natural History

Gallery, as well as an education centre with workshop and studio spaces. Curators are able to display more of the 3,000-piece permanent collection, which includes porcelain ware by Cindy Sherman, stained glass by Judith Schaechter and ceramics by James Turrell. In addition to checking out temporary shows, you can also watch resident artists create works in studios on the sixth floor, while the ninth-floor bistro has views over the park. The gift shop sells hand-crafted jewellery, among other items.

2 Columbus Circle, at Broadway (1-212 299 7777, www.madmuseum. org). Subway A, B, C, D, 1 to 59th Street-Columbus Circle. Open 10am-6pm Tue, Wed, Sat, Sun; 10am-9pm Thur, Fri. Admission $16; $12-$14 reductions; free under-19s; pay what you wish 6-9pm Thur, Fri.

New-York Historical Society

Founded in 1804 by a group of prominent New Yorkers that included Mayor DeWitt Clinton, the New-York Historical Society is the city's oldest museum, originally based at City Hall. In autumn 2011, the society's 1904 building reopened after a three-year, $70-million renovation that opened up the interior spaces to make the collection more accessible to a 21st-century audience. The Robert H and Clarice Smith New York Gallery of American History provides an overview of the collection and a broad sweep of New York's place in American history – Revolutionary-era maps are juxtaposed with a piece of the ceiling mural from Keith Haring's Pop Shop (the artist's Soho store, which closed after his death in 1990). Touch-screen monitors offer insight into artwork and documents, and large HD screens display a continuous slide show of highlights of the museum's holdings, such as original watercolours from Audubon's *Birds*

of America and some of its 132 Tiffany lamps. The auditorium screens an 18-minute film tracing the city's development, while downstairs the DiMenna Children's History Museum engages the next generation. The upper floors are devoted to changing exhibitions and the Henry Luce III Center for the Study of American Culture, a visible-storage display that spans everything from spectacles and toys to Washington's Valley Forge camp bed.

170 Central Park West, between 76th & 77th Streets (1-212 873 3400, www.nyhistory.org). Subway B, C to 81st Street-Museum of Natural History. Open 10am-6pm Tue-Thur, Sat; 10am-8pm Fri; 11am-5pm Sun. Admission $18; $6-$14 reductions; free under-4s. Pay what you wish 6-8pm Fri.

CENTRAL PARK

In 1858, the newly formed Central Park Commission chose landscape designer Frederick Law Olmsted and architect Calvert Vaux to turn a vast tract of rocky swampland into a rambling oasis of lush greenery. Inspired by the great parks of London and Paris, the Commission imagined a place that would provide city dwellers with respite from the crowded streets. It was a noble thought, but one that required the eviction of 1,600 mostly poor or immigrant inhabitants, including residents of Seneca Village, the city's oldest African-American settlement. Still, clear the area they did: when Central Park was completed in 1873, it became the first man-made public park in the US.

Although it suffered from neglect at various points in the 20th century (most recently in the 1970s and '80s, when it gained a reputation as a dangerous spot), the park has been returned to its green

glory thanks largely to the Central Park Conservancy. Since this not-for-profit civic group was formed in 1980, it has been instrumental in driving the park's restoration and maintenance.

The 1870 Victorian Gothic **Dairy** (midpark at 65th Street, 1-212 794 6564, www.centralparknyc.org, open 10am-5pm daily) houses one of Central Park Conservancy's five visitor centres and a gift shop; there are additional staffed information booths dotted around the park.

The southern section abounds with family-friendly diversions, including the **Central Park Zoo**, between 63rd & 66th Streets, the **Friedsam Memorial Carousel** (midpark, at 64th Street) and the **Trump Wollman Rink** (between 62nd & 63rd Streets; *see p88*), which doubles as a small children's amusement park in the warmer months. Come summer, kites, Frisbees and soccer balls seem to fly every which way across **Sheep Meadow**, the designated quiet zone that begins at 66th Street. Sheep did indeed graze here until 1934, but they've since been replaced by sunbathers working on their tans and scoping out the throngs. **Tavern on the Green** (Central Park West, at 67th Street), the landmark restaurant housed in the former shepherd's residence, closed in 2009, but a new seasonal eaterie should be open by publication of this guide. East of Sheep Meadow, between 66th and 72nd Streets, is the **Mall**, an elm-lined promenade that attracts street performers and in-line skaters. And just east of the Mall's Naumburg Bandshell is **Rumsey Playfield** – the main venue of the annual **SummerStage** series (*see p12*), an eclectic roster of free and benefit concerts in the city's parks.

One of the most popular meeting places (and loveliest spots) in the park is north of here, overlooking the lake: the grand **Bethesda Fountain & Terrace**, near the midpoint of the 72nd Street Transverse Road. *Angel of the Waters*, the sculpture in the centre of the fountain, was created by Emma Stebbins, the first woman to be granted a major public art commission in New York City. Be sure to admire the Minton-tiled ceiling of the ornate passageway that connects the plaza around the fountain to the Mall – after years of neglect in storage, the tiles, designed by Jacob Wrey Mould, were restored and reinstated in 2007. Mould also designed the intricate carved ornamentation of the stairways leading down to the fountain.

To the west of the fountain, near the West 72nd Street entrance, sits **Strawberry Fields**, which memorialise John Lennon, who lived in, and was shot in front of, the nearby Dakota (*see p33*). Also called the International Garden of Peace, it features a mosaic of the word 'imagine' that was donated by the city of Naples. More than 160 species of flowers and plants from all over the world flourish here, strawberries among them. Just north of the fountain is the **Loeb Boathouse** (midpark, between 74th & 75th Streets, 1-212 517 2233, www.thecentralpark boathouse.com). From here, you can take a rowing boat or a gondola out on the lake, which is crossed by the elegant Bow Bridge. The Loeb houses a restaurant and bar (closed dinner Nov-mid Apr), and lake views make it a lovely place for brunch or drinks.

Further north, the picturesque **Belvedere Castle** (see p88), a restored Victorian folly, sits atop the park's second-highest peak. Besides offering excellent views and a terrific setting for a picnic, it also houses the **Henry Luce Nature Observatory**. The nearby Delacorte Theater hosts **Shakespeare in the Park** (see p12), a summer run of free open-air performances of plays by the Bard and others. Further north still sits the **Great Lawn** (midpark, between 79th & 85th Streets), a sprawling stretch of grass that doubles as a rallying point for political protests and a concert spot for just about any act that can attract six-figure audiences. At other times, it's put to use by seriously competitive soccer, baseball and softball teams. East of the Great Lawn, behind the Metropolitan Museum of Art, is the **Obelisk**, a 69-foot hieroglyphics-covered granite monument dating from around 1500 BC, which was given to the US by the Khedive of Egypt in 1881.

In the mid 1990s, the **Reservoir** (midpark, between 85th & 96th Streets) was renamed in honour of the late Jacqueline Kennedy Onassis, who used to jog around it. A turn here gives great views of the skyscrapers rising above the park on the East and West Sides as well as midtown; in spring, the cherry trees that ring the reservoir path and the bridle path below it make it particularly beautiful.

In the northern section, the exquisite **Conservatory Garden** (entrance on Fifth Avenue, at 105th Street) comprises formal gardens inspired by English, French and Italian styles. At the top of the park, next to the **Harlem Meer**, the **Charles A Dana Discovery Center** (entrance at Malcolm X Boulevard/Lenox Avenue, at 110th Street, 1-212 860 1374, www.centralparknyc.org, open 10am-5pm daily) operates a roster of activities, events and exhibitions. It also lends out fishing rods and bait (for 'catch and release' fishing, Apr-Oct); prospective fishermen need to take photo ID.

Central Park Zoo
A collection of animals has been kept in Central Park since the 1860s. But in its current form, Central Park Zoo dates only from 1988; it was renovated when operation of the zoo was assumed by the Wildlife Conservation Society. More than 180 species inhabit its 6.5-acre corner of the park, snow leopards and penguins among them. The Tisch Children's Zoo is home to kid-friendly species, and the roving characters on the George Delacorte Musical Clock – perched atop a brick arcade between both zoos – delight little ones every half-hour. *830 Fifth Avenue, between 63rd & 66th Streets (1-212 439 6500, www. centralparkzoo.org). Subway N, Q, R to Fifth Avenue-59th Street. Open April-Nov 10am-5pm Mon-Fri; 10am-5.30pm Sat, Sun; Nov-Apr 10am-4.30pm daily. Admission (under-16s must be accompanied by an adult) $12; $7-$9 reductions; free under-3s.*

MORNINGSIDE HEIGHTS
Morningside Heights runs from 110th Street (also known west of Central Park as Cathedral Parkway) to 125th Street, between Morningside Park and the Hudson River. The campus of **Columbia University** exerts a considerable influence over the surrounding neighbourhood. One of the oldest universities in the US, Columbia was initially chartered in 1754 as King's College (the name changed after the Revolutionary War). It moved to its present location in 1897. If you wander into Columbia's campus entrance at 116th Street, you won't fail to miss the impressive Low Memorial Building, modelled on Rome's Pantheon. The former library, completed in 1897, is now an administrative building. The list of illustrious graduates includes Alexander Hamilton, Allen Ginsberg and Barack Obama.

Thanks to the large student population of Columbia and its sister school, Barnard College, the area has an academic feel, with bookshops, inexpensive restaurants and coffeehouses lining Broadway between 110th and 116th Streets. The façade of **Tom's Restaurant** (2880 Broadway, at 112th Street, 1-212 864 6137) will be familiar to *Seinfeld* aficionados, but the interior doesn't resemble Monk's Café, which was created on a studio set for the long-running sitcom.

The seat of the Episcopal Diocese of New York, the **Cathedral Church of St John the Divine**, draws visitors from all over the city. Subject to a series of construction delays and misfortunes, the enormous cathedral (larger than Paris's Notre Dame) is on a medieval schedule for completion: work is set to continue for a couple more centuries, although it has wrapped up for the time being. Just behind it Is the green expanse of **Morningside Park** (from 110th to 123rd Streets, between Morningside Avenue & Morningside Drive), while across the street is the **Hungarian Pastry Shop** (see p60), a great place for coffee and dessert and engaging graduate students in esoteric discussions.

North of Columbia, **General Grant National Memorial** (aka Grant's Tomb), the mausoleum of former president Ulysses S Grant, is located in Riverside Park. Across the street stands the towering Gothic-style **Riverside Church** (490 Riverside Drive, at 120th Street, 1-212 870 6700, www. theriversidechurchny.org), built in 1930. The tower contains the world's largest carillon: 74 bronze bells, played every Sunday at 10.30am, 12.30pm and 3pm.

Cathedral Church of St John the Divine
Construction of this massive house of worship, affectionately nicknamed 'St John the Unfinished', began in 1892 following a Romanesque-Byzantine design by George Heins and Christopher Grant LaFarge. In 1911, Ralph Adams Cram took over with a Gothic Revival redesign. Work came to a halt in 1941, when the US entered World War II. It resumed in earnest in 1979, but a fire in 2001 that destroyed the church's gift shop and damaged two 17th-century Italian tapestries further delayed completion. It's still missing a tower and a north transept, among other things, but the nave has been restored and the entire interior reopened and rededicated. No further work is planned… for now. In addition to Sunday services, the cathedral hosts concerts and tours (the Vertical Tour, which takes you to the top of the building, is a revelation). It bills itself as a place for all people – and it certainly means it. Annual events include both winter and summer solstice celebrations, the Blessing of the Animals during the Feast of St Francis, which draws pets and their people from all over the city, and even a Blessing of the Bicycles every spring. *1047 Amsterdam Avenue, at 112th Street (1-212 316 7540, www. stjohndivine.org). Subway B, C, 1 to 110th Street-Cathedral Parkway. Open 7.30am-6pm daily. Admission Suggested donation $10. Tours $6-$15; $5-$12 reductions.*

General Grant National Memorial
Although he was born in Ohio, Civil War hero and 18th president Ulysses S Grant lived in New York for the last five years of his life. More commonly referred to as Grant's Tomb, the neoclassical granite and marble mausoleum was completed in 1897; his wife, Julia, is also laid to rest here. The tomb is open for self-guided tours on the hour from 10am to 4pm; if you arrive between slots, the visitor centre offers exhibits and free talks by National Park Service rangers at 11.15am, 1.15pm and 3.15pm. *Riverside Drive, at 122nd Street (1-212 666 1640, www.nps.gov/gegr). Subway 1 to 125th Street. Open Visitor centre 9am-5pm Mon, Thur-Sun. Admission free.*

Upper East Side

Luxurious pre-war apartments owned by blue-blooded socialites, soigné restaurants filled with Botoxed ladies-who-lunch, exclusive designer boutiques… this is the clichéd image of the Upper East Side, and you'll see a lot of supporting evidence on Fifth, Madison and Park Avenues. Although Manhattan's super-rich now live all over town, the air of old money is most palpable east of Central Park. Drawn to the freshly landscaped green space in the late 19th century, the city's more affluent residents began building mansions and townhouses along Fifth Avenue. Many of these now house foreign consulates and some of the world-class institutions that draw hordes of visitors and New Yorkers to Museum Mile.

Central Park

The swathe between Fifth and Lexington Avenues in the 60s and 70s, Lenox Hill encapsulates the classic Upper East Side. Along Fifth, Madison and Park, stately mansions and townhouses rub shoulders with deluxe apartment buildings guarded by uniformed doormen. The 1916 limestone structure at 820 Fifth Avenue (at 63rd Street) was one of the earliest luxury apartment buildings on the avenue, and still has just one residence per floor. Further north, Stanford White designed 998 Fifth Avenue (at 81st Street) in the image of an Italian Renaissance palazzo. Once home to the Seventh Regiment of the National Guard, the impressive 1881 **Park Avenue Armory** (643 Park Avenue, between 66th & 67th Streets, 1-212 616 3930, www.armoryonpark.org) contains a series of period rooms from the late 19th century, designed by such luminaries as Louis Comfort Tiffany and the Herter Brothers. The vast Wade Thompson Drill Hall has become one of the city's premier alternative spaces for art, concerts and theatre.

If you head east on 59th Street, you'll eventually reach the **Ed Koch Queensboro Bridge**, which was renamed in 2011 to honour the former mayor, and links to Queens. At Second Avenue you can catch the overhead tram to **Roosevelt Island**. The two-mile-long isle between Manhattan and Queens is largely residential. However, from 1686 to 1921, it went by the name of Blackwell's Island, during which time it was the site of an insane asylum, a smallpox hospital and a prison – notable inmates included Mae West, who served eight days here after being moved from the Women's House of Detention in the Village,

and Emma Goldman, the anarchist, feminist and political agitator. In autumn 2012, **Franklin D Roosevelt Four Freedoms Park** (www.fdrfourfreedomspark.org) finally opened on the island's southern tip, 40 years after Mayor John Lindsay and Governor Nelson A Rockefeller announced the memorial. The plans languished until 2005, when an exhibition at Cooper Union revived interest in the project. Commemorating the 32nd President's famous 'four freedoms' speech, the park offers postcard-worthy skyline views.

Asia Society & Museum

The Asia Society sponsors study missions and conferences while promoting public programmes in the US and abroad. The headquarters' striking galleries host exhibitions of art from dozens of countries and time periods (from ancient India and medieval Persia to contemporary Japan); some are assembled from public and private collections, including the permanent Mr and Mrs John D Rockefeller III collection of Asian art. An attractive gift shop and a spacious, atrium-like café with a pan-Asian-inspired menu help to make the society a one-stop destination for anyone with even a passing interest in Asian culture. *725 Park Avenue, at 70th Street (1-212 288 6400, www.asiasociety.org). Subway 6 to 68th Street-Hunter College. Open July, Aug 11am-6pm Tue-Sun. Sept-June 11am-6pm Tue-Thur, Sat, Sun; 11am-9pm Fri. Admission $12; $7-$10 reductions; free under-16s (must be accompanied by an adult). Free 6-9pm Fri.*

China Institute

With two small galleries, the China Institute is somewhat overshadowed by the nearby Asia Society, but the

organisation mounts two substantial exhibitions a year, which include high-profile collections on loan from Chinese institutions. The institute also offers courses and arts events such as concerts and films. *125 E 65th Street, between Park & Lexington Avenues (1-212 744 8181, www.chinainstitute.org). Subway F to Lexington Avenue-63rd Street; 6 to 68th Street-Hunter College. Open Galleries 10am-5pm Mon, Wed, Fri-Sun; 10am-8pm Tue, Thur. Admission $7; $4 reductions; free under-12s. Free 6-8pm Tue, Thur.*

Frick Collection

Industrialist, robber baron and collector Henry Clay Frick commissioned this opulent mansion with a view to leaving his legacy to the public. Designed by Thomas Hastings of Carrère & Hastings (the firm behind the New York Public Library) and built in 1914, the building was inspired by 18th-century British and French architecture.

In an effort to preserve the feel of a private residence, labelling is minimal, but you can opt for a free audio guide or pay $2 for a booklet. Works spanning the 14th to the 19th centuries include masterpieces by Rembrandt, Vermeer, Whistler, Gainsborough, Holbein and Titian, exquisite period furniture, porcelain and other decorative objects. Aficionados of 18th-century French art will find two rooms especially enchanting: the panels of the Boucher Room (1750-52) depict children engaged in adult occupations; the Fragonard Room contains the artist's series *Progress of Love* – four of the paintings were commissioned (and rejected) by Louis XV's mistress Madame du Barry. A gallery in the enclosed garden portico is devoted to decorative arts and sculpture. For the Frick's excellent concert series, *see p102*. *1 E 70th Street, between Fifth & Madison Avenues (1-212 288 0700, www.frick.org). Subway 6 to 68th Street-Hunter College. Open 10am-6pm Tue-Sat; 11am-5pm Sun. Admission (under-10s not admitted) $20; $10-$15 reductions. Pay what you wish 11am-1pm Sun.*

Whitney Museum of American Art

945 Madison Avenue, at 75th Street (1-212 570 3600, www.whitney.org). Subway 6 to 77th Street. Open 11am-6pm Wed, Thur, Sat, Sun; 1-9pm Fri. Admission $20; $16 reductions; free under-19s. Pay what you wish 6-9pm Fri.
The Whitney is leaving the Upper East Side, but it isn't going quietly. A nearly museum-wide Jeff Koons retrospective (27 June-19 Oct 2014) is the institution's blockbuster goodbye to the Marcel-Breuer-designed premises it has occupied since 1966. In spring 2015, the new Whitney – a nine-storey building designed by Renzo Piano

at the foot of the High Line in the Meatpacking District – will open to the public. For the first time, there will be space for a comprehensive display of the collection.

When sculptor and art patron Gertrude Vanderbilt Whitney opened the museum in 1931, she dedicated it to living American artists. Today, the Whitney holds more than 19,000 pieces by around 2,900 artists, including Willem de Kooning, Edward Hopper, Jasper Johns, Georgia O'Keeffe and Claes Oldenburg. Yet its reputation rests primarily on its temporary shows – particularly the Whitney Biennial. Launched in 1932 and held in even-numbered years, it's the most prestigious and controversial assessment of contemporary art in the country.

> **TOP TIP!**
> **Night at the museum**
> Most of the city's major museums are free or pay what you wish one evening (usually Thursday or Friday) or afternoon of the week.

Philanthropic gestures made by the moneyed classes over the past 130-odd years have helped to create an impressive cluster of art collections, museums and cultural institutions on the Upper East Side. Indeed, Fifth Avenue from 82nd to 105th Streets is known as Museum Mile, and for good reason: it's lined with more than half a dozen celebrated institutions. **El Museo del Barrio** (*see p37*) used to define the Mile's northern border, but the strip is lengthening: the future home of the **New Africa Center**, which will contain a museum (www.africanart.org), is at the corner of 110th Street, although the opening has been delayed by lack of funding.

Carnegie Hill, the northern blocks of the Upper East Side between Fifth and Lexington Avenues, takes its name from early resident Andrew Carnegie. The Scottish philanthropist bought a large chunk of then-rural land in 1898 to build a 64-room mansion, which is now home to the **Smithsonian's Cooper-Hewitt, National Design Museum**.

Smithsonian's Cooper-Hewitt, National Design Museum

The Cooper-Hewitt Museum began as a collection created for students of the Cooper Union for the Advancement of Science and Art by the Hewitt sisters – grand-daughters of the institution's founder, Peter Cooper – and opened to the public in 1897. Part of the Smithsonian since the 1960s, it is the only museum in the US solely dedicated to historic and contemporary design. In 1976, it took up residence in the former home of steel magnate Andrew Carnegie. Autumn 2014 sees the completion of a three-year renovation and expansion project, which has increased the exhibition space by 60%. *See also p37* **Grand Designs**. *2 E 91st Street, at Fifth Avenue (1-212 849 8400, www.cooperhewitt.org).*

Frick Collection

Subway 4, 5, 6 to 86th Street. Closed until autumn 2014 (see website for updates and information).

El Museo del Barrio

Founded in 1969 by the artist and former MoMA curator Rafael Montañez Ortiz, El Museo del Barrio takes its name from its East Harlem locale (although this stretch of Fifth Avenue is considered to be part of the Upper East Side). Dedicated to the art and culture of Puerto Ricans and Latin Americans all over the US, El Museo reopened in autumn 2009 following a $35-million renovation. The redesigned spaces within the museum's 1921 Beaux Arts building provide a polished, contemporary showcase for the diversity and vibrancy of Hispanic art. The new galleries allow more space for rotating exhibitions from the museum's 6,500-piece holdings – from pre-Columbian artefacts to contemporary installations – as well as temporary shows.
1230 Fifth Avenue, at 104th Street (1-212 831 7272, www.elmuseo.org). Subway 6 to 103rd Street. Open 11am-6pm Wed-Sat. Admission Suggested donation $9; $5 reductions; free under-12s; free over-65s Wed. Sept-Dec, Feb-May Free 3rd Sat each mth.

Jewish Museum

The Jewish Museum is housed in a magnificent 1908 French Gothic-style mansion – the former home of the financier, collector and Jewish leader Felix Warburg. Inside, 'Culture and Continuity: The Jewish Journey' traces the evolution of Judaism from antiquity to the present day. The two-floor permanent exhibition comprises thematic displays of 800 of the museum's cache of 25,000 works of art, artefacts and media installations. The excellent temporary shows, which spotlight Jewish artists or related themes, appeal to a broad audience. The museum recently launched a series of film and video works, selected by 25 international curators, to be screened monthly over the next two years.
1109 Fifth Avenue, at 92nd Street (1-212 423 3200, www.thejewish museum.org). Subway 4, 5, 6 to 86th Street; 6 to 96th Street. Open 11am-5.45pm Mon, Tue, Sat, Sun; 11am-8pm Thur; 11am-5.45pm Fri (11am-4pm Nov-Mar). Closed on Jewish holidays. Admission $15; $7.50-$12 reductions; free under-19s. Free Sat. Pay what you wish 5-8pm Thur.

Metropolitan Museum of Art

Now occupying 13 acres of Central Park, the Metropolitan Museum of Art opened in 1880. The original Gothic Revival building was designed by Calvert Vaux and Jacob Wrey Mould, but is now almost completely hidden by subsequent additions. A redesign of the museum's four-block-long plaza is expected to be completed in autumn 2014, bringing new fountains and tree-shaded seating.

The first floor's north wing contains the collection of ancient Egyptian art and the glass-walled atrium housing

GRAND DESIGNS
The Smithsonian's Cooper-Hewitt, National Design Museum reopens.

Home to 217,000 objects, the **Smithsonian's Cooper-Hewitt, National Design Museum** (*see p36*) occupies the Carnegie mansion – itself an example of ground-breaking design. The landmark 64-room Georgian-style pile was among the first private homes to have an elevator, central heating and even a precursor of air-conditioning. Historic spaces such as the Teak Room, with its intricate wall panels and cabinets conceived by prominent interior designer Lockwood de Forest and hand-carved in India, have been painstakingly restored, and the addition of a 6,000-square-foot gallery on the third floor – formerly occupied by the National Design Library, which is now housed in an adjacent building – provides more room for rotating exhibitions.

Diller Scofidio + Renfro – the architects behind Lincoln Center's recent spruce-up – have created contemporary, interactive displays that respect the period surroundings. On the museum's reopening, the second floor will showcase a selection of 358 objects from the permanent collection – comprising wall coverings, textiles, product design, decorative arts, drawings, prints and graphic design – integrated in thematic displays. The varied holdings include an 1869 oil sketch, *Athens, from the Northwest*, by Hudson River School painter Frederic Church. Part of the museum's original collection, it reflects the museum's origins as a 'visual library' for Cooper Union students, which included preparatory sketches as well as the completed works. 'The real strength of our collection is 19th century,' says curatorial director Cara McCarty, 'although in recent years we've been making a concerted effort to add to the contemporary collection.'

You'll also see a 1996 concept design for the Air Jordan XIII sneaker, by the shoe's original designer, Tinker Hatfield, which reflects the museum's commitment to collecting not only finished objects, but drawings and prototypes that illuminate the design process. A prototype of Ingo Mauer's circuit-inspired wallpaper was first shown in 2007 as part of a retrospective of the German artist/lighting designer. 'Finally, they were able to put it into production,' says McCarty of the recently acquired wall covering. LED lights have been placed on machine-printed paper and can be programmed to illuminate specific sections.

the Temple of Dendur, moved en masse from its original Nile-side setting and now overlooking a reflective pool. The north-west corner is occupied by the American Wing, which underwent a multi-phase renovation that culminated in 2012 with the reopening of its Galleries for Paintings, Sculpture and Decorative Arts; the centrepiece is Emanuel Gottlieb Leutze's iconic 1851 painting *Washington Crossing the Delaware*. The wing's grand Engelhard Court is now more a sculpture court than an interior garden; the light-filled space is flanked by the façade of Wall Street's

Branch Bank of the United States (saved when the building was torn down in 1915) and a stunning loggia designed by Louis Comfort Tiffany for his Long Island estate.

In the southern wing are the halls housing Greek and Roman art. Turning west brings you to the Arts of Africa, Oceania and the Americas collection; it was donated by Nelson Rockefeller as a memorial to his son Michael, who disappeared while visiting New Guinea in 1961. A wider-ranging bequest, the two-storey Robert Lehman Wing, is at the western end of the floor. This eclectic collection

is housed in a recreation of the Lehman family townhouse and features works by Botticelli, Bellini, Ingres and Rembrandt, among others.

Upstairs, the central western section is dominated by the recently expanded and rehung European Paintings galleries, which hold an amazing reserve of old masters – the museum's five Vermeers are now shown together for the first time. To the south, the 19th-century European galleries contain some of the Met's most popular works – in particular the two-room Monet holdings and a colony of Van Goghs that includes his oft-reproduced *Irises*.

Walk eastward and you'll reach the galleries of the Art of the Arab Lands, Turkey, Iran, Central Asia and Later South Asia. In the north-east wing of the floor, you'll find the sprawling collection of Asian art; be sure to check out the ceiling of the Jain Meeting Hall in the South-east Asian gallery. Give your feet a well-deserved rest in the Astor Court, a tranquil recreation of a Ming Dynasty garden, or head up to the Iris & B Gerald Cantor Roof Garden (usually open May-Oct). For the Cloisters, which houses the Met's medieval art collection, *see p41*.
1000 Fifth Avenue, at 82nd Street (1-212 535 7710, www.metmuseum.org). Subway 4, 5, 6 to 86th Street. Open 10am-5.30pm Mon-Thur, Sun; 10am-9pm Fri, Sat. Admission Suggested donation (incl same-week admission to the Cloisters) $25; $12-$17 reductions; free under-12s.

Museum of the City of New York

A great introduction to the metropolis, this institution contains a wealth of city history. *Timescapes*, a 22-minute multimedia presentation that illuminates the history of NYC, is shown free with admission every half hour. The museum's holdings include prints, drawings and photos of the city, decorative arts and furnishings, and a large collection of toys. The undoubted jewel is the amazing Stettheimer Dollhouse: it was created in the 1920s by Carrie Stettheimer, whose artist friends reinterpreted their masterpieces in miniature to hang on the walls. Look closely and you'll even spy a tiny version of Marcel Duchamp's famous *Nude Descending a Staircase*.

A rolling renovation has brought new galleries for temporary exhibitions, which spotlight the city from different angles. Renovations to the museum's North Wing, due to be completed in 2015, will provide space for a core exhibition about the city.
1220 Fifth Avenue, between 103rd & 104th Streets (1-212 534 1672, www.mcny.org). Subway 6 to 103rd Street. Open 10am-6pm daily. Admission Suggested donation $10; $6 reductions; $20 family; free under-13s.

National Academy Museum

Founded in 1825, the National Academy combines an art school, a museum and a professional association – academicians include Bill Viola, Chuck Close, Cindy Sherman and Frank Gehry, to name but a few. Housed in an elegant Fifth Avenue townhouse, the museum holds more than 7,000 works of American art, from the 19th century to the present, including paintings, sculptures, engravings and architectural drawings by the likes of Louise Bourgeois, Jasper Johns, Robert Rauschenberg and John Singer Sargent. The institution also regularly hosts temporary shows. *1083 Fifth Avenue, at 89th Street (1-212 369 4880, www.nationalacademy. org). Subway 4, 5, 6 to 86th Street. Open 11am-6pm Wed-Sun. Admission $15; $10 reductions; free under-12s.*

Neue Galerie

The elegant Neue Galerie is devoted entirely to late 19th- and early 20th-century German and Austrian fine and decorative arts. The creation of the late art dealer Serge Sabarsky and cosmetics mogul Ronald S Lauder, it has the largest concentration of works by Gustav Klimt and Egon Schiele outside of Vienna. There's also a bookstore, a small design shop and the ultra-refined Café Sabarsky (see p61), serving modern Austrian cuisine and ravishing Viennese pastries. *1048 Fifth Avenue, at 86th Street (1-212 628 6200, www.neuegalerie. org). Subway 4, 5, 6 to 86th Street. Open 11am-6pm Mon, Thur-Sun; 11am-8pm 1st Fri of the mth. Admission $20; $10 reductions (under-12s not admitted). Free 6-8pm 1st Fri of the mth.*

Solomon R Guggenheim Museum

The Guggenheim is as famous for its landmark building as it is for its impressive collection and daring temporary shows. The dramatic structure, with its winding, cantilevered curves, was designed by Frank Lloyd Wright. His only NYC building, apart from a private house on Staten Island, it caused quite a stir when it debuted 1959. In 1992, the addition of a ten-storey tower provided space for a sculpture terrace (with park views), a café and an auditorium; the museum also has a more upscale restaurant. Solomon R Guggenheim's original founding collection, amassed in the 1930s, includes 150 works by Kandinsky, in addition to pieces by Chagall, Franz Marc and others; the Solomon R Guggenheim Foundation's holdings have since been enriched by subsequent bequests, including the Thannhauser Collection – which includes paintings by Impressionist and post-Impressionist masters such as Manet, Cézanne and Gaugin – and the Panza di Biumo Collection of American minimalist and conceptual art from the 1960s and '70s. *1071 Fifth Avenue, between 88th & 89th Streets (1-212 423 3500,*

Solomon R Guggenheim Museum

www.guggenheim.org). Subway 4, 5, 6 to 86th Street. Open 10am-5.45pm Mon-Wed, Fri, Sun; 10am-7.45pm Sat. Admission $22; $18 reductions; free under-13s. Pay what you wish 5.45-7.45pm Sat.

YORKVILLE

The atmosphere becomes noticeably less rarefied as you walk east from Central Park, with grand edifices giving way to bland modern apartment blocks and walk-up tenements. Not much remains of the old German and Hungarian immigrant communities that once filled Yorkville, the neighbourhood above 79th Street between Third Avenue and the East River, with delicatessens, beer halls and restaurants. However, one such flashback, open since 1936, is **Heidelberg** (1648 Second Avenue, between 85th & 86th Streets, 1-212 628 2332, www.heidelberg restaurant.com), where dirndl-wearing waitresses serve up steins of Spaten and platters of sausages from the wurst-meisters at butcher shop **Schaller & Weber** a few doors up (1654 Second Avenue, 1-212 879 3047, closed Sun). Second Avenue in the 70s and 80s throbs with rowdy pick-up bars frequented by preppy, twentysomething crowds. But new craft-beer spot the **Penrose** (*see p69*) has brought a bit of East Village chic uptown.

The only Federal-style mansion in Manhattan, **Gracie Mansion** stands at the eastern end of 88th Street. The stately pile has served as New York's official mayoral residence since 1942 – except during billionaire Michael Bloomberg's time in office. Since Bill de Blasio was elected in 2013, it is once

TOP TIP!
Roosevelt Island tram
Suspended on a cable, the tram to Roosevelt Island ascends to 250 feet. The fare is the same as the subway and the views are spectacular.

again occupied. The mansion is fenced off, but much of the exterior can be seen from surrounding Carl Schurz Park.

Gracie Mansion

This green-shuttered yellow edifice was built in 1799 by Scottish merchant Archibald Gracie as a country home. Today, the stately house is the focal point of the riverside Carl Schurz Park, named in honour of the German immigrant who became a newspaper editor and US senator. When mayor Michael Bloomberg declined to move in after taking up office in 2002, Gracie Mansion's living quarters were opened up to public tours for the first time in 60 years; tours of part of the house will continue now that Mayor de Blasio is in residence. *Carl Schurz Park, 88th Street, at East End Avenue (1-212 570 4778). Subway 4, 5, 6 to 86th Street. Tours Wed, call for information; reservations required. Admission $7; $4 reductions; free students. No credit cards.*

Harlem & Upper Manhattan

Harlem is the cultural capital of black America – a legacy of the Harlem Renaissance, the cultural movement that spanned the 1920s. During the Jazz Age, white New Yorkers accepted Ellington's famous invitation to 'Take the A Train' uptown to the neighbourhood's celebrated nightclubs, but in the 1960s and '70s, crime and urban decay kept them away. Now Harlem's second renaissance, stalled by the recession, is back on track. The area isn't packed with sights, but it offers eclectic architecture, theatrical street life, historic churches with exuberant gospel choirs and a rejuvenated restaurant and bar scene.

WEST & CENTRAL HARLEM

The village of Harlem, named by Dutch colonists after their native Haarlem, was annexed by the City of New York in 1873. The extension of the elevated subway two decades later brought eager developers who overbuilt in the suddenly accessible suburb. The consequent housing glut led to cheap rents, and Jewish, Italian and Irish immigrants escaping the tenements of the Lower East Side snapped them up.

Around the turn of the 20th century, black Americans joined the procession into Harlem, their ranks swelled by the great migration from the Deep South. By 1914, the black population of Harlem had risen well above 50,000; by the 1920s, Harlem was predominately black and the country's most populous African-American community. This prominence soon attracted some of black America's greatest artists: writers such as Langston Hughes and Zora Neale Hurston and musicians including Duke Ellington, Louis Armstrong and Cab Calloway, an unprecedented cultural gathering known as the Harlem Renaissance. White New York took notice, venturing uptown – where the enforcement of Prohibition was lax – to enjoy the Cotton Club, Connie's Inn, Smalls Paradise and the Savoy Ballroom, which supplied the beat for the city that never sleeps.

The Depression killed the Harlem Renaissance, and deeply wounded Harlem. By the 1960s, the community had been ravaged by middle-class flight and municipal neglect. Businesses closed, racial tensions ran high, and the looting during the 1977 blackout was among the worst the city had seen. However, as New York's economic standing improved in the mid '90s, investment began slowly spilling into the area, spawning new businesses and the phalanxes of renovated brownstones that beckon the middle class (white and black).

On 125th Street, Harlem's main artery, street preachers and mix-tape hawkers vie for the attentions of the human parade and the celebrated **Apollo Theater** (*see p97*) hosts concerts, a syndicated TV show and the classic Amateur Night every Wednesday – James Brown, Ella Fitzgerald, Michael Jackson and Lauryn Hill are among its starry alumni. A block east is the highly regarded **Studio Museum in Harlem**.

Although new apartment buildings, boutiques, restaurants and cafés are scattered around the neighbourhood, especially on Frederick Douglass Boulevard (Eighth Avenue) between 110th and 125th Streets, Harlem has managed to retain many of the buildings that went up around the turn of the century because redevelopers shunned it for so long. Of particular interest, the **Mount Morris Historic District** (from 119th to 124th Streets, between Malcolm X Boulevard/ Lenox Avenue & Mount Morris Park West) contains charming brownstones and a collection of religious buildings in a variety of architectural styles.

The section of West 116th Street between St Nicholas Avenue and Morningside Park is known as **Little Senegal**, a strip of West African shops and restaurants. Continue east along 116th Street West, past the domed **Masjid Malcolm Shabazz** (no.102), the mosque of Malcolm X's ministry, to the **Malcolm Shabazz Harlem Market** (no.52, 1-212 987 8131), an outdoor bazaar that buzzes with vendors, most from West Africa, selling clothes, jewellery and other goods from covered stalls.

While most of the storied jazz clubs have closed, **Showman's Bar** (375 W 125th Street, between St Nicholas & Morningside Avenues, 1-212 864 8941, www.showmans jazzclub.com, closed Sun), is a neighbourhood old-timer.

Further north is **Strivers' Row**, also known as the St Nicholas Historic District. On 138th and 139th Streets, between Adam Clayton Powell Jr Boulevard (Seventh Avenue) and Frederick Douglass Boulevard (Eighth Avenue), these harmonious blocks of brick townhouses were developed in 1891 by David H King Jr and designed by three different architects, one of whom was Stanford White. The enclave is so well preserved that the alleyway sign advising you to 'walk your horses' is still visible.

Harlem's rich history is stored in the archives of the nearby **Schomburg Center for Research in Black Culture**. This branch of the New York Public Library contains more than five million documents, artefacts, films and prints relating to the cultures of peoples of African descent, with a strong emphasis on the African-American experience.

Schomburg Center for Research in Black Culture

Part of the New York Public Library, this institution holds an extraordinary trove of vintage literature and historical memorabilia relating to black culture and the African diaspora, much of which was amassed by notable bibliophile Arturo Alfonso Schomburg, who was curator from 1932 until his death in 1938. (It was posthumously renamed in his honour.) Note that parts of the collection can only be viewed on certain days by appointment; call or refer to the website. The centre also hosts regular exhibitions, concerts, films, lectures and tours.
515 Malcolm X Boulevard (Lenox Avenue), between 135th & 136th Streets (1-212 491 2200, www.nypl.org/locations/schomburg). Subway 2, 3 to 135th Street. Open General & gallery 10am-6pm Mon, Fri, Sat; 10am-8pm Tue-Thur. Other departments times vary. Admission free.

Studio Museum in Harlem

The first black fine arts museum in the United States when it opened in 1968, the Studio Museum is an important player in the art scene of the African diaspora. Under the leadership of director and chief curator Thelma Golden (formerly of the Whitney), this vibrant institution, housed in a stripped-down, three-level space, presents shows in a variety of media by black artists from around the world. The museum supports emerging visual artists of African descent through its coveted artist-in-residence programme.
144 W 125th Street, between Adam Clayton Powell Jr Boulevard (Seventh Avenue) & Malcolm X Boulevard (Lenox Avenue) (1-212 864 4500, www.studiomuseum.org). Subway 2, 3 to 125th Street. Open noon-9pm Thur, Fri; 10am-6pm Sat; noon-6pm Sun. Admission Suggested donation $7; $3 reductions; free under-12s. Free Sun. No credit cards.

EAST HARLEM

East of Fifth Avenue is East Harlem, commonly called Spanish Harlem but also known to its primarily Puerto Rican residents as El Barrio. The traditional southern boundary with the Upper East Side is 96th Street, but is becoming increasingly blurred with the area's gentrification. The neighbourhood's main east–west cross street, East 116th Street, shows signs of a recent influx of Mexican immigrants. The modest **Graffiti Hall of Fame** (106th Street, between Madison & Park Avenues) celebrates old- and new-school taggers in a schoolyard. Be sure to check out the nearby **El Museo del Barrio** (*see p37*), too.

HAMILTON HEIGHTS

Named after Alexander Hamilton, who owned an estate here, Hamilton Heights extends from 125th Street to the Trinity Cemetery at 155th Street, between Riverside Drive and St Nicholas Avenue. Hamilton's 1802 Federal-style house, the Grange, now a national memorial, recently reopened to visitors after being moved from 287 Convent Avenue around the corner to St Nicholas Park.

The neighbourhood developed after the West Side elevated train was built in the early 20th century; it's notable for the elegant turn-of-the-20th-century row houses in the **Hamilton Heights Historic District**, centred on the side streets off scenic Convent Avenue between 140th and 145th Streets – just beyond the Gothic Revival-style campus of the City College of New York (Convent Avenue, from 135th to 140th Streets).

Hamilton Grange National Memorial

The Federal-style estate of America's first Secretary of the Treasury was completed two years before he was shot in a duel with Vice President

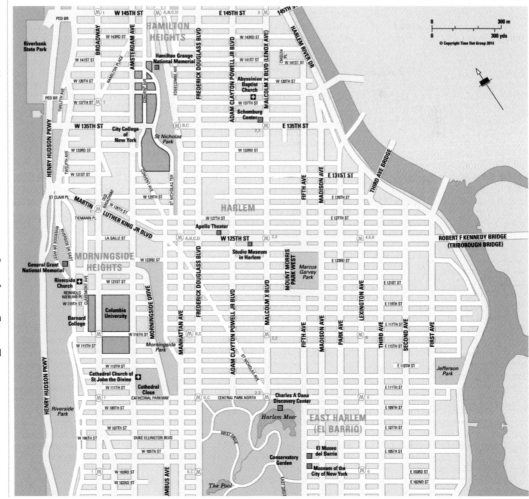

Explore

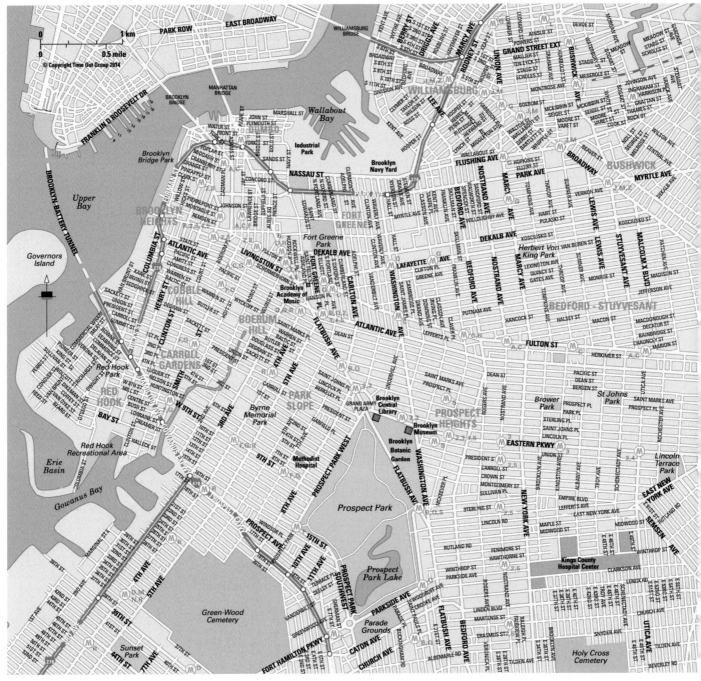

Aaron Burr. Rooms, accessed via park ranger-led tours, include Hamilton's study and the parlour, with his daughter's pianoforte. A short film about the founding father's life is shown in the visitor centre.
St Nicholas Park, 414 W 141st Street, near Convent Avenue (1-646 548 2310, www.nps.gov/hagr). Subway A, B, C, D to 145th Street. Open Visitor centre 9am-5pm Wed-Sun. Tours 11am, noon, 1pm, 2pm, 4pm. Admission free.

WASHINGTON HEIGHTS & INWOOD

The area from West 155th Street to Dyckman (200th) Street is called **Washington Heights**; venture north of that and you're in Inwood, Manhattan's northernmost neighbourhood, where the Harlem and Hudson Rivers converge. An ever-growing number of artists and young families are relocating to these parts, attracted by the spacious pre-war buildings, sprawling parks, hilly streets and (comparatively) low rents.

Washington Heights' main attraction is the **Morris-Jumel Mansion** (*see p41*), a stunning Palladian-style house that served as a swanky headquarters for George Washington during the autumn of 1776. But the small **Hispanic Society of America** (*see p41*), featuring a surprising collection of masterworks, is an overlooked gem.

Since the 1920s, waves of immigrants have settled in Washington Heights. In the post-World War II era, many German-Jewish refugees (among them Henry Kissinger and Dr Ruth Westheimer) moved to the western edge of the district. Broadway was once home to a small Greek population – opera singer Maria Callas lived here in her youth. But in the last few decades, the southern and eastern parts of the area have become predominantly Spanish-speaking due to a large Dominican population.

A trek along Fort Washington Avenue, from about 173rd Street to Fort Tryon Park, puts you in the heart of what is now called **Hudson Heights** – the posh area of Washington Heights. Start at the George Washington Bridge, the city's only bridge across the Hudson River. A pedestrian walkway (also a popular route for cyclists) allows for dazzling Manhattan views. Under the bridge on the New York side is a diminutive lighthouse. To see it up close, look for the footpath on the west side of Henry Hudson Parkway below 181st Street, which leads down to the riverside **Fort Washington Park** and the **Hudson River Greenway**, a popular route for walkers, joggers and cyclists.

North of the bridge is the beautiful **Fort Tryon Park**, and at the park's northern edge is the **Cloisters** (*see p41*), a museum built in 1938 using segments of five medieval cloisters shipped from Europe by the Rockefeller clan. It houses the Metropolitan Museum of Art's permanent medieval art collection.

Inwood stretches from Dyckman Street up to 218th Street, the last residential block in Manhattan. Dyckman buzzes with street life from river to river, but, north of that, the island narrows considerably and the parks along the western shoreline culminate in the seclusion of **Inwood Hill Park**, another Frederick Law Olmsted legacy. Some believe that this is the location of the legendary 1626 transaction between Peter Minuit and the Native American Lenapes for the purchase of a strip of land called Manahatta – a plaque at the south-west corner of the ballpark near 214th Street marks the purported spot. The 196-acre refuge contains the island's last swathes of virgin forest and salt marsh. Today, you can hike over the hilly terrain, liberally scattered with massive glacier-deposited boulders (called erratics) and picture Manhattan as it was before development.

The Cloisters

Set in a lovely park overlooking the Hudson River, the Cloisters houses the Metropolitan Museum's medieval art and architecture collections. A path winds through the peaceful grounds to a castle that looks as if it's been there since the Middle Ages. In fact, it was built in the 1930s, using pieces of five medieval French cloisters. The collection itself is an inspired trove of Romanesque, Gothic and Baroque treasures brought from Europe and assembled in a manner that somehow manages not to clash. Highlights are the famous Unicorn Tapestries (c1500), the 12th-century Fuentidueña Chapel and the Annunciation triptych by Robert Campin.
Fort Tryon Park, Fort Washington Avenue, at Margaret Corbin Plaza (1-212 923 3700, www.metmuseum. org). Subway A to 190th Street, then M4 bus or follow Margaret Corbin Drive north, for about the length of 5 city blocks, to the museum. Open Mar-Oct 10am-5.15pm daily. Nov-Feb 10am-4.45pm daily. Admission Suggested donation (incl same-day admission to Metropolitan Museum of Art) $25; $12-$17 reductions; free under-12s.

Hispanic Society of America

Though few people who pass this way seem aware of it, the Hispanic Society boasts the largest assemblage of Spanish art and manuscripts outside Spain. Goya's masterful *Duchess of Alba* greets you as you enter, while several haunting El Greco portraits can be found on the second floor. The collection is dominated by religious artefacts, including 16th-century tombs from the monastery of San Francisco in Cuéllar, Spain. Also among its holdings are decorative art objects and thousands of black and white photographs that document life in Spain and Latin America from the mid 19th century to the present. One of the highlights is Valencian painter Joaquín Sorolla y Bastida's *Vision of Spain*, comprising 14 monumental oils commissioned by the Society in 1911.
Audubon Terrace, Broadway, between 155th & 156th Streets (1-212 926 2234, www.hispanicsociety.org).

Subway 1 to 157th Street. Open 10am-4.30pm Tue-Sat; 1-4pm Sun. Admission free.

Morris-Jumel Mansion

Constructed in 1765, Manhattan's only surviving pre-Revolutionary pile was originally built for British governor Roger Morris but later served as General Washington's headquarters in the early months of the Revolutionary War. Later, an elderly Aaron Burr lived here after marrying widow Eliza Brown Jumel in 1833. (They divorced a year later.) The restored interior features many of the 19th-century French decorations of which Eliza was so fond. The handsome Palladian-style villa offers fantastic views. Its former driveway is now Sylvan Terrace, which has the longest continuous stretch (one block in total) of old wooden houses in all of Manhattan.
65 Jumel Terrace, between 160th & 162nd Streets (1-212 923 8008, www.morris jumel.org). Subway C to 163rd Street-Amsterdam Avenue. Open 10am-4pm Tue-Sun. Admission $5; $4 reductions; free under-12s.

Brooklyn

Not long ago, many Manhattanites baulked at the idea of crossing the East River for a day or night out. Times sure have changed. Not only is the second borough a destination in its own right, with a thriving cultural and food scene, but 'Brooklyn' has also become shorthand for a particular brand of indie cool, recognised the world over. Settled by the Dutch in the early 17th century, it was America's third largest municipality until its amalgamation with the four other boroughs that created New York City in 1898. Its many brownstones are a testament to a large and wealthy merchant class that made its money from the shipping trade. By the end of the 19th century, Brooklyn had become so prosperous, and its view of itself so grandiloquent, it built copies of the Arc de Triomphe (in Grand Army Plaza) and the Champs-Elysées (Eastern Parkway), and a greensward (Prospect Park) to rival Central Park.

BROOKLYN HEIGHTS & DUMBO

Home to well-to-do families and professionals lured by its proximity to Wall Street, **Brooklyn Heights** is where you'll find the idyllic leafy, brownstone-lined streets of Brooklyn legend. Thanks to the area's historic district status, it has many Greek Revival and Italianate row houses dating from the 1820s. Take a stroll down the gorgeous tree-lined streets, such as Cranberry, Hicks, Pierrepont and Willow.

Given its serenity and easy access to Manhattan, it's not surprising that Brooklyn Heights has been home to numerous illustrious (and struggling) writers. Walt Whitman printed the first edition of *Leaves of Grass* at 98 Cranberry Street (in a building since demolished); Truman Capote wrote *Breakfast at Tiffany's* at 70 Willow Street; and Thomas Wolfe penned *Of Times and the River* at 5 Montague Terrace.

Henry and Montague Streets are the prime strips for shops, restaurants and bars. At the end of Montague, the **Brooklyn Heights Promenade** offers spectacular waterfront views of lower Manhattan, New York Harbor and the nearby **Brooklyn Bridge**, a marvel of 19th-century engineering. The grand **Borough Hall** (209 Joralemon Street, at Court Street), the seat of local government, stands as a monument to Brooklyn's past as an independent municipality. Completed in 1851 but only later crowned with a Victorian cupola, the Greek Revival edifice was renovated in the late 1980s. The building is linked to the **New York State Supreme Court** (360 Adams Street, between Joralemon Street & Tech Place) by Cadman Plaza (from Prospect Street to Tech Place, between Cadman Plaza East & Cadman Plaza West).

At the turn of the 19th century, **Dumbo** (Down Under the Manhattan Bridge Overpass) was a thriving industrial district; all kinds of manufacturers, including Brillo and Benjamin Moore, were based here, leaving behind a fine collection of factory buildings and warehouses; the most famous of these, the **Eskimo Pie Building** (100 Bridge Street, at York Street), with its embellished façade, was actually built for the Thomson Meter Company in 1908-09.

In the 1970s and '80s, these warehouses were colonised by artists seeking cheap live/work spaces, but playing out a familiar New York migration pattern, the area is now bursting with million-dollar apartments and high-end design shops. The spectacular views – taking in the Statue of Liberty, the lower Manhattan skyline and the Brooklyn and Manhattan Bridges – remain the same. The best vantage point is below the Brooklyn Bridge at the **Fulton Ferry Landing**, which juts out over the East River at Old Fulton and Water Streets. It was here that General George Washington and his troops beat a hasty retreat by boat from the Battle of Brooklyn in 1776. It's now a stop on the **East River Ferry service** (see p123), which links to Manhattan and Queens. Along the same pier is the **Brooklyn Ice Cream Factory** (Fulton Ferry

TOP TIP!
Dumbo art party
Each month, around 25 Dumbo galleries stay open late – some hosting special events – for the 1st Thursday Gallery Walk (www.dumbo.is/culture).

Landing, 1 Water Street, 1-718 246 3963, closed Mon Dec-Mar), located in a 1920s fireboat house. Next door, docked at the pier, is one of the borough's great cultural jewels: **Bargemusic** (see p102), a 100-foot steel barge that was built in 1899 but has staged chamber music concerts since the 1970s.

On both sides of the landing, **Brooklyn Bridge Park** (riverside, from the Manhattan Bridge to Atlantic Avenue) has been undergoing a rolling redesign that includes lawns, freshwater gardens, a water fowl-attracting salt marsh and the Granite Prospect, a set of stairs fashioned out of salvaged granite facing the Manhattan skyline. But the undoubted centrepiece is the vintage merry-go-round known as **Jane's Carousel** (between Main Street and the Brooklyn Bridge), which made its park debut in 2011 in a Jean Nouvel-designed pavilion in the section of park alongside the post-Civil War coffee warehouses, Empire Stores.

The artists who flocked to the area en masse in the 1970s and '80s maintain a presence in the local galleries, most of which support the work of emerging talent. Dumbo is also becoming a performing arts hotspot. You can catch anything from puppet theatre to a rock concert at **St Ann's Warehouse** (see p109). Another artsy venue, which has even more diverse programming – think burlesque, camp variety and contemporary classical – is the **Galapagos Art Space** (see p97), based in quirky, LEED-certified green premises.

Head east on Water or Front Street to discover one of Brooklyn's forgotten neighbourhoods. Once a rough and bawdy patch dotted with bars and brothels frequented by sailors and dockworkers, **Vinegar Hill**, between Bridge Street and the Navy Yard, earned the moniker 'Hell's Half Acre' in the 19th century. Only fragments of the enclave remain (parts of it were designated a historic district in the late 1990s), and it's considerably quieter today. Although inhabited, the isolated strips of early-19th-century row houses and defunct storefronts on Bridge, Hudson and Plymouth Streets, and a stretch of Front Street, have a ghost-town quality, heightened by their juxtaposition with a Con Edison generating station. For refreshment, seek out the enclave's tavern-like **Vinegar Hill House** (see p64).

Brooklyn Bridge

Designed by John Roebling, the Brooklyn Bridge was built in response to the harsh winter of 1867 when the East River froze over, severing connection between Manhattan and what was then the nation's third most populous city. When it opened in 1883, the 5,989ft-long structure was the world's longest bridge, and the first in the world to use steel

Explore

suspension cables. Every day, 6,600 people walk or bike across the bridge's wide, wood-planked promenade, taking in views of New York Harbor, the Statue of Liberty and the skyscrapers of lower Manhattan. *Subway A, C to High Street; J to Chambers Street; 4, 5, 6 to Brooklyn Bridge-City Hall.*

Brooklyn Historical Society

Founded in 1863, the BHS resides in a just-renovated landmark Queen Anne-style building. In addition to a major photo and research library – featuring historic maps and newspapers, notable family histories and archives from the area's abolitionist movement – it presents ongoing and temporary exhibitions. 'Brooklyn Abolitionists/In Pursuit of Freedom', scheduled to run until 2018, examines Kings County's antislavery movement in the 19th century and includes one of the most prized items in the BHS's collection: an original copy of the Emancipation Proclamation, signed by President Lincoln. *128 Pierrepont Street, at Clinton Street, Brooklyn Heights (1-718 222 4111, www.brooklynhistory.org). Subway 2, 3, 4, 5 to Borough Hall. Open Museum noon-5pm Wed-Sat. Gift shop noon-5pm daily. Library 1-5pm Wed-Sat. Admission $10; $6 reductions; free under-13s.*

New York Transit Museum

Located in a historic 1936 IND subway station, this is the largest museum in the United States devoted to urban public transport history. Exhibits explore the social and practical impact of public transport on the development of greater New York; among the highlights is an engrossing walk-through display charting the construction of the city's century-old subway system, when fearless 'sandhogs' were engaged in dangerous tunnelling. A line-up of turnstiles shows their evolution from the 1894 'ticket chopper' to the current Automatic Fare Card model. But the best part is down another level to a real platform where you can board an exceptional collection of vintage subway and El ('Elevated') cars, some complete with vintage ads. *Corner of Boerum Place & Schermerhorn Street, Brooklyn Heights (1-718 694 1600, www.mta.info/mta/museum). Subway A, C, G to Hoyt-Schermerhorn; 2, 3, 4, 5 to Borough Hall. Open 10am-4pm Tue-Fri; 11am-5pm Sat, Sun. Admission $7; $5 reductions; free under-3s; free seniors Wed.*

A convenient if annoying real estate agents' contraction for these blurred-boundaried 'hoods, BoCoCa is a prime example of gentrification at work. Gone are the bodegas and cheap shoe shops along the stretch of Smith Street that runs from Atlantic Avenue to the Carroll Street subway stop; it's now lined with restaurants and upscale shops. The mile-long stretch of Atlantic Avenue between Henry and Nevins Streets, most of which falls under **Boerum Hill**, was once crowded with Middle Eastern restaurants and markets; one remaining stalwart is the **Sahadi Importing Company** (no.187, between Clinton & Court Streets, Cobble Hill, 1-718 624 4550, closed Sun), a neighbourhood institution that sells olives, spices, cheeses and nuts, among other foodstuffs. These days, you'll find a slew of antique and modern furniture stores on the strip, including **City Foundry** (no.365, between Bond & Hoyt Streets, Boerum Hill; 1-718 923 1786, www.cityfoundry.com), which specialises in midcentury design and industrial-style pieces. Recently, clothing stores have moved in, such as **Hollander & Lexer** (no.369; *see p84*); there's even an outpost of **Barneys New York** (no.194; *see p82*).

West of Smith Street, **Cobble Hill** has a palpable small-town feel. Here, Court Street is dotted with cafés and shops. Walk over the Brooklyn-Queens Expressway to the industrial waterfront and the excellent Thai spot **Pok Pok NY** (*see p64*).

Further south, you'll cross into the still predominantly Italian-American **Carroll Gardens**. Pick up a prosciutto loaf from **Caputo Bakery** (329 Court Street, between Sackett & Union Streets, 1-718 875 6871) or an aged soppressata salami from **G Esposito & Sons** (357 Court Street, between President & Union Streets, 1-718 875 6863); then relax in **Carroll Park** (from President to Carroll Streets, between Court & Smith Streets) and watch the old-timers play bocce (lawn bowls).

To the south-west of Carroll Gardens, beyond the Brooklyn-Queens Expressway, the formerly rough-and-tumble industrial locale of Red Hook has long avoided urban renewal. In recent years, however, the arrival of gourmet grocer Fairway and Swedish furniture superstore IKEA have served notice that gentrification is slowly moving in.

Luckily for its protective residents, the Hook still feels secluded, tucked away on a peninsula. While the area continues to evolve, its time-warp charm is still evident, and its decaying piers make a moody backdrop for empty warehouses and trucks clattering over cobblestone streets. The lack of public transport has thus far prevented it from becoming the next Williamsburg. From the Smith-9th Streets subway stop, it's either a half-hour walk south or a transfer to the B61 bus, although the **New York Water Taxi** (*see p123*) has improved the situation with its IKEA express shuttle from downtown Manhattan.

The area offers singular views of the Statue of Liberty and New York Harbor from **Valentino Pier**, and has an eclectic selection of bars, eateries and artists' studios. Look for the word 'Gallery' hand-scrawled on the doors of the **Kentler International Drawing Space** (353 Van Brunt Street, between Wolcott & Dikeman Streets, 1-718 875 2098, www.kentlergallery.org, closed Mon-Wed & Jan, Aug), or check the website of the **Brooklyn Waterfront Artists Coalition** (499 Van Brunt Street, at Beard Street Pier, 1-718 596 2506, www.bwac.org) for details of its large group shows at weekends in spring, summer and autumn; they're held in the BWAC's 25,000-square-foot exhibition space in a Civil War-era warehouse on the pier just south of Fairway.

Bustling with parents pushing baby strollers and herding lively children,

Brooklyn Bridge

Park Slope houses hip young families in Victorian brownstones and feeds them organically from the nation's oldest working food co-operative (only open to members). The neighbourhood's intellectual, progressive and lefty political heritage is palpable; local residents include Hollywood actors (Maggie Gyllenhaal and Peter Sarsgaard, John Turturro and Steve Buscemi, among others) and well-known authors (Paul Auster and Jonathan Safran Foer).

Fifth Avenue is Park Slope's main strip for restaurants, bars and shops, but recently interest has shifted west to **Gowanus**, the neighbourhood hugging the canal of the same name. It might seem baffling that anyone would want to build glitzy condos or big retail shops near a polluted waterway, but that's precisely what is happening. The canal was named a Superfund site in 2010, and the city and the Environmental Protection Agency are expected to work on clean-up for at least the next decade. That hasn't stopped businesses from moving in: all-purpose performance hub the **Bell House** (*see p97*), which opened in 2007, was among the first hotspots in the area, and the long-planned Whole Foods at the corner of Third Avenue and 3rd Street opened in 2013.

The western edge of Prospect Park is a section of the **Park Slope Historic District**. Brownstones and several fine examples of Romanesque Revival and Queen Anne residences grace these streets. Particularly charming are the brick edifices that line Carroll Street, Montgomery Place and Berkeley Place. Fans of writer-director Noah Baumbach, who grew up in these parts, may recognise the locale from 2005 hit *The Squid and the Whale*, much of which was set here.

Central Park may be bigger and far more famous, but **Prospect Park** (main entrance at Grand Army Plaza, Prospect Heights, 1-718 965 8999, www.prospectpark.org) has a more rustic quality. This masterpiece, which designers Frederick Law Olmsted and Calvert Vaux said was more in line with their vision than Central Park, is a great spot for birdwatching, especially with a little guidance from the **Prospect Park Audubon Center** at the Boathouse (*see p86*). You can pretend you've left the city altogether by hiking along the paths of the **Ravine District** (park entrances on Prospect Park West, at 3rd, 9th & 15th Streets), a landscape of dense woods, waterfalls and stone bridges in the park's centre.

Children enjoy riding the hand-carved horses at the antique carousel (Flatbush Avenue, at Empire Boulevard) and seeing real animals in the **Prospect Park Zoo** (park entrance on Flatbush Avenue, near Ocean Avenue, Prospect

Heights, 1-718 399 7339, www.prospectpark zoo.com). A 15-minute walk from Prospect Park is the verdant necropolis of **Green-Wood Cemetery**.

Near the main entrance to Prospect Park sits the massive Civil War memorial arch at **Grand Army Plaza** (intersection of Flatbush Avenue, Eastern Parkway & Prospect Park West) and the imposing art deco central branch of the **Brooklyn Public Library** (10 Grand Army Plaza, Prospect Heights, 1-718 230 2100, www.bklynpublic library.org). Around the corner are the tranquil **Brooklyn Botanic Garden** and the **Brooklyn Museum**.

To the north is the borough's biggest and most prominent new development, the 22-acre Atlantic Yards complex, on the edge of downtown Brooklyn, which encompasses more than 6,000 (yet-to-be-built) apartments and the **Barclays Center** (see p96), a major concert venue and the new home of the Brooklyn Nets. Despite nine years of local opposition, contentious legal battles and the recession, the venue was christened by Jay-Z in autumn 2012.

Brooklyn Botanic Garden
This 52-acre haven of luscious greenery was founded in 1910. In spring, when Sakura Matsuri, the annual Cherry Blossom Festival, takes place, prize buds and Japanese culture are in full bloom. Linger in serene spots like the Japanese Hill-and-Pond Garden, the first Japanese-inspired garden built in the US, and the Shakespeare Garden, brimming with plants mentioned in the Bard's works. Start your stroll at the eco-friendly visitor centre – it has a green roof filled with 45,000 plants.
990 Washington Avenue, at Eastern Parkway, Prospect Heights (1-718 623 7200, www.bbg.org). Subway B, Q, Franklin Avenue S to Prospect Park; 2, 3 to Eastern Parkway-Brooklyn Museum. Open Mar-Oct 8am-6pm Tue-Fri; 10am-6pm Sat, Sun. Nov-Feb 8am-4.30pm Tue-Fri; 10am-4.30pm Sat, Sun. Admission $10; $5 reductions; free under-12s. Free Tue; 10am-noon Sat.

Brooklyn Museum
Among the many assets of Brooklyn's premier institution are the third-floor Egyptian galleries. Highlights include the Mummy Chamber, an installation of 170 objects, including human and animal mummies. Also on this level, works by Cézanne, Monet and Degas, part of an impressive European art collection, are displayed in the museum's skylighted Beaux-Arts Court. The Elizabeth A Sackler Center for Feminist Art on the fourth floor is dominated by Judy Chicago's monumental mixed-media installation, *The Dinner Party*. The fifth floor is mainly devoted to American works, including Albert Bierstadt's immense *A Storm in the Rocky Mountains, Mt Rosalie*, and the

Brooklyn Museum

Visible Storage-Study Center, where paintings, furniture and other objects are intriguingly juxtaposed. It's always worth checking the varied schedule of temporary shows and, reflecting the trend for destination museum eateries, the institution is the new home of Michelin-starred Brooklyn restaurant Saul.
200 Eastern Parkway, at Washington Avenue, Prospect Heights (1-718 638 5000, www.brooklynmuseum.org). Subway 2, 3 to Eastern Parkway-Brooklyn Museum. Open 11am-6pm Wed, Fri-Sun; 11am-10pm Thur. Open 11am-11pm 1st Sat of mth (except Sept). Admission Suggested donation $12; $8 reductions; free under-12s. Free 5-11pm 1st Sat of mth (except Sept).

Green-Wood Cemetery
Filled with Victorian mausoleums, cherubs and gargoyles, hills and ponds, this lush 478-acre landscape is the resting place of some half-million New Yorkers, among them Jean-Michel Basquiat, Leonard Bernstein, Boss Tweed and Horace Greeley.
Fifth Avenue, at 25th Street, Sunset Park (1-718 210 3080, www.green-wood.com). Subway R to 25th Street. Open varies by season; usually 8am-5pm daily. Admission free.

FORT GREENE

With its stately Victorian brownstones and other grand buildings, Fort Greene has undergone a major revival over the past two decades. It has long been a centre of African-American life and business – Spike Lee, Branford Marsalis and Chris Rock have all lived here. **Fort Greene Park** (from Myrtle to DeKalb Avenues, between St Edwards Street & Washington Park) was conceived in 1846 at the behest of poet Walt Whitman (then editor of the *Brooklyn Daily Eagle*); its masterplan was fully realised by Olmsted and Vaux in 1867. At the centre of the park stands the Prison Ship Martyrs Monument, erected in 1909 (from a design by Stanford White) in memory of 11,000 American prisoners who died on squalid British ships that were anchored nearby during the Revolutionary War.

Despite its name, the 34-floor **Williamsburgh Savings Bank**, at the corner of Atlantic and Flatbush Avenues, is in Fort Greene, not Williamsburg. The 512-foot-high structure was long the tallest in Brooklyn and, with its four-sided clocktower, one of the most recognisable features of its skyline. The 1927 building has been renamed One Hanson Place, and converted into (what else?) luxury condominiums.

Every Saturday, New Yorkers from all across the five boroughs hit the *Brooklyn Flea* (see p84 **Superflea**) in the yard of a public high school on Lafayette Avenue between Clermont & Vanderbilt Avenues. The combination of antiques, vintage clothes, indie crafts and food has proved so popular it's sparked several other markets.

Although originally founded in Brooklyn Heights, the **Brooklyn Academy of Music** (see p101) moved to its current site on Fort Greene's southern border in 1901. America's oldest operating performing arts centre, BAM was the home of the Metropolitan Opera until 1921; today, it's at the centre of a growing cultural district (see p102 **Art of Brooklyn**). Almost as famous

is the cheesecake at nearby **Junior's** Restaurant (386 Flatbush Avenue, at DeKalb Avenue, 1-718 852 5257).

In addition to some funky shops, a slew of restaurants can be found on or near DeKalb Avenue, including South African institution **Madiba Restaurant** (see p63).

BLDG 92
Located in the grounds of the Brooklyn Navy Yard, this small museum chronicles the mighty history of the former shipbuilding centre – which, at its peak during World War II, employed close to 70,000 people. Exhibits examine the yard's origins and significance throughout history, but the institution also looks to the manufacturing future of the space and the increasing number of businesses moving in each year (including Brooklyn Grange, which operates an apiary on site). The premises also has a café and rotating exhibitions, and offers weekend bus tours.
63 Flushing Avenue, at Carlton Avenue (1-718 907 5992, www.bldg92.org). Subway A, C to High Street; F to York Street; G to Clinton-Washington Avenues. Open noon-6pm Wed-Sun. Admission free.

WILLIAMSBURG, GREENPOINT & BUSHWICK

With a thriving music scene and an abundance of laid-back bars, small galleries and independent shops, **Williamsburg** – or 'Billyburg' as it's affectionately known – channels the East Village in its heyday, and it's just one stop from the downtown Manhattan neighbourhood on the L train. But the area teeters on the brink of (or, some argue, has already fallen into) hipster cliché. Long before the trendsetters invaded, Williamsburg's waterfront location had made it ideal for industry. When the Erie Canal linked the Atlantic Ocean to the Great Lakes in 1825, the area became a bustling port. Companies such as Pfizer and Domino Sugar started here, but businesses had begun to abandon the area's huge industrial spaces by the late 20th century. The Domino refinery closed in 2004, and is currently being developed into apartments.

Bedford Avenue is the area's main thoroughfare. By day, the epicentre of the strip is the **Bedford MiniMall** (no.218, between North 4th & North 5th Streets) – you won't find a Gap or Starbucks here, but you can browse an exceptionally edited selection of titles at **Spoonbill & Sugartown, Booksellers** (1-718 387-7322, www.spoonbillbooks.com) and sip some excellent coffee at the **Verb Café** (1-718 599 0977). The area has a constantly shifting array of cafés and eateries; south of the Williamsburg Bridge on Broadway, **Marlow & Sons** (see p63) was a pioneer in the kind of rustic aesthetic and farm-to-table fare that's become the knee-jerk norm in Kings County. Nearby, New York institution

Explore

Peter Luger (see p63) grills what most carnivores consider to be the best steak in the city.

You'll find chic shops dotted around the area, and the 'hood has more than 25 art galleries, which stay open late on the second Friday of every month. Pick up the free gallery guide Wagmag at local shops and cafés or visit www.wagmag.org for listings. However, Billyburg is better known for its music scene. Local rock bands and touring indie darlings play at **Music Hall of Williamsburg**, **Pete's Candy Store** and **Knitting Factory Brooklyn** (for all, see p98).

Those with a nostalgic bent will enjoy quirky repository of NYC ephemera, **City Reliquary**. Another local gem is the **Brooklyn Brewery** (79 North 11th Street, between Berry Street & Wythe Avenue, 1-718 486 7422, www.brooklyn brewery.com), housed in a former ironworks. The tasting room is open from Friday to Sunday, but visit during the happy 'hour' (Fridays 6-11pm) for $5 drafts. You can take a tour at weekends (every 30mins 1-5pm Sat; 1-4pm Sun).

With Williamsburg approaching hipster saturation point and rents rising accordingly, many of its young, creative residents seek cheaper digs nearby – which usually starts the gentrification cycle over again. **Greenpoint**, Williamsburg's northern neighbour, has been quietly undergoing a transformation of its own in the past decade. The former Polish stronghold's cachet has risen even further, as the setting of HBO's Girls. The recently opened **WNYC Transmitter Park**, a 1.6-acre waterfront green space between Greenpoint Avenue and Kent Street that was once the site of the local public radio station's AM transmitter towers, offers a stellar view of the Manhattan skyline. Young, wealthy residents are moving into the neighbourhood in droves, leading to inevitable tensions between old and new denizens.

Bushwick has also attracted a creative demographic to its industrial spaces. In late spring, the annual **Bushwick Open Studios** (www.artsinbushwick.org) gives you a glimpse inside around 600 artists' work spaces, but you'll also see plenty of street art in the vicinity of the Morgan Avenue subway stop. Bounded by Bushwick Avenue to the north-west and Broadway to the south-west, this traditionally Latino neighbourhood has begun to sprout coffee shops, bars and vintage stores over the last few years, not mention restaurants, such as acclaimed locavore eatery **Roberta's** (see p64).

City Reliquary

This not-for-profit mini-museum of New York history reopened in 2012 after a renovation that coincided with its ten-year anniversary. Peruse Gotham ephemera such as memorabilia from both NYC World's Fairs, and hundreds of Lady Liberty figurines. Other idiosyncratic displays include a vintage barber-shop diorama furnished with a chair from Barber Hall of Famer Antonio Nobile's Bay Ridge, Brooklyn, shop, and a transplanted Chinatown newsstand. 370 Metropolitan Avenue, at Havemeyer Street, Williamsburg (1-718 782 4842, www.cityreliquary. org). Subway G to Metropolitan Avenue; L to Lorimer Street. Open noon-6pm Thur-Sun. Admission Suggested donation $5.

CONEY ISLAND & BRIGHTON BEACH

Combining old-time fairground attractions, new amusement park rides and traditional seaside pleasures against a gritty urban backdrop, **Coney Island** is a strange hybrid undergoing a revitalisation plan that also includes improvements to the surrounding residential neighbourhood. In its heyday, from the turn of the century until World War II, Coney Island was New York City's playground, drawing millions each year to its seaside amusement parks Dreamland, Luna Park and Steeplechase Park. The first two were destroyed by fire (Dreamland in 1911 and Luna Park in 1944) and not rebuilt, while Steeplechase Park staggered on until 1964. Astroland was built in 1962 in the euphoria of the World's Fair, went up in flames in 1975 and was rebuilt, only to shutter in 2008.

A few years before, a developer had bought about half the area's entertainment district with a view to transforming it into a glitzy, Las Vegas-style resort, with hotels and condos, as well as restaurants, shops and rides. But a standoff with municipal planners halted progress. Then, in 2009, the city agreed to buy almost seven acres near the boardwalk that would form the core of a 27-acre amusement district. A new incarnation of **Luna Park** (1000 Surf Avenue, at W 10th Street, 1-718 373 5862, www. lunaparknyc.com, open Apr-Oct) opened in summer 2010. It now has more than 20 rides, including the new Thunderbolt – Coney Island's first custom-built rollercoaster since the Cyclone opened in 1927. The latter whiplash-inducing ride is still going strong, along with the 1918 Deno's Wonder Wheel – both are protected landmarks.

Nostalgic visitors will enjoy a stroll along the three-mile-long boardwalk, lined with corny carnival games and souvenir shops. The iconic 1939 Parachute Jump has been restored and is illuminated at night. Non-profit arts organisation Coney Island USA keeps the torch burning for 20th-century-style attractions at its **Coney Island Museum** with seasonal Circus Sideshows, as well as kitsch summer spectacle the **Mermaid Parade** (see p12). The local baseball team, Brooklyn Cyclones, play at the seaside **MCU Park**.

Walk left along the boardwalk from Coney Island and you'll reach **Brighton Beach**, New York's Little Odessa. Groups of Russian expats (the display of big hair and garish fashion can be jaw-dropping) crowd semi-outdoor eateries such as **Tatiana** (3152 Brighton 6th Street, at the Boardwalk, 1-718 891 5151) – on weekend nights, it morphs into a glitzy club.

Coney Island Museum

Housed in a 1917 building, the Coney Island Museum acts as a repository of the district's past and the focus of its current alternative culture. From Easter to the end of September, its venue, Sideshows by the Seashore, showcases the talents of such legendary freaks as human pin-cushion Scott Baker (aka the Twisted Shockmeister), and sword swallower Betty Bloomerz, while Burlesque at the Beach slinks on to the stage on summer Thursday and Friday nights (see website for the schedule). 1208 Surf Avenue, at 12th Street, Coney Island (1-718 372 5159, www.coneyisland.com). Subway D, F, N, Q to Coney Island-Stillwell Avenue. Open Museum noon-6pm Sat, Sun. Shows vary. Admission Museum $5. Shows $12-$15.

Queens

While Queens is the point of arrival for visitors flying into JFK or La Guardia airports, the borough hasn't traditionally been on most tourists' must-see list. Now, however, cultural institutions, such as the Museum of Modern Art-affiliated MoMA PS1 and the revamped Museum of the Moving Image, are drawing both out-of-towners and Manhattanites across the Ed Koch Queensboro Bridge.

Queens is also an increasingly popular gastronomic destination. The city's largest borough is the country's most diverse urban area, with almost half its 2.3 million residents hailing from nearly 150 nations. Not for nothing is the elevated 7 subway line that serves these parts nicknamed the 'International Express'. Astoria is home to Greek tavernas and Brazilian churrascarias; Jackson Heights provides Indian, Thai and South American eateries; and Flushing has the city's second largest Chinatown.

LONG ISLAND CITY

Just across the East River from Manhattan, Long Island City has been touted as the 'next Williamsburg' for so long that several other 'hoods have since claimed and passed on the mantle. In truth, LIC's proximity to midtown and the proliferation of modern apartment towers on the waterfront have proved more of a draw to upwardly mobile professionals and young families than cutting-edge cool hunters. Nevertheless, the neighbourhood has one of the city's most adventurous museums and several interesting galleries and performance spaces.

Fronting the main stretch of residential riverside development, **Gantry Plaza State Park** (48th Avenue, at Center Boulevard) commands an impressive panorama of midtown Manhattan. The 12-acre park takes its name from the hulking industrial gantries that still stand watch over the piers and were used to haul cargo from rail barges. Wavy deckchairs offer direct views of the United Nations across the East River. While Vernon Avenue is the neighbourhood's prime restaurant, retail and bar hub, the **Waterfront Crabhouse** (2-03 Borden Avenue, at 2nd Street, 1-718 729 4862), an old-time saloon and seafood restaurant in an 1880s brick building, evokes an earlier time with a jumble of bric-a-brac dangling from the dining room ceiling.

The neighbourhood's cultural jewel is the progressive art institution **MoMA PS1**. During the summer months, the courtyard of the museum becomes a dance-music hub with its Saturday-afternoon **Warm Up** parties (see p12). Nearby, a well-preserved block of 19th-century houses constitutes the **Hunter's Point Historic District** (45th Avenue, between 21st & 23rd Streets).

With several artists' studio complexes lodged in Long Island City, a nascent art scene has taken hold. **SculptureCenter**, housed in a dramatic converted industrial space, is a great place to see new work, while the **Fisher Landau Center for Art** (38-27 30th Street, between 38th and 39th Avenues, 1-718 937 0727, www.flcart.org; closed Tue, Wed) showcases the 1,500-piece contemporary art collection of Emily Fisher Landau. For details of open-studio events in the neighbourhood, check out www.licartists.org. For the **Noguchi Museum**, see p46.

MoMA PS1

Housed in a distinctive Romanesque Revival building, MoMA PS1 mounts cutting-edge shows and hosts an acclaimed international studio programme. The contemporary art centre became an affiliate of MoMA in 1999, and the two institutions sometimes stage collaborative exhibitions. The DJed summer Warm Up parties are a fixture of the dance-music scene; eaterie M Wells Dinette is a foodie destination. 22-25 Jackson Avenue, at 46th Avenue (1-718 784 2084, www.momaps1. org). Subway E, M to Court Square-23rd Street; G to 21st Street; 7 to Court Square. Open noon-6pm Mon, Thur-Sun. Admission $10; $5 reductions; under-17s free.

SculptureCenter

One of the best places in the city to see sculpture by blossoming and mid-career artists, this non-profit space –

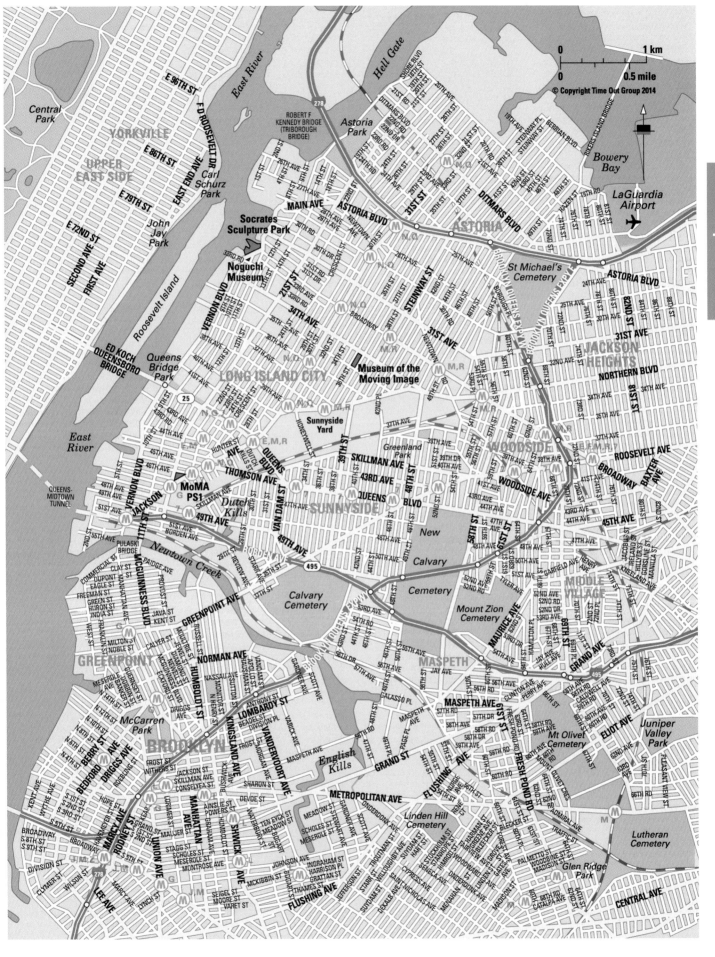

housed in an impressive former trolley-repair shop that was redesigned by acclaimed architect Maya Lin in 2002 – is known for its broad definition of the discipline. *44-19 Purves Street, at Jackson Avenue (1-718 361 1750, www.sculpture-center.org). Subway E, M to Court Square-23rd Street; G, 7 to Court Square. Open 11am-6pm Mon, Thur-Sun. Admission Suggested donation $5; $3 reductions.*

ASTORIA

A lively, traditionally Greek and Italian neighbourhood, Astoria has over the last few decades seen an influx of Brazilians, Bangladeshis, Eastern Europeans, Colombians and Egyptians; they've been joined by post-grads sharing row-house digs. A 15-minute downhill hike from Broadway subway station towards the river brings you to the **Noguchi Museum**, which was created by visionary sculptor. Nearby lies the **Socrates Sculpture Park** (Broadway, at Vernon Boulevard, www.socratessculpturepark.org), a riverfront art space in an industrial setting with great views of the Manhattan skyline.

In the early days of cinema, Astoria was a major celluloid star. Taking advantage of its proximity to talent-laden Broadway, Famous Players-Lasky (later Paramount Pictures) opened its first studios in the neighbourhood in 1920. Portions of Valentino's blockbuster *The Sheikh* (1921) were filmed there, and the studio produced the Marx Brothers' *The Cocoanuts* (1929) and *Animal Crackers* (1930) before Paramount moved its operations west. After years of neglect, the studios were declared a National Historic Landmark in 1976, and, in 1982, developer George S Kaufman bought the site and created **Kaufman Astoria Studios** (34-12 36th Street, between 34th & 35th Avenues, www.kaufmanastoria.com). Scenes for numerous films, including *The Taking of Pelham 1 2 3* (2009) and *The Bourne Legacy* (2012) were shot there, and the studios are also home to long-running kids' TV show *Sesame Street*. The recently expanded **Museum of the Moving Image** is across the street.

Still New York's Greek-American stronghold, Astoria is well known for Hellenic eateries and cafés. One of the city's last central European beer gardens, **Bohemian Hall & Beer Garden** (see p71) offers Czech-style dining and drinking. Arrive early on warm weekends to nab a picnic table in the expansive, linden tree-shaded yard. You can puff on a shisha – a (legal) hookah pipe – with thick Turkish coffee in the cafés of **'Little Egypt'** along Steinway Street, between 28th Avenue and Astoria Boulevard. At the end of the N and Q subway lines (Astoria-Ditmars Boulevard), walk west to **Astoria Park** (from Astoria

Unisphere, Flushing Meadows Corona Park

Park South to Ditmars Boulevard, between Shore Boulevard & 19th Street) for its dramatic views of two bridges: the Robert F Kennedy Bridge (formerly the Triborough), Robert Moses's automotive labyrinth connecting Queens, the Bronx and Manhattan; and the 1916 Hell Gate Bridge, a steel single-arch tour de force and template for the Sydney Harbour Bridge. On the area's north-east fringes, you can take a tour (by appointment) of the still-thriving red-brick 1871 piano factory **Steinway & Sons** (1 Steinway Place, between 19th Avenue & 38th Street, 1-718 721 2600, www.steinway.com).

Museum of the Moving Image

The Museum of the Moving Image reopened in 2011 after a major renovation that doubled its size and made it one of the foremost museums in the world dedicated to TV, film and video. The museum, with its collection and state-of-the-art screening facilities and galleries, is housed on the campus of Kaufman Astoria Studios. The upgraded core exhibition, 'Behind the Screen', on the second and third floors, contains approximately 1,400 artefacts – including the super creepy stunt doll used in *The Exorcist*, with full head-rotating capabilities, and a miniature skyscraper from *Blade Runner* – and interactive displays. A new gallery devoted to *Muppets* creator Jim Henson is expected to open in early 2015.
36-01 35th Avenue, at 36th Street (1-718 777 6888, www.moving image.us). Subway R, M to Steinway Street; N, Q to 36th Avenue. Open Galleries 10.30am-5pm Wed, Thur; 10.30am-8pm Fri; 11.30am-7pm Sat, Sun. Admission $12; $6-$9 reductions; under-3s free; free 4-8pm Fri.

Noguchi Museum

When Japanese-American sculptor and designer Isamu Noguchi (1904-88) opened his Queens museum in 1985, he became the first living artist in the US to establish such an institution. The Noguchi Museum occupies a former photo-engraving plant across the street from the studio he had occupied since the 1960s; its location allowed him to be close to stone and metal suppliers along Vernon Boulevard. Noguchi designed the entire building to be a meditative oasis amid its gritty, industrial setting. Eleven galleries – spread over two floors – and an outdoor space are filled with his sculptures, as well as drawn, painted and collaged studies, architectural models, and stage and furniture designs.
9-01 33rd Road, at Vernon Boulevard (1-718 204 7088, www.noguchi.org). Subway N, Q to Broadway, then 15min walk or Q104 bus to 11th Street; 7 to Vernon Boulevard-Jackson Avenue, then Q103 bus to 10th Street. Open 10am-5pm Wed-Fri; 11am-6pm Sat, Sun. Admission $10; $5 reductions; free under-12s; pay what you wish 1st Fri of the mth. No pushchairs/strollers.

JACKSON HEIGHTS

Dizzying even by Queens standards, Jackson Heights' multiculturalism gives it an energy all its own. Little India greets you with a cluster of small shops on 74th Street between 37th Road and 37th Avenue, selling Indian music, Bollywood DVDs, saris and glitzy jewellery. But the main appeal for visitors is culinary. The unofficial HQ of the Indian expat community, **Jackson Diner** (see p64) serves sumptuous curries. Along with neighbouring Elmhurst and Woodside, Jackson Heights has also welcomed waves of Latin American and South-east Asian immigrants. Fresh, meaty tacos – think broiled

beef and steamed tongue – give **Taqueria Coatzingo** (76-05 Roosevelt Avenue, between 76th & 77th Streets, 1-718 424 1977) an edge over the other tempting holes-in-the-wall under the 7 train track.

FLUSHING

Egalitarian Dutchmen staked their claim to 'Vlissingen' in the 1600s and were shortly joined by pacifist Friends, or Quakers, seeking religious freedom in the New World. These religious settlers promulgated the Flushing Remonstrance, a groundbreaking 1657 edict extending 'the law of love, peace and liberty' to Jews and Muslims. It's now regarded as a forerunner of the United States Constitution's First Amendment. The plain wooden **Old Quaker Meeting House** (137-16 Northern Boulevard, between Main & Union Streets), built in 1694, creates a startling juxtaposition to the prosperous Chinatown that rings its weathered wooden walls. The neighbourhood has hundreds of temples and churches used by immigrants from Korea, China and south Asia. **St George's Church** (135-32 38th Avenue, between Main & Prince Streets, 1-718 359 1171, www.saintgeorgesflushing.org), an Episcopalian church with a striking steeple, chartered by King George III, was once a dominant site, but now competes for attention with restaurants and shops. The interior is worth a brief visit if only to see the two examples of Queens-made Tiffany stained glass.

Most visitors, however, come for the restaurants and dumpling stalls of Flushing's sprawling **Chinatown**, which has a more affluent demographic than its Manhattan counterpart – a case in point is the gleaming **New World Mall** (136-20 Roosevelt Avenue, at Main Street, 1-718 353 0551, www.newworld mallny.com) and its opulent third-floor dim sum palace, **Grand Restaurant** (1-718 321 8258). Downstairs, at the spacious **JMart** supermarket, peruse such exotic produce as the formidably prickled durian and the notoriously elusive mangosteen, or gawk at buckets full of live eels and frogs.

The most visited site in Queens is rambling **Flushing Meadows Corona Park** (from 111th Street to Van Wyck Expressway, between Flushing Bay & Grand Central Parkway, 1-718 760 6565, www. nycgovparks.org), where the 1939-40 and 1964-65 World's Fairs were held. Larger than Central Park, it's home to the **Queens Zoo** (1-718 271 1500, www.queenszoo.com); **Queens Theatre in the Park** (1-718 760 0064, www.queenstheatre. org), an indoor amphitheatre designed by Philip Johnson; the **New York Hall of Science** (see p87), an acclaimed interactive museum; the **Queens Botanical Garden**, a 39-acre cavalcade of greenery; and the recently expanded **Queens Museum**. Also here are **Citi Field** (Roosevelt Avenue, near 126th Street, 1-718 507 8499, www.new york.mets.mlb.com), the home of the Mets baseball team, and the **USTA (United States Tennis Association) National Tennis Center**. The **US Open** (*see p12*) raises an almighty racket at summer's end, but the general public can play here the other 11 months of the year.

Louis Armstrong House

Pilgrims to the two-storey house where the great 'Satchmo' lived from 1943 until his death in 1971 will find a shrine to the revolutionary trumpet player – as well as his wife's passion for wallpaper. Her decorative attentions extended to the interiors of cupboards, closets and even bathroom cabinets. The 40-minute tour is enhanced by audiotapes of the jazz legend that give much insight into the tranquil domesticity he sought in the then suburban neighbourhood.
34-56 107th Street, between 34th & 37th Avenues, Corona (1-718 478 8274, www.louisarmstronghouse.org). Subway 7 to 103rd Street-Corona Plaza. Open 10am-5pm Tue-Fri; noon-5pm Sat, Sun. Tours hourly (last tour 4pm). Admission $10; $6-$7 reductions; free under-4s.

Queens Museum

Facing the Unisphere, the 140ft stainless steel globe created for the 1964 World's Fair, in Flushing Meadows Corona Park, the Queens Museum occupies the former New York City Building, a Gotham-themed pavilion built for the earlier World's Fair in 1939. In the 1940s, the structure was the first home of the United Nations. During the 1964 World's Fair, the New York City Building showcased the Panorama of the City of New York, a 9,335sq ft scale model of the city dreamed up by powerful urban planner Robert Moses. Still on display in the museum, it includes every one of the 895,000 buildings constructed before 1992.

In autumn 2013, after more than two years, the Queens Museum wrapped up an expansion-cum-renovation project that doubled its size. The centrepiece of the 50,000sq ft addition, which used to house an ice-rink, is an airy atrium. The extra space accommodates studios for Queens-based artists, a café and a museum shop selling original World's Fair memorabilia. The Panorama has had a modest makeover of its own. Its day-to-night cycle, which allowed it to be viewed as a city at night, has been restored – wait for the room to darken to see the Little Apple twinkle. The new World's Fair Visible Storage and Gallery displays more than 900 artefacts from the 1939 and 1964 fairs.
New York City Building, park entrance on 49th Avenue, at 111th Street, Flushing Meadows-Corona Park (1-718 592 9700, www.queens museum.org). Subway 7 to 111th Street, then walk south on 111th Street, turning left on to 49th Avenue; continue into the park & over Grand Central Parkway Bridge. Open noon-6pm Wed-Sun. Admission Suggested donation $8; $4 reductions; under-12s free.

The Bronx

The only NYC borough that's physically attached to the mainland of America, the Bronx seems remote to most visitors – and, indeed, many New Yorkers. Part of this perceived distance is due to the lingering of the South Bronx's global reputation for urban strife in the 1970s, which means the borough's two best-known visitor attractions, Yankee Stadium and the Bronx Zoo, are generally covered in quick trips in and out. But there's more to the boogie-down borough than gritty cityscapes: the area offers art deco architecture on the Grand Concourse, an up-and-coming art scene, old-school Italian eateries on Arthur Avenue, and some of the most exquisite gardens in the city.

Visitors should note, however, that although some parts of the Bronx are gentrifying, others, such as parts of the South Bronx and the northern swathe of the Grand Concourse, are still rough around the edges.

THE SOUTH BRONX

In the 1960s and '70s, the South Bronx was so ravaged by post-war 'white flight' and community displacement from the construction of the Cross Bronx Expressway that the neighbourhood became virtually synonymous with urban blight. Crime was rampant and arson became widespread, as landlords discovered that renovating decayed property was far less lucrative than simply burning it down to collect insurance. During a World Series game at Yankee Stadium in 1977, TV cameras caught a building on fire just blocks away. 'Ladies and gentlemen,' commentator Howard Cosell told the world, 'the Bronx is burning.'

These days, the South Bronx is rising from the ashes. In 2006, the South Bronx Initiative was formed to revitalise the area, while eco-sensitive outfits such as Sustainable South Bronx (www.ssbx.org) have helped to transform vacant lots into green spaces such as **Barretto Point Park** (between Tiffany & Barretto Streets) and **Hunts Point Riverside Park** (at the foot of Lafayette Avenue on the Bronx River). In 2005, Hunts Point became the new home to the city's **Fulton Fish Market** (1-718 378 2356, www.newfultonfishmarket.com), which moved from the site it had occupied for 180 years near South Street Seaport to a 400,000-square foot modern facility that is the largest consortium of seafood retailers in America.

Hunts Point is also becoming a creative live-work hub. In 1994, a group of artists and community leaders converted an industrial building into the **Point** (940 Garrison Avenue, at Manida Street, 1-718 542 4139, www.thepoint.org, closed Sun), an arts-based community development centre with a much-used performance space and gallery, studios for dance, theatre and photography and an environmental advocacy group. The Point also leads walking tours (call for reservations) that explore the history of locally born music, such as mambo and hip hop.

Another artistic South Bronx hotbed is simmering further south-west in Mott Haven. Here, **Longwood Art Gallery @ Hostos** (450 Grand Concourse, at 149th Street, 1-718 518 6728, www.bronxarts.org/lag.asp), the creation of the Bronx Council on the Arts, mounts top-notch exhibits in a variety of media. Yet despite developers' hopes for 'SoBro', the area has not quite turned into the Next Big Thing. Yet.

Of course, the vast majority of visitors to the South Bronx are just stopping long enough to take in a baseball game at **Yankee Stadium**, where some of baseball's most famous legends, from Babe Ruth to Derek Jeter, have made history.

Yankee Stadium

In 2009, the Yankees vacated the fabled 'House that Ruth Built' and moved into their new $1.3-billion stadium across the street. Monument Park, an open-air museum behind centre field that celebrates the exploits of past Yankee heroes, can be visited as part of a tour ($25, $23 reductions, $20 booked online; 1-646 977 8687), along with the New York Yankees Museum, the dugout, and – when the Yankees are on the road – the clubhouse.
River Avenue, at 161st Street (1-718 293 6000, www.yankees. com). Subway B, D, 4 to 161st Street-Yankee Stadium.

THE GRAND CONCOURSE

A few blocks east of Yankee Stadium runs the four-and-a-half-mile Grand Concourse, which begins at 138th Street in the South Bronx and ends at Mosholu Parkway just shy of Van Cortlandt Park. Once the most prestigious drag in the Bronx, the Grand Boulevard and Concourse (to give the artery's grandiose official title) is still a must for lovers of art deco. Engineer Louis Risse designed the boulevard in 1892, modelling it on Paris's Champs-Elysées, and it opened to traffic in 1909. Following the arrival of a new subway line nearly a decade later, rapid development along the Concourse began in the deco style so popular in the 1920s and '30s.

Starting at 161st Street and heading south, look for the permanent street plaques that make up the **Bronx Walk of Fame**, honouring famous Bronxites from Stanley Kubrick and Tony Orlando to Colin Powell and hip hop 'godfather' Afrika Bambaataa. Heading north, the buildings date mostly from the 1920s to the early '40s, and constitute the country's largest concentration of art deco housing outside Miami Beach. Erected in 1937 at the corner of 161st Street, 888 Grand Concourse has a large concave entrance of gilded mosaic and is topped by a curvy metallic marquee. Inside, the mirrored lobby's central fountain and sunburst-patterned floor could rival those of any hotel on Miami's Ocean Drive. On the south side of **Joyce Kilmer Park**, at 161st Street, is the elegant white-marble fountain of Lorelei, built in 1893 in Germany in homage to Heinrich Heine, who

Bronx Museum of the Arts. *See p48.*

wrote the poem of the same name. This was intended as the original entrance to the Concourse before it was extended south. The grandest building on the thoroughfare is the landmark **Andrew Freedman Home**, a 1924 French-inspired limestone palazzo between McClennan and 166th Streets. Freedman, a millionaire subway contractor, left the bulk of his $7 million fortune with instructions to build a poorhouse for the rich – that is, those who had lost their fortunes and were suffering an impecunious old age. In 2012, it was reborn as a '20s-inspired B&B (1-718 588 8200, www.andrewfreedman complex.com), part of a local hospitality-training scheme, and a venue for arts events and exhibitions. The lower level is occupied by the Family Preservation Center (FPC), a community-focused social service agency. Across the street is the **Bronx Museum of the Arts**, which was established in 1971 in a former synagogue.

A few blocks north, at 1150 Grand Concourse, at McClellan Place, is a 1937 art deco apartment block commonly referred to as the **'fish building'** because of the colourful marine-themed mosaic flanking its doors; pause inside the restored lobby for a glimpse of its two large murals depicting pastoral scenes. Near the intersection of Fordham Road, keep an eye out for the Italian rococo exterior of the **Paradise Theater** (2403 Grand Concourse, at 187th Street, www.paradise theater.net), once the largest cinema in the city. To see the elaborate murals, fountains and grand staircase of the interior, which was restored in 2005, you'll need to buy a ticket for one of the concerts staged here. Just north is the ten-storey **Emigrant Savings Bank**, at 2526 Grand Concourse, worth ducking into for a glimpse of five striking murals by the artist Angelo Manganti, depicting scenes of the Bronx's past. Further north to Kingsbridge Road lies the **Edgar Allan Poe Cottage**, a small wooden house where the writer lived from 1846 to 1849. It was moved to the Grand Concourse from its original spot on Fordham Road in 1913.

Bronx Museum of the Arts
Featuring more than 1,000 works, this multicultural art museum shines a spotlight on 20th- and 21st-century artists who are either Bronx-based or of African, Asian or Latino ancestry. *1040 Grand Concourse, at 165th Street (1-718 681 6000, www. bronxmuseum.org). Subway B, D to 161st Street; 4 to 161st Street-Yankee Stadium. Open 11am-6pm Thur, Sat, Sun; 11am-8pm Fri. Admission free.*

Edgar Allan Poe Cottage
Pay homage to Poe in the house where he spent the last three years of his life and wrote such literary marvels as *Annabel Lee* and *The Bells*. After a major renovation, the cottage has been restored with period furnishings, including the author's rocking chair, and a new visitors' centre complete with a sloping shingle roof designed to resemble the wings of the bird from the poet's famous *The Raven*. *2640 Grand Concourse, at Kingsbridge Road (1-718 881 8900, www.bronxhistorical society.org/ poecottage). Subway B, D, 4 to Kingsbridge Road. Open 10am-4pm Sat; 1-5pm Sun. Admission $5; $3 reductions.*

TOP TIP!
Bronx Culture Trolley
To check out SoBro's burgeoning art scene, hop on the free Bronx Culture Trolley (www.bronxarts.org; see website for info), which stops at several venues.

BELMONT & BRONX PARK

Settled in the late 19th century by Italian immigrants hired to landscape nearby Bronx Zoo, close-knit Belmont is centred on Arthur Avenue, lined with delis, bakeries, restaurants and stores selling T-shirts proclaiming the locale to be New York's 'real Little Italy'. Still celebrating Mass in Italian, neoclassical **Our Lady of Mt Carmel Church** (627 E 187th Street, at Hughes Avenue, 1-718 295 3770) has been serving the community for more than a century. Food is the main reason to visit.

Arthur Avenue Retail Market (2344 Arthur Avenue, between Crescent Avenue & E 186th Street) is a covered market built in the 1940s when Mayor Fiorello La Guardia campaigned to get the pushcarts off the street. Inside, you'll find **Mike's Deli** (*see p64*), where you can order enormous sandwiches bursting with Italian cold cuts. For a full meal, try old-school red-sauce joints such as **Mario's** (*see p64*), featured in several *Sopranos* episodes and Mario Puzo's novel *The Godfather*; or bare-bones canteen **Dominick's** (*see p64*).

Belmont is within easy walking distance of Bronx Park, home to two of the borough's most celebrated attractions. Make your way east along 187th Street, then south along Southern Boulevard, and you'll come to the **Bronx Zoo**. Opened in 1899 by Theodore Roosevelt, at 265 acres it's the largest urban zoo in the US. A 15-minute walk north of the zoo – and still in Bronx Park – brings you to the serene 250 acres of the **New York Botanical Garden**, which comprises 50 different gardens.

Bronx Zoo/Wildlife Conservation Society
The Bronx Zoo shuns cages in favour of indoor and outdoor environments that mimic natural habitats. There are more than 60,000 creatures and more than 600 species here. Monkeys, leopards and tapirs live inside the lush, steamy Jungle World, a recreation of an Asian rainforest inside a 37,000sq ft building, while lions, giraffes, zebras and other animals roam the African Plains. The popular Congo Gorilla Forest has turned 6.5 acres into a dramatic central African rainforest habitat. A glass-enclosed tunnel winds through the forest, allowing visitors to get close to the dozens of primate families in residence, including majestic western lowland gorillas. Tiger Mountain is populated by Siberian tigers, while the Himalayan Highlands features snow leopards and red pandas. *Bronx River Parkway, at Fordham Road (1-718 367 1010, www.bronxzoo. com). Subway 2, 5 to E Tremont/W Farms Square, then walk 2 blocks to the zoo's Asia entrance; or Metro-North (Harlem Line local) from Grand Central Terminal to Fordham, then take the Bx9 bus to 183rd Street and Southern Boulevard. Open Apr-Oct 10am-5pm Mon-Fri; 10am-5.30pm Sat, Sun. Nov-Mar 10am-4.30pm daily. Admission $17; $12-$15 reductions; pay what you wish Wed. Some rides & exhibitions cost extra.*

New York Botanical Garden
The serene 250 acres comprise 50 gardens and plant collections, including the Rockefeller Rose Garden, the Everett Children's Adventure Garden and the last 50 original acres of a forest that once covered the whole city area. In spring, clusters of lilac, cherry, magnolia and crab apple trees burst into bloom; in autumn you'll see vivid foliage in the oak and maple groves. The Azalea Garden features around 3,000 vivid azaleas and rhododendrons. The Enid A Haupt Conservatory – the nation's largest greenhouse, built in 1902 – contains the World of Plants, a series of environmental galleries that take you on an eco-tour through tropical rainforests, deserts and a palm tree oasis. *Bronx River Parkway, at Fordham Road (1-718 817 8700, www.nybg. org). Subway B, D, 4 to Bedford Park Boulevard, then Bx26 bus to the garden's Mosholu Gate; or Metro-North (Harlem Line local) from Grand Central Terminal to Botanical Garden. Open Jan, Feb 10am-5pm Tue-Sun. Mar-Dec 10am-6pm Tue-Sun. Admission $20-$25; $8-$22 reductions. Grounds only $13; $3-$6 reductions; grounds free Wed, 9-10am Sat.*

RIVERDALE & VAN CORTLANDT PARK

Riverdale, along the north-west coast of the Bronx, reflects the borough's suburban past; its huge homes perch on narrow, winding streets that meander towards the Hudson River. The only one you can actually visit is **Wave Hill**, an 1843 stone mansion set on a former private estate that has beautiful gardens and a gallery. The nearby 1,146-acre **Van Cortlandt Park** (entrance on Broadway, at 242nd Street) occasionally hosts cricket teams largely made up of West Indians and Indians. You can hike through a 100-year-old forest, play golf on the nation's first municipal course or ride horses hired from stables in the park.

The oldest building in the Bronx is **Van Cortlandt House Museum**, a 1749 Georgian residence that was commandeered by both sides during the Revolutionary War. Abutting the park is **Woodlawn Cemetery**, the resting place for such notable souls as Herman Melville, Duke Ellington, Miles Davis, FW Woolworth and Fiorello La Guardia. To help you to pay your respects, maps are available at the entrance at Webster Avenue and E 233rd Street. About five blocks south on Bainbridge Avenue, history buffs will also enjoy the **Museum of Bronx History**, set in a 1758 stone farmhouse.

Museum of Bronx History
Operated by the Bronx County Historical Society, the museum displays its collection of documents and photos in the Valentine-Varian House, a Federal-style fieldstone residence built in 1758. *Valentine-Varian House, 3266 Bainbridge Avenue, between Van Cortlandt Avenue East & 208th Street (1-718 881 8900, www.bronx historicalsociety.org). Subway D to Norwood-205th Street. Open 10am-4pm Sat; 1-5pm Sun. Admission $5; $3 reductions.*

Van Cortlandt House Museum
A one-time wheat plantation that has since been turned into a colonial museum, Van Cortlandt House was alternately used as headquarters by George Washington and British General Sir William Howe during the Revolutionary War. *Van Cortlandt Park, entrance on Broadway, at 246th Street (1-718 543 3344). Subway 1 to 242nd Street-Van Cortlandt Park. Open 10am-3pm Tue-Fri; 11am-4pm Sat, Sun. Admission $5; $3 reductions; free under-12s; free Wed.*

Wave Hill
Laze around in these 28 lush acres overlooking the Hudson River at Wave Hill, the setting of a Georgian Revival house that was home at various times to Mark Twain, Teddy Roosevelt and conductor Arturo Toscanini. Now open to the public, the grounds contain exquisite cultivated gardens and woodlands commanding excellent views of the river. The small on-site gallery hosts intriguing contemporary art shows inspired by nature, and the property is also a venue for concerts and other events. *W 249th Street, at Independence Avenue (1-718 549 3200, www.wavehill.org). Metro-North (Hudson Line local) from Grand Central Terminal to Riverdale. Open Mid Mar-Oct 9am-5.30pm Tue-Sun. Nov-mid Mar 9am-4.30pm Tue-Sun. Admission $8; $2-$4 reductions; free under-6s; free Tue, 9am-noon Sat.*

Consume

The city's top restaurants, cafés, bars and shops

Restaurants & Cafés

Ed's Lobster Bar

The melting pot redefined

Variety is the dominant spice in NYC's mind-bogglingly diverse food scene.

In Gotham, where apartments are as tight as sardine cans, restaurants serve as vibrant second living rooms and top chefs are elevated to rock-star status. For visitors, there's no better way to tap into the city's zeitgeist than soaking up the scene at its most beloved culinary destinations. Some of the most exciting restaurants to open in recent years include **Carbone** (see p55), a Godfather hangout on steroids, cross-cultural American canteen the **Dutch** (see p51), elegant grand-hotel throwback the **NoMad** (see p58) and Portland import Andy Ricker's Brooklyn Thai eaterie **Pok Pok NY** (see p64).

The East Village and Lower East Side tend to sprout reasonably priced eateries that draw big followings – tuck into superlative smoked meats at **Mighty Quinn's** (see p54), a standout in the latest wave of barbecue joints to hit town. While Danny Bowien's revelatory Szechuan spot, Mission Chinese Food, is on hiatus, he has followed up with popular **Mission Cantina**

(see p53). New York's farm-to-table movement is perhaps most robust in Brooklyn, where cheaper rents and a DIY spirit have made the borough a refuge for young, risk-taking chefs. The nerve centre of the movement is **Roberta's** (see p64), which grows some of its own produce and spun off a tasting-menu spot **Blanca**, in the back garden.

Elsewhere, there are cheek-by-jowl Asian restaurants in **Chinatown**, while **Koreatown**, the stretch of West 32nd Street between Fifth Avenue and Broadway, is lined with Korean barbecue joints and other eateries. Further afield, **Harlem** offers soul food and West African cooking, while the most diverse borough, **Queens**, counts Greek (in Astoria), Thai (in Elmhurst) and Indian (in Jackson Heights) among its globe-spanning cuisines.

Some of these further-flung locales are now attracting big-name chefs. Quebecois toque Hugue Dufour put Queens on the food map a few years ago with his snout-to-tail cooking at the short-lived M Wells,

which he followed up with museum eaterie **M Wells Dinette** at MoMA PS1 (see p44) and, more recently, **M Wells Steakhouse** (see p64).

Financial District

Adrienne's Pizzabar Pizza
Good, non-chain eateries are scarce in the Financial District, but this bright, modern pizzeria on quaint Stone Street provides a pleasant break from the crowded thoroughfares – there are outside tables from April to November. The kitchen prepares nicely charred pies with delectable toppings such as the rich quattro formaggi. If you're in a hurry, you can eat at the 12-seat bar, or opt for the sleek, wood-accented dining room to savour small plates and main courses such as baked sea scallops and ravioli al formaggio.
54 Stone Street, between Coenties Alley & Mill Street (1-212 248 3838). Subway R to Whitehall Street-South

Ferry; 2, 3 to Wall Street. Open 11.30am-midnight Mon-Sat; 11.30am-10pm Sun. Pizzas $14-$19.

Barbalu Italian
Former Barbarini owners Stefano Barbagallo and Adriana Luque bounced back from Hurricane Sandy with this 120-seat Italian eaterie at the same location. The husband-and-wife team scaled back the retail area, making space for a skylighted dining room packed with wooden two-tops. Slide into a brown banquette for classics such as mozzarella-and-eggplant caponatina, fettuccine with shrimp and tomatoes, and *torta di pinoli* (pine-nut cake). At the expanded bar area, find charcuterie and cheese plates along with Italian wines.
225-227 Front Street, between Beekman Street & Peck Slip (1-646 918 6565, www.barbalu.com). Subway A, C, J, Z, 2, 3, 4, 5 to Fulton Street. Open 10am-10pm daily. Main courses $14-$22.

Jack's Stir Brew Coffee Café
Java fiends convene at this award-winning caffeine spot that offers organic, shade-grown beans and a homey vibe. Coffee is served by espresso artisans with a knack for oddball concoctions, such as the super-silky Mountie latte, infused with maple syrup.
222 Front Street, between Beekman Street & Peck Slip (1-212 227 7631, www.jacksstirbrew.com). Subway A, C, J, Z, 2, 3, 4, 5 to Fulton Street. Open 6.30am-7pm Mon-Fri; 7am-7pm Sat, Sun. Coffee $2.50-$5.50. Other location 138 W 10th Street, between Greenwich Avenue & Waverly Place, West Village (1-212 929 0821).

North End Grill American
Danny Meyer brings his Midas touch to Battery Park City for this instant classic. The place has all the hallmarks of a Meyer joint: effortless, affable service; a warm, buzzy space; and cooking that's easy and accessible. Chef Floyd Cardoz puts his stamp on the seasonal menu, devoting an entire section to eggs and adding doses of fire and spice. We were impressed by composed plates such as wood-fired lamb loin shingled on a bed of green lentils seasoned with mint.
104 North End Avenue, at Murray Street (1-646 747 1600, www.north endgrillnyc.com). Subway A, C to Chambers Street; E to World Trade Center; 2, 3 to Park Place. Open 11.30am-2pm, 5.30-10pm Mon-Thur; 11.30am-2pm, 5.30-10.30pm Fri; 11am-2pm, 5.30-10.30pm Sat; 11am-2.30pm, 5.30-9pm Sun. Main courses $26-$58.

Katz's Delicatessen

Critic's choice

1 **Katz's Delicatessen** The iconic deli still serves some of the best pastrami in the city. *See p53.*

2 **Carbone** The food is as satisfying as the retro setting in this reimagined mob supper club. *See p55.*

3 **The NoMad** Elegant dining in plush, Paris-inspired surroundings. *See p58.*

4 **Pok Pok NY** A renowned Portland chef brings his touch to Thai. *See p64.*

5 **Roberta's** The laid-back locavore hangout is an essential destination for gastronauts. *See p64.*

Soho & Tribeca

Balthazar French
At dinner, this iconic faux-vintage brasserie is perennially packed with rail-thin lookers dressed to the nines. But it's not only fashionable – the kitchen rarely makes a false step and the service is surprisingly friendly. The $165 three-tiered seafood platter casts an impressive shadow, and the roast chicken with garlic mash for two is *délicieux*.
80 Spring Street, between Broadway & Crosby Street (1-212 965 1414, www.balthazarny.com). Subway N, R to Prince Street; 6 to Spring Street. Open 7.30-11.30am, noon-5pm, 6pm-midnight Mon-Thur; 7.30-11.30am, noon-5pm, 6pm-1am Fri; 8am-4pm, 6pm-1am Sat; 8am-4pm, 5.30pm-midnight Sun. Main courses $20-$45.

Brushstroke Japanese
Prominent local chef David Bouley's name may be behind this venture, but he's not in the kitchen, having handed the reins over to talented import Isao Yamada, who turns out some of the most accomplished Japanese food in the city. The ever-changing seasonal menu is best experienced as an intricate multicourse feast inspired by the Japanese *kaiseki*. A meal might start with crab *chawanmushi* (egg custard) with Oregon black truffles, before building slowly towards a subtle climax. In keeping with the basic tenets of this culinary art form, the savoury procession concludes with a rice dish – top-notch *chirashi* or seafood and rice cooked in a clay casserole – and delicate sweets such as creamy soy-milk panna cotta. The sushi bar is run by Tokyo-trained chef Eiji Ichimura, who serves a traditional Edomae-style *omakase*.
30 Hudson Street, at Duane Street (1-212 791 3771, www.davidbouley.com). Subway 1, 2, 3 to Chambers Street. Open 5.30-10pm Mon-Sat. Tasting menus $85-$135.

The Dutch American
Andrew Carmellini, Josh Pickard and Luke Ostrom – the white-hot team behind Italian hit Locanda Verde (*see right*) – turned to American eats for their sophomore effort. The Dutch offers late-night hours and a freewheeling menu, completing Carmellini's progression from haute golden boy (Café Boulud, Lespinasse) to champion of lusty plates and raucous settings. Carmellini plays off the country's diverse influences with a broad spectrum of dishes. Mini fried-oyster sandwiches, dry-aged steaks and peel 'n' eat prawns all get their due. Drop by the airy oak bar, with its adjacent oyster room, to sip one of the extensive selection of American whiskies.
131 Sullivan Street, at Prince Street (1-212 677 6200, www.thedutchnyc.com). Subway C, E to Spring Street. Open 11.30am-3pm, 5.30pm-11pm Mon-Wed; 11.30am-3pm, 5.30pm-midnight Thur, Fri; 10am-3pm, 5.30pm-midnight Sat; 10am-3pm, 5.30pm-11pm Sun. Main courses $21-$38.

Ed's Lobster Bar Seafood
If you secure a place at the 25-seat marble seafood bar or one of the few tables in the whitewashed eaterie, expect superlative raw-bar eats, delicately fried clams and lobster served every which way: steamed, grilled, broiled, chilled, stuffed into a pie and – the crowd favourite – the lobster roll. Here, it's a buttered bun stuffed with premium chunks of meat and a light coating of mayo. Note that the place serves lobster rolls only at the bar on weekday afternoons (3-5pm).
222 Lafayette Street, between Kenmare & Spring Streets (1-212 343 3236, www.lobsterbarnyc.com). Subway 6 to Spring Street. Open noon-3pm, 5-11pm Mon-Thur; noon-3pm, 5pm-midnight Fri; noon-midnight Sat; noon-9pm Sun. Main courses $18-$36.

La Esquina Mexican
La Esquina comprises three dining and drinking areas: first, a street-level taqueria, serving a short-order menu of tacos and Mexican *tortas*. Around the corner is a 30-seat café, its shelves stocked with books and old vinyl. Lastly, there's a dungeon-esque restaurant and lounge accessible through a back door of the taqueria (to enter, you have to confirm that you have a reservation). It's worth the hassle: a world of Mexican murals, fine tequilas, *huitlacoche* (Mexican truffle) quesadillas and crab tostadas awaits.
114 Kenmare Street, between Cleveland Place & Lafayette Street (1-646 613 7100, www.esquinanyc.com). Subway 6 to Spring Street. Open Taqueria 11am-2am daily. Café noon-midnight Mon-Thur; noon-1am Fri; 11am-1am Sat; 11am-midnight Sun. Restaurant 6pm-2am daily. Tacos $3.50. Main courses (café) $9-$16; (restaurant) $18-$32.

Jack's Wife Freda Café
Keith McNally protégé Dean Jankelowitz is behind this charming café. The 45-seat spot – sporting dark-green leather banquettes, brass railings and marble counters – serves homey fare, like Jankelowitz's grandmother's matzo-ball soup made with duck fat or a skirt steak sandwich served alongside hand-cut fries.
224 Lafayette Street, between Kenmare & Spring Streets (1-212 510 8550, www.jackswifefreda.com). Subway 6 to Spring Street. Open 9.45am-midnight Mon-Sat; 9.45am-10pm Sun. Main courses $15-$33.

Landmarc Tribeca Eclectic
This downtown dining destination quickly distinguished itself among its Tribeca competitors by serving heady bistro dishes (bone marrow, crispy sweetbreads) until midnight, and stocking the wine list with reasonably priced half bottles. Chef-owner Marc Murphy focuses on the tried and trusted: *frisée aux lardons*, braised lamb shank and several types of mussels. Metal beams and exposed brick add an unfinished edge to the elegant bi-level space. Those who have little restraint when it comes to sweets will appreciate the dessert menu: miniature portions cost just $4 a pop.
179 West Broadway, between Leonard & Worth Streets (1-212 343 3883, www.landmarc-restaurant.com). Subway 1 to Franklin Street. Open 11am-midnight daily. Main courses $17-$40. Other location 3rd Floor, Time Warner Center, 10 Columbus Circle, at Broadway, Upper West Side (1-212 823 6123).

Locanda Verde Italian
This buzzy eaterie in Robert De Niro's Greenwich Hotel features bold family-style fare that's best enjoyed as a bacchanalian banquet. Steak tartara piedmontese with hazelnuts, truffles and crispy guanciale (pork jowel bacon) won't last long in the middle of the table. Nor will the 'grandmother's' ravioli, stuffed with veal, pork and beef. This is one of those rare Italian restaurants with desserts worth saving room for – try the decadent La Fantasia di Tiramisu for two.
377 Greenwich Street, at North Moore Street (1-212 925 3797, www.locandaverdenyc.com). Subway 1 to Franklin Street. Open 7-11am, 11.30am-3pm, 5.30-11pm Mon-Fri; 8am-3pm, 5.30-11pm Sat, Sun. Main courses $19-$35.

Osteria Morini Italian
Michael White is one of New York's most prolific and successful Italian-American chefs, and this terrific downtown homage to a classic Bolognese tavern is his most accessible restaurant. The toque spent seven years cooking in Italy's Emilia-Romagna region, and his connection to the area surfaces in the restaurant's rustic food. Handmade pastas are fantastic across the board, while superb meats might include porchetta with crisp, crackling skin and potatoes bathed in pan drippings.
218 Lafayette Street, between Broome & Spring Streets (1-212 965 8777, www.osteriamorini.com). Subway 6 to Spring Street. Open 11.30am-11pm daily. Main courses $28-$38.

Brushstroke

Telepan Local American

Bill Telepan had a busy 2013 – along with redesigning his Michelin-starred Upper West Side flagship, the locavore champion also opened this more casual small-plates spot, with shareable snacks like foie gras doughnuts and shrimp poppers with green-chili aioli. To sate more ample appetites, it also offers heftier fare such as grilled short ribs and quail à l'orange.
329 Greenwich Street, between Duane & Jay Streets (1-212 966 9255, www.telepanlocal.com). Subway 1, 2, 3 to Chambers Street. Open 11.30am-11.30pm Mon-Thur; 11.30am-12.30am Fri, Sat; 11am-11.30pm Sun. Main courses $6-$20. Other location 72 West 69th Street, at Columbus Avenue, Upper West Side (1-212 580 4300).

Chinatown, Little Italy & Nolita

Big Wing Wong Chinese

You'll be confused when you show up to this old-school Cantonese joint – the outside inexplicably says 102 Noodles Town. But clarity hits when you taste a slice of the roasted duck, with its fatty, succulent meat and crackly, burnished mahogany skin. You can get the bird over rice or congee, but purists stick to a mere drizzle of hoisin.
102 Mott Street, between Canal & Hester Streets (1-212 274 0696). Subway J, N, Q, R, Z, 6 to Canal Street. Open 7am-9.30pm daily. Main courses $5-$20. No credit cards.

Café Habana Cuban

Trendy Nolita types storm this chrome corner fixture for a taste of the addictive grilled corn: golden ears doused in fresh mayo, chargrilled, and generously sprinkled with chilli powder and grated *cotija* cheese. Staples include a Cuban sandwich of roasted pork, ham, melted swiss and sliced pickles, and crisp beer-battered catfish with spicy mayo. At the takeaway next door, you can get that corn-on-a-stick to go.
17 Prince Street, at Elizabeth Street (1-212 625 2001, www.ecoeatery. com). Subway N, R to Prince Street; 6 to Spring Street. Open 9am-midnight daily. Main courses $10-$17.50.

Estela American

The fashionable cookie-cutter decor – exposed brick, globe lights, hulking marble bar – may suggest you've stumbled into yet another bustling rustic restaurant-cum-bar that's not worth the wait. But there is more to this Mediterranean-tinged spot than meets the eye: primarily, the talent of Ignacio Mattos, the imaginative Uruguayan-born chef, who strained to sell his brand of 'primitive modern' cooking to a Williamsburg crowd at Isa. Here, he has reined in his modernist tendencies with an ever-changing, mostly small-plates menu that pivots from avant-garde towards

intimate. Highlights might include beef tartare with tart pickled elderberries, a musty baseline note from fish sauce and crunchy sunchoke (Jerusalem artichoke) chips, egg with gigante beans and cured tuna, and a creamy panna cotta with honey.
47 E Houston Street, between Mott & Mulberry Streets (1-212 219 7693, www.estelanyc.com). Subway B, D, F, M to Broadway-Lafayette Street; 6 to Bleecker Street. Open 5.30-11pm Mon-Sat; 5.30-10.30pm Sun. Main courses $16-$33.

Nom Wah Tea Parlor Chinese

New York's first dim sum house, Nom Wah opened in 1920 and was owned by the same family for more than three decades. The current owner, Wilson Tang, has revamped it in a vintage style true to the restaurant's archival photographs. He also updated the kitchen and did away with cooking dim sum en masse. Now, each plate (ultra-fluffy oversized roasted-pork buns, flaky fried crêpe egg rolls) is cooked to order.
13 Doyers Street, between Bowery & Pell Street (1-212 962 6047, www.nomwah.com). Subway J, N, Q, R, Z, 6 to Canal Street; J, Z to Chambers Street. Open 10.30am-9pm Mon-Thur, Sun; 10.30am-10pm Fri, Sat. Main courses $2-$10.

Parm & Torrisi Italian Specialties Italian

Young guns Mario Carbone and Rich Torrisi, two fine-dining vets, brought a cool-kid sheen to red-sauce plates in 2010, when they debuted Torrisi Italian Specialties, a deli by day and haute eaterie by night. People lined up for their buzzworthy sandwiches (outstanding herb-rubbed roast turkey, classic cold cuts or chicken

parmesan) and hard-to score dinner seats, packing the joint until it outgrew the space. The pair smartly split the operations, devoting their original flagship to tasting menus and transplanting the sandwich offerings to fetching diner digs next door.
Parm *248 Mulberry Street, between Prince & Spring Streets (1-212 993 7189, www.parmnyc.com). Open 11am-11pm Mon-Wed, Sun; 11am-midnight Thur-Sat. Sandwiches $9-$14.*
Torrisi Italian Specialties *250 Mulberry Street, between Prince & Spring Streets (1-212 965 0955, www.torrisinyc.com). Open 5.30-11pm Mon-Thur; noon-2pm, 5.30-11pm Fri-Sun. Prix fixe $100. Subway N, R to Prince Street; 6 to Spring Street.*

Ping's Chinese

The bank of fish tanks near the entrance suggests the speciality. Go for something you haven't tried: bite-sized pieces of boneless smelt deep-fried to a golden yellow and served with a mix of Szechuan peppercorns and salt. Big steamed oysters benefit from a splash of Ping's celebrated house-made XO sauce – a spicy condiment made of dried shrimp, scallops and garlic. The sliced sautéed conch is set off by snappy snow peas and a tangy fermented shrimp sauce. Those exotic flavours, plus touches like tablecloths, justify prices that are a notch above the Chinatown norm.
22 Mott Street, between Mosco & Pell Streets (1-212 602 9988, www. pingsnyc.com). Subway J, N, Q, R, Z, 6 to Canal Street. Open 10.30am-11pm Mon-Fri; 9am-11pm Sat, Sun. Main courses $7-$80.

Prosperity Dumpling Chinese

This pint-size dumpling den serves one of the best budget meals in

Chinatown: four pan-fried pot stickers for a buck. A plump, hand-made wrapper – chewy with crisp, griddle-pressed edges – is folded around a juicy pork-and-chive filling, its rich flavour at odds with the cheap price.
46 Eldridge Street, between Canal & Hester Streets (1-212 343 0683). Subway J, N, Q, R, Z, 6 to Canal Street. Open 7am-9.30pm daily. Dumplings $1/4. No credit cards.

Public Eclectic

This sceney restaurant is moodily lit and industrially chic. Reflecting pan-Pacific, Middle Eastern and South-east Asian influences, the menu offers creative dishes such as grilled kangaroo on coriander falafel, or ricotta cavatelli with carrot bolognese, Thai basil and cashew pesto, all paired with interesting wines.
210 Elizabeth Street, between Prince & Spring Streets (1-212 343 7011, www.public-nyc.com). Subway N, R to Prince Street; 6 to Spring Street. Open 6pm-1am Mon-Thur; 6pm-2am Fri; 10.30am-3.30pm, 6pm-2am Sat; 10.30am-3.30pm, 6pm-midnight Sun. Main courses $21-$35.

Super Taste Restaurant Chinese

In a sea of cheap Chinatown noodle bars, Super Taste stands out. Watch the cook hand-pull your Lanzhou-style *la mian*, the Chinese relative of Japanese ramen, which is served in a soup with toppings that vary from beef tendon to eel – for little more than $5.
26 Eldridge Street, at Canal Street (1-646 283 0999). Subway F to East Broadway. Open 10.30am-10.30pm daily. Main courses $4.50-$6. No credit cards.

Xi'an Famous Foods Chinese

This cheap Chinese chainlet, which got the seal of approval from celebrity chef

Alder

Anthony Bourdain, highlights the mouth-tingling cuisine of Xi'an, an ancient capital along China's Silk Road. Claim one of the 35 stools and nosh on spicy noodles or a cumin-spiced burger for less than $5. *67 Bayard Street, between Elizabeth & Mott Streets (no phone, www. xianfoods.com). Subway J, N, Q, R, Z, 6 to Canal Street. Open 11.30am-9pm Mon-Thur, Sun; 11.30am-9.30pm Fri, Sat. Main courses $3-$10. No credit cards.*

Lower East Side

Clinton Street Baking Company & Restaurant American/Café
The warm buttermilk biscuits and fluffy plate-size pancakes at this pioneering little eaterie are reason enough to face the brunch-time crowds. If you want to avoid the onslaught, the homey place is just as reliable for both lunch and dinner. Try the $15 beer and burger special (6-8pm Mon-Thur): 8oz of Black Angus topped with swiss cheese and caramelised onions, served with a beer. *4 Clinton Street, between E Houston & Stanton Streets (1-646 602 6263, www.clintonstreetbaking.com). Subway F to Lower East Side-Second Avenue; J, M, Z to Delancey-Essex Streets. Open 8am-4pm, 6-11pm Mon-Fri; 9am-4pm, 6-11pm Sat; 8am-6pm Sun. Main courses $9-$23. No credit cards before 6pm.*

Freemans American creative
Located at the end of a graffiti-marked alley, Freemans, with its colonial tavern meets hunting lodge style, is an enduring hit with retro-loving New Yorkers. Garage-sale oil paintings and moose antlers serve as backdrops to a curved zinc bar, while the menu recalls a simpler time – devils on horseback (prunes stuffed with stilton cheese and wrapped in bacon); rum-soaked ribs, the meat falling off the bone with a gentle nudge of the fork; and stiff cocktails that'll get you good and sauced. *2 Freeman Alley, off Rivington Street, between Bowery & Chrystie Street (1-212 420 0012, www.freemans restaurant.com). Subway F to Lower East Side-Second Avenue; J, Z to Bowery. Open 11am-4pm, 6-11.30pm Mon-Fri; 10am-4pm, 6-11.30pm Sat, Sun. Main courses $15-$32.*

Katz's Delicatessen American
A visit to Gotham isn't complete without a stop at a quintessential New York deli, and this Lower East Side survivor is the real deal. You might get a kick out of the famous faces (from Bill Clinton to Ben Stiller) plastered to the panelled walls, or the spot where Meg Ryan faked it in *When Harry Met Sally…*, but the real stars of this cavernous cafeteria are the thick-cut pastrami sandwiches and crisp-skinned all-beef hot dogs – the latter a mere $3.45.

Rock-star chef Danny Bowien has changed the tune for his sophomore act, turning from Szechuan eats to Mexican fare. At a 40-seat hangout down the block from Mission Chinese Food (currently closed), he reworks classic dishes like rotisserie chicken stuffed with rice. Tacos also get the Bowien touch: tortillas made with Anson Mills corn are topped with such rotating fillings as rotisserie pork and house-made Oaxacan-style cheese. Yet, where the cooking at his first NYC spot launched a Szechuan reformation, his creative Mexican plates are merely a slight evolution. It stands to reason: Bowien brought Mission Chinese Food east after years of experimentation in San Francisco; his latest venture has had a much shorter incubation period. *172 Orchard Street, at Stanton Street (1-212 254 2233, www.mission cantinanyc.com). Subway F to Lower East Side-Second Avenue. Open noon-3pm, 5.30pm-midnight Tue-Sun. Tacos $5-$6. Shared plates $35.*

205 E Houston Street, at Ludlow Street (1-212 254 2246, www.katz delicatessen.com). Subway F to Lower East Side-Second Avenue. Open 8am-10.45pm Mon-Wed; 8am-2.45am Thur; 24hrs Fri (from 8am), Sat; closes 10.45pm Sun. Sandwiches $12-$18.

Schiller's Liquor Bar Eclectic
At this artfully reconstructed faux-vintage hangout, the menu is a mix of French bistro (steak frites), British pub (fish and chips) and good ol' American (cheeseburger), while the wine menu famously hawks a down-to-earth hierarchy: Good, Decent, Cheap. As at Keith McNally's other establishments, folks pack in for the scene, triple-parking at the curved central bar for elaborate cocktails and star sightings. *131 Rivington Street, at Norfolk Street (1-212 260 4555, www.schillersny. com). Subway F to Delancey Street; J, M, Z to Delancey-Essex Streets. Open 11am-1am Mon-Thur; 11am-3am Fri; 10am-3am Sat; 10am-1am Sun. Main courses $15-$27.*

Yonah Schimmel Knish Bakery Café
This neighbourhood stalwart has been doling out its carb-laden goodies since 1910. About 20 rotating varieties are available, including blueberry, chocolate-cheese and pizza flavour, but traditional potato, kasha and spinach knishes are the most popular. *137 E Houston Street, between Eldridge & Forsyth Streets (1-212 477 2858, www.knishery.com). Subway F to Lower East Side-Second Avenue. Open 9am-7pm Mon-Thur, Sun; 9am-9pm Fri, Sat (extended hours in summer). Knishes $3.50-$5.*

East Village

Acme Scandinavian
The Scandinavian food scene – known for the extreme locavore cooking showcased at restaurants such as Copenhagen's Noma – is suddenly the hottest on earth. And Nordic cuisine has finally arrived in NYC, thanks to Danish chef Mads Refslund, who co-founded Noma with superstar René Redzepi (but left after a year to do his own thing). Formerly a Cajun dive, the once-grungy spot has been transformed into a raffish and chic downtown bistro, featuring a retro mix of contemporary art and antiques. Refslund's menu delivers an easy introduction to the avant-garde cuisine of Northern Europe, unpretentious and moderately priced. The chef's new-wave bistro fare features some unusual pairings, but even the most oddball combinations work. His spin on steak tartare marries hand-cut raw bison with delicious sweet shrimp – an elemental surf-and-turf spooned into retro canapés into bitter endive and radicchio leaves. The big family-style portions of meat, fish and fowl that round out the collection of shareable plates are even more down-to-earth. *9 Great Jones Street, between Broadway & Lafayette Street (1-212*

203 2121, www.acmenyc.com). Subway B, D, F, M to Broadway-Lafayette Street; 6 to Bleecker Street. Open 6-11pm Mon-Wed; 6pm-midnight Thur, Fri; 11am-3pm, 6pm-midnight Sat; 11am-3pm, 6-11pm Sun. Main courses $10-$38.

Alder Gastropub
James Beard Award-winning chef Wylie Dufresne cultivated his modernist, tongue-in-cheek approach at wd~50 (50 Clinton Street, between Rivington & Stanton Streets, 1-212 477 2900, www.wd-50.com). At the original nucleus of North American avant-garde cuisine, which opened in 2003, he created curiosities such as deep-fried mayonnaise and scrambled-egg ravioli. At his gastropub, Alder, Dufresne is still challenging the orthodoxy of serious cooking, presenting familiar flavours in new frameworks: the wrappers in a pigs-in-a-blanket riff are Pepperidge Farm hot-dog buns, flattened in a pasta machine and fried into crisp jackets as gratifying as any puff pastry. But you can also eat quite simply here if you want to, with a pub cheese platter or bowl of New England clam chowder. Intriguing tapped cocktails like the Dr Dave's 'Scrip Pad, made with rye, amaro, smoked maple and yuzu, are sold in full-size or short portions, so you can taste your way through the lot. *157 Second Avenue, between 9th & 10th Streets (1-212 539 1900, www.aldernyc.com). Subway L to Third Avenue; 6 to Astor Place. Open 6-11pm daily. Main courses $11-$25.*

Back Forty American
Peter Hoffman (the pioneering chef who launched the market-driven restaurant Savoy, now occupied by his second Back Forty location) is behind this East Village seasonal-eats tavern. Pared-down farmhouse chic prevails in the decor and on the menu. House specialities include juicy grass-fed burgers, served with a spicy home-made ketchup and pickle. The spacious back garden, open during warmer months, is a bonus. *190 Avenue B, at 12th Street (1-212 388 1990, www.backfortynyc.com). Subway L to First Avenue. Open 6-11pm Mon-Thur; 6pm-midnight Fri; 11am-3pm, 6pm-midnight Sat; 11am-3.30pm, 6-10pm Sun. Main courses $12-$38. Other location 70 Prince Street, at Crosby Street, Soho (1-212 219 8570).*

Big Gay Ice Cream Shop Ice-cream
Ice-cream truckers Doug Quint and Bryan Petroff now have two bricks-and-mortar shops dispensing their quirky soft-serve creations. Toppings run the gamut from cayenne pepper to bourbon-butterscotch sauce, or opt for one of the signature combos like the Salty Pimp (vanilla ice-cream, dulce de leche, sea salt and chocolate dip) or the Bea Arthur (vanilla ice-cream, dulce de leche and crushed Nilla wafers). *125 E 7th Street, between First Avenue & Avenue A (1-212 533 9333,*

www.biggayicecream.com). Subway
L to First Avenue. Open 1pm-
midnight daily (see website for reduced
winter hours). Ice-cream $4-$8.
Other location 61 Grove Street,
at Seventh Avenue South, West
Village (1-212 533 9333).

Caracas Arepa Bar Venezuelan
This endearing spot, with bare-brick
walls and tables covered with flower-
patterned vinyl, zaps you straight to
Caracas. Each *arepa* is made from
scratch daily; the pita-like pockets are
stuffed with a choice of a dozen fillings,
such as the classic beef with black
beans, cheese and plantain, or chicken
with chorizo and avocado. Top off
your snack with a *cocada*, a thick and
creamy coconut milkshake made with
freshly grated cinnamon.
93½ E 7th Street, between First
Avenue & Avenue A (1-212 228 5062,
www.caracasarepabar.com). Subway
F to Lower East Side-Second Avenue;
6 to Astor Place. Open noon-11pm
daily. Arepas $7-$8.50.

Crif Dogs American
You'll recognise this place by the
giant hot dog outside, bearing the
come-on 'Eat me'. Crif offers the best
Jersey-style dogs this side of the
Hudson: handmade smoked pork
tube-steaks that are deep-fried until
they're bursting out of their skins.
While they're served in various
guises, including the Spicy Redneck
(bacon-wrapped and covered in chilli,
coleslaw and jalapeños) and the
Chihuahua (bacon-wrapped with
sour cream and avocado), the classic
with mustard and kraut is the most
popular. If you're wondering why
there are so many people hanging
around near the public phone booth
at night, it's because there's a trendy
cocktail bar, PDT (see p67), concealed
behind it.
113 St Marks Place, between First
Avenue & Avenue A (1-212 614
2728, www.crifdogs.com). Subway
L to First Avenue; 6 to Astor Place.
Open noon-2am Mon-Thur, Sun;
noon-4am Fri, Sat. Hot dogs $2.50-
$5. Other location 555 Driggs Avenue,
at North 7th Street, Williamsburg,
Brooklyn (1-718 302 3200).

DBGB Kitchen & Bar French
This big, buzzy brasserie – chef Daniel
Boulud's most populist venture –
stands out for its kitchen-sink scope.
Around ten rotating types of sausage,
from Thai-accented to Tunisian, are
served alongside burgers, various
pieces of offal and haute bistro fare.
The best way to get your head around
it all is to bring a large group and
sample as much of the range as
possible, including ice cream sundaes
or sumptuous cakes.
299 Bowery, at E Houston Street
(1-212 933 5300, www.dbgb.com/nyc).
Subway B, D, F, M to Broadway-
Lafayette Street; 6 to Bleecker Street.
Open noon-11pm Mon; noon-midnight
Tue-Thur; noon-1am Fri; 11am-
1am Sat; 11am-11pm Sun. Main
courses $14-$42.

Dirt Candy Vegetarian
The shiny, futuristic environment here
makes the place look more like a chic
nail salon than a restaurant. Chef-
owner Amanda Cohen has created an
unlikely space to execute her ambition:
to make people crave vegetables. And
she mostly succeeds. Elaborate dishes
might include a pungent portobello
mousse accompanied by truffled pear
and fennel compote, or stone-ground
grits served with corn cream, pickled
shiitake mushrooms, *huitlacoche*
(Mexican truffle) and a tempura
poached egg. With vegan-friendly
options for desserts, Cohen has created
a menu that's suitable for omnivores.
Note that the restaurant may be
relocating later in 2014.
430 E 9th Street, between First
Avenue & Avenue A (1-212 228 7732,
www.dirtcandynyc.com). Subway L to
First Avenue; 6 to Astor Place. Open
5.30-10pm Tue, Wed; 5.30-10.30pm
Thur-Sat. Main courses $18-$21.

Il Buco Alimentari & Vineria
Italian
Il Buco has been a mainstay of the
downtown dining scene since the
1990s and a pioneer in the sort of
rustic Italian food now ubiquitous in
the city. Owner Donna Leonard took
her sweet time (18 years, to be exact)
to unveil her first offshoot, Il Buco
Alimentari & Vineria. It was worth
the wait: the new hybrid bakery, food
shop, café and trattoria is as confident
as its decades-old sibling with sure-
footed service, the familial bustle of
a neighbourhood pillar, and heady
aromas of wood-fired short ribs
and salt-crusted fish drifting from
an open kitchen.
53 Great Jones Street, between
Bowery & Lafayette Streets
(1-212 837 2622, www.
ilbucovineria.com).
Subway B, D, F, M
to Broadway-Lafayette
Street; 6 to Bleecker
Street. Open 7am-
midnight Mon-Thur;
7am-1am Fri;
9am-1am Sat; 9am-
11pm Sun. Main courses
$19-$45. Other location
47 Bond Street, between
Bowery & Lafayette Street,
East Village (1-212 533 1932).

Ippudo NY Japanese
This sleek outpost of a Japanese ramen
chain is packed mostly with Nippon
natives who queue up for a taste of
'Ramen King' Shigemi Kawahara's
tonkotsu – a pork-based broth. About
half a dozen varieties include the
Akamaru Modern, a smooth, buttery
soup topped with scallions, cabbage,
a slice of roasted pork and pleasantly
elastic noodles. Avoid non-soup dishes
such as the oily fried-chicken wings.
Long live the Ramen King – just don't
ask him to move beyond his speciality.
65 Fourth Avenue, between 9th &
10th Streets (1-212 388 0088,
www.ippudony.com). Subway 6 to
Astor Place. Open 11am-3.30pm, 5-
11.30pm Mon-Thur; 11am-3.30pm,

Mighty Quinn's

5pm-12.30am Fri, Sat; 11am-
10.30pm Sun. Ramen $15-$16.
Other location 321 W 51st Street,
between Eighth & Ninth Avenues,
Midtown West (1-212 974 2500).

Kyo Ya Japanese
The city's most ambitious Japanese
speakeasy is marked only by an
'Open' sign, but in-the-know diners
still find their way inside. The food,
presented on beautiful handmade
plates, is gorgeous: maitake
mushrooms are fried in the lightest
tempura batter and delivered on a
polished stone bed. Sushi is pressed
with a hot iron on to sticky vinegar
rice. The few desserts are just as
ethereal as the savoury food.
94 E 7th Street, between
First Avenue & Avenue
A (1-212 982 4140).
Subway 6 to Astor
Place. Open 5.30-
11.30pm Mon-Sat;
5.30-10.30pm Sun.
Main courses $28-$42.

TOP TIP!
The prix fixe is right
Visit during Summer or
Winter Restaurant Week
(www.nycgo.com/
restaurantweek) for
affordable deals
at hundreds of
eateries.

Mighty Quinn's
Barbecue
Drummer-turned-chef Hugh
Mangum first hawked his Texalina
(Texas spice meets Carolina vinegar)
specialities at his immensely popular
stand at Smorgasburg (see p84
Superflea). When the operation went
bricks-and-mortar, the hungry throngs
followed. Lines of customers snake
through the steel-tinged East Village
joint, watching as black-gloved carvers
give glistening meat porn a dash of
Maldon salt before slinging it down
the assembly line. Dry-rubbed brisket
is slow-smoked for 22 hours, and the
Jurassic-sized beef rib is so impossibly
tender that one bite will quieten the
pickiest barbecue connoisseur.
103 Second Avenue, at E 6th Street
(1-212 677 3733, www.mightyquinns
bbq.com). Subway 6 to Astor Place.
Open 11.30am-11pm Mon-Thur,
Sun; 11.30am-midnight Fri, Sat.
Barbecue $6.50-$23.

Momofuku Ssäm Bar Korean
At celebrated chef David Chang's
second modern Korean restaurant,
waiters hustle to loud rock music in the
50-seat space, which feels expansive
compared with the crowded counter
dining of its nearby predecessor,
Momofuku Noodle Bar (171 First
Avenue, between 10th & 11th Streets,
1-212 777 7773). Try the wonderfully
fatty pork-belly steamed bun with
hoisin sauce and cucumbers, or one
of the ham platters. But you'll need to
come with a crowd to sample the house
speciality, *bo ssäm* (a slow-roasted hog
butt that is consumed wrapped in
lettuce leaves, with a dozen oysters
and other accompaniments); it serves
six to eight people and must be ordered
in advance. David Chang has further
expanded his E Vill empire with a
bar, Booker and Dax (see p66) at
this location, and a sweet annexe,
Milk Bar (one of several in the city),
across the street.
207 Second Avenue, at 13th Street
(1-212 254 3500, www.momofuku.
com). Subway L to First or Third
Avenue; L, N, Q, R, 4, 5, 6 to 14th
Street-Union Square. Open 11.30am-
3.30pm, 5pm-midnight Mon-Thur,
Sun; 11.30am-3.30pm, 5pm-1am
Fri, Sat. Main courses $20-$25.

Northern Spy Food Co
American
Named after an apple indigenous to
the North-east, Northern Spy serves
locally sourced meals at reasonable
prices. The frequently changing menu
is based almost entirely on what's
in season. The food isn't fancy, but
it satisfies: a recent dish paired
toothsome pastured pork loin in a rich
pork jus with sautéed leeks, green
cabbage and brussels-sprout leaves.
511 E 12th Street, between Avenues
A & B (1-212 228 5100, www.
northernspyfoodco.com). Subway
L to First Avenue. Open 10am-
4pm, 5.30-11pm Mon-Fri; 10am-
3.30pm, 5.30-11pm Sat, Sun.
Main courses $22-$27.

Porchetta Italian/Sandwiches

This small, subway-tiled space has a narrow focus: central Italy's classic boneless roasted pork. The meat – available as a sandwich or a platter – is amazingly moist and tender, having been slowly roasted with rendered pork fat, seasoned with fennel pollen, herbs and spices and flecked with brittle shards of skin. The other menu items (a mozzarella sandwich, humdrum sides) seem incidental; the pig is the point.
110 E 7th Street, between First Avenue & Avenue A (1-212 777 2151, www.porchettanyc.com). Subway F to Lower East Side-Second Avenue; L to First Avenue; 6 to Astor Place. Open 11.30am-10pm Mon-Thur, Sun; 11.30am-11pm Fri, Sat. Sandwiches $10-$12.

Veselka Eastern European

When you need food to soak up the mess of drinks you've consumed in the East Village in the early hours, it's worth remembering Veselka: a relatively inexpensive Eastern European restaurant with plenty of seats, which is open 24 hours a day. Hearty appetites can get a platter of classic Ukrainian grub: pierogies, goulash, kielbasa, beef stroganoff or bigos stew. For dessert, try the *kutya* (traditional Ukrainian pudding made with berries, walnuts, poppy seeds and honey).
144 Second Avenue, at 9th Street (1-212 228 9682, www.veselka.com). Subway L to Third Avenue; 6 to Astor Place. Open 24hrs daily. Main courses $14-$18.

Greenwich Village & West Village

Blue Hill American

More than a mere crusader for sustainability, Dan Barber is also one of the most talented cooks in town, building his menu around whatever's at its peak on the family farm in Great Barrington, Massachusetts, and the not-for-profit Stone Barns Center for Food and Agriculture in Westchester, New York (home to a sibling restaurant), among other suppliers. The evening may begin with a sophisticated seasonal spin on a pig-liver terrine and move on to a sweet slow-roasted parsnip 'steak' with creamed spinach and beet ketchup.
75 Washington Place, between Washington Square West & Sixth Avenue (1-212 539 1776, www.bluehillfarm.com). Subway A, B, C, D, E, F, M to W 4th Street. Open 5-11pm Mon-Sat; 5-10pm Sun. Main courses $32-$38.

Buvette French

Chef Jody Williams has filled every nook of tiny, Gallic-themed Buvette with old picnic baskets, teapots and silver trays, among other vintage ephemera. The food is just as thoughtfully curated – Williams's immaculate renditions of coq au vin, duck rillettes or intense, lacquered wedges of tarte Tatin arrive on tiny plates, in petite jars or in miniature casseroles, her time-warp flavours recalling an era when there were still classic bistros on every corner.
42 Grove Street, between Bedford & Bleecker Streets (1-212 255 3590, www.ilovebuvette.com). Subway 1 to Christopher Street-Sheridan Square. Open 8am-2am Mon-Fri; 10am-2am Sat, Sun. Main courses $12-$15.

Caffe Reggio Café

Legend has it that the original owner of this classic café introduced Americans to the cappuccino in 1927 and, apart from its acquired patina, we bet the interior hasn't changed much since then. It's since traded in the coal-fuelled espresso machine for a sleeker Caffè Sacco model, but you can still admire the old custom chrome-and-bronze contraption on the bar. Tuck into a house-made tiramisu and espresso under the Italian Renaissance paintings.
119 MacDougal Street, at W 3rd Street (1-212 475 9557, www.caffereggio.com). Subway A, B, C, D, E, F, M to W 4th Street. Open 8am-3am Mon-Thur; 8am-4am Fri, Sat; 9am-3am Sun. Main courses $10-$11. No credit cards.

Chez Sardine Eclectic/Japanese

Prolific restaurateur Gabriel Stulman's fifth Village venture is a cross-cultural *izakaya*. The slim restaurant's sardine-can-size kitchen, run by Fedora's (*see below*) Mehdi Brunet-Benkritly, sends out wild riffs on sushi, like Scottish salmon with pretzels and lime cream or chopped beef with sea urchin. The inspiration and compact dimensions are steeped in Japan. The execution, though, is pure Quebecois gluttony, with a smoked cheddar grilled cheese sandwich oozing melted foie gras; and pancakes stacked with briny roe, fish tartare and tangy yoghurt.
183 W 10th Street, at W 4th Street (1-646 360 3705, www.chezsardine.com). Subway A, B, C, D, E, F, M to W 4th Street; 1 to Christopher Street-Sheridan Square. Open 5.30-11pm Mon-Wed; 5.30pm-1am Thur, Fri; 11am-2.45pm, 5.30pm-1am Sat; 11am-2.45pm, 5.30-11pm Sun. Main courses $19-$24.

Corner Bistro American

There's one compelling reason to come to this legendary pub: it serves what some New Yorkers say are the city's best burgers – plus the beer is just $3 for a mug of McSorley's. The patties are no-frills and served on a flimsy paper plate. To get one, you may have to queue for a good hour, especially on weekend nights; if the wait is too long for a table, try to slip into a space at the bar.
331 W 4th Street, at Jane Street (1-212 242 9502). Subway A, C, E to 14th Street; L to Eighth Avenue. Open 11.30am-4am Mon-Sat; noon-4am Sun. Burgers $6.75-$8.75. No credit cards. Other location 47-18 Vernon Boulevard, at 47th Road, Long Island City, Queens (1-718 606 6500).

EN Japanese Brasserie Japanese

The owners of this popular spot aim to evoke a sense of Japanese living in the multi-level space. On the ground floor are *tatami*-style rooms; on the mezzanine are recreations of a living room, dining room and library of a Japanese home from the Meiji era. But the spacious main dining room is where the action is. Highlights of chef Abe Hiroki's menu include freshly made scooped tofu served with a soy-dashi mix; miso-marinated, broiled Alaskan black cod; and Berkshire pork belly braised in sansho miso. Try the saké and shochu flights.
435 Hudson Street, at Leroy Street (1-212 647 9196, www.enjb.com). Subway 1 to Houston Street. Open noon-2.30pm, 5.30-10.30pm Mon-Thur; noon-2.30pm, 5.30-11.30pm Fri; 11am-2.30pm, 5.30-11.30pm Sat; 11am-2.30pm, 5.30-10.30pm Sun. Main courses $14-$34.

Fatty Crab Malaysian

This Malaysian-inspired eaterie reflects chef Zak Pelaccio's cunning take on South-east Asian cuisine: who knew you could squeeze slow-cooked lamb, shallot raisin sambal, chillies and Vietnamese mint between slices of Pepperidge Farm bread for a killer tea sandwich? The classic Malaysian chilli crab makes an appearance, but it doesn't come cheap. Far better bang for your buck is the short rib *rendang*, a tender chunk of meat braised in lemongrass-chilli and coconut. This packed spot takes no reservations, but turnover is quick – hard wooden chairs squeezed behind tiny tables in the single red-walled room don't encourage tarrying.
643 Hudson Street, between Gansevoort & Horatio Streets (1-212 352 3592, www.fattycrab.com). Subway A, C, E to 14th St; L to Eighth Avenue. Open noon-11pm Mon-Wed; noon-midnight Thur, Fri; 11am-midnight Sat; 11am-11pm Sun. Main courses $16-$35.

Fedora Eclectic

This French-Canadian knockout is part of restaurateur Gabriel Stulman's West Village mini-empire (his other local eateries are Joseph Leonard, Jeffrey's Grocery, Italian spot Perla and eclectic Japanese joint Chez Sardine; *see above*). Mehdi Brunet-Benkritly produces some of the most exciting toe-to-tongue cooking in town, plying epicurean hipsters with Quebecois party food that's eccentric, excessive and fun – crisp pig's head with enoki, for example, or maple-smoked salmon with almonds and curry cream.
239 W 4th Street, between Charles & W 10th Streets (1-646 449 9336, www.fedoranyc.com). Subway A, B, C, D, E, F, M to W 4th Street; 1 to Christopher Street-Sheridan Square. Open 5.30pm-midnight Mon, Sun; 5.30pm-2am Tue-Sat. Main courses $24-$30.

RECOMMENDED
Carbone

Nostalgia specialists Rich Torrisi and Mario Carbone honour Gotham's legendary red-sauce relics (Rao's, Bamonte's) with their high-profile revamp of historic Rocco's Ristorante. Suave, tuxedo-clad waiters – Bronx accents intact, but their burgundy threads designed by Zac Posen – tote an avalanche of complimentary extras: chunks of chianti-infused parmesan, olive oil-soaked 'Grandma Bread' and slivers of smoky prosciutto. Follow updated renditions of classic pasta like a spicy, über-rich rigatoni vodka with mains such as sticky cherry-pepper ribs and lavish takes on tiramisu for dessert.
181 Thompson Street, between Bleecker & Houston Streets (1-212 254 3000, www.carbonenewyork.com). Subway C, E to Spring Street. Open noon-2pm, 5.30pm-midnight Mon-Fri; 5.30pm-midnight Sat, Sun. Main courses $21-$52.

Kesté Pizza & Vino Pizza

If anyone can claim to be an expert on Neapolitan pizza, it's Kesté's Roberto Caporuscio: as president of the US branch of the Associazione Pizzaiuoli Napoletani, he's the top dog for the training and certification of *pizzaioli*. At his intimate, 46-seat space, it's all about the crust – blistered, salty and elastic, it could easily be eaten plain. Add ace toppings such as sweet-tart San Marzano tomato sauce, milky mozzarella and fresh basil, and you have one of New York's finest pies. *271 Bleecker Street, between Cornelia & Jones Streets (1-212 243 1500, www.kestepizzeria.com). Subway 1 to Christopher Street-Sheridan Square. Open noon-3.30pm, 5-11pm Mon-Thur; noon-11.30pm Fri, Sat; noon-10.30pm Sun. Pizzas $13-$23.*

Kin Shop Thai

Top Chef champ Harold Dieterle channels his South-east Asian travels into the menu at this eatery, which serves classic Thai street food alongside more upmarket Thai-inspired dishes. The traditional fare seems extraneous, but Dieterle's auteur creations are often inspired. A salad of crispy oysters, slivered celery and fried pork belly is bright and refreshing, while a sophisticated riff on massaman curry features long-braised goat with a silky sauce infused with toasted coconut, fried shallots and purple yams. *469 Sixth Avenue, between 11th & 12th Streets (1-212 675 4295, www.kinshopnyc.com). Subway F, M to 14th Street; L to Sixth Avenue. Open 11.30am-3pm, 5.30-10pm Mon-Wed; 11.30am-3pm, 5.30-11pm Thur-Sat; 11.30am-3pm, 5-10pm Sun. Main courses $19-$32.*

Lupa Italian

No mere 'poor man's Babbo' (Mario Batali's other and pricier restaurant around the corner), this convivial trattoria offers communal dining, reasonably priced wines and hit-the-spot comfort food. Come for classic Roman fare such as punchy rigatoni with skate and broccoli rabe, or gumdrop-shaped ricotta gnocchi. *170 Thompson Street, between Bleecker & W Houston Streets (1-212 982 5089, www.luparestaurant.com). Subway A, B, C, D, E, F, M to W 4th Street. Open 11.30am-midnight daily. Main courses $18-$25.*

Minetta Tavern Eclectic

Thanks to restaurateur extraordinaire Keith McNally's spot-on restoration, the Minetta is as buzzy now as it must have been when it was frequented by Hemingway and Fitzgerald in its heyday. The big-flavoured bistro fare includes classics such as roasted bone marrow, trout meunière topped with crabmeat, and an airy Grand Marnier soufflé. But the most illustrious thing on the menu is the Black Label burger. You might find the $28 price tag a little hard to swallow, but the superbly tender sandwich – essentially chopped steak in a bun smothered in caramelised onions – is worth every penny. *113 MacDougal Street, between Bleecker & W 3rd Streets (1-212 475 3850, www.minettatavernny.com). Subway A, B, C, D, E, F, M to W 4th Street. Open 5.30pm-1am Mon, Tue; noon-2.30pm, 5.30-1am Wed-Fri; 11am-3pm, 5.30pm-1am Sat, Sun. Main courses $19-$35.*

Num Pang Sandwich Shop Cambodian

At this small shop, the rotating varieties of *num pang* (Cambodia's answer to the Vietnamese *banh mi*) include pulled duroc pork with spiced honey, peppercorn catfish, and hoisin veal meatballs, each stuffed into crusty baguettes. There's counter seating upstairs, or get it to go and eat in nearby Washington Square Park. *21 E 12th Street, between Fifth Avenue & University Place (1-212 255 3271, www.numpangnyc.com). Subway L, N, Q, R, 4, 5, 6 to 14th Street-Union Square. Open 11am-10pm Mon-Sat; noon-9pm Sun. Sandwiches $7.50-$12. No credit cards. Other locations throughout the city.*

Pearl Oyster Bar Seafood

There's a good reason this convivial, no-reservations, New England-style fish joint always has a queue – the food is outstanding. Signature dishes include the lobster roll (sweet, lemon-scented meat laced with mayonnaise on a butter-enriched bun) and a contemporary take on bouillabaisse: a briny lobster broth packed with mussels, cod, scallops and clams, topped with an aïoli-smothered croûton. *18 Cornelia Street, between Bleecker & W 4th Streets (1-212 691 8211, www.pearloysterbar.com). Subway A, B, C, D, E, F, M to W 4th Street. Open noon-2.30pm, 6-11pm Mon-Fri; 6-11pm Sat. Main courses $23-$36.*

RedFarm Chinese

The high-end ingredients and whimsical plating at Ed Schoenfeld's interpretive Chinese restaurant have helped to pack the dining room since opening night. Chef Joe Ng is known for his dim sum artistry: scallop and squid shu mai come skewered over shot glasses of warm carrot and ginger bisque – designed to be eaten and gulped in rapid succession; other nouveau creations include Katz's pastrami-stuffed egg rolls and shrimp dumplings decorated with 'eyes' and pursued on the plate by a sweet-potato Pac-Man. *529 Hudson Street, between Charles & W 10th Streets (1-212 792 9700, www.redfarmnyc.com). Subway 1 to Christopher Street-Sheridan Square. Open 5-11.45pm Mon-Fri; 11am-2.30pm, 5-11.45pm Sat; 11am-2.30pm, 5-11pm Sun. Main courses $19-$49. Other location 2170 Broadway, between 76th & 77th Streets, Upper West Side (1-212 724 9700).*

Rosemary's Italian

While gastronomy isn't the primary focus in most of the pheromone factories clustered on this stretch of Seventh Avenue, this rustic, farmhouse-vibe celebrity magnet ought to be packed with food fanatics. Chef Wade Moises, who worked for Mario Batali at Babbo and Lupa, is a talent to watch. Pair pasta with one of the showstopping large-format feasts – big platters for two that in fact serve three or four. House-made cavatelli with braised beef, heirloom tomato sauce and fresh cherry tomatoes is a mellow foil for the chef's *carne misti*, a mountain of espresso-glazed pork ribs, smoky lamb shoulder and super-succulent whey-brined chicken. *18 Greenwich Avenue, at 10th Street (1-212 647 1818, www.rosemarys nyc.com). Subway A, B, C, D, E, F, M to W 4th Street. Open 11.30am-4.30pm, 5pm-midnight Mon-Fri; 10am-4pm, 5pm-midnight Sat, Sun. Main courses $12-$24.*

'sNice Café/Vegetarian

If you're looking for a laid-back place in which to read the papers, do a little laptopping, and enjoy cheap, simple and satisfying veggie fare, then 'sNice is nice indeed. Far roomier than it appears from its windows, the bare-brick café has what may well be the largest menu in the city, scrawled on the wall, giving thorough descriptions of each sandwich and salad. *45 Eighth Avenue, at 4th Street (1-212 645 0310, www.snicecafe.com). Subway A, C, E to 14th Street; L to Eighth Avenue. Open 7.30am-10pm daily. Sandwiches/salads $9.25. Other locations 150 Sullivan Street, between Houston & Prince Streets, Soho (1-212 253 5405); 315 Fifth Avenue, at 3rd Street, Park Slope, Brooklyn (1-718 788 2121).*

The Spotted Pig Eclectic

With a creaky interior that recalls an ancient pub, this Anglo-Italian hybrid from Ken Friedman and chef April Bloomfield is still hopping more than a decade after opening. The gastropub doesn't take reservations and a wait can always be expected. The burger is a must-order: a secret blend of ground beef grilled rare (unless otherwise specified) and covered with gobs of pungent roquefort. It arrives with a tower of crispy shoestring fries tossed with rosemary. Indulgent desserts, like the flourless chocolate cake, are worth loosening your belt for. *314 W 11th Street, at Greenwich Street (1-212 620 0393, www.the spottedpig.com). Subway A, C, E to 14th Street; L to Eighth Avenue. Open noon-2am Mon-Fri; 11am-2am Sat, Sun. Main courses $20-$32.*

Stumptown Coffee Roasters Café

The lauded Portland, Oregon, outfit has expanded its New York holdings – which include a branch inside the Ace Hotel – with this stand-alone café. Coffee purists can find single-origin espresso from a La Marzocco GS3 machine and slow brews prepared via java-geek speciality drips like Chemex pour-overs, ceramic filter-cone Bee House drippers or a siphon vacuum brewer. It also offers the chain's full line of 20 seasonal coffees, plus pastries from Momofuku Milk Bar, Ovenly and Doughnut Plant. *30 W 8th Street, at MacDougal Street (1-347 414 7802, www.stumptown coffee.com). Subway A, B, C, D, E, F, M to W 4th Street. Open 7am-8pm daily. Coffee $2.50-$5.50.*

Sweet Revenge Café

Baker Marlo Scott steamrollered over the cupcake's innocent charms – at

Rosemary's

er café/bar, she pairs her confections with wine or beer; instead of pretty pastel swirls of frosting, you're more likely to find anarchic spikes of peanut butter, cream cheese and milk-chocolate icing. In the process, she saved the ubiquitous treat from becoming a cloying cliché. Gourmet sandwiches and other plates cater to non-sweet-tooths.
2 Carmine Street, between Bedford Street & Seventh Avenue (1-212 242 2240, www.sweetrevengenyc.com). Subway A, B, C, D, E, F, M to W 4th Street; 1 to Christopher Street-Sheridan Square. Open 7am-11pm Mon-Thur; 7am-12.30am Fri; 10.30am-12.30am Sat; 10.30am-10pm Sun. Cupcakes $3.50.

ZZ's Clam Bar Seafood
A powerhouse trio – Rich Torrisi, Mario Carbone and Jeff 'ZZ' Zalaznick – continues its neo-Italian-American hot streak (including Carbone and Parm) with a 12-seat raw bar highlighting first-rate cocktails and crudo. At the marble bar, acclaimed barman Thomas Waugh (Death & Company) concocts the likes of rum, house-made coconut cream, acacia honey and lime juice served in a frozen coconut. In bar-friendly small plates, the chefs explore raw fish in all forms, with East Coast oysters on the half-shell and the titular clams. Composed crudos might feature *shimaaji* (striped horse mackerel) tartare topped with whipped ricotta and Petrossian caviar.
169 Thompson Street, between Bleecker & W Houston Streets (1-212 254 3000, www.zzsclambar.com). Subway B, D, F, M to Broadway-Lafayette Street; 6 to Bleecker Street. Open 6pm-1am Tue-Sat. Main courses $18-$56.

Chelsea

Co Pizza
This unassuming pizzeria was the restaurant debut of Jim Lahey, whose Sullivan Street Bakery supplies bread to many top restaurants. Lahey's crust is so good, in fact, it doesn't need any toppings (try the Pizza Bianca, sprinkled with sea salt and olive oil). The most compelling individual-sized pies come from non-traditional sources, such as the ham and cheese, essentially a croque-monsieur in pizza form.
230 Ninth Avenue, at 24th Street (1-212 243 1105, www.co-pane.com). Subway C, E to 23rd Street. Open 5-11pm Mon; 11.30am-11pm Tue-Sat; 11am-10pm Sun. Pizzas $9-$20.

Cookshop American creative
Chef Marc Meyer and his wife/co-owner Vicki Freeman want Cookshop to be a platform for sustainable ingredients from independent farmers. True to this mission, the ingredients are consistently top-notch, and the menu changes daily. While organic ingredients alone don't guarantee a great meal, Meyer knows how to let

The **Empire Diner** (*see below*) has been a Chelsea fixture since 1976, when three partners took over a run-down former greasy spoon. The interior of the 1940s Fodero dining car was an Edward Hopper time-warp of rotating stools, leather booths and subway tiles, with a dash of piano-parlour elegance – a 1930 Steck upright regularly provided mood music. Despite the retro space, the round-the-clock eaterie reflected the ever-changing character of the area. During the disco-ball decadence of the '70s, counter stools were dominated by club-hopping drag queens and leather daddies hungry for after-hours chilli sundaes. In the 1980s the boxcar mellowed into a coffee-pouring haven until the '90s art-world boom, which ushered in gallery glitterati and celebrities including Madonna, Steven Spielberg and Woody Allen (who immortalised the iconic spot in his 1979 film, *Manhattan*). The haute hash house remained a tourist destination until lease issues forced it to close in 2010. After an unsuccessful reboot by the team behind the Coffee Shop in Union Square, the diner remained shuttered, its future uncertain.

Despite attaining celebrity-chef status through appearances on *Chopped* and *Iron Chef*, Amanda Freitag, former executive chef of the Harrison, had one space left to fill on her résumé – running her own restaurant. In 2013, the Chelsea resident announced she was taking over the Empire, preserving its vintage looks but giving the menu a contemporary, locavore revamp. Fare includes smoked whitefish wrapped up with radishes in crêpes and Greek salad studded with charred octopus, and the ice-cream for the banana splits is churned in house.

the flavours speak for themselves, and Cookshop scores points for getting the house-made ice-cream to taste as good as Ben & Jerry's.
156 Tenth Avenue, at 20th Street (1-212 924 4440, www.cookshopny.com). Subway C, E to 23rd Street. Open 8-11am, 11.30am-4pm, 5.30-11.30pm Mon-Fri; 10.30am-4pm, 5.30-11.30pm Sat; 10.30am-4pm, 5.30-10pm Sun. Main courses $22-$42.

Empire Diner American
See above **The Non-Greasy Spoon**.
210 Tenth Avenue, at 22nd Street (1-212 596 7523, www.empire-diner.com). Subway C, E to 23rd Street. Open 5.30-10pm Mon-Thur, Sun; 5.30-11pm Fri, Sat (hrs may be extended). Main courses $17-$28.

The Heath American/British
Punchdrunk – the London troupe behind the hit *Macbeth*-inspired

production *Sleep No More* (*see p107*) – has premiered a 150-seat restaurant underneath its seasonal rooftop bar, Gallow Green. Chef RL King crafts a menu of modern American and British fare, such as chicken with charred broccoli, apples and hazelnuts, and a short-rib-and-chanterelle-mushroom pie. Cocktails with names like the gin-based Hull Executive and the Aberdonian Sour (Scotch, orgeat syrup, red wine float) bow to the company's UK roots.
McKittrick Hotel, 530 W 27th Street, between Tenth & Eleventh Avenues (1-212 564 1662, www.theheath nyc.com). Subway 1 to 28th Street. Open 5-11pm daily. Main courses $18-$35.

Tipsy Parson American regional
Julie Wallach's Chelsea restaurant channels the experience of dining at home – if home happens to be a charming country cottage stocked with knick-knacks, that is. The nostalgic food is grounded firmly in the Deep South. A tasty down-home twist on a burger comes topped with pimento cheese (grits and bacon optional), accompanied by batter-fried pickles. Macaroni and cheese features a complex medley of cheddar, gruyère and grana padano, with crumbled corn bread and fresh cavatelli. For dessert, try the namesake Tipsy Parson – a boozy trifle.
156 Ninth Avenue, between 19th & 20th Streets (1-212 620 4545, www.tipsyparson.com). Subway C, E to 23rd Street. Open 11.30am-midnight Mon-Fri; 10am-1am Sat; 10am-11pm Sun. Main courses $24-$34.

Gramercy & Flatiron

71 Irving Place Coffee & Tea Bar Café
Irving Farm's beans are roasted in a 100-year-old carriage house in the Hudson Valley; fittingly, its Gramercy Park café, which occupies the ground floor of a stately brownstone, also has a rustic edge. Breakfast (the likes of granola, oatmeal, croissants, bagels), sandwiches and salads accompany the excellent java.
71 Irving Place, between 18th & 19th Streets (1-212 995 5252, www.irvingfarm.com). Subway L, N, Q, R, 4, 5, 6 to 14th Street-Union Square. Open 7am-10pm Mon-Fri; 8am-10pm Sat. Sandwiches $10-$11. Other locations 88 Orchard Street, at Broome Street, Lower East Side (1-212 228 8880); 89 E 42nd Street, Grand Central Terminal, Midtown (1-212 983 4242); 224 W 79th Street, between Amsterdam Avenue & Broadway, Upper West Side (1-212 874 7979).

ABC Kitchen Eclectic
The haute green cooking at Jean-Georges Vongerichten's artfully decorated restaurant inside landmark Flatiron furniture store ABC Carpet & Home is based on the most gorgeous ingredients from up and down the East Coast. Local, seasonal bounty finds its way into the menu of salads, house-made pastas, whole-wheat pizzas and meat and fish dishes. A signature sundae of salted caramel ice-cream, candied peanuts and popcorn with chocolate sauce reworks the kids' treat to thrill a grown-up palate. ABC delivers one message overall: food that's good for the planet needn't be any less opulent, flavourful or stunning to look at.
35 E 18th Street, between Broadway & Park Avenue South (1-212 475 5829, www.abckitchennyc.com). Subway L, N, Q, R, 4, 5, 6 to 14th Street-Union Square. Open noon-3pm, 5.30-10.30pm Mon-Wed; noon-3pm, 5.30-11pm Thur; noon-3pm, 5.30-11.30pm Fri; 11am-3.30pm, 5.30-11.30pm Sat; 11am-3.30pm, 5.30-10pm Sun. Main courses $15-$39.

The Breslin Bar & Dining Room
Eclectic

The third project from restaurant savant Ken Friedman and Anglo chef April Bloomfield, the Breslin broke gluttonous new ground. Expect a wait at this no-reservations hotspot – quell your appetite at the bar with an order of scrumpets (fried strips of lamb belly). The overall ethos might well be described as late-period Henry VIII: groaning boards of house-made terrines feature thick slices of guinea hen, rabbit and pork. The pig's foot for two – half a leg, really – could feed the full Tudor court. Desserts include amped-up childhood treats like ice-cream sundaes.
Ace Hotel New York, 16 W 29th Street, at Broadway (1-212 679 1939, www.thebreslin.com). Subway N, R to 28th Street. Open 7am-4pm, 5.30pm-midnight daily. Main courses $21-$48.

The Cannibal **American creative**
Run by restaurateur Christian Pappanicholas and connected to his Belgian-American eaterie, Resto, the Cannibal is an unusual retail-restaurant hybrid – a beer store and a butcher but also a laid-back place to eat and drink. The meat counter supplies whole beasts for Resto's large-format feasts, but the carnivore's paradise is otherwise autonomous, with its own chef, Preston Clark (formerly of Jean-Georges), and beer director, Julian Kurland. The food is best ordered in rounds, pairing beer and bites – wispy shavings of Kentucky ham, pâtés, sausages and tartares – as you sample some of the 450 selections on the drinks list.
113 E 29th Street, between Park & Lexington Avenues (1-212 686 5480, www.thecannibalnyc.com). Subway 6 to 28th Street. Open 11am-11.30pm daily. Small plates $11-$18.

Casa Mono **Spanish**
Offal-loving chef-partners Mario Batali and Andy Nusser broke new ground in NYC with their adventurous Spanish fare: crispy pigs' ears, fried sweetbreads with fennel, foie gras with *cinco cebollas* (five types of onion), or fried duck egg with black truffles. For a somewhat cheaper option, the attached Bar Jamón (125 E 17th Street; open 5pm-2am Mon-Fri; noon-2am Sat, Sun) offers tapas, Ibérico hams and Spanish cheeses.
52 Irving Place, at 17th Street (1-212 253 2773, www.casamononyc.com). Subway L to Third Avenue; N, Q, R, 4, 5, 6 to 14th Street-Union Square. Open noon-midnight daily. Small plates $9-$25.

City Bakery Café
Pastry genius Maury Rubin's loft-size City Bakery is jammed with shoppers loading up on creative baked goods such as maple bacon biscuits and unusual salad bar choices (grilled pineapple with ancho chilli, or beansprouts with smoked tofu, for example). There's also a small selection of soups, pizzas and hot dishes. But

never mind all that: the thick, incredibly rich hot chocolate with fat house-made marshmallows is justly famed, and the moist 'melted' chocolate-chip cookies are divinely decadent.
3 W 18th Street, between Fifth & Sixth Avenues (1-212 366 1414, www.thecitybakery.com). Subway L, N, Q, R, 4, 5, 6 to 14th Street-Union Square. Open 7.30am-7pm Mon-Fri; 8am-7pm Sat; 9am-6pm Sun. Salad bar $14/lb.

Eleven Madison Park
American creative
Chef Daniel Humm and impresario partner Will Guidara – who bought Eleven Madison Park from their old boss, legendary restaurateur Danny Meyer – are masters of reinvention. And once again, they've hit on a winning formula, this time for a 16-course Gotham-themed meal – marked by stagecraft and tricks – that departs from the city's upper echelons of Old World-dominated fine dining. During a recent meal, a glass cloche rose over a puff of smoke, unveiling smoked sturgeon above smouldering embers. Rib-eye, aged an astonishing 140 days, was served with a side of oxtail jam with melted foie gras and whipped potato icing that's as rich as it sounds, and a waiter performed a card trick with a chocolate pay-off – a nod to the city's old street-corner shysters.
11 Madison Avenue, at E 24th Street (1-212 889 0905, www.elevenmadisonpark.com). Subway N, R, 6 to 23rd Street. Open 5.30-10pm Mon-Wed, Sun; noon-1pm, 5.30-10pm Thur-Sat. Tasting menu $225.

Hanjan **Korean**
Hanjan is a shining example of a *joomak*, the Korean equivalent of the English gastropub. Expect a barrage of deeply satisfying dishes: glutinous rice cakes licked with spicy pork fat; crispy scallion pancakes studded with local squid; and skewers of fresh chicken thighs that you can swab with funky *ssam-jang*. Each plate packs its own surprises, but the whole feast is tied together by a soulful bass note melding sweetness, spice and just the right amount of fishy funk.
36 W 26th Street, between Broadway & Sixth Avenue (1-212 206 7226, www.hanjan26.com). Subway N, R to 28th Street. Open noon-2.15pm, 5.30pm-1am Mon-Fri; 5.30pm-1am Sat. Main courses $10-$24.

Hill Country **Barbecue**
The guys behind Hill Country are about as Texan as Donald Trump in a stetson, but the cooking is an authentic, world-class take on the restaurant's namesake region. Dishes feature sausages imported from barbecue stalwart Kreuz Market of Lockhart, Texas, and two options for brisket: go for the 'moist' (read: fatty) version for full flavour. Beef shoulder emerges from the smoker in 20lb slabs, and tips-on pork ribs are hefty, with just enough fat to imbue proper flavour. Desserts, such as jelly-filled cupcakes with peanut butter frosting, live out some kind of *Leave*

It to Beaver fantasy, though June Cleaver wouldn't approve of the two dozen tequilas and bourbons on offer.
30 W 26th Street, between Broadway & Sixth Avenue (1-212 255 4544, www.hillcountryny.com). Subway N, R to 28th Street. Open noon-10pm Mon-Wed, Sun; noon-11pm Thur; noon-midnight Fri, Sat. Main courses $12-$30.

The John Dory Oyster Bar **Seafood**
April Bloomfield and Ken Friedman's original John Dory in the Meatpacking District was an ambitious, pricey endeavour, but its reincarnation in the Ace Hotel is an understated success. Tall stools face a raw bar stocked with a rotating mix of East and West Coast oysters, all expertly handled and impeccably sourced. True to form, the rest of Bloomfield's tapas-style seafood dishes are intensely flavoured – cold poached lobster with tomalley vinaigrette, for example, or chorizo-stuffed squid with smoked tomato.
Ace Hotel New York, 1196 Broadway, at 29th Street (1-212 792 9000, www.thejohndory.com). Subway N, R to 28th Street. Open noon-midnight daily. Small plates $11-$29.

Maialino **Italian**
Danny Meyer's first full-fledged foray into Italian cuisine is a dedicated homage to the neighbourhood trattorias that kept him well fed as a 20-year-old tour guide in Rome. Salumi and bakery stations between the front bar and the wood-beamed dining room – hog jowls and sausages dangling near shelves stacked with crusty loaves of bread – mimic a market off the Appian Way. Executive chef Nick Anderer's menu offers exceptional facsimiles of dishes specific to Rome, such as carbonara, braised tripe and suckling pig.
Gramercy Park Hotel, 2 Lexington Avenue, between E 21st & E 22nd Streets (1-212 777 2410, www.maialinonyc.com). Subway 6 to 23rd Street. Open 7.30-10am, noon-2pm, 5.30-10.30pm Mon-Thur; 7.30-10am, noon-2pm, 5.30-11pm Fri; 10am-2.30pm, 5.30-11pm Sat; 10am-2.30pm, 5.30-10.30pm Sun. Main courses $23-$72.

The NoMad **American**
Another restaurant from chef Daniel Humm and front-of-house partner Will Guidara, also behind Eleven Madison Park (*see left*), the NoMad features plush armchairs around well-spaced tables and a stylish return to three-course dining. The food, like the space, exudes decadence: a slow-cooked egg stars in one over-the-top starter, with mushrooms, black garlic and kale for crunch. And while there are plenty of rich-man roast chickens for two in New York, the amber-hued bird here – with a foie gras, brioche and black truffle stuffing – is surely the new gold standard, well worth its $79 price tag.
1170 Broadway, at 28th Street (1-212 796 1500, www.thenomadhotel.com). Subway N, R to 28th Street. Open

5.30-10.30pm Mon-Thur; 5.30-11pm Fri, Sat; 5.30-10pm Sun. Main courses $20-$37.

Pure Food & Wine **Vegetarian**
The dishes delivered to your table – whether out on the leafy patio or inside the ambient dining room – are minor miracles, not only because they look gorgeous and taste terrific, but also because they come from a kitchen that lacks a stove. Everything at Pure is raw and vegan, including the lasagne (with creamy macadamia nut and pumpkin seed 'ricotta'). Wines, most of which are organic, are top-notch, as are the desserts, including a classic vegan ice-cream sundae.
54 Irving Place, between 17th & 18th Streets (1-212 477 1010, www.purefoodandwine.com). Subway L, N, Q, R, 4, 5, 6 to 14th Street-Union Square. Open noon-4pm, 5.30-11pm daily. Main courses $22-$26.

Midtown

Artisanal **French**
As New York's bistros veer towards uniformity, Terrance Brennan's high-ceilinged deco gem makes its mark with an all-out homage to *fromage*. Skip the appetisers and open with fondue, which comes in three varieties. Familiar bistro fare awaits, with such dishes as steak frites, mussels, and chicken baked 'under a brick', but the curd gets the last word with the cheese and wine pairings. These selections of three cheeses – chosen by region, style or theme (for example, each one produced in a monastery) – are matched with three wines (or beers or even sakés) for a sumptuous and intriguing finale.
2 Park Avenue, at 32nd Street (1-212 725 8585, www.artisanalbistro.com). Subway 6 to 33rd Street. Open 11.45am-2.45pm, 5-9.45pm Mon-Wed; 11.45am-2.45pm, 5-10.45pm Thur, Fri; 11am-3.45pm, 5-10.45pm Sat; 10.30am-3.45pm, 5-8.45pm Sun. Main courses $24-$50.

Bar Room at the Modern
American creative
Those who can't afford to drop a pay cheque at award-winning chef Gabriel Kreuther's formal MoMA dining room the Modern, can still dine in the equally stunning and less pricey bar at the front. The Alsatian-inspired menu is constructed of around 30 small- and medium-sized plates (for example, liverwurst with pickled vegetables; slow-poached egg with lobster; spicy steak tartare with quail egg; and house-made country sausage with sauerkraut), which can be mixed and shared. Desserts come courtesy of pastry chef Marc Aumont, and the wine list is extensive, to say the least.
9 W 53rd Street, between Fifth & Sixth Avenues (1-212 333 1220, www.themodernnyc.com). Subway E, M to Fifth Avenue-53rd Street. Open 11.30am-3pm, 5-10.30pm Mon-Sat; 11.30am-3pm, 5-9.30pm Sun. Main courses $16-$35.

Hanjan

Benoit French
Alain Ducasse's classic brasserie attempts to reclaim 55th Street's former Francophile row. Come for successful, seasonality-snubbing relics like a cassoulet packed with hearty meat (pork loin, garlic sausage, duck confit) under a canopy of white beans. At the Sunday-only brunch, the dessert bar (per item $6, all-you-can-eat $18) offers a dozen seasonal pastries and tarts.
60 W 55th Street, between Fifth & Sixth Avenues (1-646 943 7373, www.benoitny.com). Subway E, M to Fifth Avenue-53rd Street; F to 57th Street. Open 11.45am-3pm, 5.30-11pm Mon-Sat; 11.30am-3.30pm, 5.30-11pm Sun. Main courses $26-$48.

Betony American creative
Eleven Madison Park alums Bryce Shuman and Eamon Rockey have created a rare treat: a serious New American restaurant that doesn't take itself too seriously. Hyper-professional service is softened with a heaping dose of humanity, and the fun-loving à la carte menu includes stellar riffs on crunchy fried pickles and toasty tuna melts. Dishes such as seared foie gras plugged with smoked ham hock and draped with crisp, vinegar-twanged kale combine upmarket cachet with down-home comforts.
41 W 57th Street, between Fifth & Sixth Avenues (1-212 465 2400, www.betony-nyc.com). Subway F, N, Q, R to 57th Street. Open noon-2pm, 5.30-10pm Mon-Thur; noon-2pm, 5.30-10.30pm Fri; 5.30-10.30pm Sat. Main courses $28-$37.

Café Edison American
This old-school no-frills eaterie draws tourists, theatregoers, actors and just about everyone else in search of deli staples such as cheese blintzes and giant Reuben sandwiches. The matzo ball soup is so restorative, you can almost feel it bolstering your immune system.
Hotel Edison, 228 W 47th Street, between Broadway & Eighth Avenue (1-212 354 0368). Subway N, Q, R to 49th Street; 1 to 50th Street. Open 6am-9.30pm Mon-Sat; 6am-7.30pm Sun. Main courses $7-$13. No credit cards.

Don Antonio by Starita Italian/Pizza
Pizza aficionados have been busy colonising this pedigreed recent arrival, a collaboration between Kesté's (*see p56*) talented Roberto Caporuscio and his decorated Naples mentor, Antonio Starita. Start with tasty bites like the *fritattine* (a deep-fried spaghetti cake oozing *prosciutto cotto* and mozzarella sauce). The main event should be the habit-forming Montanara Starita, which gets a quick dip in the deep fryer before hitting the oven to develop its puffy, golden crust. Topped with tomato sauce, basil and intensely smoky buffalo mozzarella, it's a worthy new addition to the pantheon of classic New York pies.
309 W 50th Street, between Eighth & Ninth Avenues (1-646 719 1043, www.donantoniopizza.com). Subway C, E to 50th Street. Open 11.30am-11pm Mon-Thur; 11.30am-midnight Fri, Sat; 11.30am-10.30pm Sun. Pizzas $9-$23.

Gotham West Market Eclectic
In 2013, Hell's Kitchen welcomed this hip take on a food court, perfect for lunch or a quick pre-theatre bite. The 15,000sq ft retail-dining mecca is divided into eight culinary stalls – such as Blue Bottle Coffee and an outpost of gourmet grocer/cooking-supply store Brooklyn Kitchen – as well as a full-service NYC Velo bike shop. Dine-in or take-out options include Ivan Ramen Slurp Shop, where Tokyo noodle guru Ivan Orkin offers his famed shio, shoyu and chilli-sesame varieties; Little Chef, the salad-and-soup-focused offshoot of Caroline Fidanza's Saltie sandwich shop; El Colmado tapas bar from Seamus Mullen of Tertulia; and a cocktail-and-charcuterie outpost of the Cannibal (*see p58*). Seating is at chef's counters or communal tables.
600 Eleventh Avenue, between 44th & 45th Streets (1-212 582 7940, www.gothamwestmarket.com). A, C, E to 42nd Street-Port Authority. Open 7am-11pm Mon-Fri; 8am-11pm Sat, Sun.

Grand Central Oyster Bar & Restaurant Seafood
The legendary Grand Central Oyster Bar has been a fixture of the gorgeous hub that shares its name since 1913. The surly countermen at the mile-long bar (the best seats in the house) are part of the charm. Avoid the more complicated fish concoctions and play it safe with a reliably awe-inspiring platter of iced, just-shucked oysters (there can be a whopping 30 varieties to choose from, including many from nearby Long Island).
Grand Central Terminal, Lower Level, 42nd Street, at Park Avenue (1-212 490 6650, www.oysterbarny. com). Subway S, 4, 5, 6, 7 to 42nd Street-Grand Central. Open 11.30am-9.30pm Mon-Sat. Main courses $18-$32.

Kajitsu Japanese/Vegetarian
There's no shortage of cheap ramen joints in postgrad mecca Murray Hill, but house-made soba crowned with shaved black truffles? That's only at Kajitsu. The minimalist, Michelin-starred den displays a devotion to produce, influenced by the monk-approved *shojin-ryori* (vegetarian) tradition. The sublime fare has made it a cult favourite among top-notch toques like Momofuku's David Chang. In the small, bare dining room or at the eight-seat chef's counter, choose from three ever-changing menus – four courses, eight or a counter-only *omakase* – each paired with saké if you like.
125 E 39th Street, between Park & Lexington Avenues (1-212 228 4873, www.kajitsunyc.com). Subway S, 4, 5, 6, 7 to 42nd Street-Grand Central. Open 11.45am-1.45pm, 5.30-10pm Tue-Sat; 5.30-10pm Sun (closed 1st day of each month). Tasting menus $55-$85.

Kashkaval Garden Mediterranean
This charming tapas and wine bar evokes fondue's peasant origins, with deep cast-iron pots and generous baskets of crusty bread. Steer clear of the bland and rubbery kashkaval (a Balkan sheep's-milk cheese) and order the gooey gruyère and truffle. Or choose from the selection of tangy Mediterranean spreads – roasted artichoke dip with breadcrumbs or beet hummus – and the impressive roster of skewers. End the meal with the crowd-pleasing chocolate torte.
852 Ninth Avenue, between 55th & 56th Streets (1-212 245 1758, www.kashkavalgarden.com). Subway C, E to 50th Street. Open 4pm-2am daily. Main courses $12-$17.

Keens Steakhouse Steakhouse
The ceiling and walls are hung with pipes, some from such long-ago Keens regulars as Babe Ruth, JP Morgan and Teddy Roosevelt. Even in these nonsmoking days, you can catch a whiff of the restaurant's 125-plus years of history. Bevelled-glass doors, two working fireplaces and a forest's worth of dark wood suggest a time when 'Diamond Jim' Brady piled his table with bushels of oysters, slabs of seared beef and troughs of ale. The menu still lists a three-inch-thick mutton chop and the porterhouse (for two or three) holds its own against any steak in the city.
72 W 36th Street, at Sixth Avenue (1-212 947 3636, www.keens.com). Subway B, D, F, M, N, Q, R to 34th Street-Herald Square. Open 11.45am-10.30pm Mon-Fri; 5-10.30pm Sat; 5-9.30pm Sun. Main courses $26-$58.

Mandoo Bar Korean
If the staff members filling and crimping dough squares in the front window don't give it away, we will – this wood-wrapped industrial-style spot elevates mandoo (Korean dumplings) above mere appetiser status. Six varieties of the tasty morsels are filled with such delights as subtly piquant kimchi, juicy pork, succulent shrimp and vegetables. Try them miniaturised, as in the Baby Mandoo, swimming in a soothing beef broth or atop soupy ramen noodles.
2 W 32nd Street, between Fifth Avenue & Broadway (1-212 279 3075, www. mandoobarnyc.com). Subway B, D, F,

M, N, Q, R to 34th Street-Herald Square. Open 11.30am-10pm daily. Main courses $12-$20.

The Monkey Bar American
After the repeal of Prohibition in 1933, this one-time piano bar in the swank Hotel Elysée (*see p117*) became a boozy clubhouse for the glitzy artistic figures of the age, among them Tallulah Bankhead, Dorothy Parker and Tennessee Williams. The Monkey Bar is now owned by publishing titan Graydon Carter, who has brought new buzz to the historic space. Perched at the bar with a pitch-perfect glass of Gonet-Medeville champagne or ensconced in a red leather booth with a plate of fettuccine carbonara with bacon lardons, you'll find yourself seduced by that rare alchemy of old New York luxury and new-school flair.
Hotel Elysée, 60 E 54th Street, between Madison & Park Avenues (1-212 288 1010, www.monkeybarnewyork.com). Subway E, M to Lexington Avenue-53rd Street; 6 to 51st Street. Open 11.30am-10pm Mon-Fri; 5.30-10pm Sat. Main courses $25-$55.

Quality Meats Steakhouse
Michael Stillman – son of the founder of landmark steakhouse Smith & Wollensky – is behind this highly stylised industrial theme park complete with meat-hook light fixtures, wooden butcher blocks, white tiles and exposed brick. Lespinasse-trained chef Craig Koketsu nails the steaks (including a $110 double-rib steak) and breathes new life into traditional side dishes. Pudding-like corn crème brûlée and the airy 'gnocchi & cheese', a clever take on mac and cheese, are terrific. High-concept desserts are best exemplified by the outstanding coffee-and-doughnuts ice-cream crammed with chunks of the fritters and crowned with a miniature doughnut.
57 W 58th Street, between Fifth & Sixth Avenues (1-212 371 7777, www.qualitymeatsnyc.com). Subway F, N, Q, R to 57th Street; N, Q, R to Fifth Avenue-59th Street. Open 11.30am-3pm, 5-10.30pm Mon-Wed; 11.30am-3pm, 5-11.30pm Thur, Fri; 5-11.30pm Sat; 5-10pm Sun. Main courses $21-$47.

Salvation Taco Mexican
The decor – coloured Christmas lights, fake fruit – may evoke that Cancun vacation, but the fiesta fare doled out at this Murray Hill cantina off the lobby of the Pod 39 hotel (*see p118*) has an upscale bent, thanks to April Bloomfield and Ken Friedman (of the Spotted Pig and the Ace Hotel's Breslin). Exotic fillings include Moroccan-spiced lamb and Korean-barbecue-style beef. Even a margarita gets a chefly update with a zippy guajillo chili salt rim.
145 E 39th Street, between Lexington & Third Avenues (1-212 865 5800, www.salvationtaco.com). Subway S, 4, 5, 6, 7 to 42nd Street-Grand Central. Open 7am-5pm, 5.30pm-midnight daily. Main courses $13-$38.

Upper West Side

Barney Greengrass American
Despite decor that Jewish mothers might call 'schmutzy', this legendary deli is a madhouse at breakfast and brunch. Enormous egg platters come with the usual choice of smoked fish (such as sturgeon or Nova Scotia salmon). Prices are on the high side, but portions are large, and that goes for the sandwiches too. Or try the less costly items: matzo-ball soup, creamy egg salad or cold pink borscht served in a glass.
541 Amsterdam Avenue, between 86th & 87th Streets (1-212 724 4707, www.barneygreengrass.com). Subway B, C, 1 to 86th Street. Open 8.30am-6pm Tue-Sun. Sandwiches $9-$21. No credit cards.

Bouchon Bakery Café
Chef Thomas Keller's café, in the same mall as his lauded fine-dining room Per Se (*see right*), lacks ambience, and the menu (soups, tartines, salads, sandwiches) is basic. But prices are much more palatable – a dry-cured ham and emmenthal baguette is around a tenner. Baked goods, including Keller's takes on American classics like Oreo cookies, are the highlights.
3rd Floor, Time Warner Center, 10 Columbus Circle, at Broadway (1-212 823 9366, www.bouchonbakery.com). Subway A, B, C, D, 1 to 59th Street-Columbus Circle. Open 8am-9pm Mon-Sat; 8am-7pm Sun. Pastries $1-$7. Other location 1 Rockefeller Plaza, at 49th Street, Midtown (1-212 782 3890).

Boulud Sud Mediterranean
At his most international restaurant yet, superchef Daniel Boulud highlights the new French cuisine of melting-pot cities like Marseille and Nice. With his executive chef, Travis Swikard, he casts a wide net – looking to Egypt, Turkey and Greece. Diners can build a full tapas meal from shareable snacks like octopus *a la plancha*, with marcona almonds and arugula. Heartier dishes combine Gallic finesse with polyglot flavours: sweet-spicy chicken tagine with harira soup borrows from Morocco. Desserts – such as grapefruit givré stuffed with sorbet, sesame mousse and rose-scented nuggets of Turkish delight – take the exotic mix to even loftier heights.
20 W 64th Street, between Broadway & Central Park West (1-212 595 1313, www.danielnyc.com). Subway 1 to 66th Street-Lincoln Center. Open noon-11pm Mon-Fri; 11.30am-11pm Sat; 11.30am-10pm Sun. Main courses $22-$41.

Celeste Italian
This popular spot, offering authentic fare in a rustic setting, doesn't take reservations so a wait is to be expected. Once you're in, start with *carciofi fritti*: fried artichokes that are so light, they're evanescent. Three house-made pastas are prepared daily – the tagliatelle with shrimp, cabbage and pecorino stands out. Those who can manage a few more bites are advised to try the *pastiera*, a grain-and-ricotta cake flavoured with candied fruit and orange-blossom water.
502 Amsterdam Avenue, between 84th & 85th Streets (1-212 874 4559, www.celestenewyork.com). Subway 1 to 86th Street. Open 5-11pm Mon-Thur; 5-11.30pm Fri; noon-3pm, 5-11.30pm Sat; noon-3pm, 5-10.30pm Sun. Main courses $9-$16. No credit cards.

Community Food & Juice American
Clinton Street Baking Company's Upper West Side sibling is a neighbourhood brunch destination, but there's more to eating here than eggs and pancakes. Chef and co-owner Neil Kleinberg's dinner menu of global comfort food includes a formidable matzo-ball soup and a top-notch grass-fed burger with caramelised onions and Vermont cheddar. Vegetarians will be pleased by a range of creative salads and meatless sandwiches and main dishes.
2893 Broadway, between 112th & 113th Streets (1-212 665 2800, www.communityrestaurant.com). Subway 1 to 110th Street-Cathedral Parkway. Open 8am-3.30pm, 9.30pm Mon-Thur, Sun; 8am-3.30pm, 5-10pm Fri; 9am-3.30pm, 5-10pm Sat; 9am-3.30pm, 5-9.30pm Sun. Main courses $14-$29.

Hungarian Pastry Shop Café
So many theses have been dreamed up, procrastinated over or tossed aside in the Hungarian Pastry Shop since it opened more than five decades ago that the Columbia University neighbourhood institution merits its own dissertation. The java is strong enough to make up for the erratic array of pastries, and the Euro feel is enhanced by the view of St John the Divine cathedral from outdoor tables.
1030 Amsterdam Avenue, between 110th & 111th Streets (1-212 866 4230). Subway 1 to 110th Street-Cathedral Parkway. Open 7.30am-11.30pm Mon-Fri; 8.30am-11.30pm Sat; 8.30am-10.30pm Sun. Pastries $1-$4.

Jean-Georges French
Unlike many of its vaunted peers, the flagship of celebrated chef Jean-Georges Vongerichten has not become a shadow of itself: the top-rated food is still breathtaking. Velvety foie gras terrine is coated in a thin brûlée shell; other signature dishes include ginger-marinated yellowfin tuna ribbons with avocado and spicy radish. Pastry chef Joseph Murphy's inventive seasonal quartets, comprising four mini desserts, are always a delight. The more casual on-site Nougatine café is less expensive, but still provides a taste of its big brother.
Trump International Hotel & Tower, 1 Central Park West, at Columbus Circle (1-212 299 3900, www.jean-georges restaurant.com). Subway A, B, C, D, 1 to 59th Street-Columbus Circle. Open noon-2.30pm, 5.30-11pm Mon-Thur; noon-2.30pm, 5-11pm Fri-Sun. Three-course prix fixe $118. Seven-course prix fixe $198.

Ouest American creative
A prototypical local clientele calls chef-owner Tom Valenti's uptown stalwart – one of the neighbourhood's most celebrated restaurants – its local canteen. And why not? The friendly servers ferry pitch-perfect cocktails and rich, Italian-inflected cuisine from the open kitchen to immensely comfortable round red booths. Valenti adds some unexpected flourishes to the soothing formula: salmon gravadlax is served with a chickpea pancake topped with caviar and potent mustard oil, while the house-smoked sturgeon presides over frisée, lardons and a poached egg.
2315 Broadway, between 83rd & 84th Streets (1-212 580 8700, www.ouestny.com). Subway 1 to 86th Street. Open 5.30-9.30pm Mon, Tue; 5.30-10pm Wed, Thur; 5.30-11pm Fri; 5-11pm Sat; 11am-2pm, 5-9pm Sun. Main courses $27-$36.

Per Se French
Expectations are high at Per Se – and that goes both ways. You're expected to wear the right clothes (jackets are required for men), pay a non-negotiable service charge, and pretend you aren't eating in a shopping mall. The restaurant, in turn, is expected to deliver one hell of a tasting menu for $310. And it does. Dish after dish is flawless, beginning with Thomas Keller's signature Oysters and Pearls (a sabayon of pearl tapioca with oysters and caviar); an all-vegetable version is also available. If you can afford it, it's worth every penny, but avoid the à la carte option in the lounge, which offers miserly portions at high prices, making it less of a deal than the celebrated tasting menu in the formal dining room.
4th Floor, Time Warner Center, 10 Columbus Circle, at Broadway (1-212 823 9335, www.perseny.com). Subway A, B, C, D, 1 to 59th Street-Columbus Circle. Open 5.30-10pm Mon-Thur; 11.30am-1.30pm, 5.30-10pm Fri-Sun. Main courses (in lounge) $30-$125. Five-course prix fixe $205 (Fri-Sun lunch only). Nine-course tasting menu $310.

Shake Shack American
The spacious offspring of Danny Meyer's wildly popular Madison Square Park concession stand is now one of several locations across the city. Shake Shack gets several local critics' votes for New York's best burger. Patties are made from fresh-ground, all-natural Angus beef, and the franks are served Chicago-style on potato buns and topped with Rick's Picks Shack relish. Frozen-custard shakes hit the spot, and there's beer and wine if you want something stronger.
366 Columbus Avenue, at 77th Street (1-646 747 8770, www.shakeshack. com). Subway B, C to 81st Street-

Museum of Natural History; 1 to 79th Street. Open 10.45am-11pm daily. Burgers $5-$9. Other locations throughout the city.

Upper East Side

Café Sabarsky Austrian/Café
Purveyor of indulgent pastries and whipped cream-topped *einspänner* coffee for Neue Galerie patrons by day, this sophisticated, high-ceilinged restaurant, inspired by a classic Viennese *kaffeehaus*, is helmed by chef Kurt Gutenbrunner of modern Austrian restaurant Wallsé. Appetisers are most adventurous – the creaminess of the *spätzle* is a perfect base for sweetcorn, tarragon and wild mushrooms – while main course specials, such as the *wiener schnitzel* tartly garnished with lingonberries, are capable yet ultimately feel like the calm before the *Sturm und Drang* of dessert. Try the *klimttorte*, which masterfully alternates layers of hazelnut cake with chocolate. Note that Café Sabarsky is closed on Tuesdays. *Neue Galerie, 1048 Fifth Avenue, at 86th Street (1-212 288 0665, www.cafesabarsky.com). Subway 4, 5, 6 to 86th Street. Open 9am-6pm Mon, Wed; 9am-9pm Thur-Sun. Main courses $16-$30.*

Daniel French
The cuisine at Daniel Boulud's elegant fine-dining flagship, designed by Adam Tihany, is rooted in French technique with contemporary flourishes like fusion elements and an emphasis on local produce. Although the menu changes seasonally, it always includes a few signature dishes, such as the chef's oven-baked black sea bass with Syrah sauce, or the duo of beef – a sumptuous pairing of Black Angus short ribs and seared Wagyu tenderloin. *60 E 65th Street, between Madison & Park Avenues (1-212 288 0033,*

www.danielnyc.com). Subway F to Lexington Avenue-63rd Street; 6 to 68th Street-Hunter College. Open 5.30-11pm Mon-Sat. Three-course prix fixe $125.

Dough Loco Café
Chef Corey Cova (Earl's Beer & Cheese, ABV) – known for funky dishes like a Spam-and-octopus salad and a foie gras Fluffernutter – rolls out eccentric haute doughnuts at this seven-seat bakery. Behind a counter crafted from old bowling alley lanes, find a rotating selection of oddball flavours like miso-maple and raspberrry-Sriracha alongside more traditional ones like cinnamon-sugar and chocolate. To drink: pour-overs and espressos made from Blue Bottle beans. *1261 Park Avenue, between 97th & 98th Streets (1-212 876 1980, www.doughloco.com). Subway 6 to 96th Street. Open 7am-7pm daily. Doughnuts $3.*

Lexington Candy Shop American
You won't see much candy for sale here. Instead, you'll find a wonderfully preserved retro diner (it was founded in 1925), its long counter lined with chatty locals on their lunch hours, tucking into burgers and chocolate malts. If you come for breakfast, order the doorstop slabs of french toast. *1226 Lexington Avenue, at 83rd Street (1-212 288 0057, www.lexington candyshop.net). Subway 4, 5, 6 to 86th Street. Open 7am-7pm Mon-Sat; 8am-6pm Sun. Main courses $6-$14.*

Rôtisserie Georgette French/American
Two Daniel Boulud vets strike out on their own with this 90-seat rotisserie, decorated with steel columns and caramel-coloured banquettes. Led by Georgette Farkas – the toque's publicist for nearly two decades – the restaurant showcases spit-fired roasts, including organic Zimmerman Farm chicken and rib-eye steak with béarnaise sauce. Former Boulud banquet chef David Malbequi helms

the kitchen, turning out seasonal sides like pancetta-studded brussels sprouts and four takes on potatoes (roasted, fried, puréed and stuffed with black truffles). Legendary Daniel sommelier Jean-Luc Le Dû, now a wine shop owner, curates a vino list showcasing lesser-known French producers. *14 E 60th Street, between Fifth & Madison Avenues (1-212 390 8060, www.rotisserieg.com). Subway N, Q, R to Fifth Avenue-59th Street. Open noon-2.30pm, 5.45-10pm Mon; noon-2.30pm, 5.45-11pm Tue-Fri; noon-3pm, 5.45-11pm Sat; 5.45-10pm Sun. Main courses $25-$45.*

Harlem & Upper Manhattan

Amy Ruth's American regional
This popular no-reservations spot is a prime place for soul food in Harlem. Delicately fried okra is delivered without a hint of slime, and the mac and cheese is gooey inside and crunchy-brown on top. Dishes take their names from notable African-Americans – vote for the President Barack Obama (fried, smothered, baked or barbecued chicken). *113 W 116th Street, between Malcolm X Boulevard (Lenox Avenue) & Adam Clayton Powell Jr Boulevard (Seventh Avenue) (1-212 280 8779, www. amyruthsharlem.com). Subway 2, 3 to 116th Street. Open 11am-11pm Mon; 8.30am-11pm Tue-Thur; 8.30am-5.30am Fri; 7.30am-5.30am Sat; 7.30am-11pm Sun. Main courses $12.25-$23.*

The Cecil Eclectic
The Cecil may lack celebrated Harlem toque Marcus Samuelsson's culinary star power – chef Alexander Smalls and his fat-cat partner, former Time Warner CEO Richard Parsons, are mostly unknown entities in the food world – but it's nevertheless a worthwhile dining option uptown. The menu braids together the far-reaching flavours of the African diaspora (citrus jerk bass, roasted *poussin yassa*) in a polished, gold-accented dining room. Ella Fitzgerald and Billie Holiday once crooned next door at legendary jazz club Minton's Playhouse (206 W 118th Street, 1-212 243 2222, www.mintonsharlem.com), also recently revamped by Parsons. *210 W 118th Street, between Adam Clayton Powell Jr Boulevard (Seventh Avenue) and St Nicholas Avenue (1-212 866 1262, www.thececil harlem.com). Subway B, C to 116th Street. Open 5pm-midnight Mon-Thur; 5pm-1am Fri; 10am-1am Sat; 11am-11pm Sun. Main courses $19-$36.*

Charles' Country Panfried Chicken American regional
Fried chicken has made quite the comeback, and the guru of moist flesh and crackly skin, Charles Gabriel,

has also made a triumphant return to Harlem with his resurrected restaurant. In addition to the poultry, you can feast on barbecued ribs, mac and cheese, collard greens, yams and other Southern favourites. *2841 Frederick Douglass Boulevard (Eighth Avenue), between 151st & 152nd Streets (1-212 281 1800). Subway B, D to 155th Street. Open 11am-1am Mon-Thur; 11am-2am Fri, Sat; 11am-9pm Sun. Main courses $10.50-11.50.*

The Grange Bar & Eatery American
Harlem goes back to its rural roots at this locavore bistro and bar, outfitted with Mason jars, white-oak floors and chandeliers. Aric Sassi oversees a comfort-food menu rooted in seasonal produce; having scoured nearby farms, the chef dispatches dishes such as seared crab cakes with celery-parsnip slaw and a roast-beet salad with lime yogurt, almonds and goat-cheese croutons. At the 40ft-long butcher-block bar, cocktails designed by Dead Rabbit head bartender Jack McGarry include the Grange Collins (Farmer's Gin, pomegranate liqueur, basil, lemon juice and soda) and the Convent Stroll (Heaven Hill whiskey, ginger, honey, lemon juice and soda). *1635 Amsterdam Ave at 141st St (212-491 1635, www.thegrange barnyc.com). Subway A, B, C, D to 145th Street; 1 to 137th Street-City College. Open 11.30am-4am Mon-Fri; 10.30am-4am Sat, Sun. Main courses $11-$25.*

New Leaf Restaurant & Bar American
At this seasonal American restaurant in lush Fort Tryon Park you can have brunch on the patio in the warmer months; dinner in the 1930s former concessions building sees dishes such as own-made pappardelle with jumbo shrimp. Profits go to the New York Restoration Project, dedicated to the greening of the city. *Fort Tryon Park, 1 Margaret Corbin Drive (212 568 5323, www.new leafrestaurant.com). Subway A to 190th Street; 1 to 191st Street. Open noon-3.30pm Mon; noon-9pm Tue-Thur; noon-10pm Fri; 11am-3.30pm, 6-10pm Sat; 11am-3.30pm, 6-9pm Sun. Main courses $18-$30.*

Red Rooster Harlem American
With its hobnobbing bar scrum, potent cocktails and regular jazz sets, this upbeat eatery serves as a worthy clubhouse for the new Harlem. Superstar chef Marcus Samuelsson is at his most populist here, drawing on a mix of Southern-fried, East African, Scandinavian and French flavours. Harlem politicos mix at the teardrop bar with downtown fashionistas, swilling cocktails and gorging on rib-sticking food. *310 Malcolm X Boulevard (Lenox Avenue), between 125th & 126th Streets (1-212 792 9001, www. redroosterharlem.com). Subway 2, 3 to 125th Street. Open 11.30am-3pm,*

Salvation Taco

5.30-10.30pm Mon-Thur; 11.30am-3pm, 5.30-11.30pm Fri; 10am-3pm, 5-11.30pm Sat; 10am-3pm, 5-10pm Sun. Main courses $18-$36.

Rusty Mackerel Eclectic
Uptown native James 'Mac' Moran (Olives, Chanterelle) plies Mediterranean small plates at this 35-seat Washington Heights restaurant. From an open kitchen, the chef sends out dishes that honour the neighbourhood's diversity: organic chicken with green harissa, octopus with romesco sauce, and cauliflower in a golden-raisin chimichurri. The drinks list includes a rhubarb-strawberry sangria on tap and six draught wines.
209 Pinehurst Avenue, between 186th & 187th Streets (1-212 928 0584, www.rustymackerelny.com). Subway A to 190th Street. Open 5pm-11pm Mon-Wed; 5pm-midnight Thur, Fri; 11am-3pm, 5pm-midnight Sat; 11am-3pm, 5-11pm Sun. Small plates $5-$30.

Brooklyn

Al di là Italian
A fixture on the Slope's Fifth Avenue for more than a decade, this convivial, no-reservations restaurant is still wildly popular. Affable owner Emiliano Coppa orchestrates the inevitable wait with panache. Coppa's wife, co-owner and chef, Anna Klinger, produces northern Italian dishes with a Venetian slant. It would be hard to better her braised rabbit with black olives atop polenta, and even simple pastas, such as own-made *tagliatelle al ragù*, are superb. The full menu is also served in the restaurant's bar, which has a separate entrance around the corner on Carroll Street.
248 Fifth Avenue, at Carroll Street, Park Slope (1-718 783 4565, www.aldilatrattoria.com). Subway R to Union Street. Open noon-3pm, 10.30pm Mon-Thur; noon-3pm, 6-11pm Fri; 11am-3.30pm, 5.30-11pm Sat; 11am-3.30pm, 5-10pm Sun. Main courses $10-$27.

Allswell American
Chef-owner Nate Smith, who earned his gastropub stripes at the Spotted Pig, broke out on his own with this laid-back Williamsburg tavern. The 47-seat space is done up with a reclaimed pine bar, vintage wallpaper in different patterns and brass-hunting-horn chandeliers with matching sconces. Choose from chefly bar grub (like smoked-trout spread or spicy pork-stuffed pastry rounds); heartier dishes (such as roasted lamb or shellfish stew); and greens (including a chicory salad with figs and pomegranate). The drinks list takes a locavore slant with small-production wines and craft beers on tap, plus a selection of market-driven cocktails.
124 Bedford Avenue, at North 10th Street, Williamsburg (1-347 799 2743, http://allswellnyc.com).

Subway L to Bedford Avenue. Open 10am-2am Mon-Thur; 10am-4am Fri; 9am-4am Sat; 9am-2am Sun. Main courses $14-$36.

Blue Marble Ice Cream Ice-cream
With 30 rotating seasonal flavours, including sweet-tart strawberry, maple-toffee popcorn and sea salt caramel, Blue Marble is beloved by locals of all ages. Produced in NYC's only certified-organic ice-cream plant, it's a cut above standard scoops, and the shop also serves superior La Colombe coffee.
196 Court Street, between Bergen & Warren Streets, Cobble Hill (1-718 858 0408, www.bluemarbleicecream.com). Subway F, G to Bergen Street. Open varies by season; usually 8am-10pm daily. Ice-cream $4-$8.

BrisketTown Barbecue
New Jersey-born Daniel Delaney – a former journalist – might not seem like an obvious poster child for purist Texan 'cue. But the Yankee is turning out some seriously crave-worthy meat. Delaney takes the traditionalist route, coating chunks of heritage beef in salt and pepper before smoking them over oak-fuelled fire for 16 hours. That deep-pink brisket, along with remarkably tender pork ribs, draws Williamsburg's jeans-and-plaid set, who tuck in while indie tunes jangle over the speakers.
359 Bedford Avenue, between South 4th & 5th Streets, Williamsburg (1-718 701 8909, http://delaneybbq.com). Subway L to Bedford Avenue. Open 11am-11pm Mon-Thur, Sun; 11am-midnight Fri, Sat. Main courses $12-$25.

Brooklyn Crab Seafood
Channelling Maine's minigolf clam shacks, this hulking 250-seat spot brings games and seaside flavours to Red Hook's waterfront. Elevated on stilts, the three-storey stand-alone restaurant is done up with wharf-themed flourishes: lobster traps,

fishing rods and a mounted shark's head. Gather friends for a round of minigolf, shuffleboard or cornhole (beanbag toss) outdoors, then grab a picnic table and dig into simple coastal fare, such as peel-and-eat shrimp, and steam pots brimming with crabs and lobster. Drinkers can sip margaritas and piña coladas or split a mixed bucket of five beers on the open-air roof deck, while taking in views of New York's Upper Bay.
24 Reed Street, between Conover & Van Brunt Streets, Red Hook (1-718 643 2722, www.brooklyncrab.com). Subway F, G to Smith-9th Streets, then B61 bus. Open Mid Mar-mid Oct 11.30am-10pm Mon-Thur, Sun; 11.30am-11pm Fri, Sat. Mid Oct-mid Mar 11.30am-10pm Wed, Thur, Sun; 11.30am-11pm Fri, Sat. Main courses $11-$47.

Brooklyn Roasting Company Café
If you need a caffeine fix in Dumbo, stop by Brooklyn Roasting Company, supplier of Fairtrade, organic beans to many of the borough's best cafés. Savour the aromas wafting from the fuel-efficient roasting machine in the on-site 'espresso lab' and accompany your brew with baked goods or a sandwich from Brooklyn's Dough or Margo Patisserie.
25 Jay Street, between John & Plymouth Streets, Dumbo (1-718 522 2664, www.brooklynroasting.com). Subway A, C to High Street; F to York Street. Open 7am-7pm daily. Coffee $1.50-$5.25.

Chef's Table at Brooklyn Fare Eclectic
Scoring a place at chef César Ramirez's 18-seat restaurant within the Brooklyn Fare supermarket takes determination: reservations are only taken on Mondays at 10.30am, six weeks before your desired booking. But the luxurious set dinner of approximately 20 courses is among the best small-plate cuisine in New

York, and the dinner-party vibe is convivial: diners perch on stools around a prep table. The menu changes weekly, but might include such delicacies as a Kumamoto oyster reclining on crème fraîche and yuzu gelée or halibut served in a miraculous broth of dashi and summer truffles.
200 Schermerhorn Street, at Hoyt Street, Boerum Hill (1-718 243 0050, www.brooklynfare.com/chefs-table). Subway A, C, G to Hoyt-Schermerhorn; B, N, Q, R to DeKalb Avenue; 2, 3 to Hoyt Street; 2, 3, 4, 5 to Nevins Street. Open Seatings 7pm & 7.45pm Tue, Wed; 6pm, 6.45pm, 9.30pm & 9.55pm Thur-Sat. Prix fixe $255.

The Elm French
The ingenious and notoriously bullish Paul Liebrandt recently departed Tribeca's Corton – and the two Michelin stars he earned there – to bring a softened rendition of his art-cum-cuisine to the gleaming King & Grove hotel. Bare-wood tables and a wall of living vines make for pleasant gazing, but the tidy room feels as sterile and listless as an architectural rendering. A deeply soothing shellfish stew was anchored by brackish seaweed butter and crowned with a meaty hunk of halibut-like amadai, whose feathery scales boast a 'how did he do that?' crunch. On occasion, function succumbs to form on Liebrandt's painterly plates. Yet despite its fussiness, Liebrandt's food is too inspired to be stifled by the bland space.
160 North 12th Street, between Bedford Avenue & Berry Street, Williamsburg (1-718 218 1088, www.theelmnyc.com). Subway L to Bedford Avenue. Open 7am-11am, 6-10pm Mon-Wed; 7am-11am, 6-11pm Thur-Sat; 7am-10.45am, 11.30am-3pm, 6-10pm Sun. Main courses $18-$26.

Four & Twenty Blackbirds Café
Emily and Melissa Elsen, the South Dakota-reared sisters who opened this cult bakery, learned pie-baking from their grandma, and her expert instruction is evident in varieties like lemon chess, salted caramel apple and the rich chocolate-and-custard Black Bottom Oatmeal. Settle in at one of the communal tables in the homey space and savour a slice.
439 Third Avenue, at 8th Street, Gowanus (1-718 499 2917, www.birdsblack.com). Subway F, G, R to Fourth Ave-9th Street. Open 8am-7pm Mon-Fri; 9am-7pm Sat; 10am-6pm Sun. Pie $5.25/slice.

Frankies 457 Spuntino Italian
This casual eaterie was an instant classic when it debuted in Carroll Gardens in 2004. The mavericks behind the place – collectively referred to as 'the Franks' Castronovo and Falcinelli went on to become neighbourhood pillars, opening German-leaning steakhouse Prime Meats down the block and a coffee shop, Café Pedlar, in Cobble Hill. But their flagship remains

Grange Bar & Eatery. *See p61.*

s alluring as ever, turning out an mpressive selection of cheeses, ntipasti and cured meats, distinctive alads and exceptional pastas to a nostly local crowd. Cavatelli with hot ausage and browned sage butter is a taple, as are the flawless meatballs – eather-light orbs stuffed into a andwich or served solo.
57 Court Street, between Lucquer treet & 4th Place, Carroll Gardens (1- '18 403 0033, www.frankiesspuntino. om). Subway F, G to Carroll Street.)pen 11am-11pm Mon-Thur, Sun; 1am-midnight Fri, Sat. Main courses 15-$20.

ilasserie Eclectic
n an old industrial glass factory, Sara ramer (Reynard, Blue Hill) and Sara onklin (Cipriani) bring a touch of the reezy Mediterranean coast to the ritty Greenpoint waterfront. Kramer versees a small-plates spread with a eavy emphasis on produce sourced om Pennsylvania's Lancaster Farm nd upstate's Blooming Hill Farm. he menu spans Spain, Greece and ne Middle East, in dishes such as imb tartare alongside bulgur rackers, and a whole rabbit for two, erved with flaky flatbread. At the orseshoe-shaped bar, the wine list ocuses on exotic locales, including roatia, Portugal and Morocco, and ocktails follow suit, spiced with igredients like Aleppo peppers and uddled mint. Sea-foam-green walls onjure the ocean, and potted plants nliven the rustic 72-seat interior, utfitted in whitewashed brick and ramed catalogue prints from the rstwhile factory. A terrace, ransformed from the loading dock, rovides coastal breezes.
5 Commercial Street, between lox Street & Manhattan Avenue, reenpoint (1-718 389 0640, ww.glasserienyc.com). Subway G to reenpoint Avenue. Open 5.30-11pm lon-Thur; 5.30pm-midnight Fri; 0am-4pm, 5.30pm-midnight Sat; 0am-4pm, 5.30-11pm Sun. Shared lates $19-$22.

uliana's Pizza
or years, Manhattanites and tourists ave crossed the Brooklyn Bridge and ned up for pizza at venerated Dumbo xture Grimaldi's – but they may not e aware that founder Patsy Grimaldi old the place more than a decade ago. 2012, he burst out of retirement to eclaim his shop's first location, along ith its original coal oven. This time, rimaldi – who learned to spin dough t age 13 in his Uncle Patsy Lancieri's larlem institution – named the spot fter his mother. At Juliana's, the menu potlights iconic red-sauce fare, icluding classic pizzas, such as ausage and broccoli rabe. But he's also ixed in a few nods to modern times: reative pizzas (such as a bagel-like riff rith lox and goat cheese) and a roprietary chocolate-and-raspberry avour from nearby Brooklyn Ice ream Factory. Another throwback ouch: an antique jukebox plays Patsy's avourite Sinatra tunes.

19 Old Fulton Street, between Front & Water Streets, Dumbo (1-718 596 6700, www.julianaspizza.com). Subway A, C to High Street; F to York Street. Open 11.30am-11pm daily. Pizzas $16-$30.

Madiba Restaurant
South African
Brooklyn's first South African eaterie honours the spirit of the late Nelson Mandela – Madiba is the legendary leader's clan name. Wooden chairs and folk art grace the convivial, high-ceilinged space, and live music ranges from Afrobeat to Afropop. The menu features fragrant curries and stews, as well as offbeat eats like thin, pleasantly gamey ostrich carpaccio and spicy prawns piri piri. The safari platter, loaded with cured, salted and dried beef tenderloin, is a presidential feast.
195 DeKalb Avenue, between Carlton Avenue & Adelphi Street, Fort Greene (1-718 855 9190, www.madiba restaurant.com). C to Lafayette Avenue; C, G to Clinton-Washington Avenues. Open 11am-11pm Mon- Thur, Sun; 11am-midnight Fri, Sat. Main courses $13-$25.

Marlow & Sons American
creative
In this charming oyster bar, restaurant and café, diners wolf down market- fresh salads, succulent brick chicken and the creative crostini of the moment (such as goat's cheese with flash-fried strawberries). In the back, an oyster shucker cracks open the catch of the day, while the bartender mixes the kind of potent drinks that helped to make the owners' earlier ventures (including the next-door Diner, a tricked-out 1920s dining car) successes.
81 Broadway, between Berry Street & Wythe Avenue, Williamsburg (1-718 384 1441, www.marlowand sons.com). Subway J, M, Z to Marcy Avenue. Open 8am-midnight daily. Main courses $20-$30.

Mile End Deli Canadian
New Yorkers have pastrami, Montrealers have smoked meat – luscious brisket that's been dry- rubbed, cured, smoked, steamed and hand cut, resulting in flavourful, delicious slices bound for mustard- slathered rye. This Montreal-style deli from Québécois Noah Bernamoff and his wife, Rae Cohen, serves the sandwiches in old-school fashion, along with other regional specialities – like the excellent poutine (including a smoked-meat riff), and, at brunch, a killer hash.
97A Hoyt Street, between Atlantic Avenue and Pacific Street, Boerum Hill (1-718 852 7510, www. enddeli.com). Subway A, C, G to Hoyt-Schermerhorn; 2, 3 to Hoyt Street. Open 11am-4pm, 5pm- midnight Tue-Fri; 10am-4pm, 5pm-midnight Sat; 10am-4pm, 5-10pm Sun. Sandwiches $9-$14. Other location 53 Bond Street, between Bowery & Lafayette Street, East Village (1-212 529 2990).

Glasserie

Nathan's Famous American
Opened in 1916, the famed frank joint has retained its subway tiles and iconic signage, as well as staples like crinkle- cut fries and thick-battered corn dogs. But there's one shiny 'new' addition: a curbside clam bar, a revival of the restaurant's 1950s raw bar. East Coast oysters and littlenecks are shucked over a mountain of ice, served with chowder crackers, lemon wedges, sinus-clearing horseradish and cocktail sauce.
1310 Surf Avenue, at Stillwell Avenue, Coney Island (1-718 333 2202, www. nathansfamous.com). Subway D, F, N, Q to Coney Island-Stillwell Avenue. Open 9am-midnight Mon-Thur, Sun; 9am-1am Fri, Sat. Hot dogs $3.50.

No.7 Eclectic
Given the constraints of this restaurant's tiny kitchen, chef Tyler Kord's eclectic cuisine – influenced by Asian and Eastern European flavours among others – is impressively bold. The menu changes frequently; on a recent visit, an unforgettable starter of crisp broccoli tempura was served with black-bean purée and a vinegary, citrus-spiked salad, and a hanger steak entrée featured pink slices of beef and toothsome kimchi-stuffed pierogi.
7 Greene Avenue, between Cumberland & Fulton Streets, Fort Greene (1-718 522 6370, www.no7restaurant.com). C to Lafayette Avenue; C, G to Clinton- Washington Avenues. Open 5.30- 11pm Tue-Fri; noon-3pm, 5.30-11pm Sat; noon-3pm, 4-9pm Sun. Main courses $16-$25.

Northeast Kingdom American
The mood inside this 28-seat eaterie is half cabin in the woods (wide-plank wood floors, clunky butcher-block tables) and half Grandma's living room (quaint sconces). In keeping with the country vibe, chef Kevin Adey uses meat and produce from local farms, including Brooklyn Grange, and

foraged ingredients. The seasonal menu features such elevated fare as Hudson Valley foie gras and Rhode Island scallops alongside classics like an excellent burger.
18 Wyckoff Avenue, at Troutman Street, Bushwick (1-718 386 3864, www.north-eastkingdom.com). Subway L to Jefferson Street. Open 11.30am-2.30pm, 6-11pm Mon-Wed; 11.30am-2.30pm, 6-11.30pm Thur, Fri; 11am-3pm, 6-11.30pm Sat; 11am-3pm, 6-11pm Sun. Main courses $15-$30.

One Girl Cookies Café
Dawn Casale started baking cookies out of her Greenwich Village apartment in 2000 (hence the name), before hiring chef David Crofton to help – now married, they run two bakery-cafés. Pair your tea cookies or a whoopie pie with Red Hook-roasted Stumptown coffee. The spot also serves a rotating selection of craft beer, wine and snacks, such as a cheese plate in collaboration with Stinky Bklyn.
33 Main Street, at Water Street, Dumbo (1-347 338 1268, www. onegirlcookies.com). Subway A, C to High Street; F to York Street. Open 8am-7pm Mon-Thur; 8am-8pm Fri; 9am-8pm Sat; 9am-7pm Sun. Cookies $2.75-$4. Other location 68 Dean Street, between Smith Street & Boerum Place, Cobble Hill (1-212 675 4996).

Peter Luger Steakhouse
At Luger's old-school steakhouse, the choice is limited, but the porterhouse is justly famed. Choose from various sizes, from a small single steak to 'steak for four'. Although a slew of Luger copycats have prospered in the last several years, none has captured the elusive charm of this stucco- walled, beer hall-style eaterie, with worn wooden floors and tables, and waiters in waistcoats and bow ties.
178 Broadway, at Driggs Avenue, Williamsburg (1-718 387 7400,

www.peterluger.com). Subway J, M, Z to Marcy Avenue. Open 11.45am-10pm Mon-Thur; 11.45am-10.45pm Fri, Sat; 12.45-9.45pm Sun. Steaks $49-$199. No credit cards.

Pok Pok NY Thai
James Beard Award-winning chef Andy Ricker's Brooklyn restaurant replicates the indigenous dives of Chiang Mai – a seasonal outdoor dining area is festooned with dangling plants, colourful oilcloths on the tables and second-hand seats. But what separates Pok Pok from other cultish Thai restaurants is the curatorial role of its minutiae-mad chef. Ricker highlights a host of surprisingly mild northern-Thai dishes, including a delicious sweet-and-sour Burmese-inflected pork curry, *kaeng hung leh*. His *khao soi*, the beloved meal-in-a-bowl from Chiang Mai – chicken noodle soup delicately spiced with yellow curry and topped with fried noodles for crunch – is accompanied here with raw shallots and pickled mustard greens.
117 Columbia Street, at Kane Street, Cobble Hill (1-718 923 9322, www.pokpokny.com). Subway F, G to Bergen Street. Open 5.30-10.30pm daily. Main courses $10-$21.

Reynard American
The Wythe Hotel's sprawling restaurant is a Balthazar for Brooklyn, urbane and ambitious, mature and low-key. Its chef, Sean Rembold, serves casual breakfast and lunch to a drop-in crowd, including a terrifically earthy grass-fed burger. His menu, which changes often – sometimes daily – becomes much more serious at night. There's no fanfare at any time to his spare list of dishes, no trendy buzzwords, barely any descriptions at all. Rembold's thoughtful food, portioned to satisfy and priced to move, mostly speaks for itself.
Wythe Hotel, 80 Wythe Avenue, at North 11th Street, Williamsburg (1-718 460 8004,www.wythehotel. com). Subway L to Bedford Avenue. Open 7am-midnight daily. Main courses $20-$30.

Roberta's Italian
This sprawling hangout has become the unofficial meeting place for Brooklyn's sustainable-food movement. Opened in 2008 by a trio of friends, Roberta's has its own on-site garden that provides some of the ingredients for its locally sourced dishes. The pizzas – like the Cheeses Christ, topped with mozzarella, taleggio, parmesan, black pepper and cream – are among Brooklyn's finest. The team recently opened Blanca, a sleek spot in the back, to showcase chef Carlo Mirarchi's acclaimed evening-only tasting menu (6-9pm Wed-Fri; 5-8pm Sat; $195).
261 Moore Street, between Bogart & White Streets, Bushwick (1-718 417 1118, www.robertaspizza.com). Subway L to Morgan Avenue. Open 11am-midnight Mon-Fri; 10am-midnight Sat, Sun. Pizzas $9-$16.

Vinegar Hill House American
As it's tucked away in a residential street in the forgotten namesake neighbourhood (now essentially part of Dumbo), tracking down Vinegar Hill House engenders a treasure-hunt thrill. In the cosy, tavern-like space, the daily-changing menu focuses on seasonal comfort foods. In the warmer months, linger over brunch in the secluded back garden.
72 Hudson Avenue, between Front & Water Streets, Dumbo (1-718 522 1018, www.vinegarhillhouse.com). Subway A, C to High Street; F to York Street. Open 6-11pm Mon-Thur; 6-11.30pm Fri; 10.30am-3.30pm, 6-11.30pm Sat; 10.30am-3.30pm, 5.30-11pm Sun. Main courses $16-$30.

Queens

Fu Run Chinese
Thanks to a change in immigration patterns, Flushing has seen an increase in Northern Chinese restaurants like Fu Run, whose owners are from Dongbei (what was once known as Manchuria). They call their justly celebrated dish the 'Muslim lamb chop', but it's more like a half rack of ribs: a platter of bone-in, fatty meat is braised, then battered and deep-fried, the whole juicy slab blanketed with cumin seeds, chilli powder and flakes, and black and white sesame seeds.
40-09 Prince Street between Roosevelt Avenue and 40th Road, Flushing (1-718 321 1363, www.furunflushing. com). Subway 7 to Flushing-Main Street. Open 11.30am-midnight daily. Main courses $10-$23.

Jackson Diner Indian
Harried waiters and Formica-topped tables evoke a diner experience at this weekend meet-and-eat headquarters for New York's Indian expat community. Watch Hindi soaps on Zee TV while enjoying *samosa chat* topped with chickpeas, yoghurt, onion, tomato, and a sweet-spicy mix of tamarind and mint chutneys. Specials such as *murgh tikka makhanwala*, tender pieces of marinated chicken simmered in curry and cream, are fiery and flavourful – ask for mild if you're susceptible to chilli.
37-47 74th Street, between 37th Avenue & 37th Road, Jackson Heights (1-718 672 1232, www.jacksondiner.com). Subway E, F, M, R to Jackson Heights-Roosevelt Avenue; 7 to 74th Street-Broadway. Open 11.30am-10pm Mon-Thur, Sun; 11.30am-10.30pm Fri, Sat. Main courses $10-$22.

M Wells Steakhouse
Steakhouse/Eclectic
Just after we got hooked on the eccentric, carnivorous fare and penchant for excess at the original M Wells, the renegade LIC diner gave up its lease, and one of the most exciting restaurants New York had seen in years disappeared. Quirk power couple Hugue Dufour and Sarah Obraitis opened a more subdued venture – MoMA PS1's lunchtime cafeteria, M Wells Dinette – in 2012. But M Wells Steakhouse is their full-fledged return. Housed in a former auto-body shop, the spot splices class with irreverence; black-tie waiters and a besuited sommelier dart around a room where trout swim in a concrete tank and Canadian-lumberjack movies project onto the wall. Charred iceberg salad, with creamy blue-cheese dressing and sweet dehydrated ketchup meringue chips, is a striking, whimsical wedge. The likes of dry-aged Nebraska *côte de boeuf* for two recall the gluttonous communal spirit of the first M Wells, while other dishes capture the madcap opulence that made it special.
43-15 Crescent Street, between 43rd Avenue & 44th Drive, Long Island City (1-718 786 9060, www.magasinwells. com). Subway N, Q, 7 to Queensboro Plaza. Open 5.30-11.30pm Mon, Wed-Sat; 5.30-10.30pm Sun. Main courses $17-$75.

The Queens Kickshaw Café
Serious java draws caffeine fiends to this airy café, which also specialises in grilled cheese sandwiches. While the pedigreed beans – from Counter Culture Coffee – are brewed with Hario V60 drip cones and a La Marzocco Strada espresso machine, there's no coffee-snob attitude here. Fancy grilled cheese choices include a weekend-morning offering of soft egg folded with ricotta, a gruyère crisp and maple hot sauce between thick, buttery slices of brioche.
40-17 Broadway, between Steinway & 41st Streets, Astoria (1-718 777 0913, www.thequeenskickshaw.com). Subway M, R to Steinway Street. Open 7.30am-1am Mon-Fri; 9am-1am Sat, Sun. Sandwiches $8-$11.

Spicy & Tasty Chinese
Any serious trip to Flushing for spicy Szechuan food should begin here. Revered by in-the-know regulars, this brightly lit eatery serves plates of peppercorn-laden pork and lamb swimming in a chilli sauce that's sure to set even the most seasoned palate aflame. Stock up on cold-bar options, like zesty sesame noodles, crunchy chopped cucumbers and smooth, delicate tofu – you'll need the relief. Service is speedy and mercifully attentive to water requests.
39-07 Prince Street, between Roosevelt & 39th Avenues, Flushing (1-718 359 1601, www.spicyandtasty.com). Subway 7 to Flushing-Main Street. Open 11.30am-10.30pm Mon-Thur, Sun; 11.30am-11pm Fri, Sat. Main courses $9-$19. No credit cards.

Zenon Taverna Greek
The faux-stone entryway and murals of ancient ruins don't detract from the Mediterranean charm of this humble place that's been serving Greek and Cypriot food for more than 25 years. Specials rotate daily, embracing all the classics – stuffed grape leaves, *keftedes* (Cypriot meatballs), *spanakopita* (spinach pie) – and less ubiquitous dishes such as rabbit stew and plump *loukaniko* (pork sausages). Filling sweets include *galaktopoureko* (syrupy layers of filo baked with custard cream).
34-10 31st Avenue, at 34th Street, Astoria (1-718 956 0133, www.zenontaverna.com). Subway N, Q to Broadway. Open noon-11pm daily. Main courses $11-$18. No credit cards.

The Bronx

Dominick's Italian
At Charlie DiPaolo's pinewood dining room – one of the most popular on Arthur Avenue – neighbourhood folks, out-of-towners and tracksuited wiseguys feast at long, crowded tables on massive platters of veal parmigiana, steaming bowls of mussels marinara and linguine with white clam sauce. There's no written menu, but you can trust your waiter's advice.
2335 Arthur Avenue, between Crescent Avenue & E 186th Street, 1-718 733 2807). Subway B, D, 4 to Fordham Road, then Bx12 bus to Arthur Avenue. Open noon-10pm Mon, Wed, Thur, Sat; noon-11pm Fri; 1-9pm Sun. Main courses $15-$42. No credit cards

Mario's Italian
The Migliucci family has stayed in business since 1919 by pleasing the customer; if you don't see what you want on the menu, feel free to ask for embellishments or modifications to the Neapolitan-inspired cuisine. Do as the regulars do and order the signature gnocchi, which arrive perfectly light and plump with a deliciously savoury and tangy sauce. For something more hearty, try the *saltimbocca alla romana* (veal braised in Marsala wine and served over spinach sautéed with prosciutto).
2342 Arthur Avenue, between Crescent Avenue & E 186th Street (1-718 584 1188, www.mariosrest arthurave.com). Subway B, D, 4 to Fordham Road, then Bx12 bus to Arthur Avenue. Open noon-9pm Tue-Thur, Sun; noon-10pm Fri, Sat. Main courses $13.75-$35.

Mike's Deli Café/Deli
This venerable delicatessen, overstocked butcher and café may leave you paralysed with indecision: the glossy menu lists more than 50 sandwiches, plus platters, pastas, soups, salads, *stromboli* (a kind of cheese turnover) and sides. Try the Yankee Stadium Big Boy hero sandwich, filled with prosciutto, soppressata, mozzarella, capicola, mortadella, peppers and lettuce.
Arthur Avenue Retail Market, 2344 Arthur Avenue, between Crescent Avenue & E 186th Street (1-718 295 5033, www.arthuravenue.com). Subway B, D, 4 to Fordham Road, then Bx12 bus to Arthur Avenue. Open 7am-7pm Mon-Wed; 7am-9pm Thur-Sat; 10am-7pm Sun. Sandwiches $6.50-$13.

Bars

Milk & Honey. See p68.

The big tipple

Choose your poison, neighbourhood and vibe.

New York continues to be a cradle of cocktail culture. Standard bearers like Audrey Saunders' renowned **Pegu Club** (see right) still offer fine drinks, but new life is brought to the scene by newcomers, including **Attaboy** (see p66), a sultry den in the former Milk and Honey space from two of its longtime bartenders, the **Dead Rabbit** (see right), a Financial District barroom with a sprawling historical menu, and 1970s homage **Golden Cadillac** (see p66). The craft-beer revolution that's swept the country has a firm foothold in NYC, too. Scrappy producers in Brooklyn and, recently, Queens (see p69), have brought attention to the local brewing scene. The most dependable spots to sample the local offerings are hops-head havens like **Jimmy's No 43** (see p66) and **Blind Tiger Ale House** (see p67), while the pint-size den **Proletariat** (see p67) offers an intimate experience. Recent Brooklyn arrival **Tørst** (see p71), meanwhile, elevates beer-drinking to new heights.

While wine doesn't drive the boozing scene like cocktails and beer, a new breed of vino bars is tossing out the pretence and putting an emphasis on well-chosen but affordable lists. The poster child of this movement is **Terroir** (see p67), which opened its fourth location in Park Slope, Brooklyn, after conquering the East Village, Tribeca and Murray Hill.

For gay bars, see pp92-93.

The Financial District

Dead Rabbit Grocery & Grog
At this time-capsule nook, you can drink like a boss – Boss Tweed, that is. Belfast bar vets Sean Muldoon and Jack McGarry have conjured up a rough-and-tumble 19th-century tavern in a red-brick landmark. Resurrecting long-forgotten quaffs is nothing new in NYC, but the Dead Rabbit's sheer breadth of mid 19th-century libations eclipses the competition, spanning 100-odd bishops, fixes, nogs and smashes. The fruit-forward Byrrh Wine Daisy, era-appropriate in its china teacup with moustache guard, is particularly well wrought. *30 Water Street, at Broad Street (1-646 422 7906, www.deadrabbitnyc.com). Subway R to Whitehall Street-South Ferry. Open 11am-4am daily.*

Watermark
Sip local craft beers accompanied by sea-inspired bar bites like lobster rolls and crab cakes at this contemporary waterfront bar – the skyline views through the floor-to-ceiling windows are spectacular. In summer, the bar also doles out cones of Ben & Jerry's ice-cream, sorbets and frozen yoghurt, fit for indulging your inner kid as you soak up rays on the outdoor deck. *Pier 15, between Fletcher Street & Maiden Lane (1-212 742 8200, www.watermarkny.com). Subway A, C, J, Z, 2, 3, 4, 5 to Fulton Street; 2, 3 to Wall Street. Open Apr-Dec 11am-11pm daily. Jan-Mar 11am-6pm daily.*

Bohemian Hall & Beer Garden

Critic's choice

1 **Golden Cadillac** Indulge in guilty-pleasure cocktails at this homage to '70s tippling. See p66.

2 **PDT** The 'secret' entrance only thrills once, but the drinks warrant return visits. See p67.

3 **Terroir** Well-picked wines and nibbles in a down-to-earth setting. See p67.

4 **The Commodore** The ultimate Brooklyn neo-dive. See p70.

5 **Bohemian Hall & Beer Garden** Experience a remnant of Queens' quaffing history. See p71.

Soho & Tribeca

Pegu Club
Audrey Saunders, the drinks maven who turned Bemelmans Bar (see p69) into one of the city's most respected cocktail lounges, is behind this sleek liquid destination. Tucked away on the second floor, the sophisticated spot was inspired by a British officers' club in Burma. The cocktail list features classics culled from decades-old booze bibles, and gin is the key ingredient – these are serious drinks for grown-up tastes. *2nd Floor, 77 W Houston Street, at West Broadway (1-212 473 7348, www.peguclub.com). Subway B, D, F, M to Broadway-Lafayette Street; N, R to Prince Street. Open 5pm-2am Mon-Thur, Sun; 5pm-4am Fri, Sat.*

Weather Up Tribeca
At Kathryn Weatherup's tony Manhattan drinkery, a spin-off of her popular Prospect Heights bar, the well-balanced cocktail list features a regularly rotating mix of classics and

original quaffs. Pair the booze with smart snacks such as grilled cheese sandwiches and steak tartare.
159 Duane Street, between Hudson Street & West Broadway (1-212 766 3202, www.weatherupnyc.com). Subway 1, 2, 3 to Chambers Street. Open 5pm-2am daily.
Other location 589 Vanderbilt Avenue, between Bergen & Dean Streets, Prospect Heights, Brooklyn (no phone).

Chinatown, Little Italy & Nolita

Mother's Ruin
At this airy Nolita drinkery, co-owners Timothy Lynch and Richard Knapp bring in a rotating cast of star bartenders to sling classic and contemporary drinks. The laid-back space – done up with a cream tin ceiling, exposed brick and weathered-wood bar – also offers a full menu of globally inflected bites.
18 Spring Street, between Elizabeth & Mott Streets (no phone, www.mothers ruinnyc.com). Subway J, Z to Bowery; 6 to Spring Street. Open 11am-4am Mon-Fri; noon-4am Sat, Sun.

Lower East Side

Attaboy
Occupying the original Milk and Honey (*see p68*) digs and run by alums Sam Ross and Michael McIlroy, Attaboy has a livelier, lighter air than Sasha Petraske's big-league cocktail den. The tucked-away haunt has kept the same bespoke protocol as its forebear: at the brushed-steel bar, suspender-clad drinks slingers stir off-the-cuff riffs to suit each customer's preference. Wistful boozers can seek solace in Petraske-era standard-bearers, like Ross's signature Penicillin, a still-inspiring blend of Laphroaig ten-year, honey-ginger syrup and lemon.
134 Eldridge Street, between Broome & Delancey Streets (no phone). Subway F to Delancey Street; J, M, Z to Delancey-Essex Streets. Open 6.45pm-3.30am daily.

Back Room
For access to this ersatz speakeasy, look for a sign that reads 'The Lower East Side Toy Company'. Pass through the gate, walk down an alleyway, up a metal staircase and open an unmarked door to find a convincing replica of a 1920s watering hole. Cocktails are poured into teacups, and bottled beer is brown-bagged before being served. Patrons must be 25 or older on Fridays and Saturdays. The dress code is casual, but note that in a departure from the Jazz Age sensibility, real fur is banned in the bar.
102 Norfolk Street, between Delancey & Rivington Streets (1-212 228 5098).

Nostalgic for the 1970s, drinks historian Greg Boehm (owner of barware emporium Cocktail Kingdom) and James True (former manager of the Pegu Club) have joined forces for this ode to the seedy decade. At the 55-seat spot – outfitted with a wooden canopy bar and patterned wallpaper – the powerhouse duo revives maligned classics like the Harvey Wallbanger, whiskey sour and Disco Daiquiri (a frosty mix of overproof rum, lime and sugar). To match the throwback quaffs, executive chef Miguel Trinidad crafts a menu of retro comfort eats from vintage food magazines – devilled eggs, a shrimp Louie salad with Treasure Island dressing, and deep-fried Monte Cristo sliders with maple syrup.
13 First Avenue, at 1st Street (1-212 995 5151, www.goldencadillac nyc.com). Subway F to Lower East Side-Second Avenue. Open 5pm-2am Mon-Wed; 5pm-4am Thur-Fri; 11am-4am Sat; 11am-2am Sun.

Subway F to Delancey Street; J, M, Z to Delancey-Essex Streets. Open 7.30pm-3am Mon-Thur, Sun; 7.30pm-4am Fri, Sat.

Loreley
Perhaps bar owner Michael Momm, aka DJ Foosh, wanted a place where he could spin to his heart's content. Maybe he missed the *biergartens* of his youth in Cologne. Whatever. Just rejoice that he opened Loreley. Twelve draughts and eight bottled varieties of Germany's finest brews are available, along with wines from the country's Loreley region and a full roster of spirits. Or try one of the speciality cocktails, such as the Zimtschnitte with Captain Morgan, Cointreau, cinnamon and fresh orange.
7 Rivington Street, between Bowery & Chrystie Street (1-212 253 7077, www.loreleynyc.com). Subway J, Z to Bowery. Open noon-1am Mon, Tue, Sun; noon-2am Wed; noon-3am Thur; noon-4am Fri, Sat.

Spitzer's Corner
Referencing the Lower East Side's pickle-making heritage, the walls at this rustic gastropub are made from salvaged wooden barrels. The formidable beer list – 40 rotating draughts – includes New York's Southern Tier IPA. Mull over your selection, with the help of appetising tasting notes, at one of the wide communal tables. The gastro end of things is manifest in the menu of quality pub grub, such as truffle mac and cheese or grilled fish sliders.
101 Rivington Street, at Ludlow Street (1-212 228 0027, www.spitzers corner.com). Subway F to Delancey Street; J, M, Z to Delancey-Essex Streets. Open noon-4am Mon-Fri; 10am-4am Sat, Sun.

Two-Bit's Retro Arcade
Joystick addicts, take note: this gamer haven offers titles dating back to the 1980s (Pac-Man, Popeye, Final Fight, Donkey Kong), as well as pinball (Fun House, Twilight Zone). After you've grabbed a beer, pause for a moment to admire the video-game-character illustrations inlaid in the bar. One tip: try to make it here by early evening, before the lines to play become three dudes deep.
153 Essex Street, between Rivington & Stanton Streets (1-212 477 8161, www.twobitsretroarcade.com). Subway F to Lower East Side-Second Avenue; J, M, Z to Delancey-Essex Streets. Open 5pm-2am Mon-Thur; 5pm-4am Fri; 1pm-4am Sat; 1pm-2am Sun.

East Village

Booker and Dax
This tech-forward cocktail joint, housed next to Momofuku Ssäm Bar (*see p54*), showcases the boozy tinkerings of wizardly Dave Arnold, the International Culinary Center

director of culinary technology. Glasses are chilled with a pour of liquid nitrogen, and winter warmers, like the Friend of the Devil (Campari, sweet vermouth, rye, Pernod, bitters, absinthe), are scorched with a Red Hot Poker, a rod with a built-in 1,500-degree heater created by Arnold. He also showcases new techniques for creating fizzy drinks, like the Gin and Juice, made with Tanqueray gin and grapefruit juice that is clarified in a centrifuge, then carbonated in a CO_2-pressurised cocktail shaker.
207 Second Avenue, at 13th Street (entrance on 13th Street) (1-212 254 3500, www.momofuku.com). Subway L to Third Ave; L, N, Q, R, 4, 5, 6 to 14th Street-Union Square. Open 6pm-2am Mon-Thur, Sun; 6pm-3am Fri, Sat.

Bourgeois Pig
Ornate mirrors and antique chairs give this small, red-lit wine and fondue joint a decidedly decadent feel. The wine list is well chosen, and although the hard stuff is verboten here, mixed concoctions based on wine, champagne or beer – such as the Provence Punch, featuring champagne, elderflower, white peach, lemon and orange bitters – cater to cocktail aficionados.
111 E 7th Street, between First Avenue & Avenue A (1-212 475 2246, www. bourgeoispigny.com). Subway F to Lower East Side-Second Avenue; 6 to Astor Place. Open 6pm-2am daily.

Death & Company
The nattily attired mixologists are deadly serious about drinks at this pseudo speakeasy with gothic flair (don't be intimidated by the imposing wooden door). Black walls and cushy booths combine with chandeliers to set a luxuriously sombre mood. The inventive cocktails are matched by top-notch food, including crispy oysters with pickled jalapeño relish and lime cream.
433 E 6th Street, between First Avenue & Avenue A (1-212 388 0882, www. deathandcompany.com). Subway F to Lower East Side-Second Avenue; 6 to Astor Place. Open 6pm-2am Mon-Thur, Sun; 6pm-3am Fri, Sat.

Elsa
At this stylish *boîte*, named for the iconoclastic 1930s clothing designer Elsa Schiaparelli, nods to couture include framed fashion sketches and three tap lines that flow through a vintage sewing machine. Perch on a white wooden banquette to enjoy speciality cocktails such as the Black Book (bourbon, jalapeño and spices, including cinnamon and cardamom).
217 E 3rd Street, between Avenues B & C (1-917 882 7395, www.elsabar. com). Subway F to Lower East Side-Second Avenue. Open 6pm-4am daily.

Jimmy's No. 43
You could easily miss this worthy subterranean spot if it weren't for the sign painted on a doorway over an inconspicuous set of stairs. Descend them and you'll encounter burnt-

Bars

ellow walls displaying taxidermy, mismatched wood tables and medieval-style arched passageways that lead to different rooms. Beer is a big attraction here, with about a dozen quality selections on tap (and more in the bottle), many of which also make it into the slow-food dishes filled with organic ingredients.
3 E 7th Street, between Second & Third Avenues (1-212 982 3006, www.jimmysno43.com). Subway F to Lower East Side-Second Avenue; 6 to Astor Place. Open noon-2am Mon-Thur; noon-4am Fri, Sat; 1.30am-2am Sun.

Mayahuel
Tequila and its cousin, mezcal, are the focus at this haute cantina. The inventive cocktail menu features the Red Baron, a smoky, spicy mix of mezcal, red pepper, basil, lemon, absinthe and cayenne salt. The East 8th cocktail is a liquid campfire of tequila, Jamaican rum, apple brandy, sweet vermouth, cynar and smoked salt. The craftsmanship in the drinks is equalled in the bar menu, which features juicy pork bellies with papaya and mango salsa.
304 E 6th Street, between First & Second Avenues (1-212 253 5888, www.mayahuelny.com). Subway F to Lower East Side-Second Avenue; 6 to Astor Place. Open 6pm-2am daily.

McSorley's Old Ale House
Ladies should probably leave the Blahniks at home. In traditional Irish-pub fashion, McSorley's floor has been thoroughly scattered with sawdust to take care of the spills and other messes that often accompany the consumption of large quantities of cheap beer. Established in 1854, McSorley's became an institution by remaining steadfastly authentic and providing only two choices: McSorley's Dark Ale and McSorley's Light Ale.
15 E 7th Street, between Second & Third Avenues (1-212 473 9148,

www.mcsorleysnewyork.com). Subway F to Lower East Side-Second Avenue. Open 11am-1am Mon-Sat; 1pm-1am Sun. No credit cards.

PDT
Word has gotten out about 'Please Don't Tell', the faux speakeasy inside gourmet hot dog joint Crif Dogs (*see p54*), so it's a good idea to reserve a booth in advance. Once you arrive, you'll notice people lingering outside an old wooden phonebooth near the front. Slip inside, pick up the receiver and the host opens a secret panel to the dark, narrow space. The serious cocktails surpass the gimmicky entry: try the house old-fashioned, made with bacon-infused bourbon, which leaves a smoky aftertaste.
113 St Marks Place, between First Avenue & Avenue A (1-212 614 0386, www.pdtnyc.com). Subway L to First Avenue; 6 to Astor Place. Open 6pm-2am Mon-Thur, Sun; 6pm-4am Fri, Sat.

Proletariat
Proletariat is a much-deserved look into no-holds-barred beer geekdom, blissfully free of TVs and generic pub grub. With just 12 stools and a space so tight that clunky menus have been replaced with a QR code (scan it with your smartphone), brewhounds get the type of intimacy usually afforded only to the cocktail and wine crowds. The expert servers have a story for every keg they tap, from the newest local brews to obscure New Zealand ales and deep cuts from the Belgian canon. Sure, the name out front may feel ironic when you're sipping a $10 pour of a Norwegian saison you can't pronounce, but Gotham's beer scene is ready for a place that doesn't compromise.

102 St Marks Place, between First Avenue & Avenue A (1-212 777 6707, www.proletariatny.com). Subway 6 to Astor Place. Open 5pm-2am daily.

Terroir
The surroundings are stripped-back basic at this wine-bar offspring of nearby restaurant Hearth – the focus is squarely on the drinks. Co-owner and oeno-evangelist Paul Grieco preaches the powers of *terroir* – grapes that express a sense of place – and the knowledgeable waitstaff deftly help patrons to navigate nearly 50 by-the-glass options. Pair the stellar sips with the restaurant-calibre small plates.
413 E 12th Street, between First Avenue & Avenue A (1-646 602 1300, www.wineisterroir.com). Subway L to First Avenue; L, N, Q, R, 4, 5, 6 to 14th Street-Union Square. Open 5pm-2am Mon-Sat; 5pm-midnight Sun. Other locations 24 Harrison Street, between Greenwich & Hudson Streets, Tribeca (1-212 625 9463); 439 Third Avenue, between 30th & 31st Streets, Murray Hill (1-212 481 1920); 284 Fifth Avenue, at 1st Street, Park Slope, Brooklyn (1-718 832 9463).

The Wayland
East Village boozers have been stumbling further down the alphabet for years now, but it's taken evolving Avenue C time to develop the critical mass necessary to attract a late-night buzz. At this fun-loving bar, solicitous staff, a young and attractive crowd and the likelihood of a spontaneous sing-along around the piano all contribute to a convivial vibe that makes you want to call for another round. An old-fashioned riff called I Hear Banjos ($12) – made with apple pie moonshine, rye whiskey and apple-spice bitters – comes with

a ceremonious puff of applewood smoke, captured in an overturned glass that's placed over the drink.
700 E 9th Street, at Avenue C (1-212 777 7022, www.thewaylandnyc.com). Subway L to First Avenue. Open 5pm-4am daily.

TOP TIP!
Where there's smoke…
There are still a few bars where you can light up, including Circa Tabac (32 Watts Street, between Sixth Avenue & Thompson Street, Soho, 1-212 941 1781).

Greenwich Village & West Village

Blind Tiger Ale House
Brew geeks descend upon this hops heaven for boutique ales and more than two dozen daily rotating, hard-to-find drafts (like Southern Tier Krampus and Singlecut Half-Stack). The clubby room features windows that open on to the street. Late afternoons and early evenings are ideal for serious sippers enjoying plates of Murray's Cheese, while the after-dark set veers dangerously close to Phi Kappa territory.
281 Bleecker Street, at Jones Street (1-212 462 4682, www.blindtigeralehouse.com). Subway A, B, C, D, E, F, M to W 4th Street; 1 to Christopher Street-Sheridan Square. Open 11.30am-4am daily.

Corkbuzz Wine Studio
This intriguing and elegant hybrid, owned by the world's youngest female master sommelier, Laura Maniec, comprises a restaurant, wine bar and educational centre. Staff preach the Maniec gospel to patrons as they navigate 35 by-the-glass options and around 250 bottles.
13 E 13th Street, between Fifth Avenue & University Place (1-646 873 6071, www.corkbuzz.com). Subway L, N, Q, R, 4, 5, 6 to 14th Street-Union Square. Open 4.30pm-midnight, Mon-Wed; 4.30pm-1am Thur-Sat; 11am-3pm, 4.30pm-midnight Sun. (Call or see website for summer hours.)

Employees Only
This Prohibition-themed bar cultivates an exclusive vibe, but there's no cover and no hassle at the door. Pass by the palm reader in the window (it's a front) and you'll find an amber-lit art deco interior where formality continues to flourish: servers wear custom-designed frocks and bartenders are in waitstaff whites. But the real stars are cocktails such as the West Side, a lethal mix of lemon vodka, lemon juice, fresh mint and club soda.
510 Hudson Street, between Christopher & W 10th Streets (1-212 242 3021, www.employees onlynyc.com). Subway 1 to Christopher Street-Sheridan Square. Open 6pm-3.30am daily.

Gottino
Jockey for a seat at this narrow enoteca – there are just five tables in addition to the long marble bar. It's worth the crush. The all-Italian wine list is complemented by a menu of choice nibbles, divided into salumi and cheese

Proletariat

on one side, and delectable prepared bites on the other.

52 Greenwich Avenue, between Charles & Perry Streets (1-212 633 2590, www.gottinony.com). Subway 1 to Christopher Street-Sheridan Square. Open 8am-2am Mon-Fri; 10am-2am Sat, Sun.

Vol de Nuit Bar (aka Belgian Beer Lounge)

148 W 4th Street, between Sixth Avenue & MacDougal Street (1-212 982 3388, www.voldenuitbar.com). Subway A, B, C, D, E, F, M to W 4th Street. Open 4pm-midnight Mon-Wed, Sun; 4pm-1am Thur; 4pm-2am Fri, Sat.

Duck through an unmarked doorway and find yourself in a red-walled Belgian bar that serves brews exclusively from the motherland. Clusters of European grad students knock back glasses of Corsendork and Triple Kermeliet – just two of 13 beers on tap and 22 by the bottle. Moules and frites – served with one of a dozen sauces – are the only eats available (not Monday).

White Horse Tavern

Popular lore tells us that in 1953, Dylan Thomas pounded 18 straight whiskeys here before expiring in his Chelsea Hotel residence – a portrait of him now hangs in the middle room, above his favourite table in the corner. Now the old-school bar and its adjacent outdoor patio play host to a yuppie crowd and clutches of tourists, drawn by the outdoor seating, a fine selection of beers – and the legend.

567 Hudson Street, at 11th Street (1-212 989 3956). Subway 1 to Christopher Street-Sheridan Square. Open 11am-2am Mon-Thur, Sun; 11am-4am Fri, Sat. No credit cards.

Chelsea

Half King

Don't let their blasé appearance fool you – the creative types gathered at the Half King's yellow pine bar are probably as excited as you are to catch a glimpse of the part-owner, author Sebastian Junger. While you're waiting, order one of the 16 draught beers – including several local brews – or a seasonal cocktail.

505 W 23rd Street, between Tenth & Eleventh Avenues (1-212 462 4300, www.thehalfking.com). Subway C, E to 23rd Street. Open 11am-4am Mon-Fri; 9am-4am Sat, Sun.

The Tippler

Even at its most packed, there's still a fair amount of room to manoeuvre in this expansive lounge, which means you won't have too much trouble finding a space at the long marble bar. The menu includes draft and bottled beers, plus wines from around the world, but you'd be remiss not to try at least one of the speciality cocktails, such as the Gin & Chronic (Plymouth gin, hops, spiced lime, tonic).

Chelsea Market, 425 W 15th Street, between Ninth & Tenth Avenues

(1-212 206 0000, www.thetippler. com). Subway A, C, E to 14th Street; L to Eighth Avenue. Open 4pm-2am Mon-Thur, Sun; 4pm-4am Fri, Sat.

Gramercy & Flatiron

230 Fifth

The 14,000sq ft roof garden atop an anonymous office building dazzles with truly spectacular views, including a close-up of the Empire State Building, but the glitzy indoor lounge – with floor-to-ceiling windows, wraparound sofas and bold lighting – shouldn't be overlooked. While the sprawling outdoor space gets mobbed on sultry nights, it's less crowded during the cooler months when heaters, fleece robes and hot ciders turn it into a winter hotspot.

230 Fifth Avenue, at 27th Street (1-212 725 4300, www.230-fifth.com). Subway N, R to 28th Street. Open 4pm-4am Mon-Fri; 10am-4am Sat, Sun.

Milk & Honey

In 2000, Sasha Petraske recast the mould for the Gotham cocktail bar with Milk & Honey, the reservations-only temple of mixology guarded by a secret phone number. More than a decade and countless imitations later, he shocked the booze cognoscenti by moving his legendary bar to the Flatiron neighbourhood. Ditching the reservations-only policy, the relocated, expanded and now democratic drinkery now operates on a first come, first served basis, but cocktail menus are still absent. Ask for one of the bar's contemporary classics like the ginger-and-Scotch Penicillin.

30 E 23rd Street, between Madison Avenue & Park Avenue South (no phone, www.mlkhny.com). Subway N, R, 6 to 23rd Street. Open 6.15pm-3am daily.

Old Town Bar & Grill

Amid the swank food and drink sanctums sprouting around Park Avenue South, this classic tavern remains a shrine to unchanging values. Belly up to the bar and drain a few pints alongside the regulars who gather on stools 'south of the pumps' (their lingo for taps). If you work up an appetite, skip the much-praised burger in favour of the chilli dog: a grilled and scored all-beef Sabrett with spicy homemade beef-and-red-kidney-bean chilli.

45 E 18th Street, between Broadway & Park Avenue South (1-212 529 6732, www.oldtownbar.com). Subway L, N, Q, R, 4, 5, 6 to 14th Street-Union Square. Open 11.30am-11.30pm Mon-Fri; 10am-11.30pm Sat; 11am-10pm Sun.

Pete's Tavern

According to history buffs, in 1904, O Henry wrote his sentimental short story 'The Gift of the Magi' in what was then a quiet Gramercy pub. Today it's three deep at the bar, and O Henry would have a hard time parking it anywhere. Although Pete's – a Civil War-era survivor – draws its share of tourists, you'll also rub shoulders with neighbourhood types who slide into the wooden booths to snack on affordable Italian eats with standard suds (16 beers on tap include a hoppy house ale) bubbling in frosty mugs.

129 E 18th Street, at Irving Place (1-212 473 7676, www.petestavern. com). Subway L, N, Q, R, W, 4, 5, 6 to 14th Street-Union Square. Open 11am-2.30am daily.

Raines Law Room

There's no bar to belly up to at this louche lounge. In deference to its name (which refers to an 1896 law that was designed to curb liquor consumption), drinks are prepared in a half-hidden back room known as 'the kitchen'. While this reduces the noise level in the

plush, upholstered space, it also robs you of the opportunity to watch the bar staff at work. The cocktail list includes classics, and variations thereof.

48 W 17th Street, between Fifth & Sixth Avenues (no phone, www.raineslawroom.com). Subway F, M to 14th Street; L to Sixth Avenue. Open 5pm-2am Mon-Thur; 5pm-3am Fri, Sat; 8pm-1am Sun.

Rye House

11 W 17th Street, between Fifth & Sixth Avenues (1-212 255 7260, www.ryehousenyc.com). Subway F, M to 14th Street; L to Sixth Avenue. Open noon-2am Mon-Thur; noon-midnight Fri; 11am-midnight Sat; 11am-11pm Sun.

As the name suggests, American spirits are the emphasis at this dark, sultry bar. As well as bourbons and ryes, there are gins, vodkas and rums, most distilled in the States. Check out the jalapeño-infused Wake-up Call, one of the venue's most popular bourbon cocktails. While the focus is clearly on drinking, there's excellent upscale pub grub, such as truffle grilled cheese or potato pierogies.

Midtown

Ardesia

Le Bernardin vet Mandy Oser's iron-and-marble gem, tucked away on a quiet Hell's Kitchen street, offers superior wines in a relaxed setting. The 75-strong collection of international bottles is a smart balance of Old and New World options that pair beautifully with the varied selection of small plates. A grüner veltliner – a dry, oaky white from Austria – had enough backbone to stand up to a duck *banh mi* layered with spicy duck pâté and Sriracha aioli. One for the serious oenophile.

510 W 52nd Street, between Tenth & Eleventh Avenues (1-212 247 9191, www.ardesia-ny.com). Subway C, E to 50th Street. Open 5pm-midnight Mon-Wed; 5pm-2am Thur, Fri; 2pm-2am Sat; 2-11pm Sun.

Middle Branch

In 2000, visionary barman Sasha Petraske paved the way for the modern cocktail bar with members-only Milk & Honey (*see above*); since then, he and his acolytes have spread the liquid gospel with a rapidly expanding web of standout watering holes. His latest bar, Middle Branch – run by longtime Little Branch lieutenants Lucinda Sterling and Benjamin Schwartz – plants a flag for artisanal cocktails in post-frat epicentre Murray Hill. Unlike Little Branch, this is no sly speakeasy, hidden from the masses with a windowless façade and an unmarked ingress: the bi-level drinkery, sporting French doors that offer a glimpse inside, practically beckons passersby. As at Petraske's other highfalutin' joints, the razor-sharp focus is on classic cocktails and riffs (all $12), built with hand-cut ice and superior spirits.

Ginny's Supper Club. See p70.

154 E 33rd Street, between Lexington & Third Avenues (1-212 213 1350). Subway 6 to 33rd Street. Open 5pm-2am daily.

Pony Bar
The Theater District isn't known for civilised, non-chain bars, but you need only walk a couple of blocks west to this convivial paean to American microbrews. Choose from a constantly changing selection of two cask ales and 20 beers on tap; daily selections are artfully listed on signboards according to provenance and potency. Despite the expert curation, the prices are kept low (all beers cost $6). 637 Tenth Avenue, at 45th Street (1-212 586 2707, www.theponybar.com). Subway C, E to 50th Street. Open 3pm-4am Mon-Fri; noon-4am Sat, Sun.

Rum House
In 2009, this rakish, 1970s-vintage piano bar in the Edison Hotel seemed destined to go the way of the Times Square peep show. But the team behind Tribeca mixology den Ward III has ushered in a second act, introducing some key upgrades (including serious cocktails) while maintaining the charmingly offbeat flavour of the place. Sip dark spirit-heavy tipples, such as a funky old-fashioned riff that showcases the rich, tropical complexity of Banks 5 Island Rum, while listening to a pianist or jazz trio most nights of the week. 228 W 47th Street, between Seventh & Eighth Avenues (1-646 490 6924, www.edisonrumhouse.com). Subway N, Q, R to 49th Street. Open noon-4am daily.

Upper West Side

Ding Dong Lounge
Goth chandeliers and kick-ass music mark this dark dive as punk – with broadened horizons. The tap pulls, dispensing half a dozen beers including Guinness, are sawn-off guitar necks, and the walls are covered with vintage concert posters (from Dylan to the Damned). The affable local clientele and mood-lit conversation nooks make it surprisingly accessible (even without a working knowledge of Dee Dee Ramone). 929 Columbus Avenue, between 105th & 106th Streets (1-212 663 2600, www.dingdonglounge.com). Subway B, C to 103rd Street. Open 4pm-4am daily.

Jacob's Pickles
This craft-beer-and-biscuit-slinging gastropub shoehorns a grab bag of tippling memes – Dixieland grub, house-made bitters, local wines on tap – into one rustic barroom. But while it may be trying a little too hard, there's plenty for brew geeks to get excited about, with more than two dozen taps offering an all-domestic lineup. The list is broken down by state, with a stable of Empire State breweries (Barrier,

BEER KINGS OF QUEENS
The pre-Prohibition brewery hub makes a comeback.

SingleCut Beersmiths

Watch your back, Brooklyn. Among Queens' new crop of craft breweries, Astoria's **SingleCut Beersmiths** (19-33 37th Street, between 19th & 20th Avenues, 1-718 606 0788, www.single cutbeer.com) is the biggest, producing 700 kegs each month. Owner Rich Buceta specialises in lagers; try the aggressively hoppy 19-33 Lagrrr! or John Michael Dark Lyric Lagrrr!, a coffee-inflected seasonal black, in the 90-seat tasting room Thursday to Sunday (see website for hours).

Ethan Long and Marcus Burnett – a set designer and cinematographer, respectively – decided to go pro after three and a half years of home-brewing in their Rockaway Beach bungalows. Their first beer, the mellow English ale ESB got a bump from the community when Rockaway Taco and Caracas Arepa started pouring the easy-drinking sipper at their boardwalk stands. Now based in Long Island City, **Rockaway Brewing Company** (46-01 5th Street, at 46th Avenue, 1-718 482 6528, www.rockawaybrewco.com) produces six beers available in such varied establishments as the **Queens Kickshaw** (*see p64*) and East Village bar **Jimmy's No.43** (*see p66*) – or stop by the growler room for a taste on weekend afternoons (see website for hours).

After winning Heartland's 2011 home-brewing contest, amateurs Kyle Hurst, Robby Crafton and Scott Berger bought a 1,000-square-foot former Bible warehouse to turn their shared hobby into a career. **Big Alice Brewing** (8-08 43rd Road, at Vernon Boulevard, 1-347 688 2337, www.bigalicebrewing.com) makes eight to ten one-off beers every month. Some offerings draw on New York purveyors, such as a coffee-wheat stout infused with beans from Park Slope's Gorilla. The brewery opens its doors for tastings and purchases every Friday night.

Radiant Pig, SingleCut) complemented by a constantly rotating roster of cross-country favourites from the likes of Maine Beer Co and Virginia's Blue Mountain Brewery. If you're feeling peckish, go for the namesake pickles or the biscuits in sausage gravy. 509 Amsterdam Avenue, between 84th and 85th Streets (212 470 5566, www.jacobspickles.com). Subway 1 to 86th Street. Open 11am-2am Mon-Thur; 11am-4am Fri; 9am-4am Sat; 9am-2am Sun.

Manhattan Cricket Club
Upstairs from Australian bistro Burke & Wills, this gold-brocaded, cricket-inspired cocktail parlour is a polished upgrade from the shrimp-on-the-barbie kitsch that often plagues Aussie efforts. Summit Bar founder Greg Seider offers pricey but potent quaffs inspired by cricket hubs like India and South Africa. The I'll Have Another jolts a dark-and-stormy base of sweet rum and shaved ginger with the spice-heavy bite of garam masala-infused agave, while the kafir lime's sweetness tempers a smoky spritz of campfire essence in the vodka-based Bonfire of the Calamities. 226 W 79th Street, between Amsterdam Avenue & Broadway (1-646 823 9252, www.burkeand willsny.com). Subway 1 to 79th Street. Open 7pm-2am daily.

Upper East Side

Bar Pleiades
Designed as a nod to Coco Chanel, Daniel Boulud's bar is framed in black lacquered panels that recall an elegant make-up compact. The luxe setting and moneyed crowd might seem a little stiff, but the seasonally rotating cocktails are so exquisitely executed you won't mind sharing your banquette with a suit. Light eats are provided by Café Boulud next door. The Surrey, 20 E 76th Street, between Fifth & Madison Avenues (1-212 772 2600, www.danielnyc.com). Subway 6 to 77th Street. Open noon-midnight daily.

Bemelmans Bar
The Plaza may have Eloise, but the Carlyle has its own children's book connection – the wonderful 1947 murals of Central Park by *Madeline* creator Ludwig Bemelmans in this, the quintessential classy New York bar. A jazz trio adds to the atmosphere every night at 9.30pm (a cover charge of $15-$30 applies when the musicians take up residence). The Carlyle, 35 E 76th Street, at Madison Avenue (1-212 744 1600, www.thecarlyle.com). Subway 6 to 77th Street. Open 11am-midnight Mon, Sun; 11am-12.30am Tue-Thur; 11am-1am Fri, Sat.

Earl's Beer & Cheese
Tucked into the no-man's land between the Upper East Side and Spanish Harlem, this craft-beer cubby hole has the sort of community-hub vibe that makes you want to settle in. The well-priced rotating selection of American craft brews and slapdash set-up appeal to a neighbourhood crowd, but it's Momofuku Ssäm Bar alum Corey Cova's madcap bar menu that makes it destination-worthy. Try the NY State Cheddar – a grilled cheese with braised pork belly, fried egg and house-made kimchi. (Note that the kitchen closes at 11pm.) The crew has since opened a cocktail bar, the Guthrie Inn, next door (at the same address, 1-212 423 9900) and a wine bar, ABV (1504 Lexington Avenue, at 97th Street, 1-212 722 8959, www.abvny.com), a block east. 1259 Park Avenue, between 97th & 98th Street (1-212 289 1581, www.earlsny.com). Subway 6 to 96th Street. Open 4pm-midnight Mon, Tue; 11am-midnight Wed, Thur, Sun; 11am-2am Fri, Sat.

Penrose
Named for a neighbourhood in Cork, Ireland, where two of the owners grew up, the Penrose stands apart from the Upper East Side's sports bars and fancier joints – its exposed-brick walls, retro decorative touches and curved wooden bar are casually sophisticated. The craft-brew list includes the malty NewBurgh Brown Ale from upstate New York; there's also Murphy's Stout and an extensive whiskey selection (Irish, American and Scotch). The comfort-food-heavy menu includes a thick, juicy Pat LaFrieda blend house burger. 1590 Second Avenue, between 82nd & 83rd Streets (1-212 203 2751, www.penrosebar.com). Subway 4, 5, 6 to 86th Street. Open 3pm-4am Mon-Thur; noon-4am Fri; 10.30am-4am Sat, Sun.

Bars

Harlem & Upper Manhattan

For bars around the border of the Upper East Side and East Harlem, *see p69.*

Camaradas el Barrio Bar Restaurant

Owner Orlando Plaza pays tribute to his Puerto Rican heritage at this lively bar, eaterie and nightspot. The look is downtown chic: exposed brick, rough-hewn wooden benches and a modest gallery. Grab a seat and sample 'Puerto Rican pub fare' from the tapas-style menu, or kick back over a pitcher of sangria and take in some live salsa or jazz.
2241 First Avenue, at 115th Street (1-212 348 2703, www.camaradas elbarrio.com). Subway 6 to 116th Street. Open 3pm-3am Mon-Thur; 3pm-3.30am Fri, Sat; 3pm-midnight Sun.

Ginny's Supper Club

This sprawling basement lounge is modelled after the Harlem speakeasies of the '20s. The menu, eclectic cocktails and a steady line-up of live music revive the sophisticated supper club experience.
310 Malcolm X Boulevard (Lenox Avenue), between 125th & 126th Streets (1-212 421 3821, www. redroosterharlem.com). Subway 2, 3 to 125th Street. Open 6-10pm Mon-Wed 7pm-2am Thur; 6pm-3am Fri, Sat; 10am & 12.30pm brunch seatings, 6-10pm Sun.

Park 112

Styled with illuminated communal tables and brown-leather banquettes, this 90-seat restaurant and bar is equipped with a self-serve Enomatic wine machine. In addition to the 60-bottle wine list, you'll find global fare from Aquavit alum Kingsley John. Note that the kitchen closes at 11pm Mon-Wed, midnight Thur-Sat and 10pm Sun.
2080 Fredrick Douglass Boulevard (Eighth Avenue), at 112th Street (1-646 524 6610, www.thepark112. com). Subway B, C to 110th Street-Cathedral Parkway. Open 5.30pm-midnight Mon-Wed; 5.30pm-2am Thur, Fri; 11am-2am Sat; 11am-11pm Sun.

Shrine

Playfully adapting a sign left over from the previous tenants (the Black United Foundation), the Shrine advertises itself as a 'Black United Fun Plaza'. The interior is tricked out with African art and vintage album covers, and actual vinyl adorns the ceiling. Nightly concerts might feature indie rock, jazz, reggae or DJ sets. The cocktail menu aspires to similar diversity.
2271 Adam Clayton Powell Jr Boulevard (Seventh Avenue), between

Bars

BROOKLYN SHUFFLE
The latest nostalgic game spot proves shuffleboard isn't just for old folks.

Royal Palms Shuffleboard Club

The relentlessly competitive metropolis has a league of game-focused watering holes, from Lower East Side joystick mecca **Two-Bit's Retro Arcade** (*see p66*) and Williamsburg Skee-Ball hub **Full Circle Bar** (318 Grand Street, between Havemeyer Street & Marcy Avenue, 1-347 725 4588, www.fullcirclebar.com) to Susan Sarandon-backed Flatiron Ping-Pong spot **SPiN New York** (48 E 23rd Street, between Madison & Park Avenues, 1-212 982 8802, www.spinyc.com).

The newest addition to the pantheon of play brings the sport of seniors to the unlikely post-industrial environs of Gowanus, Brooklyn: the **Royal Palms Shuffleboard Club** (514 Union Street, between Nevins Street & Third Avenue, 1-347 233 4410, www.royalpalmsshuffle.com) is a Floridian oasis with ten sunken aquamarine courts and black-and-white cabanas. Launched to the sound of a thousand hacks screeching 'hipster!', the place isn't merely a posing ground, thanks to the genuine passion of owners Jonathan Schnapp and Ashley Albert (ranked the men's 82nd and women's 68th in the world, respectively). In the hangar-like space, bag a first-come first-served court ($40 an hour, split between four players). White-clad staff initiate newbies into the rules and lingo – the stick is called a 'tang', the puck is a 'biscuit'. If you're looking for pointers, watch the pros during league nights on Monday and Tuesday, then practice with gratis court time between 10pm and midnight.

Even if you don't take to the game like a retiree to an early-bird special, there are ample reasons to visit: a rotating array of food trucks purveying cult local eats, including Red Hook Lobster Pound, Crif Dogs and Solber Pupusas, a Wednesday bingo night with drag king and queen Murray Hill and Linda Simpson and a regular roster of DJs and local bands.

133rd & 134th Streets (1-212 690 7807, www.shrinenyc.com). Subway B, C, 2, 3 to 135th Street. Open 4pm-4am daily. No credit cards.

Brooklyn

Clover Club

Classic concoctions are the signature tipples at Julie Reiner's Victorian-styled cocktail parlour. Sours, fizzes, mules, punches and cobblers all get their due at the 19th-century mahogany bar. Highbrow snacks (fried oysters, steak tartare) accompany drinks like the eponymous Clover Club (with gin, raspberry syrup, egg whites, dry vermouth and lemon juice).
210 Smith Street, between Baltic & Butler Streets, Cobble Hill (1-718 855 7939, www.cloverclub ny.com). Subway F, G to Bergen
Street. Open 4pm-2am Mon-Thur; noon-4am Fri; 10.30am-4am Sat; 10.30am-1am Sun.

The Commodore

With its old arcade games, cheap Schaefer in a can and stereo pumping out the *Knight Rider* theme song, this Williamsburg gastrodive offers some of the city's best cheap-ass bar eats. The 'hot fish' sandwich, for one, is a fresh, flaky, cayenne-rubbed catfish fillet poking out of both sides of a butter-griddled sesame-seed roll. You'll be thankful it's available after you've had a few rounds of the Commodore's house drink – a slushy, frozen piña colada.
366 Metropolitan Avenue, at Havemeyer Street, Williamsburg (1-718 218 7632). Subway J, M, Z to Marcy Avenue; L to Bedford Avenue. Open 4pm-4am Mon-Fri; 3pm-4am Sat, Sun.

Long Island Bar

A revivalist spirit is at the core of this retro-fitted bar from Toby Cecchini, which took over midcentury greasy spoon the Long Island Restaurant. But the cocktail vet does more than simply dig up old bones. The menu swaps the *tortas* that once powered neighbourhood blue-collars for Cecchini's fine-tuned list of six bedrock quaffs. Cecchini is a bit of a legend in cocktail-swilling circles – he created the modern Cosmo at the Odeon in 1987. Here you'll find a biting but balanced rye-and-Campari Boulevardier and a tart gimlet, given a fiery kick from ginger grated into the lime cordial. The iconic signage and old-line interior – terrazzo floors, Formica walls – have been preserved with an almost religious reverence, down to the faded cigarette burns that still cheetah-spot the gleaming art deco bar.
110 Atlantic Avenue, at Henry Street, Cobble Hill (1-718 625 8908). Subway F, G to Bergen Street; 2, 3, 4, 5 to Borough Hall. Open 5.30pm-midnight Mon-Thur, Sun; 5.30pm-2am Fri, Sat.

Maison Premiere

Most of NYC's New Orleans-inspired watering holes choose debauched Bourbon Street as their muse, but this gorgeous salon embraces the romance found in the Crescent City's historic haunts. Belly up to the oval, marble-topped bar and get familiar with the twin pleasures of oysters and absinthe: two French Quarter staples with plenty of appeal in Brooklyn. The mythical anise-flavoured liqueur appears in 22 international varieties, in addition to a trim list of cerebral cocktails.
298 Bedford Avenue, between Grand & South 1st Streets, Williamsburg (1-347 335 0446, www.maison premiere.com). Subway L to Bedford Avenue. Open 4pm-2am Mon-Wed; 4pm-4am Thur, Fri; 11am-4am Sat; 11am-2am Sun.

Sunny's Bar

Restored after 2012's Hurricane Sandy dealt it a devastating blow, this unassuming wharfside tavern, which has been passed down in the Balzano family since 1890, is back in business. The bar buzzes with middle-aged and new-generation bohemians. Despite the nautical feel, you're more likely to hear bossa nova or bluegrass than sea shanties from the speakers.
253 Conover Street, between Beard & Reed Streets, Red Hook (1-718 625 8211, www.sunnysredhook.com). Subway F, G to Smith-9th Streets, then B61 bus. Open 8pm-4am Wed-Fri; 4pm-4am Sat; 4pm-11pm Sun (extended hrs in summer). No credit cards.

Spuyten Duyvil

Don't arrive thirsty. It takes at least ten minutes to choose from roughly 150 quaffs, a list that impresses even microbrew mavens. Most selections are middle-European regionals, and bartenders are eager to explain the differences among them. The cosy

interior is chock-full of flea market finds, most of which are for sale. There's also a tasty bar menu of smoked meats, pâtés and cheeses.
359 Metropolitan Avenue, at Havermeyer Street, Williamsburg (1-718 963 4140, www.spuytenduyvil nyc.com). Subway L to Bedford Avenue; G to Metropolitan Avenue. Open 5pm-2am Mon-Thur; 5pm-4am Fri; 1pm-4am Sat; 1pm-2am Sun.

Tørst
Danish for 'thirst', Tørst is helmed by legendary 'gypsy brewer' Jeppe Jarnit-Bjergsø and chef Daniel Burns, formerly of Noma in Copenhagen. These warriors are laying waste to tired ideas of what a great taproom should be, with a minimalist space that looks like a modernist log cabin, and rare brews from throughout Europe and North America. The ever-changing, 21-tap draft menu can move faster than a Swedish vallhund, but usually includes selections from Jarnit-Bjergsø's own Evil Twin Brewing. More than 100 bottled beers are also available. Tørst has more in common with a high-end wine bar than with your average local watering hole – well-heeled locals and pilgrimaging brew buffs quietly sip from designer wineglasses at the sleek white marble counter. Luksus, the restaurant hidden away in the back room, offers a tasting menu for $95 from 6.30pm to midnight Tuesday through Saturday.
615 Manhattan Avenue, between Driggs & Nassau Avenues, Greenpoint (1-718 389 6034). Subway G to Nassau Avenue. Open noon-midnight Mon-Wed, Sun; noon-2am Thur-Sat.

Union Hall
Upstairs at Union Hall, couples chomp on mini burgers and sip microbrews in the gentlemen's club anteroom (decorated with Soviet-era globes, paintings of fez-capped men, fireplaces) – before battling it out on the clay bocce courts. Downstairs, in the taxidermy-filled basement, the stage hosts bands, comedians and offbeat events.
702 Union Street, between Fifth & Sixth Avenues, Park Slope (1-718 638 4400, www.unionhallny.com). Subway R to Union Street. Open 4pm-4am Mon-Fri; 1pm-4am Sat, Sun.

Union Pool
This former pool-supply outlet now supplies booze to scruffy Williamsburgers, who pack the tin-walled main room's half-moon booths and snap saucy photo-kiosk pics. Bands strum away on the adjacent stage, while the spacious courtyard and outdoor bar is popular during the warmer months. Arrive early to kick back $5 draft beers and $6 house cocktails – happy hour is 5pm to 9pm weeknights.
484 Union Avenue, at Meeker Avenue, Williamsburg (1-718 609 0484, www.union-pool.com). Subway L to Lorimer Street; G to Metropolitan Avenue. Open 5pm-4am Mon-Fri; 1pm-4am Sat, Sun.

Queens

Alewife
A serious craft-beer selection is the draw at this bi-level beer hall, which comes from a team of hops zealots with ties to Alewife Baltimore and the cultish Lord Hobo in Cambridge, Massachusetts. It's a generic-looking gastropub, and we could do without the poppy soundtrack and truffle oil on our fries. But the owners come through where it counts, curating a balanced and worldly beer list (28 taps and casks and 100-plus bottles) that can go toe-to-toe with the most pedigreed suds haunts.
5-14 51st Avenue, between Vernon Boulevard & 5th Street, Long Island City (1-718 937 7494, www.alewife nyc.com). Subway 7 to Vernon Boulevard-Jackson Avenue. Open 4pm-1am Mon-Thur; 4pm-3am Fri; 11am-3am Sat; 11am-1am Sun.

Dutch Kills
What separates Dutch Kills from other mixology temples modelled after vintage saloons is the abundance of elbow room. Settle into one of the deep, dark-wood booths in the front, or perch at the bar. Another bonus: the cocktails – mostly riffs on the classics – come with slightly lower prices than in similar establishments in Manhattan.
27-24 Jackson Avenue, at Dutch Kills Street, Long Island City (1-718 383 2724, www.dutchkillsbar.com). Subway E, M, R to Queens Plaza. Open 5pm-2am Mon-Thur, Sun; 5pm-3am Fri, Sat.

Garden at Studio Square
35-33 36th Street, between 35th & 36th Avenues, Long Island City (1-718 383 1001, www.studiosquarenyc. com). Subway M, R to 36th Street; N, Q to 36th Avenue. Open 1pm-3am Mon-Thur; 1pm-4am Fri-Sun. A contemporary interpretation of a classic beer garden, Studio Square's grand cobblestoned courtyard is lined with communal picnic tables. Three modern fire pits keep out evening chills, but there is also an indoor bar. The 20-strong list includes European classics and American microbrews. Basic pub grub is supplemented by sausages (kielbasas and brats), and the party-hearty ambience is fuelled by DJs and bands.

Astoria Bier & Cheese
Manhattan's hybrid bar-shop trend comes to Queens with this funky curds-and-brew haven, which sports a bathroom mural of Kim Jong-il milking a cow. At the marble bar, grab one of the ten seasonal, mostly local drafts, like Greenport Harbor's Gobsmacked IPA, from Long Island. There are close to 300 bottles and cans – organised by style and offered in mix-and-match six packs – that can be purchased to go or opened on-site for a $2 corking fee. Fromage buff Mike Fisher (a Bedford Cheese Shop vet) culls close to 100 selections for the refrigerated case, some of which are worked into a sit-down menu that includes a selection of grilled cheese melts.
34-14 Broadway, between 34th & 35th Streets, Astoria (1-718 545 5588, www.astoriabierandcheese.com). Subway M, R to Steinway Street; N, Q to Broadway. Open noon-11pm Mon-Thur; noon-midnight Fri, Sat; noon-10pm Sun.

Bohemian Hall & Beer Garden
This authentic Czech beer garden features plenty of mingle-friendly picnic tables, where you can sample cheap, robust platters of sausage and 16 mainly European drafts. Though the huge, tree-canopied garden is open year-round (in winter, it's tented and heated), summer is prime time to visit.
29-19 24th Avenue, between 29th & 31st Streets, Astoria (1-718 274 4925, www.bohemianhall.com). Subway N, Q to Astoria Boulevard. Open 5pm-1am Mon-Thur; 5pm-3am Fri; noon-3am Sat; noon-1am Sun (hrs vary seasonally).

Sweet Afton
This Queens gastropub combines an industrial feel – lots of concrete and massive beams – with the dim, dark-wood cosiness of an Irish pub. The bar's smartly curated array of reasonably priced suds includes strong selections from craft breweries like Ommegang, Sixpoint and Captain Lawrence, but the bartender will just as happily mix a cocktail. The satisfying food menu is highlighted by the beer-battered McClure's pickles – an epic bar snack.
30-09 34th Street, between 30th & 31st Avenue, Astoria (1-718 777 2570, www.sweetaftonbar.com). Subway N, Q to 30th Avenue. Open 4pm-4am Mon-Fri; 11am-4am Sat, Sun.

The Bronx

Bruckner Bar & Grill
This popular neighbourhood hangout has eight beers on tap, including Bronx Brewery Pale Ale, plus a wide range of bottled craft beers, and an eclectic menu of bar snacks, sandwiches and burgers. The culture hub also serves as a gallery spotlighting local talent.
1 Bruckner Boulevard, at Third Avenue (1-718 665 2001, www.the brucknerbar.com). Subway 6 to Third Avenue-138th Street. Open 11am-1.30am daily.

Bronx Beer Hall
Surrounded by the cigar makers and meat and cheese counters of the septuagenarian Arthur Avenue Market, patrons can sit at BBH's stand-alone rustic wooden bar and imbibe one of five New York State choices on draft – there's a particular emphasis on the borough's own Jonas Bronck's Beer Co. Try the brewery's New York Chocolate Egg Cream Stout, a bi-borough creation made with Brooklyn's Fox's U-bet chocolate syrup, or another local favourite, City Island Beer Company's balanced pale ale. Mike's Deli (see p64) supplies the grub, like cheese boards and sausages.
2344 Arthur Avenue, between Crescent Avenue & E 186th Street (1-347 396 0555, www.thebronxbeer hall.com). Open 11am-3am Mon-Sat; 11am-9pm Sun.

RECOMMENDED
Whiskey Soda Lounge NY

Andy Ricker's Thai canteen was conceived as a spillover spot for Pok Pok NY hopefuls, but the boozier kid bro is a destination in its own right, offering a highlight reel of *ahaan kap klaem* (Thai drinking food) and smartly tweaked cocktails. Not surprisingly, whiskey – commonly drunk with fizzy water in Thailand – is front and centre. There's a 30-plus roster of American slugs, as well as selections from Japan, Ireland and Canada. The low-ceilinged rec room is sparse – wood-panelled walls, drooping Christmas lights – but dashed with poppy touches of Bangkok-in-Brooklyn kitsch.
115 Columbia Street, at Kane Street, Cobble Hill (1-718 797 4120, www.whiskeysodalounge-ny.com). Subway F, G to Bergen Street. Open 5.30pm-midnight daily.

Printed Matter. See p79.

Get the goods

Whatever you're looking for, you'll find it (and much more) in this retail paradise.

One of the best cities in the world to drop some of your hard-earned cash, New York offers anything you could possibly want to buy, and – as long as you're prepared to shop around or hit some sample sales – at the best prices. Locals may complain about the 'mallification' of certain areas such as **Soho**, but for visitors (and, if they're honest, many New Yorkers), these retail-rich neighbourhoods are intoxicating consumer playgrounds. Other prime downtown shopping destinations include the **Lower East Side**, **Nolita**, the **West Village** and the **Meatpacking District**.

As America's fashion capital, and the site of the prestigious Fashion Institute of Technology and other high-profile art colleges, the metropolis is a magnet for creative young designers from around the country. This ensures that the shops and markets are stuffed with unique finds, and it also means that the Garment District is a hotbed of open-to-the-public showroom sales. The best are listed at www.timeout.com/newyork. Other terrific resources are **Racked** (www.ny.racked.com), **Top Button** (www.topbutton.com) and **Clothing Line** (1-212 947 8748, www.clothingline.com), which holds sales for a variety of labels – from J.Crew and Theory to Helmut Lang and Rag & Bone, at its Garment District showroom.

Chief among the permanent sale stores is the famous **Century 21** (*see right*). A second Manhattan location opened on the Upper West Side in 2011, but we recommend braving the original for breadth of stock and, sometimes, deeper discounts. Union Square's **Nordstrom Rack** (60 E 14th Street, between Broadway & Fourth Avenue, 1-212 220 2080, www.nordstrom rack.com), the discount arm of the department store, is worth checking out too. Appealing to the environmentally aware and budget-conscious alike, the vintage trend is stronger than ever. See page 75 for our favourite under-the-radar troves.

Of course, many visitors to New York will simply be looking to make the most of the incredible variety of big brands on offer in the city. For young, casual and streetwear labels, head to Broadway in Soho. **Fifth Avenue** heaves with a mix of designer showcases and mall-level megastores. **Madison Avenue** is more consistently posh, with a further line-up of deluxe labels. If you prefer to do all your shopping under one roof, famous department stores **Macy's** (good for mid-range brands), Bloomingdale's (a mix of mid-range and designer), **Barneys** (cutting-edge and high-fashion) and **Bergdorf Goodman** (luxury goods and international designer) are all stuffed with desirable items.

The Financial District

Bowne Printers and Bowne & Co Stationers Gifts & souvenirs
South Street Seaport Museum's re-creation of a 19th-century print shop doesn't just look the part: the platen presses – hand-set using antique letterpress and type from the museum's collection – also turn out custom and small-batch stationery and cards. Next door, Bowne & Co Stationers, founded in 1775, sells hand-printed cards, prints journals and other gifts.
209-211 Water Street, between Fulton & Beekman Streets (1-646 628 2707). Subway A, C, J, Z, 2, 3, 4, 5 to Fulton Street. Open 11am-7pm daily.

Century 21 Fashion
A Marc Jacobs cashmere sweater for less than $200? Stella McCartney sunglasses for a mere $40? No, you're not dreaming – you're shopping at Century 21. You may have to rummage to unearth a treasure, but with savings of up to 65% off regular prices, it's worth it.
22 Cortlandt Street, between Broadway & Church Street (1-212 227 9092, www.c21stores.com). Subway A, C, J, Z, 2, 3, 4, 5 to Fulton Street; E to World Trade Center; R to Cortlandt Street. Open 7.45am-9pm Mon-Wed; 7.45am-9.30pm Thur, Fri; 10am-9pm Sat; 11am-8pm Sun. Other location 1972 Broadway, between 66th & 67th Streets, Upper West Side (1-212 518 2121).

J&R Music & Computer World Electronics
This block-long electronics emporium stocks a plethora of electronic and electrical goods – from MP3 players and TVs to kitchen appliances.
1 Park Row, at Beekman Street (1-212 238 9000, www.jr.com). Subway A, C to Broadway-Nassau Street. Open 10am-7pm Mon-Wed; 10am-7.30pm Thur, Fri; 11am-7pm Sat, Sun.

Soho & Tribeca

Soho's converted warehouses are packed with just about every major fashion brand you can think of, from budget and mid-priced international chains such as H&M and Topshop to A-list designer labels like Chanel and Prada, plus stores selling home goods, cosmetics, food and more. Listed below is a selection of our favourite independent shops.

3.1 Phillip Lim Fashion
Since Phillip Lim debuted his collection in 2005, the New York-based designer has amassed a devoted international following for his simple yet strong silhouettes and beautifully constructed tailoring with a twist. His Soho boutique gathers together his award-winning collections for men and women, plus his cult accessories, under one roof.

115 Mercer Street, between Prince & Spring Streets (1-212 334 1160, www.31philliplim.com). Subway N, R to Prince Street; 6 to Spring Street. Open 11am-7pm Mon-Sat; noon-6pm Sun.

(3x1) Fashion

Denim obsessives who are always looking for the next It jeans have another place to splurge: (3x1) creates entirely limited-edition styles sewn in the store. Designer Scott Morrison, who previously launched Paper Denim & Cloth and Earnest Sewn, fills the large, gallery-like space with a variety of jeans (prices start at $185 for women, $265 for men) and other denim pieces such as shorts and miniskirts. Watch the construction process take place in a glass-walled design studio in the middle of the boutique.

15 Mercer Street, between Howard & Grand Streets (1-212 391 6969, www.3x1.us). Subway A, C, E, J, N, Q, R, Z, 1, 6 to Canal Street. Open 11am-7pm Mon-Sat; noon-6pm Sun.

Alexander Wang Fashion

Anna Wintour-approved designer Alexander Wang has amassed a cult-like following of voguish downtown types. The Parsons dropout, who launched his eponymous line in 2007, was propelled to fashion royalty the following year after scoring a Council of Fashion Designers of America award. With chalky-white marble display pedestals and overstuffed leather couches, his luxurious flagship boutique offers the wunderkind's chic-but-casual men's and women's clothing, handbags and showstopping shoes, plus the lower-priced T by Alexander Wang line.

103 Grand Street, between Greene & Mercer Street (1-212 977 9683, www.alexanderwang.com). Subway J, N, Q, R, Z, 6 to Canal Street. Open 11am-7pm Mon-Sat; noon-6pm Sun.

Babesta Threads Children

Husband-and-wife team Aslan and Jenn Cattaui fill their cosy store with the stuff kids love – Rowdy Sprout concert tees, Uglydolls and eco-friendly clothing that'll make parents envious. The shop focuses on the under-six set, but there are also pieces for children aged up to 12 from popular lines such as Mini Rodini.

66 West Broadway, between Murray & Warren Streets (1-212 608 4522, www.babesta.com). Subway 1, 2, 3 to Chambers Street. Open 11am-7pm Mon-Fri; noon-6pm Sat, Sun.

Dominique Ansel Bakery
Food & drink

Dominique Ansel honed his skills as executive pastry chef at Daniel for six years before opening this innovative patisserie. In 2013, his croissant-doughnut hybrid, the Cronut, created a frenzy in foodie circles and put his ingenious creations into the spotlight. If you can't get your hands on a Cronut, try the DKA – a caramelised, flaky take on the croissant-like Breton speciality *kouign amann*. And his cotton-soft mini cheesecake, an ethereally light gâteau with a brûléed top, leaves the dense old New York classic sputtering in its dust.

189 Spring Street, between Sullivan & Thompson Streets (1-212 219 2773, www.dominiqueansel.com). Subway C, E to Spring Street. Open 8am-7pm Mon-Sat; 9am-7pm Sun.

Housing Works Bookstore Café
Books & music

This endearing two-level space – which stocks literary fiction, non-fiction, rare books and collectibles – is also a peaceful spot to relax in over coffee or wine. All proceeds go to providing support services for people living with HIV/AIDS. Both emerging writers and the literati take the mic at the store's readings.

126 Crosby Street, between Houston & Prince Streets (1-212 334 3324, www.housingworksbookstore.org). Subway B, D, F, M to Broadway-Lafayette Street; N, R to Prince Street; 6 to Bleecker Street. Open 10am-9pm Mon-Fri; 10am-5pm Sat, Sun.

In God We Trust Fashion

Designer Shana Tabor's cosy antique-furnished stores cater to that appealing vintage-intellectual aesthetic, offering locally crafted collections for men and women. The store's line of well-priced, cheeky accessories is a highlight – for example, gold heart-shaped pendants engraved with blunt sayings like 'Boring' or 'Blah Blah Blah', rifle-

Dover Street Market New York

Critic's choice

1 **Century 21** Bargains galore at this rummagers' paradise. *See p72.*

2 **Russ & Daughters** This 100-year-old purveyor offers a taste of the old Lower East Side. *See p76.*

3 **Strand Book Store** A multi-floor NYC literary institution. *See p77.*

4 **Dover Street Market New York** Rei Kawakubo's arty Comme concept store has arrived in Manhattan. *See p80.*

5 **Brooklyn Flea** The game-changing market makes a great day out. *See p84.*

In God We Trust

shaped tie bars, and a wide selection of retro sunglasses for only $20 a pair.

265 Lafayette Street, between Prince & Spring Streets (1-212 966 9010, www.ingodwetrustnyc.com). Subway N, R to Prince Street; 6 to Spring Street. Open noon-8pm Mon-Sat; noon-7pm Sun. Other locations 129 Bedford Avenue, between North 9th & 10th Streets, Williamsburg, Brooklyn (1-718 384 0700); 70 Greenpoint Avenue, between Milton & Franklin Streets, Greenpoint, Brooklyn (1-718 389 3545).

Jacques Torres Chocolate
Food & drink

Walk into Jacques Torres's glass-walled shop and café, and you'll be surrounded by a Willy Wonka-esque factory that turns raw cocoa beans into luscious chocolate goodies before your eyes. As well as selling the usual assortments, truffles and bars (plus more unusual delicacies such as chocolate-covered cornflakes and Cheerios), the shop serves deliciously rich hot chocolate, steamed to order.

350 Hudson Street, between Charlton & King Streets, entrance on King Street (1-212 414 2462, www.mrchocolate.com). Subway 1 to Houston Street. Open 8.30am-7pm Mon-Fri; 9am-7pm Sat; 10.30am-6.30pm Sun. Other locations throughout the city.

Kiki de Montparnasse Lingerie

This erotic luxury boutique channels the spirit of its namesake, a 1920s sexual icon and Man Ray muse, with a posh array of tastefully provocative contemporary lingerie in satin and French lace. Look out for novelties such as cotton tank tops with built-in garters and panties embroidered with saucy legends.

79 Greene Street, between Broome & Spring Streets (1-212 965 8150, *www.kikidm.com). Subway N, R to Prince Street; 6 to Spring Street. Open 11am-7pm Mon, Sun; 11am-8pm Tue-Sat.*

Kirna Zabete Fashion

Since relocating a block from their original boutique, founders Beth Buccini and Sarah Easley have more space to display their edited collection of coveted designer clothing and accessories – more than 25 labels are new to the store, including Valentino, Nina Ricci and Roland Mouret. True to the duo's aesthetic, the 10,000sq ft space features black-and-white striped hardwood floors and neon signs displaying quirky mantras such as 'life is short, buy the shoes'.

477 Broome Street, between Greene & Wooster Streets (1-212 941 9656, www.kirnazabete.com). Subway N, R to Prince Street. Open 11am-7pm Mon-Sat; noon-6pm Sun.

Nili Lotan Fashion

The sparsely hung women's garments in Israeli designer Nili Lotan's airy, all-white store and studio look like art pieces on display in a gallery. Perfectly cut, largely monochrome wardrobe staples such as silk camisoles and dresses, oversized cashmere sweaters and crisply tailored menswear-inspired shirts appeal to minimalists with a penchant for luxury.

188 Duane Street, between Greenwich & Hudson Streets (1-212 219 9784, www.nililotan.com). Subway 1, 2, 3 to Chambers Street. Open noon-7pm Mon-Sat; noon-6pm Sun.

Odin Fashion

The Norse god Odin is often portrayed sporting an eye patch and shabby robes. That may have been stylish back in medieval Scandinavia, but to make it in NYC, he'd have to pick up

some Engineered Garments, Rag & Bone or Our Legacy gear from this upscale men's boutique. Also keep an eye out for White Mountaineering, a Japanese brand that successfully combines high-function fabrics with a fashionable aesthetic.
199 Lafayette Street, between Broome & Kenmare Streets (1-212 966 0026, www.odinnewyork.com). Subway 6 to Spring Street. Open 11am-8pm Mon-Sat; noon-7pm Sun. Other locations 328 E 11th Street, between First & Second Avenues, East Village (1-212 475 0666); 106 Greenwich Avenue, between Jane & W 13th Streets, West Village (1-212 243 4724).

Opening Ceremony Fashion
The name references the Olympic Games; each year the store assembles hip US designers (Band of Outsiders, Alexander Wang, Patrik Ervell, Rodarte and its own house label) and pits them against the competition from abroad. The store is so popular it has expanded, adding a book and music section upstairs and a men's shop next door. There's an additional OC outpost at the Ace Hotel (*see p116*).
33-35 Howard Street, between Broadway & Lafayette Street (1-212 219 2688, www.opening ceremony.us). Subway J, N, Q, R, Z, 6 to Canal Street. Open 11am-8pm Mon-Sat; noon-7pm Sun.

Patron of the New Fashion
This avant-garde fashion emporium showcases an international collection of unique guys' and gals' clothing, accessories, beauty products and housewares from both illustrious and under-the-radar designers, including Balmain, Nicolas Andreas Taralis and Denis Colomb. Most goods carry hefty price tags, but there are some affordable jewellery, accessories and gifts such as soaps and candles.
151 Franklin Street, between Hudson & Varick Streets (1-212 966 7144, www.patronofthenew.com). Subway A, C, E to Canal Street; 1 to Franklin Street. Open 11am-7pm Mon-Sat; noon-6pm Sun.

Shinola Accessories/ gifts & souvenirs
Motor City may be in dire financial straits but there is no denying the cool factor of the struggling metropolis. The first NYC location of the Detroit-based brand Shinola showcases a range of American-manufactured watches, bicycles, leather goods and other items. A 1930s bronze map that used to hang in Rockefeller Center adorns the industrial-edged store, which includes an outpost of cult East Village café the Smile.
177 Franklin Street, between Greenwich & Hudson Streets (1-917 728 3000, www.shinola.com). Subway A, C, E to Canal Street; 1 to Franklin Street. Open 11am-7pm Mon-Sat; noon-6pm Sun.

Steven Alan Fashion
Known for well-crafted cotton shirts in an array of stripes, checks and solid colours, Steven Alan also assembles cultish boutique brands for men and women in its flagship store. In addition to the house label, browse clothing by Acne, Band of Outsiders and Engineered Garments, plus a range of handbags and shoes.
103 Franklin Street, between West Broadway & Church Street (1-212 343 0692, www.stevenalan.com). Subway 1 to Franklin Street. Open 11.30am-7pm Mon-Wed, Fri, Sat; 11.30am-8pm Thur; noon-6pm Sun.

What Goes Around Comes Around Fashion
A favourite among the city's fashion cognoscenti, this downtown vintage destination sells highly curated stock alongside its own retro label. Style mavens particularly recommend it for 1960s, '70s and '80s rock T-shirts, pristine Alaïa clothing and vintage fur coats.
351 West Broadway, between Broome & Grand Streets (1-212 343 1225, www.whatgoesaround nyc.com). Subway A, C, E, 1 to Canal Street. Open 11am-8pm Mon-Sat; noon-7pm Sun.

Chinatown, Little Italy & Nolita

Christian Siriano Fashion
This 1,000sq ft flagship boutique was personally designed by the hotshot Project Runway season-four winner. You'll find the glam evening wear that propelled Siriano to success – such as beaded gowns and cocktail dresses – displayed on mannequins throughout the shop, but if you don't have a red-carpet event on your calendar, there are plenty of reasonably priced separates and accessories to paw through, along with the designer's current Payless footwear collection (starting at just $30).
252 Elizabeth Street, between E Houston & Prince Streets (1-212 775 8494, www.christiansiriano. com). Subway B, D, F, M to Broadway-Lafayette Street. Open 11.30am-7pm Mon-Sat; noon-6pm Sun.

Creatures of Comfort Fashion
Jade Lai opened Creatures of Comfort in Los Angeles in 2005 and brought her cool-girl aesthetic east five years later. Occupying the former home of the 12th police precinct, the New York offshoot offers a similar mix of pricey but oh-so-desirable pieces from avant-garde lines – such as MM6 Maison Martin Margiela, Acne and Isabel Marant's Etoile – alongside the store's own-label bohemian basics and a selection of shoes and accessories.
205 Mulberry Street, between Kenmare & Spring Streets (1-212 925 1005, www.creaturesofcomfort.us). Subway 6 to Spring Street; N, R to Prince Street. Open 11am-7pm Mon-Sat; noon-7pm Sun.

Downtown Music Gallery Books & music
Many landmarks of the so-called downtown music scene have closed down, but as long as DMG persists, the community will have a sturdy anchor. The shop stocks the city's finest selection of avant-garde jazz, contemporary classical, progressive rock and related styles.
13 Monroe Street, between Catherine & Market Streets (1-212 473 0043, www.downtownmusicgallery.com). Subway J, Z to Chambers Street; 4, 5, 6 to Brooklyn Bridge-City Hall. Open noon-6pm Mon-Wed; noon-7pm Thur-Sun.

TOP TIP!
Counter culture
Museum shops are great places to pick up unique souvenirs. The Museum of Arts & Design (*see p34*) has an impressive array of artisan-made jewellery.

Erica Weiner Accessories
Erica Weiner sells her own bronze, brass, silver and gold creations – many under $100 – alongside vintage and reworked baubles. Old wooden cabinets and stacked crates showcase rings and charm-laden necklaces, the latter featuring the likes of tiny dangling harmonicas and steel penknives. Other popular items include brass ginkgo-leaf earrings, and moveable-type-letter necklaces for your favourite wordsmith.
173 Elizabeth Street, between Kenmare & Spring Streets (1-212 334 6383, www.ericaweiner.com). Subway C, E to Spring Street. Open noon-8pm daily.

McNally Jackson Books & music
Owned by Sarah McNally, daughter of the folks behind Canada's fine independent McNally Robinson, this appealing bookstore stocks a distinctly international selection of novels and non-fiction titles. A wide range of readings and events – which

Creatures of Comfort

have included such well-known figures as Garrison Keillor, Hari Kunzru and Siri Hustvedt – take place in its comfortable downstairs space.
52 Prince Street, between Lafayette & Mulberry Streets (1-212 274 1160, www.mcnallyjackson.com). Subway N, R to Prince Street; 6 to Spring Street. Open 10am-10pm Mon-Sat; 10am-9pm Sun.

New & Almost New Fashion

Germophobe label-lovers, rejoice: 40 per cent of the merchandise on sale at this resale shop is actually brand new. Owner Maggie Chan hand-selects every piece, ensuring its quality and authenticity. Among the items hanging on the racks you'll find pieces from lofty labels such as Prada, Chanel and Hermès. Prices range from as low as $15 up to around $600.
171 Mott Street, between Broome & Grand Streets (1-212 226 6677, www.newandalmostnew.com). Subway B, D to Grand Street; J, Z to Bowery; 6 to Spring Street. Open 1-5pm Mon, Sun; noon-6.30pm Tue-Sat.

Sun's Organic Garden
Food & drink

Owner Lorna Lai knows her teas the way a sommelier knows *terroir*. Curious sippers peruse the well-stocked shelves of the Hong Kong native's nook, which boasts more than a thousand jarred loose-leaf varieties from around the world, available by the ounce. Lai's house-made herbal blends are standouts, in exotic flavours like holy basil and bilberry.
79 Bayard Street, between Mott and Mulberry Streets (1-212 566 3260). Subway J, N, Q, R, Z, 6 to Canal Street. Open 10.30am-7.30pm daily.

Warm Fashion/accessories

The husband-and-wife owners of this appealing boutique, Rob Magnotta and Winnie Beattie, curate an eclectic selection of women's threads and accessories, alongside fragrances and body products, vintage books and items for the home, all influenced by the couple's globe-trotting surfer lifestyle. The laid-back looks include urban boho-chic clothing from designers such as Vanessa Bruno, Giada Forte and Maison Olga, and handcrafted jewellery by artist Suzannah Wainhouse.
181 Mott Street, between Broome & Kenmare Streets (1-212 925 200, www.warmny.com). Subway J, Z to Bowery; 6 to Spring Street. Open noon-7pm Mon-Sat; noon-6pm Sun.

Lower East Side

Alife Rivington Club
Accessories

Whether you're looking for a simple white trainer or a trendy graphic style, you'll want to gain entry to this 'club', which stocks a wide range of major brands such as Nike (including sought-after reissues like Air Jordan), Adidas

and New Balance. You'll also find lesser-known names including the shop's own label.
158 Rivington Street, between Clinton & Suffolk Streets (1-212 432 7200, www.alifenewyork.com). Subway F to Delancey Street; J, M, Z to Delancey-Essex Streets. Open noon-7pm Mon-Sat; noon-6pm Sun.

The Cast Fashion

At the core of Chuck Guarino's rock 'n' roll-inspired collection is the trinity of well-cut denim, superior leather jackets based on classic motorcycle styles, and the artful T-shirts that launched the label in 2004. The ladies have their own line, covering similar ground.
71 Orchard Street, between Broome & Grand Streets (1-212 228 2020, www.thecast.com). Subway F to Delancey Street; J, M, Z to Delancey-Essex Streets; B, D to Grand Street. Open noon-8pm Mon-Sat; noon-6pm Sun.

Curvaceous K Fashion

Lifelong New Yorker Kathy Sanchez ditched her desk job in marketing to bring NYC something it was missing – a full-figure fashion boutique, catering to a considerably underserved market of plus-size women (US sizes 14-24). She searched high and low for the best, most affordable curvy-girl threads, by labels such as Melissa Masse, Igigi, Mynt 1792 and Jessica Simpson.
179 Stanton Street, between Attorney & Clinton Streets (1-646 684 3175, www.curvaceousk.com). Subway F to Delancey Street; J, M, Z to Delancey-Essex Streets. Open 2-7pm Mon, Tue, Sun; 2-8pm Thur, Fri, Sat.

Dear: Rivington
Fashion/homewares

The glass storefront is a stage for Moon Rhee and Hey Ja Do's art installation-like displays; inside the white bi-level space, head downstairs for their own Victorian-inspired line and select pieces by avant-garde Japanese labels such as Comme des Garçons and Yohji Yamamoto. Upstairs is a fascinating archive of vintage homewares, art and objects, including framed antique silhouettes, old globes and tins, plus contemporary handmade pottery.
95 Rivington Street, between Ludlow & Orchard Streets (1-212 673 3494, www.dearrivington.com). Subway F to Delancey Street; J, M, Z to Delancey-Essex Streets. Open noon-7pm daily.

The Dressing Room Fashion

At first glance, the Dressing Room may look like any Lower East side lounge, thanks to a handsome wood bar, but this co-op cum watering hole rewards the curious. The adjoining room displays designs by indie labels alongside select vintage pieces, and there's a second-hand clothing exchange downstairs.
75A Orchard Street, between Broome & Grand Streets (1-212 966 7330, www.thedressingroomnyc.com). Subway B, D to Grand Street; F to

VINTAGE STYLE SECRETS
Sleuth out these lesser-known thrift stores for retro treasures and great deals.

Antoinette

Antoinette

Store namesake Antoinette Oliveri worked as an apprentice to milliner Lilly Daché in the 1950s, and was a clothing hoarder in the best sense of the word. Her daughter, Lexi Oliveri, put her pack-rat tendencies to good use by opening this shop, filled with all of her mother's finds from her years toiling in the fashion business – all under $100. Oliveri now supplements the store's stock with finds from her buying trips upstate. There's also a small men's section from – you guessed it – her dad's wardrobe.
119 Grand Street, between Berry & Wythe Avenues, Williamsburg, Brooklyn (1-718 387 8664, www.antoinettebrooklyn.com).

Bopkat Vintage

If you've ever lusted over a pair of Betty Draper's cigarette pants or Peggy Olson's working-girl suits, it's possible that they may have come from the racks of this unassuming shop – a go-to for *Mad Men*'s wardrobe department. Owner Laura Buscaglia combs estate sales, flea markets and thrift stores for pristine pieces from the '50s and '60s, such as a beaded-chiffon cocktail dress and plaid capri pants for gals and tiki-print shirts and fedoras for guys.
117 Union Street, between Columbia & Van Brunt Streets, Red Hook, Brooklyn (1-718 222 1820).

David Owens Vintage

Unlike many vintage stores that traffic in '80s and '90s garb, David Owens's eponymous boutique carries items exclusively from the '30s to the '70s. The small space is stuffed to the gills with rare and unique pieces, such as a '30s printed dress with the original store tags attached and a '60s

clutch made to look like a rolled-up *Harper's Bazaar* magazine. Men will find just as many interesting items, including pin-up girl ties from the '40s to the '70s and leather motorcycle jackets.
154 Orchard Street, between Rivington & Stanton Streets, Lower East Side (1-212 677 3301).

Grand Street Bakery

Despite the Grand Street Bakery signage, this storefront churns out not sweets but clothing and accessories for both sexes from the '60s to the '90s that are almost exclusively made in the US. Many of the original bakery fixtures – including metal baking racks that hold stacks of Levi's 501s – remain intact. Former Urban Outfitters vintage buyer Neal Mello and his girlfriend, Cyd Mullen, scour the country for classic Americana garb, such as ladies' fisherman knit sweaters and denim overalls. Guys' buys include Pendleton plaid wool shirts and denim jackets.
602 Grand Street, between Leonard & Lorimer Streets, Williamsburg, Brooklyn (1-718 387 2390, www.grandstbakery.com).

Rue St Denis

Jean-Paul Buthier searches the US and Europe for unworn dead-stock garb, culled from long-closed factories and stores. Film, TV and Broadway costume departments frequently source pieces here. Menswear is the speciality – the back room is filled with pristine suits from the '40s to the '90s, organised by era – but ladies will still find plenty to ogle. Two in-house tailors are on hand to ensure you get the perfect fit.
170 Ave B, between 10th & 11th Streets, East Village (1-212 260 3388, www.ruestdenis.com).

Delancey Street; J, M, Z to Delancey-Essex Streets. Open 1pm-midnight Tue, Wed; 1pm-2am Thur-Sat; 1-8pm Sun.

Edith Machinist
Fashion/accessories
An impeccable assemblage of leather bags, shoes and boots is the main draw here, but you'll also find a whittled-down collection of clothes, including a small men's section. The store is closed some Mondays, so call before visiting. *104 Rivington Street, between Essex & Ludlow Streets (1-212 979 9992, www.edithmachinist.com). Subway F to Delancey Street; J, M, Z to Delancey-Essex Streets. Open noon-7pm Tue, Thur, Sat; noon-6pm Fri, Sun.*

The Hoodie Shop **Fashion**
Up to 50 different brands of hooded apparel for both men and women are showcased in this 1970s-inspired boutique, from retro zip-ups to army-print utility jackets. The shop has a DJ booth and movie screen for late-night shopping parties and other in-store events. *181 Orchard Street, between E Houston & Stanton Streets (1-646 559 2716, www.thehoodieshop.com). Subway F to Lower East Side-Second Avenue. Open noon-9pm Mon-Sat; noon-7pm Sun.*

Moo Shoes **Accessories**
Cruelty-free footwear is far more fashionable than it once was. Moo stocks a variety of brands for men and women, such as Vegetarian Shoes and Novacas, plus styles from independent designers such as Elizabeth Olsen, whose arty line of high heels and handbags is anything but hippyish. *78 Orchard Street, between Broome & Grand Streets (1-212 254 6512, www.mooshoes.com). Subway F to Delancey Street; J, M, Z to Delancey-Essex Streets. Open 11.30am-7.30pm Mon-Sat; noon-6pm Sun.*

Obsessive Compulsive
Cosmetics Health & beauty
Creator David Klasfeld founded OCC in the kitchen of his Lower East Side apartment in 2004. The make-up artist has since expanded his 100% vegan and cruelty-free cosmetics line from just two shades of lip balm to an extensive assortment of bang-for-your-buck beauty products. In the downtown flagship, you can browse more than 40 shades of nail polish and nearly 40 loose eye-shadow powders, among other products, but we especially like the Lip Tars, which glide on like a gloss but have the matte finish and saturated pigmentation of a lipstick. *174 Ludlow Street, between E Houston & Stanton Streets (1-212 675 2404, www.occmakeup.com). Subway F to Lower East Side-Second Avenue. Open 11am-7pm Mon-Sat; noon-6pm Sun.*

Reed Space
Fashion/accessories
Reed Space is the brainchild of Jeff Ng (AKA Jeff Staple), who has worked on product design and branding with the likes of Nike and Timberland. The store stocks local and international urban clothing brands – such as 10.Deep and Undefeated – and footwear, including exclusive Staple collaborations. Art books and culture mags are shelved on an eye-popping installation of four stacked rows of white chairs fixed to one wall. *151 Orchard Street, between Rivington & Stanton Streets (1-212 253 0588, www.thereedspace.com). Subway F to Delancey Street; J, M, Z to Delancey-Essex Streets. Open 1-7pm Mon-Fri; noon-7pm Sat, Sun.*

Russ & Daughters **Food & drink**
The daughters in the shop's name have given way to great-grandchildren, but this Lower East Side institution (established 1914) is still run by the same family. Specialising in smoked and cured fish and caviar, it sells about ten varieties of smoked salmon, eight types of herring (pickled, salt-cured, smoked and so on) and many other Jewish-inflected Eastern European delectables. Bagels are available to take away – try the Super Heebster, filled with baked salmon, fluffy whitefish salad, horseradish-dill cream cheese and wasabi-infused flying-fish roe. *179 E Houston Street, between Allen & Orchard Streets (1-212 475 4880, www.russ anddaughters.com). Subway F to Lower East Side-Second Avenue. Open 8am-8pm Mon-Fri; 9am-7pm Sat; 8am-5.30pm Sun.*

Spiritual America
Fashion/accessories
Housed in the same storefront (and operating under the same name) as artist Richard Prince's original pop-up exhibition in 1983, this minimalist shop stocks a mix of European and American labels (Vanessa Bruno, Damir Doma, Derek Lam) and wares by up-and-coming designers. Using the airy feel of a gallery as inspiration, Parisian-born owner Claire Lemétais has outfitted the space with custom light-sculpture installations and rammed-earth-crafted countertops. We're especially taken with the boutique's selection of cool shoes and accessories. *5 Rivington Street, between Bowery & Chrystie Street (1-212 960 8564, www.spiritualameri.ca). Subway F to Lower East Side-Second Avenue; J, Z to Bowery; 6 to Spring Street. Open noon-8pm Mon-Fri; 11am-7pm Sat, Sun.*

East Village

Astor Place Hairstylists
Health & beauty
The army of barbers at Astor Place does everything from neat trims to more complicated and creative shaved designs. You can't make an appointment, but you can call ahead; otherwise, just take a number and wait outside with the crowd. Sunday mornings are usually quieter. Cuts start at $16. *2 Astor Place, at Broadway (1-212 475 9854, www.astorplacehairnyc.com).*

Russ & Daughters

Subway N, R to 8th Street-NYU; 6 to Astor Place. Open 8am-8pm Mon, Sat; 8am-9pm Tue-Fri; 9am-6pm Sun. No credit cards.

Astor Wines & Spirits
Food & drink
High-ceilinged, wide-aisled Astor Wines is a terrific place to browse for wines of every price range, vineyard and year – which makes it a favourite hunting ground for the city's top sommeliers. Sakés and spirits are also well represented. *399 Lafayette Street, at 4th Street (1-212 674 7500, www.astorwines.com). Subway N, R to 8th Street-NYU; 6 to Astor Place. Open 9am-9pm Mon-Sat; noon-6pm Sun.*

Bond No. 9 **Health & beauty**
The collection of scents here pays olfactory homage to New York City. Choose from more than 60 'neighbourhoods' and 'sensibilities', including Wall Street, Park Avenue, Eau de Noho, High Line – even Chinatown (but don't worry, it smells of peach blossoms, gardenia and patchouli, not fish stands). The arty bottles and neat, colourful packaging are particularly gift-friendly. *9 Bond Street, between Broadway & Lafayette Street (1-212 228 1732, www.bondno9.com). Subway B, D, F, M to Broadway-Lafayette Street; 6 to Bleecker Street. Open 11am-8pm Mon-Fri; 10am-7pm Sat; noon-6pm Sun. Other locations throughout the city.*

Bond Street Chocolate
Food & drink
Former pastry chef Lynda Stern's East Village spot is a grown-up's candy store, with quirky chocolate confections in shapes ranging from gilded Buddhas (and other religious figures) to skulls, and flavours from elderflower to bourbon and absinthe. *63 E 4th Street, between Bowery & Second Avenue (1-212 677 5103, www.bondstchocolate.com). Subway 6 to Bleecker Street. Open noon-8pm Tue-Sat; 1-6pm Sun.*

Buffalo Exchange **Fashion**
This popular buy-sell-trade clothing shop spans all sartorial tastes, from Forever 21 to Marc Jacobs. You could score a pair of 7 for All Mankind jeans for $25, current-season Manolo Blahniks for $250 or a Burberry men's wool coat for $135. *332 E 11th Street, between First & Second Avenues (1-212 260 9340, www.buffaloexchange.com). Subway L to First Avenue. Open 11am-8pm Mon-Sat; noon-7pm Sun. Other locations throughout the city.*

DQM **Fashion**
DQM founder – and professional skateboarder – Chris Keeffe stocks a range of top-shelf streetwear in this wittily designed shop. As well as a line-up of the latest sneaks by Adidas and Vans, DQM sells its own-label T-shirts, chinos and button-downs. *7 E 3rd Street, between Bowery & Second Avenue (1-212 505 7551, www.dqmnewyork.com). Subway F to Lower East Side-Second Avenue. Open 11.30am-7.30pm Mon-Sat; noon-6pm Sun.*

Fabulous Fanny's
Accessories
Formerly a Chelsea flea market booth, this two-room shop is the city's best source of period glasses, stocking more than 30,000 pairs of spectacles, from Jules Verne-esque wire rims to 1970s rhinestone-encrusted Versace shades.

335 E 9th Street, between First &
Second Avenues (1-212 533 0637,
www.fabulousfannys.com). Subway
L to First Avenue; 6 to Astor Place.
Open noon-8pm daily.

Fun City Tattoo Tattoo parlour
Jonathan Shaw started inking locals
from his apartment nearly 40 years
ago (back when tattooing was illegal)
and then opened the storefront Fun
City in the early 1990s. The legendary
figure has retired to South America,
but his New York City institution –
which has served the likes of Johnny
Depp, Jim Jarmusch and Dee Dee
Ramone – continues its operations
in the East Village. The current artists
– 'Big' Steve Pedone, Mina Aoki,
Claire Vuillemot, Benjamin Haft and
John Raftery – can do almost anything,
from lettering and Japanese to
American traditional.
94 St Marks Place, between First
Avenue & Avenue A (1-212 353
8282, www.funcitytattoo.com).
Subway N, R to 8th Street-NYU;
6 to Astor Place. Open noon-10pm
daily. No credit cards.

Future Perfect Homewares
Championing avant-garde interior
design, this innovative store showcases
international and local talent – it's the
exclusive US stockist of Dutch designer
Piet Hein Eek's furniture and pottery.
Look out for Kiel Mead's quirky gold
and silver jewellery.
55 Great Jones Street, between Bowery
& Lafayette Street (1-212 473 2500,
www.thefutureperfect.com). Subway 6
to Bleecker Street. Open 10am-7pm
Mon-Fri; noon-7pm Sat; noon-5pm
Sun; also by appointment.

Great Jones Spa Health & beauty
Based on the theory that water brings
health, Great Jones has a popular water
lounge complete with subterranean
pools, saunas, steam rooms and a
three-and-a-half-storey waterfall.
Access to the 15,000sq ft paradise is
free with services over $100 – treat
yourself to a divinely scented body
scrub, a massage or one of the many
indulgent packages. Alternatively,
a three-hour pass costs $50.
29 Great Jones Street, at Lafayette
Street (1-212 505 3185, www.
greatjonesspa.com). Subway 6 to
Astor Place. Open 9am-10pm daily.

Kiehl's Health & beauty
The apothecary founded on this East
Village site in 1851 has morphed
into a major skincare brand, but the
products, in their minimal packaging,
are still good value and effective. Lip
balms and the thick-as-custard Creme
de Corps have become cult classics.
The Upper East Side location (157 E
64th Street, between Lexington &
Third Avenues, 1-917 432 2503) houses
the first Kiehl's spa; the Hell's Kitchen
store (678 Ninth Avenue, at 47th Street,
1-212 956 2891) has a barber shop.
109 Third Avenue, between 13th &
14th Streets (1-212 677 3171,
www.kiehls.com). Subway L to Third
Avenue; N, Q, R, 4, 5, 6 to 14th Street-

Union Square. Open 10am-8pm
Mon-Sat; 11am-6pm Sun. Other
locations throughout the city.

Other Music Books & music
Other Music opened in the shadow of
Tower Records in the mid 1990s, a
pocket of resistance to chain-store
tedium. Now the Goliath across the
street is gone, but tiny Other Music
carries on. Whereas the shop's mishmash of indie rock, experimental
music and stray slabs of rock's past
once seemed adventurous, the
curatorial foundation has proved
prescient amid the emergence of
mixed-genre venues in the city.
15 E 4th Street, between Broadway
& Lafayette Street (1-212 477 8150,
www.othermusic.com). Subway
B, D, F, M to Broadway-Lafayette
Street; 6 to Bleecker Street. Open
11am-9pm Mon-Fri; noon-8pm Sat;
noon-7pm Sun.

Patricia Field Fashion
The iconic redheaded designer and
stylist has moved her boutique two
doors down from the original, into a
space that's nearly double the size,
combining Field's former apartment
with a vacated store behind it – her old
bedroom is now a full-service hair
salon. Funky ladies' threads include
daringly short crop tops and thigh-high
faux snake boots, while flamboyant
fellas will find Keith Haring for House
of Field T-shirts and Joy Rich sweat
pants. Stock up on whimsical
accessories such as polka-dot shades,
taxi cab-shaped wristlets by Betsey
Johnson and cube-shaped rings.
306 Bowery, between Bleecker & E
Houston Streets (1-212 966 4066,
www.patriciafield.com). Subway 6
to Bleecker Street. Open 11am-8pm
Mon-Thur, Sun; 11am-9pm Fri, Sat.

Screaming Mimi's Fashion
This vintage mecca has been peddling
men's and women's clothing and
accessories since 1978. Owner Laura
Wills travels the world, scouting eclectic
finds that span the 1950s to the 1990s,
and organises clothing racks by decade.
Do you need sunglasses from the 1970s?
How about a Duran Duran T-shirt from
the '80s? Head upstairs to check out
higher-end garments by designers such
as Hattie Carnegie, Jean Paul Gaultier
and Vivienne Westwood.
382 Lafayette Street, at 4th Street (1-
212 677 6464, www.screamingmimis.
com). Subway B, D, F, M to Broadway-
Lafayette Street; N, R to Prince Street;
6 to Bleecker Street. Open noon-8pm
Mon-Sat; 1-7pm Sun.

Strand Book Store
Books & music
Established in 1927, the Strand has a
mammoth collection of more than two
million discount volumes (both new
and used), and the store is made all the
more daunting by its chaotic, towering
shelves and sometimes crotchety staff.
You can find just about anything here,
from that out-of-print Victorian book on
manners to the kitschiest of sci-fi pulp.
The rare book room upstairs closes at

6.15pm. There's a seasonal Strand
kiosk on the edge of Central Park at
Fifth Avenue and 60th Street (Apr-Dec
10am-dusk, weather permitting).
828 Broadway, at 12th Street (1-212
473 1452, www.strandbooks.com).
Subway L, N, Q, R, 4, 5, 6 to 14th Street-
Union Square. Open 9.30am-10.30pm
Mon-Sat; 11am-10.30pm Sun.

Sustainable NYC Gifts &
souvenirs
This gift-centric shop houses a wealth
of eco-minded goods within its green
walls: organic shampoos and beauty
products; fair-trade chocolate; frames,
jewellery, clutch bags and other gifts
made from recycled metals and
materials such as computer keys; and
sun-powered BlackBerry chargers.
The on-site café serves fair-trade
coffee and locally made treats.
139 Avenue A, between 9th Street & St
Marks Place (1-212 254 5400, www.
sustainable-nyc.com). Subway L to First
Avenue; 6 to Astor Place. Open 8am-
10pm Mon-Fri; 9am-10pm Sat, Sun.

Greenwich Village & West Village

Aedes de Venustas
Health & beauty
Decked out like a 19th-century
boudoir, this extravagant perfume
collector's palace devotes itself to
ultra-sophisticated fragrances and
high-end skincare lines, such as
Diptyque, Santa Maria Novella and its
own glamorously packaged range of
fragrances, candles and room sprays.
Hard-to-find scents, such as Serge
Lutens perfumes, line the walls.
9 Christopher Street, between
Greenwich Avenue & Waverly Place
(1-212 206 8674, www.aedes.com).
Subway A, B, C, D, F, M to W 4th
Street; 1 to Christopher Street-

Sheridan Square. Open noon-8pm
Mon-Sat; 1-7pm Sun.

Blow Health & beauty
Launched as a scissor-free blow-dry
bar in 2005, this award-winning salon
was at the vanguard of the trend. It
later diversifed into other services,
but has recently returned to its roots,
so to speak, to concentrate on expertly
executed 'blowouts' ($50), to use the
local parlance. You can also opt for an
updo, such as a chic ponytail, twist or
chignon. There's now a Blow outpost
in Macy's (see p81) should you require
grooming in midtown.
Second Floor, 34 Gansevoort Street,
at Hudson Street (1-212 989 6282,
www.blowny.com). Subway A, C, E to
14th Street. Open 7.30am-8pm Mon-
Fri; 10am-8pm Sat; noon-6pm Sun.

CO Bigelow Chemists
Health & beauty
Established in 1838, Bigelow is
the oldest apothecary in America.
Its appealingly old-school line of
toiletries includes such tried-and-
trusted favourites as Mentha Lip
Shine, Barber Cologne Elixirs and
Lemon Body Cream. The spacious,
chandelier-lit store is packed with
natural and homeopathic remedies,
organic skincare products and
drugstore essentials – and the place
still fills prescriptions.
414 Sixth Avenue, between 8th & 9th
Streets (1-212 533 2700, www.bigelow
chemists.com). Subway A, B, C, D, F,
M to W 4th Street; 1 to Christopher
Street. Open 7.30am-9pm Mon-Fri;
8.30am-7pm Sat; 8.30am-5pm Sun.

Darling Fashion
Ann Emonts Sherman's two-floor
boutique is a great place to pick up a
special-occasion number. Not only is
the lower level stocked with dramatic
pieces from the 1950s to the recent
past, the former Broadway and
Off-Broadway costume designer
has a discerning eye for cherry-picking

Patricia Field

reasonably priced dresses from popular labels like BB Dakota, Karina and Bailey 44 that meet her girly aesthetic. For a finishing touch, check out the jewellery by Lotus, Alosh and Sally Kay displayed near the register. *1 Horatio Street, at Eighth Avenue (1-646 336 6966, www.darlingnyc.com). Subway A, C, E to 14th Street; L to Eighth Avenue. Open noon-7pm Mon-Sat; noon-6pm Sun.*

Doyle & Doyle Accessories
Whether your taste is art deco or nouveau, Victorian or Edwardian, gemologist sisters Elizabeth and Pamela Doyle, who specialise in vintage and antique jewellery, will have that one-of-a-kind item you're looking for, including engagement and eternity rings. In 2013, they packed up their curated archive and moved from the Lower East Side to larger premises in the Meatpacking District. The sisters have also launched their own collection of new heirlooms. *412 W 13th Street, between Ninth Avenue & Washington Street (1-212 677 9991, www.doyledoyle.com). Subway A, C, E to 14th Street; L to Eighth Avenue. Open noon-7pm Mon-Wed, Fri-Sun; noon-8pm Thur.*

Flight 001 Travel
As well as a tasteful selection of luggage by the likes of Lipault, Rimowa and Hideo, this one-stop shop carries everything for the chic jet-setter, including fun travel products such as novelty patterned eye masks and emergency totes that squash down to tennis ball size, plus 'essentials' such as expanding hand-towel tablets and single-use packets of Woolite. *96 Greenwich Avenue, between Jane & W 12th Streets (1-212 989 0001, www.flight001.com). Subway A, C, E to 14th Street; L to Eighth Avenue. Open 11am-8pm Mon-Sat; noon-6pm Sun. Other location 132 Smith Street, between Bergen & Dean Streets, Boerum Hill, Brooklyn (1-718 243 0001).*

Forbidden Planet Books & music
Embracing both pop culture and the cult underground, the Planet takes comics seriously. You'll also find graphic novels, manga, action figures, DVDs and more. *832 Broadway, between 12th & 13th Streets (1-212 473 1576, www.fpnyc.com). Subway L, N, Q, R, 4, 5, 6 to 14th Street-Union Square. Open 9am-10pm Mon, Tue, Sun; 9am-midnight Wed-Sat.*

Harry's Corner Shop
Health & beauty
Warby Parker co-founder Jeff Raider and business partner Andy Katz-Mayfield launched grooming brand Harry's in 2013 and opened the e-commerce platform's first 1920s-esque barbershop. Aside from affordable haircuts ($35) and shaves ($30), the shop offers clients a completely individualised appointment: barbers use iPads to snap headshots and update digital profiles of each customer. The merchandise stocked on ash-wood shelves includes Harry's razors and shave cream, plus gents' essentials like Hanes white cotton tees, Sleepy Jones striped socks, and Best Made Belgian dart sets. *64 MacDougal Street, at Houston Street (1-646 964 5193, www.harrys.com/cornershop). Subway 1 to Houston Street. Open 11am-8pm Mon-Fri; 10am-7pm Sat.*

Jeffrey New York
Fashion/accessories
Jeffrey Kalinsky, a former Barneys shoe buyer, was a Meatpacking District pioneer when he opened his namesake store in 1999. Designer clothing abounds here – by Yves Saint Laurent, L'Wren Scott, Céline and Christopher Kane, among others. But the centrepiece is without doubt the shoe salon, which features the work of Manolo Blahnik, Prada and Christian Louboutin, as well as newer names to watch. *449 W 14th Street, between Ninth & Tenth Avenues (1-212 206 1272, www.jeffreynewyork.com). Subway A, C, E to 14th Street; L to Eighth Avenue. Open 10am-8pm Mon-Wed, Fri; 10am-9pm Thur; 10am-7pm Sat; 12.30-6pm Sun.*

Meurice Garment Care
Drycleaner
This longstanding family-run dry cleaners prides itself on attention to detail. Knitwear is cleaned using a hydrocarbon process, which substitutes a gentler petroleum-based solvent for the traditional perchloroethylene, and very delicate fabrics, including vintage items and shearlings, are hand-cleaned. Be prepared to pay for this superior service; dry cleaning starts at about $15 for a skirt.

31 University Place, between 8th & 9th Streets (1-212 475 2778, www.garmentcare.com). Subway N, R to 8th Street-NYU. Open 7.30am-6pm Mon-Fri; 9am-6pm Sat; 10am-3pm Sun. Other location 245 E 57th Street, between Second & Third Avenues, Midtown (1-212 759 9057).

Murray's Cheese Food & drink
For the last word in curd, New Yorkers have been flocking to Murray's since 1940 to sniff out the best international and domestic cheeses. The helpful staff will guide you through hundreds of stinky, runny, washed-rind and aged comestibles. Murray's also has an outpost in Grand Central Terminal, plus a Cheese Bar near the original store at at 264 Bleecker Street serving cheese-focused dishes. *254 Bleecker Street, between Sixth & Seventh Avenues (1-212 243 3289, www.murrayscheese.com). Subway A, B, C, D, E, F, M to W 4th Street. Open 8am-8pm Mon-Sat; 9am-7pm Sun.*

Owen Fashion
FIT grad Phillip Salem founded this upscale boutique featuring more than 30 emerging and already-established brands. Anchoring the stock is Phillip Lim's cool, urban menswear and edgy dresses by Alexander Wang. The modern threads for both genders are displayed atop quartz slab tables and hung on blackened steel bars. *809 Washington Street, between Gansevoort & Horatio Streets (1-212 524 9770, www.owennyc.com). Subway A, C, E to 14th Street; L to Eighth Avenue. Open 11am 7pm Mon-Sat; noon-6pm Sun.*

Porto Rico Importing Co
Food & drink
This family-run store, established in 1907, has earned a large following for its terrific range of coffee beans,

Owen

including its own prepared blends. Prices are reasonable, and the selection of teas also warrants exploration. *201 Bleecker Street, between Sixth Avenue & MacDougal Street (1-212 477 5421, www.portorico.com). Subway A, B, C, D, E, F, M to W 4th Street. Open 8am-9pm Mon-Sat; noon-7pm Sun. Other locations throughout the city.*

Rag & Bone General Store
Fashion
The Meatpacking District location of this enduringly hip brand, which began as a denim line in 2002, retains much of the former factory's industrial vibe with unfinished concrete floors, brick walls and an original Dave's Quality Veal sign. Sip a latte from the in-store Jack's Stir Brew Coffee before or after browsing the impeccably cut jeans, luxurious knitwear and well-tailored jackets for men and women. *425 W 13th Street, at Washington Street (1-212 249 3331, www.rag-bone.com). Subway A, C, E to 14th Street. Open 11am-8pm Mon-Sat; noon-7pm Sun. Other locations throughout the city.*

Reminiscence
Fashion/accessories
When Stewart Richer began crafting newsboy hats out of salvaged denim in the 1970s, he had no intention of starting a lifelong business. But his designs proved so popular with buyers, he decided to open his own storefront, selling his handmade clothing and accessories alongside vintage items. Having held four locations around the city, the shop recently relocated to its original Greenwich Village spot. Specialising in quirky threads from the 1960s to the '80s, Reminiscence is known for its inexpensive collection of street-ready and costume duds for both men and women. Snatch up unisex deep-dyed cotton tie-string overalls, Hawaiian-print skirts and authentic Swiss Army surplus bags. *74 Fifth Avenue, between 13th & 14th Streets (1-212 243 2292, www.reminiscence.com). Subway L, N, Q, R, 4, 5, 6 to 14th Street-Union Square. Open 10am-8pm Mon-Sat; noon-7pm Sun.*

Whittemore House
Health & beauty
Victoria Hunter and Larry Raspanti, who each spent more than 15 years at Bumble & Bumble, opened this hair salon in an 1830s mansion (one of the oldest buildings in Manhattan). The decor features faux-decayed stencilled walls and boudoir chairs. Cuts (from $105) and natural-looking colour, achieved through the house hair-painting technique (from $225), come courtesy of some of the city's best stylists. *45 Grove Street, at Bleecker Street (1-212 242 8880, www.whittemorehouse salon.com). Subway 1 to Christopher Street-Sheridan Square. Open 11am-8pm Tue; noon-8pm Wed; noon-9pm Thur, Fri; 10am-6pm Sat.*

Shops & Services

Chelsea

192 Books Books & music
In an era when many an indie bookshop has closed, 192, open since 2003, is proving that quirky boutique booksellers can make it after all. Owned and 'curated' by art dealer Paula Cooper and her husband, editor Jack Macrae, the store offers a strong selection of art books and literature, as well as tomes on history, current affairs, music, science and nature. The phenomenal reading series brings in top authors of the calibre of Joan Didion, Zadie Smith and Mark Strand.
192 Tenth Avenue, between 21st & 22nd Streets (1-212 255 4022, www.192books.com). Subway C, E to 23rd Street. Open 11am-7pm daily.

Antiques Garage Homewares
Designers (and the occasional celebrity) hunt regularly at this flea market in a vacant parking garage. Strengths include old prints, vintage clothing and household paraphernalia. The weekend outdoor Hell's Kitchen Flea Market, run by the same people, features a mix of vintage clothing and textiles, furniture and bric-a-brac.
112 W 25th Street, between Sixth & Seventh Avenues (1-212 243 5343, www.annexmarkets.com). Subway F, M to 14th Street. Open 9am-5pm Sat, Sun. No credit cards. Other location 39th Street, between Ninth & Tenth Avenues, Hell's Kitchen.

Billy's Bakery Food & drink
If you crave a large serving of nostalgia, come here for such super-sweet delights as classic cupcakes, coconut cream pie, Hello Dollies (indulgent graham cracker treats) and Famous Chocolate Icebox Cake, all dispensed in a retro setting.
184 Ninth Avenue, between 21st & 22nd Streets (1-212 647 9956, www.billysbakerynyc.com). Subway C, E to 23rd Street. Open 9.30am-11pm Mon-Thur; 9.30am-midnight Fri, Sat; 9am-9pm Sun.

Chelsea Piers Sport & fitness
Chelsea Piers is still the most impressive all-in-one athletic facility in New York. Between the ice rink (Pier 61, 1-212 336 6100), the bowling alley (between Piers 59 & 60, 1-212 835 2695), the driving range (Pier 59, 1-212 336 6400) and scads of other choices, there's definitely something for everyone. The Field House (between Piers 61 & 62, 1-212 336 6500) has a climbing wall, a gymnastics centre, batting cages, basketball courts and indoor turf fields. At the Sports Center Health Club (Pier 60, 1-212 336 6000), you'll find a gym complete with comprehensive weight deck and cardiovascular machines, plus classes covering everything from boxing to triathlon training in the pool.
Piers 59-62, W 18th to 23rd Streets, at Twelfth Avenue (1-212 336 6666, www.chelseapiers.com). Subway C, E to 23rd Street. Open times vary; phone or check website for details.

Mantiques Modern

Mantiques Modern Homewares
Walking into this two-level shop is a little like stumbling upon the private collection of a mad professor. Specialising in industrial and modernist furnishings, art and accessories from the 1880s to the 1980s, Mantiques Modern is a fantastic repository of beautiful and bizarre items, from kinetic sculptures and early 20th-century wooden artists' mannequins to a Soviet World War II telescope. Pieces by famous designers such as Hermès sit side by side with natural curiosities, and skulls (in metal or Lucite), crabs, animal horns and robots are all recurring themes.
146 W 22nd Street, between Sixth & Seventh Avenues (1-212 206 1494, www.mantiquesmodern.com). Subway 1 to 23rd Street. Open 10.30am-6.30pm Mon-Fri; 11am-7pm Sat, Sun.

Printed Matter Books & music
This non-profit organisation is devoted to artists' books – from David Shrigley's deceptively naïve illustrations to provocative photographic self-portraits by Matthias Herrmann – and operates a public reading room as well as a shop. Works by unknown and emerging artists share shelf space with those by veterans such as Yoko Ono and Edward Ruscha.
195 Tenth Avenue, between 21st & 22nd Streets (1-212 925 0325, www.printedmatter.org). Subway C, E to 23rd Street. Open 11am-7pm Mon-Wed, Sat; 11am-8pm Thur, Fri.

Gramercy & Flatiron

ABC Carpet & Home Homewares
Most of ABC's 35,000-strong carpet range is housed in the store across the street at no.881 – except the rarest rugs, which reside on the sixth floor of the main store. Browse everything from organic soap to hand-beaded lampshades on the bazaar-style ground floor. On the upper floors, furniture spans every style, from slick European minimalism to antique oriental and mid-century modern. The Bronx warehouse outlet (1055 Bronx River Avenue, between Bruckner Boulevard & Westchester Avenue, 1-718 842 8772) has discounted furnishings, but prices are still steep.
888 Broadway, at 19th Street (1-212 473 3000, www.abchome.com). Subway L, N, Q, R, 4, 5, 6 to 14th Street-Union Square. Open 10am-7pm Mon-Wed, Fri, Sat; 10am-8pm Thur; 11am-6.30pm Sun.

Books of Wonder Books & music
The only independent children's bookstore in the city features titles new and old (rare and out-of-print editions), plus a special collection of Oz books. The store also always has a good stock of signed books and children's book art, and the on-site bakery makes a visit even more of a treat.
18 W 18th Street, between Fifth & Sixth Avenues, Flatiron District (1-212 989 3270, www.booksofwonder.com). Subway F, M to 14th Street; L to Sixth Avenue; 1 to 18th Street. Open 10am-7pm Mon-Sat; 11am-6pm Sun.

Eataly Food & drink
This massive foodie destination from Mario Batali and Joe and Lidia Bastianich sprawls across 50,000sq ft. A spin-off of an operation by the same name just outside of Turin, the complex encompasses six restaurants and a rooftop beer garden. Adjacent retail areas offer gourmet provisions, including artisanal breads baked on the premises, fresh mozzarella, salumi and a vast array of olive oils.
200 Fifth Avenue, between 23rd & 24th Streets (1-212 229 2560,

www.eataly.com). Subway F, M, N, R to 23rd Street. Open 10am-11pm daily.

Fishs Eddy Homewares
Penny-pinchers frequent this barn-like space for sturdy dishware and glasses – surplus stock or recycled from restaurants, ocean liners and hotels (plain white side plates are a mere 99¢). But there are plenty of affordable, freshly minted kitchen goods too. Add spice to mealtime with glasses adorned with male or female pole-dancers, plates printed with the Brooklyn or Manhattan skyline and Floor Plan dinnerware – from $10 for a 'studio' side plate, NYC real estate has never been so cheap.
889 Broadway, at 19th Street (1-212 420 9020, www.fishseddy.com). Subway N, R to 23rd Street. Open 10am-9pm Mon; 9am-9pm Tue-Sat; 10am-8pm Sun.

Idlewild Books Books & music
Idlewild stocks travel guides to more than 100 countries and all 50 US states, which are grouped with related works of fiction and non-fiction. The shop also has a large selection of works in French, Spanish and Italian.
12 W 19th Street, between Fifth & Sixth Avenues (1-212 414 8888, www.idlewildbooks.com). Subway F, M to 14th Street; L to Sixth Avenue. Open noon-7.30pm Mon-Thur; noon-6pm Fri, Sat; noon-5pm Sun. Other location 249 Warren Street, between Court & Smith Streets, Cobble Hill, Brooklyn (1-718 403 9600).

JJ Hat Center Accessories
Trad hats may be back in fashion, but this venerable shop, in business since 1911, is oblivious to passing trends. Dapper gents sporting the shop's wares will help you choose from more than 4,000 fedoras, pork pies, caps and other styles on display in the splendid, chandelier-illuminated, wood-panelled

showroom. Prices start at $35 for a wool-blend cap.
310 Fifth Avenue, between 31st & 32nd Streets (1-212 239 4368, www.porkpiehatters.com). Subway B, D, F, M, N, Q, R to 34th Street-Herald Square. Open Jan-Sept 9am-6pm Mon-Fri; 9.30am-5.30pm Sat. Oct-Dec 9am-6pm Mon-Fri; 9.30am-5.30pm Sat; noon-5pm Sun.

Kiosk Accessories/homewares
Alisa Grifo has collected an array of inexpensive items – mostly simple and functional but with a strong design aesthetic – from around the world. At her gem of a shop, you can pick up anything from cool Japanese can openers to colourful net bags from Germany and Shaker onion baskets handmade in New Hampshire. Kiosk was relocating to the address below as this guide went to press, so call or check the website for details.
Room 925, 41 Union Square West, at 17th Street (1-212 226 8601, http://kioskkiosk.com). Subway N, Q, R, 4, 5, 6 to 14th Street-Union Square. Open call or see website for hours.

LA Burdick Food & drink
Best known for its petite chocolate penguins and mice, the family-owned, New Hampshire-based chocolatier now has a shop and café in NYC. Pastries share space in the display cases with marzipan, dipped caramels and a selection of truffles. Ponder the choices over a cup of dark, white or milk hot chocolate, or plump for dealer's choice with the assorted boxes.
5 E 20th Street, between Fifth Avenue & Broadway (1-212 796 0143, www.burdickchocolate.com). Subway N, R to 23rd Street. Open 8.30am-9pm Mon-Sat; 10am-7pm Sun.

Paragon Sporting Goods Sports equipment
Three floors of equipment and clothing for almost every activity, from the everyday (a slew of gym gear and trainers) to the more niche (badminton, kayaking) make this a prime one-stop sports-gear spot.
867 Broadway, at 18th Street (1-212 255 8889, www.paragonsports.com). Subway L, N, Q, R, 4, 5, 6 to 14th Street-Union Square. Open 10am-8.30pm Mon-Fri; 10am-8pm Sat; 11am-7pm Sun.

Showplace Antique & Design Center Fashion/homewares
Set over four expansive floors, this indoor market houses more than 200 high-quality dealers selling everything from Greek and Roman antiquities to vintage radios. Among the highlights are Joe Sundlie's spot-on trend vintage pieces from Lanvin and Alaïa, and Mood Indigo – arguably the best source in the city for collectable bar accessories and dinnerware. The array of Bakelite jewellery and table accessories, Fiestaware and novelty cocktail glasses is dazzling, and it's a wonderful repository of art deco cigarette cases, lighters and New York City memorabilia.

40 W 25th Street, between Fifth & Sixth Avenues (1-212 633 6063, www.nyshowplace.com). Subway F, M to 23rd Street. Open 10am-6pm Mon-Fri; 8.30am-5.30pm Sat, Sun.

Union Square Greenmarket Food & drink
Shop elbow-to-elbow with top chefs for locally grown produce, handmade breads and baked goods, preserves and cheeses at the city's flagship farmers' market around the periphery of Union Square Park. Between Thanksgiving and Christmas, a holiday market sets up shop.
From 16th to 17th Streets, between Union Square East & Union Square West (1-212 788 7476, www.grownyc.org/greenmarket). Subway L, N, Q, R, 4, 5, 6 to 14th Street-Union Square. Open 8am-6pm Mon, Wed, Fri, Sat.

Midtown

Amy's Bread Food & drink
Whether you want sweet (double-chocolate pecan Chubbie cookies) or savoury (hefty French sourdough boules), Amy's never disappoints. Breakfast and snacks such as the grilled cheese sandwich (made with New York State cheddar) are served in the on-site café.
672 Ninth Avenue, between 46th & 47th Streets (1-212 977 2670, www.amysbread.com). Subway C, E to 50th Street; N, Q, R to 49th Street. Open 7.30am-10pm Mon, Tue; 7.30am-11pm Wed-Fri; 8am-11pm Sat; 8am-10pm Sun. Other locations Chelsea Market, 75 Ninth Avenue, between 15th & 16th Streets, Chelsea (1-212 462 4338); 250 Bleecker

Street, at Leroy Street, West Village (1-212 675 7802).

B&H Electronics & photography
The ultimate one-stop shop for all your photographic, video and audio needs. In this huge store, goods are transported from the stock room via an overhead conveyor belt. Due to the largely Hasidic Jewish staff, the store is closed on Saturdays and Jewish holidays.
420 Ninth Avenue, at 34th Street (1-212 444 6615, www.bhphotovideo. com). Subway A, C, E to 34th Street-Penn Station. Open 9am-7pm Mon-Thur; 9am-1pm Fri; 10am-6pm Sun.

Bergdorf Goodman Department store
Synonymous with understated luxury, Bergdorf's is known for designer clothes (the fifth floor is dedicated to younger, trend-driven labels) and accessories. For something more unusual, seek out Kentshire's wonderful cache of vintage jewellery on the ground floor. Descend to the basement for the wide-ranging beauty department. The men's store is across the street at 745 Fifth Avenue.
754 Fifth Avenue, between 57th & 58th Streets (1-212 753 7300, www.bergdorfgoodman.com). Subway E, M to Fifth Avenue-53rd Street; N, Q, R to Fifth Avenue-59th Street. Open 10am-8pm Mon-Fri; 10am-7pm Sat; noon-6pm Sun.

Domus Homewares
Each year, the owners of this tucked-away Hell's Kitchen store, Luisa Cerutti and Nicki Lindheimer, visit a far-flung part of the world to forge links with and support co-operatives and individual craftspeople. The beautiful results, such as vivid baskets

woven from telephone wire by South African Zulu tribespeople, reflect a fine attention to detail and a sense of place. It's a great spot for reasonably priced home goods and gifts, from Tunisian bath towels to Italian throws.
413 W 44th Street, at Ninth Avenue, Hell's Kitchen (1-212 581 8099, www. domusnewyork.com). Subway A, C, E to 42nd Street-Port Authority. Open noon-8pm Tue-Sat; noon-6pm Sun.

Dover Street Market New York
The third location of Rei Kawakubo's quirky designer market sells an eclectic mix of 75-plus labels, including all of the Comme des Garçons lines. *See p5*
Clash of the Concept Stores.
160 Lexington Avenue, at 30th Street (1-646 837 7750, www.newyork.dover streetmarket.com). Subway 6 to 28th or 33rd Street. Open 11am-7pm Mon-Sat; noon-6pm Sun.

FAO Schwarz Children
Although it's now owned by the ubiquitous Toys 'R' Us company, this three-storey emporium is still the ultimate NYC toy box. Most people head straight to the 22ft-long floor piano that Tom Hanks famously tinkled in *Big*. Children will marvel at the giant stuffed animals, the detailed and imaginative Lego figures and the revolving Barbie fashion catwalk.
767 Fifth Avenue, at 58th Street (1-212 644 9400, www.fao.com). Subway N, Q, R to Lexington Avenue-59th Street; 4, 5, 6 to 59th Street. Open 10am-8pm Mon-Thur, Sun; 10am-9pm Fri, Sat.

Fine and Dandy Accessories
Following the success of several pop-ups around the city, owner Matt Fox opened his first permanent location in

Macy's

Magpie

Upper West Side

Alexis Bittar Accessories

Alexis Bittar started out selling his jewellery from a humble Soho street stall, but now the designer has four shops in which to show off his flamboyant pieces, such as sculptural Lucite cuffs and oversized crystal-encrusted earrings. This uptown boutique is twice the size of the West Village, Upper East Side and Soho locations, and is meant to resemble a 1940s powder room, with silk wallpaper and art deco-style lights. *410 Columbus Avenue, at 80th Street (1-646 590 4142, www. alexisbittar.com). Subway B, C to 81st Street-Museum of Natural History. Open 11am-7pm Mon-Sat; noon-6pm Sun. Other locations throughout the city.*

Levain Bakery Food & drink

Levain sells a variety of breads, muffins, brioche and other delectable baked goods, but we're crazy about the cookies. A full 6oz, the massive mounds stay gooey in the middle. The lush, brownie-like double-chocolate variety, made with extra-dark French cocoa and semi-sweet chocolate chips, is a truly decadent treat. *167 W 74th Street, between Columbus & Amsterdam Avenues (1-212 874 6080, www.levainbakery.com). Subway 1 to 79th Street. Open 8am-7pm Mon-Sat; 9am-7pm Sun. Other location 2167 Frederick Douglass Boulevard (Eighth Avenue), between 116th & 117th Streets, Harlem (1-646 455 0952).*

Magpie Gifts & souvenirs

Sylvia Parker worked as a buyer at the American Folk Art Museum gift shop before opening this eco-friendly boutique. The funky space, which is decorated with bamboo shelving and recycled Hudson River driftwood, is packed with locally made, handcrafted, sustainable and fair-trade items. Finds include vintage quilts, recycled-resin cuff bracelets, and Meow Meow Tweet soaps and candles, handmade in Brooklyn. *488 Amsterdam Avenue, between 83rd & 84th Streets (1-646 998 3002, www.magpienewyork.com). Subway 1 to 86th Street. Open 11am-7pm Mon-Sat; 11am-6pm Sun.*

Shops at Columbus Circle Mall

Classier than your average mall, the retail contingent of the 2.8 million-sq-ft Time Warner Center features upscale stores such as Coach, Cole Haan and LK Bennett for accessories and shoes, London shirtmaker Thomas Pink, Bose home entertainment, the fancy kitchenware purveyor Williams-Sonoma, as well as shopping centre staples J.Crew, Aveda, and organic grocer Whole Foods. Some of the city's top restaurants (including Thomas Keller's gourmet destination Per Se

---

Hell's Kitchen. The accessories-only shop – decked out in flourishes such as collegiate trophies and ironing boards repurposed as tables – is a prime location for the modern gent to score of-the-moment retro accoutrements like bow ties, suspenders (braces) and spats. House-label printed ties are hung in propped-open vintage trunks, while patterned socks are displayed in old briefcases. *445 W 49th Street, between Ninth & Tenth Avenues (1-212 247 4847, www.fineanddandyshop.com). Subway C, E to 50th Street. Open noon-8pm Mon, Wed-Sat; 1-8pm Sun.*

Henri Bendel Department store

While Bendel's merchandise (a mix of jewellery, accessories, cosmetics and fragrances) is comparable to that of other upscale stores, it somehow seems more desirable when viewed in its opulent premises, a conglomeration of three 19th-century townhouses – and those darling brown-and-white striped shopping bags don't hurt, either. If you find you haven't a thing to wear while you're in NYC, but don't want to add to your luggage, you can select designer duds and accessories in the on-site showroom of popular e-tailer Rent the Runway. Bendel's is also the home of celebrity hairdresser Frédéric Fekkai's flagship salon. *712 Fifth Avenue, at 56th Street (1-212 247 1100, www.henribendel.com). Subway E, M to Fifth Avenue-53rd Street; N, Q, R to Fifth Avenue-59th Street. Open 10am-8pm Mon-Sat; noon-7pm Sun.*

Juvenex Health & beauty

This bustling Koreatown relaxation hub may be slightly rough around the edges (frayed towels, dingy sandals), but we embrace it for its bathhouse-meets-Epcot feel (igloo saunas, tiled 'soaking ponds' and a slatted bridge), and 24-hour availability (it's women only between 7am and 5pm). A basic Purification Program – including soak and sauna, face, body and hair cleansing and a salt scrub – is great value at $115. *5th Floor, 25 W 32nd Street, between Fifth Avenue & Broadway (1-646 733 1330, www.juvenexspa.com). Subway B, D, F, M, N, Q, R to 34th Street-Herald Square. Open 24hrs daily.*

Macy's Department store

It may not be as glamorous as New York's other famous stores but for sheer breadth of stock, the 34th Street behemoth is hard to beat. Mid-price fashion for all ages, big beauty names and housewares have traditionally been the store's bread and butter, but a $400 million redesign, wrapping up in late 2015, has introduced new luxury boutiques including Gucci and Burberry. The cosmetics department has been luxed up with high-end brands such as Jo Malone London and Laura Mercier, plus a Blow hair-styling bar. If you need tourist guidance, stop by the store's Official NYC Information Center. *151 W 34th Street, between Broadway & Seventh Avenue (1-212 695 4400, www.macys.com). Subway B, D, F, M, N, Q, R to 34th Street-Herald Square; 1, 2, 3 to 34th Street-Penn Station. Open 9am-9.30pm Mon-Sat; 11am-8.30pm Sun.*

Nepenthes New York Fashion

Well-dressed dudes with an eye on the Japanese style scene will already be familiar with this Tokyo fashion retailer. The narrow Garment District shop – its first US location – showcases expertly crafted urban-rustic menswear from house label Engineered Garments, such as plaid flannel shirts and workwear-inspired jackets. There is also a small selection of its women's line, FWK. *307 W 38th Street, between Eighth & Ninth Avenues (1-212 643 9540, www.nepenthesny.com). Subway A, C, E, 1, 2, 3 to 34th Street-Penn Station. Open noon-7pm Mon-Sat; noon-5pm Sun.*

Saks Fifth Avenue Department store

Although Saks maintains a presence in more than 30 American states, the Fifth Avenue location is the original, established in 1924 by New York retailers Horace Saks and Bernard Gimbel. The store features all the big names in fashion, from Armani to Yves Saint Laurent, including an expansive shoe salon that shares the eighth floor with a shop-cum-café from deluxe chocolatier Charbonnel et Walker. The opulent beauty hall is fun to peruse, and customer service is excellent, though retiring types might find it too aggressive. *611 Fifth Avenue, between 49th & 50th Streets, (1-212 753 4000, www.saksfifthavenue.com). Subway E, M to Fifth Avenue-53rd Street. Open 10am-8pm Mon-Sat; 11am-7pm Sun.*

Sam Ash Music Books & music

Established in Brooklyn in 1924, this musical instrument emporium moved from Times Square's now-silent 'music row' in 2013. The 30,000sq ft store offers new, vintage and custom guitars of all varieties, along with amps, DJ equipment, drums, keyboards, recording equipment, turntables and an array of sheet music. *333 W 34th Street, between Eighth & Ninth Avenues (1-212 719 2299, www.samashmusic.com). Subway A, C, E to 34th Street-Penn Station. Open 10am-8pm Mon-Sat; 11am-7pm Sun.*

GALLERY-HOPPING GUIDE
Hit these essential stops on our curated contemporary art crawl.

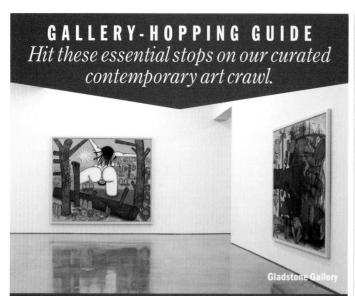

Gladstone Gallery

CHELSEA

From West 19th Street to West 29th Street, between Tenth and Eleventh Avenues, converted industrial spaces are crammed with around 200 art spaces. Most are open 10am-6pm Tuesday to Saturday, though in summer many keep different hours and close at weekends, so call before visiting.

David Zwirner
Zwirner mixes museum-quality shows of historical figures with head-turning contemporary artists. *519, 525 & 533 W 19th Street, between Tenth & Eleventh Avenues (1-212 727 2070, www.davidzwirner.com).*

Gagosian Gallery
Larry Gagosian's mammoth (20,000sq ft) contribution to 24th Street's galleries opened in 1999. *555 W 24th Street, between Tenth & Eleventh Avenues (1-212 741 1111, www.gagosian.com).*

Gladstone Gallery
Gladstone is strictly blue-chip, with an emphasis on daring conceptual art. *515 W 24th Street, between Tenth & Eleventh Avenues (1-212 206 9300, www.gladstonegallery.com).*

Luhring Augustine
An impressive index of artists includes Rachel Whiteread, Christopher Wool and Pipilotti Rist. *531 W 24th Street, between Tenth & Eleventh Avenues (1-212 206 9100, www.luhringaugustine.com).*

Mary Boone Gallery
Boone made her name in the 1980s, representing Julian Schnabel and Jean-Michel Basquiat, and continues to produce hit shows featuring young artists. *541 W 24th Street, between Tenth & Eleventh Avenues (1-212 752 2929, www.maryboonegallery.com).*

Matthew Marks Gallery
Opened in 1991, the gallery was a driving force behind Chelsea's transformation into an art mecca. *523 W 24th Street, between Tenth & Eleventh Avenues (1-212 243 0200, www.matthewmarks.com).*

LOWER EAST SIDE

Over the past ten years, the area has seen a steady migration of young dealers, aided by the relocation of the New Museum of Contemporary Art to the Bowery.

Canada
One of the first of the Lower East Side galleries, Canada continues to keep it real with a programme that reflects a funky DIY aesthetic. *333 Broome Street, between Bowery & Chrystie Street (1-212 925 4631, www.canadanewyork.com). Open 11am-6pm Wed-Sun.*

Eleven Rivington
The Van Doren Waxter Gallery offshoot offers an elegant uptown vibe in small-storefront form. *11 Rivington Street, between Bowery & Chrystie Street (1-212 982 1930, www.elevenrivington.com). Open noon-6pm Wed-Sun.*

Miguel Abreu Gallery
A filmmaker and founding member of the legendary Threadwaxing alternative space in Soho (now closed), Miguel Abreu represents conceptually inspired artists. *136 Orchard Street, between Canal & Hester Streets (1-212 995 1774, www.miguelabreugallery.com). Open 11am-6.30pm Wed-Sun.*

Rachel Uffner Gallery
Uffner, who cut her teeth at Christies, showcases a small but eclectic stable. *170 Suffolk Street, between E Houston & Stanton Streets (1-212 274 0064, www.racheluffnergallery.com). Open 10am-6pm Wed-Sun.*

and his café Bouchon Bakery; for both, *see p60*) have made it a dining destination that transcends the stigma of eating at the mall. *Time Warner Center, 10 Columbus Circle, at 59th Street (1-212 823 6300, www.theshopsatcolumbuscircle.com). Subway A, B, C, D, 1 to 59th Street-Columbus Circle. Open 10am-9pm Mon-Sat; 11am-7pm Sun (hours vary for some businesses).*

Zabar's Food & drink
Zabar's is more than just a market – it's a genuine New York City landmark. It began life in 1934 as a tiny storefront specialising in Jewish 'appetising' delicacies and has gradually expanded to take over half a block of prime Upper West Side real estate. What never ceases to surprise, however, is its reasonable prices – even for high-end foods. Besides the famous smoked fish and rafts of delicacies, Zabar's has fabulous bread, cheese, olives and coffee, and an entire floor dedicated to gadgets and homewares. *2245 Broadway, at 80th Street (1-212 787 2000, www.zabars.com). Subway 1 to 79th Street. Open 8am-7.30pm Mon-Fri; 8am-8pm Sat; 9am-6pm Sun.*

Upper East Side

Madison Avenue, between 57th and 86th Streets, is packed with international designer names: Alexander McQueen, Chloé, Derek Lam, Gucci, Prada, Lanvin, Ralph Lauren, Valentino and more.

Barneys New York
Department store
Barneys has a reputation for spotlighting more independent designer labels than other upmarket department stores, and has its own quirky-classic collection. The ground floor showcases luxe accessories, and cult beauty brands are in the basement. Head to the seventh and eighth floors for contemporary designer and denim lines. There are several smaller Barneys around town. *660 Madison Avenue, at 61st Street, Upper East Side (1-212 826 8900, www.barneys.com). Subway N, Q, R to Fifth Avenue-59th Street; 4, 5, 6 to 59th Street. Open 10am-8pm Mon-Fri; 10am-7pm Sat; 11am-6pm Sun. Other locations throughout the city.*

Bloomingdale's
Department store
Ranking among the city's top tourist attractions, Bloomie's is a gigantic, glitzy department store stocked with everything from handbags to home furnishings. The glam beauty section includes an outpost of globe-spanning apothecary Space NK, and you can get a mid-shopping sugar fix at the on-site Magnolia Bakery. The hipper, compact Soho outpost concentrates on contemporary fashion and accessories, denim and cosmetics.

1000 Third Avenue, at 59th Street (1-212 705 2000, www.bloomingdales.com). Subway N, Q, R to Lexington Avenue-59th Street; 4, 5, 6 to 59th Street. Open 10am-8.30pm Mon-Sat; 10am-7pm Sun. Other location 504 Broadway, between Broome & Spring Streets, Soho (1-212 729 5900).

Cornelia Spa at the Surrey
Health & beauty
Husband and wife Rick Aidekman and Ellen Sackoff have reopened this popular boutique spa, which closed in 2009, in a smaller space in upscale hotel the Surrey. The intimate yet luxurious oasis is designed to make you feel like you're lounging in your own living space, while a 'botanical tasting bar' serves savoury and sweet treats. Splurge on the Reparative Caviar and Oxygen Quench facial ($325), or a signature massage ($175), which combines deep-tissue, Swedish and shiatsu techniques. *2nd Floor, 20 E 76th Street, between Fifth & Madison Avenues (1-646 358 3600, www.corneliaspaathesurrey.com). Subway 6 to 77th Street. Open 10am-8pm Mon-Fri; 9am-7pm Sat, Sun.*

Fivestory Fashion
At just 26 years old (and with a little help from her fashion-industry insider dad), Claire Distenfeld opened this glamorous, grown-up boutique just off Madison Avenue's swanky designer row. Sprawling over two and a half floors of – you guessed it – a five-storey townhouse, the space is stocked with clothing, shoes and accessories for men, women and children, plus select home items. The emphasis is on less ubiquitous American and European labels, including Alexander Wang, Giambattista Valli and Acne, and Gianvito Rossi's seductively sleek footwear. *18 E 69th Street, between Fifth & Madison Avenues (1-212 288 1338, www.fivestoryny.com). Subway 6 to 68th Street-Hunter College. Open 10am-6pm Mon-Wed, Fri; 10am-7pm Thur; noon-6pm Sat, Sun.*

Fix Beauty Bar
Health & beauty
Writer Karol Markowicz and Michelle Breskin, whose background is in real estate and finance, are taking the blow-dry bar phenomenon one step further, offering busy New Yorkers manicures ($15) and pedicures ($35) to accompany the affordable flat-rate blow-dries ($40) at their chic lavender-and-grey salon. Hairstyles are named after celebrities with instantly recognisable tresses, such as the Jen (sleek and pin-straight), the Taylor (soft, styled curls) and the Kim (full, dramatic waves). *2nd Floor, 847 Lexington Avenue, between 64th & 65th Streets (1-212 744 0800, www.fixbeautybar.com). Subway F to Lexington Avenue-63rd Street. Open 9am-7pm Mon, Tue; 9am-8pm Wed, Thur; 9am-9pm Fri, Sat; 9am-6pm Sun.*

Gagosian Shop
Gifts & souvenirs

The art-gallery giant recently opened a 600sq ft gift shop, designed by Selldorf Architects, on the ground floor of its Upper East Side location. Posters, prints and publications are the main focus, but artist-designed home decor and objects pepper the offerings. *976 Madison Avenue, between 76th & 77th Streets (1-212 796 1224, www.gagosian.com). Subway 6 to 77th Street. Open 10am-7pm Mon-Sat.*

Lisa Perry
Fashion

Upon graduation from FIT in 1981, designer Lisa Perry launched her line of retro women's threads inspired by her massive personal collection of 1960s and '70s fashion. Ultrabright pieces, such as her signature colour-blocked minidresses, pop against the stark white walls of her Madison Avenue flagship. You'll also find the designer's cheerful accessories, such as candy-coloured duffel bags, and her mod home collection, which includes place mats and pillows. *988 Madison Avenue, at 77th Street (1-212 431 7467, www.lisaperrystyle.com). Subway 6 to 77th Street. Open 10am-6pm Mon-Sat; noon-5pm Sun.*

Malin + Goetz
Health & beauty

Matthew Malin and Andrew Goetz recently opened the third Manhattan location of their modern apothecary, showcasing their natural, locally manufactured line of unisex skin and hair products. You'll find the full collection, including glycolic-acid peel pads, aluminium-free eucalyptus deodorant and sage styling cream. An alcove in the back displays candles and fragrances in unusual scents. *1266B Madison Avenue, between 90th & 91st Streets (1-212 226 1310, www.malinandgoetz.com). Subway 4, 5, 6 to 86th Street. Open 11am-7pm Mon-Fri; noon-7pm Sat; noon-6pm Sun.*

Paul Molé Barber Shop
Health & beauty

Best known for its precise shaves, this nostalgic barbers' has been grooming men since 1913 (John Steinbeck used to come here to be debearded). As well as its signature Deluxe Open Razor Shave ($40), you can get a haircut (from $39) and other services such as a scalp massage ($10). *1034 Lexington Avenue, at 74th Street (1-212 535 8461, www.paulmole.com). Subway 6 to 77th Street. Open 7.30am-8pm Mon-Fri; 7.30am-6pm Sat; 9am-4pm Sun (except July, Aug). No credit cards.*

Harlem & Upper Manhattan

Trunk Show Designer Consignment
Fashion

Modelling agent Heather Jones went from hosting oversubscribed pop-up trunk shows to co-opening this small Harlem storefront. Men's and women's threads and accessories range from edgier brands (Margiela, Rick Owens) to Madison Avenue labels (Gucci, Chanel, Céline), with in-season items marked down between 20 per cent and 70 per cent. The shop sometimes keeps erratic hours, so it's wise to call before making a special trip. *275-277 W 113th Street, between Adam Clayton Powell Jr Boulevard (Seventh Avenue) & Frederick Douglass Boulevard (Eighth Avenue) (1-212 662 0009, www.trunkshowconsignment.com). Subway B, C to 110th Street-Cathedral Parkway. Open 1-8.30pm Tue-Fri; 1-7.30pm Sat; noon-6.30pm Sun.*

Brooklyn

Bird
Fashion

A former assistant buyer at Barneys, Jen Mankins opened her first Bird boutique in Park Slope in 1999. Now fashion-forward Brooklynites – and residents from NYC's other boroughs – flock to three locations for up-and-coming local and international designers. The spacious Williamsburg store stocks clothing and accessories for men and women. Rubbing shoulders on the racks are eclectic pieces by well-known and not-so-familiar names such as Acne, Isabel Marant, A Détacher, Tsumori Chisato and Black Crane. *203 Grand Street, between Bedford & Driggs Avenues, Williamsburg (1-718 388 1655, www.shopbird.com). Subway L to Bedford Avenue. Open noon-8pm Mon-Fri; 11am-7pm Sat; noon-7pm Sun. Other locations 220 Smith Street, at Butler Street, Cobble Hill (1-718 797 3774); 316 Fifth Avenue, between 2nd & 3rd Streets, Park Slope (1-718 768 4940).*

TOP TIP!
On the record
Greenpoint, Brooklyn is vinyl central – also check out Permanent Records (www.permanentrecords.info) and Academy Record Annex (www.academyannex.com).

Brooklyn Superhero Supply Company
Gifts & souvenirs

To unleash your inner superhero, stop by this purveyor of capes, X-ray goggles, truth serum and gallon tins of Immortality. Just be sure you adhere to the Vow of Heroism you must recite before your purchases are handed over. Proceeds benefit the 826NYC kids' writing centre behind a concealed door in the back, so you can feel super about that, too. *372 Fifth Avenue, between 5th & 6th Streets, Park Slope (1-718 499 9884, www.superherosupplies.com). Subway F, G, R to Fourth Ave-9th Street. Open varies; call before visiting.*

By Brooklyn
Gifts & souvenirs

Gaia DiLoreto's modern-day general store offers an array of New York-made goods, including pickles, soaps, T-shirts, jewellery, housewares, accessories and cookbooks by Brooklyn authors. Look out for Maptote borough-specific bags and Brooklyn Slate Co's burlap-wrapped reclaimed slate cheese boards. *261 Smith Street, between DeGraw & Douglass Streets, Carroll Gardens (1-718 643 0606, www.bybrooklyn.com). Subway F, G to Carroll Street. Open 11am-7pm Mon-Wed, Sun; 11am-8pm Thur-Sat.*

Captured Tracks
Books & music

A crop of record stores has sprung up in already cratedigger-friendly North Brooklyn within the last year. The flagship of the trendsetting label of the same name, Captured Tracks stocks an ever-changing trove of vinyl, plus cassettes, art books, vintage recording equipment and curated listening booths from local musicians. Don't be surprised to find yourself browsing alongside artists from the top-shelf Captured Tracks roster, such as DIIV's Zachary Cole Smith and Canadian troubadour Mac DeMarco. *195 Calyer Street, between Manhattan Avenue & Leonard Street, Greenpoint (1-718 609 0871, www.capturedtracks.com). Subway G to Greenpoint Avenue or Nassau Avenue. Open noon-8pm daily.*

CB I Hate Perfume
Health & beauty

Contrary to the name of his shop, Christopher Brosius doesn't actually hate what he sells; he just despises the concept of mass-produced fragrances. While the one-on-one custom perfume service, which allows you to collaborate with Brosius to create your own signature scent, starts at a lofty $10,000, there is already a waiting list of several months. However, you can choose from nearly 40 evocative ready-to-wear fragrances, such as Gathering Apples or At the Beach 1966, which start at less than $100. *3rd Floor, 318 Maujer Street, between Morgan Avenue & Waterbury Street, Bushwick (1-718 384 6890, www.cbihateperfume.com). Subway L to Bedford Avenue. Open by appointment noon-6pm Tue-Thur; noon-6pm Fri, Sat.*

Cog & Pearl
Gifts & souvenirs

This gift shop sells a melange of artist-made items including jewellery, fine art, home accessories and greetings cards. Look out for embroidered linen pillows by Brooklyn-based Coral & Tusk, gemstone rings by local jeweller Emily Amey and cool terrariums, complete with miniature figures, by Twig Terrariums. *190 Fifth Avenue, at Sackett Street, Park Slope (1-718 623 8200, www.cogandpearl.com). Subway R to Union Street. Open noon-8pm Tue-Sat; noon-6pm Sun (reduced hrs in winter).*

Egg Children

Set in the old HQ of the Grand Union Tea Company, designer Susan Lazar's NYC store has a retro garment-factory

---

RECOMMENDED
Rough Trade

In late 2013, revered UK indie music retailer Rough Trade opened its first Stateside outpost in a 15,000-square-foot Williamsburg warehouse, complete with in-house café. In addition to tens of thousands of all-new titles – roughly half of them vinyl and half CDs – the megastore sells music books, magazines and equipment, curates rotating art installations, and hosts gigs both ticketed and free from the likes of Television, Sky Ferreira and Sondre Lerche. The selection spans genres and decades, from buzzy indie pop to used funk, psychedelic and world music, and the insanely knowledgeable staff can always be counted on to provide some tuneful inspiration. **64 North 9th Street, between Kent & Wythe Avenues, Williamsburg (1-718 388 4111, www.roughtrade.com). Subway L to Bedford Avenue. Open 9am-11pm Mon-Sat; 10am-9pm Sun.**

vibe. Among her seasonally changing creations for babies and children up to age eight, you might find striped infant bodysuits, cute print jersey dresses, and classic peacoats for both boys and girls.
72 Jay Street, between Front & Water Streets, Dumbo (1-347 356 4097, www.egg-baby.com). Subway A, C to High Street; F to York Street. Open 10am-6pm Mon-Wed, Sun; 10am-7pm Thur-Sat.

Erie Basin Accessories
For a unique keepsake, check out Russell Whitmore's finely honed collection of jewellery dating from the 18th century to the 1940s, from fin de siècle tortoiseshell studs to art deco cocktail rings (vintage engagement and wedding rings are a speciality). There's also a selection of furniture and decorative objects.
388 Van Brunt Street, at Dikeman Street, Red Hook (1-718 554 6147, www.eriebasin.com). Subway F, G to Smith-9th Streets, then B61 bus. Open varies seasonally; usually noon-6pm Wed-Sat.

Hollander & Lexer Fashion
Most of the men's and women's clothing displayed on vintage iron racks in this black-walled store is designed in Manhattan's Garment District. Owner Brian Cousins stocks lines, such as Kai D, Seyrig and his New York-made house label, which exude an old-fashioned focus on craftsmanship and high-quality fabrics that is also utterly contemporary.
369 Atlantic Avenue, between Bond & Hoyt Streets, Boerum Hill (1-718 797 9739, www.hollanderandlexer.com). Open 11am-7pm Mon-Sat; noon-6pm Sun.

Modern Anthology Fashion/homewares
Owners Becka Citron and John Marsala – the creative force behind the *Man Caves* TV series – have created a one-stop lifestyle shop that brings together vintage and contemporary homewares, alongside clothing, accessories and grooming products. Understatedly stylish dudes can update their wardrobes with classic shirts and sweaters by New York designers Ernest Alexander and Todd Snyder and USA-crafted footwear by Oak Street Bootmakers, among other labels. And what hip bachelor pad is complete without a stack of vintage issues of *Playboy* and barware?
68 Jay Street, between Front & Water Streets, Dumbo (1-718 522 3020, www.modernanthology.com). Subway A, C to High Street; F to York Street. Open 11am-7pm Mon-Sat; noon-6pm Sun.

Powerhouse Arena Books & music
Also serving as a gallery and performance space, the Arena is the cavernous retail arm of Powerhouse Books, which produces coffee-table tomes on such diverse subjects as

SUPERFLEA
Flea markets have morphed into food-and-culture destinations.

Brooklyn Flea

Rummaging in the city's outdoor flea markets has long been a favourite New York weekend pastime, but the past several years have seen the emergence of a more sophisticated breed of bazaar, offering high-quality crafts, gourmet snacks and even arts and entertainment, alongside vintage clothing, furniture and bric-a-brac. The popular **Brooklyn Flea** (www.brooklynflea.com) was launched in 2008 by Jonathan Butler, founder of Brooklyn real-estate blog Brownstoner.com, and Eric Demby, former PR man for the Brooklyn borough president, who identified Brooklyn as being ripe for a destination market. The original location (176 Lafayette Avenue, between Clermont & Vanderbilt Avenues, Fort Greene) is open from April until the third week of November on Saturdays, and includes around 150 vendors, selling a mix of vintage clothing, records, furnishings, locally designed fashion and crafts. Another location runs on Sundays, while the Williamsburg waterfront is the site of the nosh-only Saturday spin-off, **Smorgasburg**, where you can sample NYC grub such as Red Hook Lobster Pound lobster rolls and Mighty Quinn's barbecue. In winter, the flea market moves indoors, to a sprawling space in Williamsburg (see website for addresses and hours).

In autumn 2013, the crowd-pleasing pop-up **Brooklyn Night Bazaar** (www.bkbazaar.com) found a permanent home in a 24,000-square-foot Greenpoint warehouse at 165 Banker Street, at Norman Avenue. On Friday nights from 7pm to 1am and Saturdays from 6pm to midnight, the market features a locally focused lineup of art, crafts and food, including BrisketTown's top-flight barbecue and Ample Hills Creamery ice-cream. It also adds music to the mix – four to five bands, curated by a record label or publication, play each night – and Kelso and 21st Amendment are on tap in the beer garden. The sprawling emporium is also equipped with a minigolf course, ping-pong tables and arcade games.

The phenomenon isn't limited to Brooklyn – on Saturdays from May to October, you can nosh on everything from locally made ice-cream to tacos as you browse vintage fashion, handmade jewellery, skincare and more at **Hester Street Fair** (Hester Street, at Essex Street, www.hesterstreetfair.com). Located on the site of a former Lower East Side pushcart market, it has around 60 vendors.

New York laundromats, celebrity dogs and the Brooklyn Navy Yard.
37 Main Street, between Front & Water Streets, Dumbo (1-718 666 3049, www.powerhousearena.com). Subway A, C to High Street; F to York Street. Open 10am-7pm Mon-Fri; 11am-7pm Sat, Sun (extended hours in summer).

Steve's Authentic Key Lime Pie Food & drink
Flooding ravaged the original factory on Pier 41 during Hurricane Sandy, putting owner Steve Tarpin and his pastry lieutenants out of commission. They made their comeback on the next pier over. Inside the orange-hued bakery, you'll find Tarpin's signature graham-cracker-crusted pies, filled with a condensed-milk custard laced with zesty lime juice, plus the Swingle, a tartlet dipped in dark Belgian chocolate.
185 Van Dyke Street, at Ferris Street, Red Hook (1-718 858 5333, www.stevesauthentic.com). Subway F, G to Smith-9th Streets, then B61 bus. Open varies; usually 11am-5pm Fri-Sun.

Swords-Smith Fashion
Fashion vets Briana Swords (a former womenswear designer for

Levi Strauss) and R Smith (a graphic designer whose credits include *Vogue*) are behind this boutique for men and women. The duo offers a carefully curated collection of clothing and accessories from between 70 and 80 up-and-coming designers – many of them locally based, such as Lucio Castro and Samantha Pleet – in the skylighted, minimalist space.
98 South 4th Street, between Bedford Avenue & Berry Street, Williamsburg (1-347 599 2969, www.swords-smith.com). Subway L to Bedford Avenue; J, M, Z to Marcy Avenue. Open noon-8pm Mon-Fri, Sun; 11am-8pm Sat.

Woodley & Bunny Health & beauty
With a prime Williamsburg location, Woodley & Bunny is the place to get the most cutting-edge crop (from $86 for women, from $66 for men) or colour, but there's a welcome emphasis on individuality at this laid-back beauty spot. Part hair salon, part apothecary, it also offers beauty treatments such as mini facials and eyebrow tweezing.
196 North 10th Street, at Driggs Avenue, Williamsburg (1-718 218 6588, www.woodleyandbunny.com). Subway L to Bedford Avenue; G to Nassau Avenue. Open 10am-9pm Mon-Fri; 9am-8pm Sat; 11am-7pm Sun.

Queens

LIC: living Fashion/homewares
Neighbours-turned-business partners Rebekah Witzke and Jillian Tangen opened this lifestyle boutique, featuring women's clothing (including several hard-to-find Scandinavian brands) and accessories for both guys and gals, plus noteworthy household items. The latter, including Tocca candles and fun barware, are displayed in a 1940s vintage cabinet.
5-35 51st Avenue, between Vernon Boulevard & 5th Street, Long Island City (1-718 361 5650, www.licliving.com). Subway 7 to Vernon Boulevard-Jackson Avenue. Open 11am-7pm Tue-Sat; 11am-5pm Sun.

Long Island City Kleaners Fashion
Frustrated by the sparse streetwear options in his neighbourhood, Mark Garcia brought his favourite local brands together in this cosy lifestyle boutique. Inspired by gritty NYC storefronts from the 1980s and '90s that posed as dry cleaners but hosted illegal activities, Garcia decorated the space with vintage sewing machines and for sale T-shirts displayed in plastic dry-cleaner bags. But the goods here are completely legit: clothing, skating-related items and limited-edition collectibles.
45-03 Broadway, between 45th & 46th Streets, Astoria (1-718 606 0540, www.licnyc.com). Subway M, R to 46th Street. Open 11am-8pm Mon, Wed-Sat; noon-6pm Sun.

Arts & Entertainment

For live arts, nights on the town and fun for the kids

Children

Sand toys like this make a day at the beach lots of fun.

Brooklyn Children's Museum

Bronx Zoo

Critic's choice

1 **Bronx Zoo** All creatures great and small, from majestic lions to exotic cockroaches. *See left.*

2 **Brooklyn Children's Museum** Local-centric displays for the younger generation. *See p87.*

3 **Children's Museum of the Arts** See and do at this creativity-inspiring institution. *See p87.*

4 **New York Hall of Science** Proof that science can be fun. *See p87.*

5 **New Victory Theater** Off Broadway for young culture lovers. *See p87.*

Moppets take Manhattan

The best of the Big Apple for little ones.

The crowded and fast-paced metropolis may not seem like the world's most child-friendly place at first glance, but its 21st-century baby boom has given rise to myriad cultural, culinary and just plain fun offerings for families. Such icons as the Ellis Island Immigration Museum and the American Museum of Natural History are must-sees, but they are just the beginning. Among the most frequented corners of the city are its green spaces and playgrounds – seek one out when you're in need of a breather from the relentless urban buzz.

Sightseeing & entertainment

ANIMALS & NATURE

See also pp34-35 **Central Park**.

Bronx Zoo

Step aboard the Wild Asia Monorail (open May-Oct, admission $5), which tours 38 acres of exhibits housing Indo-Chinese tigers, elephants, Mongolian wild horses and more. Madagascar! is a permanent home to exotic animals from that lush island. Among its residents are lemurs, giant crocodiles, lovebirds, radiated tortoises and, coolest (and grossest) of all, hissing cockroaches. Five lemurs were born in the exhibit in its first year. *For listings, see p48.*

New York Aquarium

Just weeks after announcing the construction of a 57,000sq ft building that will house a new 'Ocean Wonders: Sharks!' exhibition, slated to open in 2015, the seaside aquarium was hit hard by Hurricane Sandy, which unleashed its fury on New York in autumn 2012. It has since partially reopened with a new sea lion theatre and reduced pricing that reflects the institution's limited offerings during construction. *610 Surf Avenue, at West 8th Street, Coney Island, Brooklyn (1-718 265 3474, www.nyaquarium.com). Subway D, N, Q to Coney Island-Stillwell Avenue; F, Q to W 8th Street-NY Aquarium. Open Sept-May 10am-4.30pm daily.*

June-Aug 10am-6pm daily. Admission $9.95; free under-3s. Pay what you wish after 3pm Fri.

Prospect Park Audubon Center

Overlooking Prospect Lake, the child-oriented Audubon Center is dedicated to nature education and wildlife preservation. Start at the visitor centre, featuring a giant interactive microscope and animal presentations, and stick around for woodland tours, storytelling and birdwatching walks. *Prospect Park, enter from Ocean Avenue, at Lincoln Road, Brooklyn (1-718 287 3400, www.prospectpark. org/audubon). Subway B, Q to Prospect Park. Open Feb, Mar, Nov, Dec noon-4pm Sat, Sun. Apr, June, Sept, Oct noon-4pm Thur-Sun. July, Aug noon-5pm Thur-Sun. Closed Jan. Admission free.*

MUSEUMS

Defying the stuffy cliché, many of Manhattan's most venerable institutions are extremely child-friendly. The **DiMenna Children's**

History Museum inside the **New-York Historical Society** (*see p34*) engages kids with New York's past by looking at the childhoods of various residents, some famous (Alexander Hamilton), others anonymous (child newspaper sellers in the early 20th century). For years, workshops for kids of all ages have been offered at the the **Metropolitan Museum of Art** (*see p37*), the **Whitney Museum of American Art** (*see p36*), the **Museum of Modern Art** (*see p31*), the **Rubin Museum** (*see p27*) and the **Museum of Arts and Design** (*see p34*); check their websites for schedules. The Met, with its mummies and Temple of Dendur, an ancient Egyptian temple, is a particular hit with children.

Even very young kids love exploring the **American Museum of Natural History** (*see p34*). The Fossil Halls are home to the museum's huge, beloved dinosaurs – most reconstructed from actual fossils – and the myriad wildlife dioramas are a fascinating (and astonishingly lifelike) peek at the world's fauna.

Firefighter wannabes will enjoy the **New York City Fire Museum**, housed in a historic fire station (*see p22*); kids can check out uniforms and equipment from the late 18th century to the present, including a hand-pumped fire engine. The highlight at the aircraft carrier-turned-attraction **Intrepid Sea, Air & Space Museum** (*see p30*) is the Space Shuttle Pavilion, housing the Enterprise, an original prototype. With 30-plus interactive exhibits, the new **Museum of Mathematics (MoMath)** (*see p28*) will probably win round refuseniks.

In the boroughs, the excellent core exhibition 'Behind the Screen' at the **Museum of the Moving Image** (*see p46*), outfitted with state-of-the-art movie-making stations, makes it worth the trek to Astoria, Queens. Both children and adults will be fascinated by the amazing scale-model Panorama of the City of New York at the recently renovated and expanded **Queens Museum** (*see p47*), while youngsters can pretend to drive a real bus and board vintage subway cars at Brooklyn's **New York Transit Museum** (*see p42*).

Brooklyn Children's Museum
The city's oldest museum for kids is also one of its best after a major renovation that wrapped up in 2008. The star attraction, 'World Brooklyn', is an interactive maze of small mom-and-pop shops based on real-world Brooklyn businesses. 'Neighborhood Nature' puts the spotlight on the borough's diverse ecosystems with a collection of pond critters in terrariums and a tide-pool touch tank. Under-fives will delight in 'Totally Tots', a sun-drenched play space with a water station, a sand zone, and a special hub for babies aged 18 months and under. *145 Brooklyn Avenue, at St Marks Avenue, Crown Heights, Brooklyn (1-718 735 4400, www.brooklyn kids.org). Subway A, C to Nostrand Avenue; C to Kingston-Throop Avenues; 3 to Kingston Avenue. Open 10am-5pm Tue-Sun; 10am-7pm 3rd Thur of each mth. Admission $9; free under-1s; free 3-5pm Thur (4-7pm 3rd Thur of each mth).*

Children's Museum of Manhattan
This museum customises its themed exhibits by age group. 'PlayWorks', an imaginative play environment, is for babies and toddlers up to four; 'Adventures with Dora and Diego', a bilingual playspace that transports visitors to some of the Nickelodeon TV show's settings, is for ages two to six. 'EatSleepPlay: Building Health Every Day', for all ages, is an interactive exhibit that gives families strategies for taking up a more healthy lifestyle. *212 W 83rd Street, between Amsterdam Avenue & Broadway, Upper West Side (1-212 721 1234, www.cmom.org). Subway B, C to 81st Street-Museum of Natural History; 1 to 86th Street. Open 10am-5pm Tue-Fri, Sun; 10am-7pm Sat. Admission $11; $7 reductions; free under-1s.*

New York Hall of Science
Known for the 1964 World's Fair pavilion in which it is housed and the rockets from the US space programme that flank it, this museum has always been worth a visit for its discovery-based interactive exhibits. Expansion in 2005 added a new building that houses such permanent exhibits as 'Hidden Kingdoms', where children can get their hands on microscopes, and 'Search for Life Beyond Earth', which investigates the solar system and the different planetary environments. The 30,000sq ft outdoor Science Playground teaches children the principles of balance, gravity and energy, while a mini-golf course in Rocket Park lets families play surrounded by refurbished rockets from the 1960s space race. *47-01 111th Street, at 47th Avenue, Flushing Meadows Corona Park, Queens (1-718 699 0005, www. nysci.org). Subway 7 to 111th Street. Open Sept-Mar 9.30am-5pm Tue-Fri; 10am-6pm Sat, Sun. Apr-Aug 9.30am-5pm Mon-Fri; 10am-6pm Sat, Sun. Admission $11; $8 reductions. Sept-June free 2-5pm Fri; 10-11am Sun. Science playground (open Mar-Dec) extra $4. Rocket Park Mini Golf extra $6; $5 reductions.*

PERFORMING ARTS

Broadway is packed with excellent, if pricey, family fare, from long-runners like *The Lion King* and *Wicked* to London import *Matilda*, based on the book by Roald Dahl. *The Nutcracker* (*see p104* **David H Koch Theater**) is an annual Christmas family tradition. In summer, **Madison Square Park** (*see p27*) hosts regular children's concerts, and warm-weather events such as the **River to River Festival** (*see p12*) and **SummerStage** (*see p12*) always include music and theatre tailored to little ones.

Big Apple Circus
This travelling circus was founded in 1977 as an intimate answer to the scale of the Ringling Bros operation; it typically runs from October to mid January. The non-profit organisation's clowns are among the most creative in the country. *Damrosch Park, Lincoln Center, 62nd Street, between Columbus & Amsterdam Avenues, Upper West Side (1-212 268 2500, www.bigapplecircus.org). Subway 1 to 66th Street-Lincoln Center. Shows Oct-Jan times vary. Tickets $25-$175.*

Carnegie Hall Family Concerts
Even children who solemnly profess to hate classical music are usually impressed by a visit to Carnegie Hall. This series builds on that, featuring first-rate classical, world music and jazz performers, plus a pre-concert workshop an hour before the show. It runs roughly monthly from November to May. Recommended for five to 12s. *For listings, see p101. Tickets $12-$18.*

Galli Theater
Classic fairy tales such as *Rapunzel*, *Snow White* and *Hansel and Gretel* come to life through kid-oriented, often musical adaptations written by playwright and theatre founder Johannes Galli. A hallmark of each show is audience participation. *347 W 36th Street, between Eighth & Ninth Avenues, Hell's Kitchen (1-212 731 0668, www.galli theaterny.com). Subway A, C, E to 34th Street-Penn Station. Shows 2pm Sat, Sun (see website for additional shows). Tickets $20; $15 under-18s.*

Just Kidding at Symphony Space
In Manhattan, children can spend their Saturday mornings grooving to live concerts or watching theatre, dance or a puppet show. Symphony Space's Just Kidding series features both local and nationally recognised talent, from kid rockers and bluegrass bands to hip hop storytellers and NYC star Gustaver Yellowgold. *For listings, see p105. Shows Oct-early May Sat (times vary). Tickets $20-$55; $15 reductions.*

New Victory Theater
As New York's only full-scale young people's theatre, the New Victory presents international theatre and dance companies at junior prices. Recent shows have included Circus der Sinne, a Tanzanian troupe presenting a show of acrobatics, dance and live music with an African twist; Cre8ion, an Australia-based company, in a performance about a family that takes in all long-lost and misfit toys; and Hyperish, a presentation by the Netherlands-based ISH, a multi-disciplinary troupe blending hip hop, acrobatics, martial arts and basketball to explore questions of identity. Shows often sell out, so book well in advance. *For listings, see p109.*

Puppetworks
The Brooklyn company puts on musicals adapted from fairy tales and children's stories that feature a cast of marionettes operated by two puppeteers (the voice and music track is pre-recorded). At the beginning of each performance, they demonstrate how the puppets work. *338 Sixth Avenue, at 4th Street, Park Slope, Brooklyn (1-718 965 3391, www.puppetworks.org). Subway F to Seventh Avenue. Shows 12.30pm, 2.30pm Sat, Sun. Tickets $9; $8 under-12s. No credit cards.*

Vital Theatre Company
Founded in 1999, Vital has produced a series of original theatrical hits for kids, the biggest of which it reprises often – including *Angelina Ballerina*

TOP TIP!
More kids' stuff
For additional ideas, guides and the latest child-centric events, visit www.timeout.com/ newyorkkids.

RECOMMENDED
Children's Museum of the Arts

The creativity-inspiring Soho mainstay, whose focus is on teaching, creating, collecting and exhibiting kids' artwork, moved into a much larger (10,000sq ft) space in 2011. Engaging temporary exhibits are juxtaposed with works from the museum's collection of more than 2,000 pieces of children's art. For kids, the most exciting aspects of the museum are its hands-on art workshops, clay lab and interactive media lab, plus the ball pit for letting off steam.
103 Charlton Street, between Greenwich & Hudson Streets, Soho (1-212 274 0986, www.cmany.org). Subway A, B, C, D, E, F, M to W 4th Street; C, E to Spring Street; 1 to Houston Street. Open noon-5pm Mon, Wed; noon-6pm Thur, Fri; 10am-5pm Sat, Sun. Admission $11; free under-1s; pay what you wish 4-6pm Thur.

Children

and *Fancy Nancy the Musical.* Its most popular creation, *Pinkalicious*, about a girl who comes down with a case of 'pinkitis', tends to play elsewhere, most recently midtown's Jacqueline Kennedy Onassis Theater, at 120 W 46th Street, between Sixth and Seventh Avenues.
McGinn/Cazale Theatre, 4th floor, 2162 Broadway, at 76th Street, Upper West Side (1-212 579 0528, www.vital theatre.org). Subway 1 to 79th Street; 2, 3 to 72nd Street. Shows vary. Tickets $39.50-$89.50.

Parks & play spaces

Most New Yorkers don't have their own garden – instead, they run around and relax in parks. The most popular of all is Central Park (*see pp34-35*), which has places and programmes just for kids.

Battery Park City Parks

Besides watching the boats along the Hudson, kids can enjoy Teardrop Park – a hidden urban oasis with a huge slide – and Nelson A Rockefeller Park, which has an open field for Frisbee and lazing, plus a playground with a unique pedal carousel and a duck pond. Don't miss Pier 25, just north of BPC: a top-to-bottom renovation added a new playground, a mini-golf course and snack bar, an Astroturf area and a skate park.
Hudson River, between Chambers Street & Battery Place, Financial District (1-212 267 9700, www.bpc parks.org). Subway A, C, 1, 2, 3 to Chambers Street; 1 to Rector Street. Open 6am-1am daily. Admission free.

Chelsea Piers

This vast and bustling complex on the Hudson River is ideal in the colder months, thanks to its bowling alley, roller rink, pool, toddler gym, ice-skating rink and climbing walls.
For listings, see p79.

CENTRAL PARK

For more information and a calendar of events, visit www.centralpark nyc.org. Don't miss the antique **Friedsam Memorial Carousel** (midpark at 64th Street, open Apr-Oct, $3). There are 21 playgrounds in the park; the large Heckscher Playground, in the south-west corner (between Seventh Avenue & Central Park West, from 61st to 63rd Streets), sprawls over more than three acres and has an adventure area and restrooms.

Belvedere Castle

Central Park designer Frederick Law Olmsted planned this fanciful structure to lend his masterful creation a pastoral, fairy tale-like quality. Three viewing platforms give little visitors a stunning view of Turtle Pond below and, in the distance, the expansive, tree-lined Great Lawn (the two higher terraces are accessed from within the castle's turret). Budding naturalists can borrow nature kits equipped with binoculars and field guides with which to explore the castle's dominion.
Midpark, off the 79th Street Transverse Road (1-212 772 0210, www.centralparknyc.org). Subway B, C to 81st Street-Museum of Natural History. Open 10am-5pm daily. Admission free.

Central Park Zoo

The stars here are the penguins and the polar bear, which live in glass-enclosed habitats so you can watch their underwater antics. The creation of a snow leopard environment has added a breathtaking endangered animal to Central Park's menagerie. Among the zoo's most engaging offerings for kids are the sea lion and penguin feedings, and the mist-filled Tropic Zone: the Rainforest, which has free-flying birds, plus lots of tropical vegetation, monkeys and lemurs. The Tisch Children's Zoo houses species that enjoy being petted – and fed – among them alpacas, sheep and goats.
For listings, see p35.

Central Park Zoo

Conservatory Water

Nicknamed Stuart Little Pond after EB White's story-book mouse, Conservatory Water is a mecca for model-yacht racers. When the boatmaster is around (daily from April through October, weather permitting), you can rent a remote-controlled vessel ($11/30mins; see www.centralparknyc.org for hours). Kids are drawn to two statues near the pond: the bronze rendering of Lewis Carroll's Alice, the Mad Hatter and the White Rabbit is an irresistible climbing spot, while the Hans Christian Andersen statue is a gathering point for free storytelling sessions (June-Sept 11am-noon Sat, www.hcastorycenter.org).
Central Park, entrance on Fifth Avenue, at 72nd Street. Subway 6 to 68th Street-Hunter College.

Swedish Cottage Marionette Theater

Tucked just inside the western boundary of Central Park is a curiously incongruous old wooden structure. Designed as a schoolhouse, the building was Sweden's entry in the 1876 Centennial Exposition in Philadelphia (it was moved to NYC a year later). Inside is one of the best-kept secrets (and deals) in town: a tiny marionette theatre with regular shows. Reservations are recommended.
Central Park West, at 81st Street (1-212 988 9093). Subway B, C to 81st Street-Museum of Natural History. Shows Oct-June 10.30am, noon Tue, Thur, Fri; 10.30am, noon, 2.30pm Wed; 1pm Sat, Sun. July, Aug 10.30am, noon Mon-Fri. Tickets $10; $7 reductions.

Trump Rink & Victorian Gardens

Skating in Central Park is a New York tradition. This popular (read: crowded) skating rink offers lessons and skate rentals, plus a snack bar where you can warm up with hot chocolate. In summer, the site hosts Victorian Gardens, a quaint amusement park for younger children. It's hardly white-knuckle stuff, but the mini-teacup carousel and Rio Grande train will satisfy little thrill-seekers.
Trump Rink, midpark at 62nd Street (1-212 439 6900, www.wollman skatingrink.com). Subway N, Q, R to Fifth Avenue-59th Street. Open Late Oct-Apr 10am-2.30pm Mon, Tue; 10am-10pm Wed, Thur; 10am-11pm Fri, Sat; 10am-9pm Sun. Rates $11.25-$18; $5-$9 reductions; $5 spectators. Skate rental $8. No credit cards. Victorian Gardens 1-212 982 2229, www. victoriangardensnyc.com. Open Mid May-mid Sept 11am-7pm Mon-Thur; 11am-8pm Fri; 10am-9pm Sat; 10am-8pm Sun. Admission $7 Mon-Fri; $8 Sat, Sun; free children under 36in tall. Games & rides cost extra.

TOP TIP!
Horsing around
Don't miss Jane's Carousel, a vintage merry-go-round in a Jean Nouvel-designed pavilion in Brooklyn Bridge Park (*see p41*).

Restaurants & cafés

Alice's Teacup

Beloved by Alice-loving and Disney-adoring children, this magical spot serves much more than tea (though the three-tiered version – sandwiches, scones and desserts – truly is a treat). The brunch menu offers Alice's Curious French Toast (drenched in fruit coulis, crème anglaise and syrup) and scones in scrumptious flavours like blueberry and pumpkin. At a little shop in the front, you can outfit your fairy princess in training with a pair of bright, glittery wings.
102 W 73rd Street, at Columbus Avenue, Upper West Side (1-212 799 3006, www.alicesteacup.com). Subway B, C to 72nd Street. Open 8am-8pm daily. Main courses $10-$14. Other locations 156 E 64th Street, at Lexington Avenue, Upper East Side (1-212 486 9200); 220 E 81st Street, between Second & Third Avenues, Upper East Side (1-212 734 4832).

Cowgirl

This neighbourhood favourite is one of those rare spots that appeals to both adults and children. Grown-ups can unwind with a pitcher of potent margaritas amid the charming 1950s-era ranch decor. The whimsical setting, along with a small old-time candy shop and plenty of crayons, means the whole crowd will remain buoyant while waiting for rib-sticking fare such as quesadillas, pulled-pork sandwiches and gooey mac and cheese.
519 Hudson Street, at 10th Street, West Village (1-212 633 1133, www.cowgirlnyc.com). Subway 1 to Christopher Street-Sheridan Square. Open 11am-11pm Mon-Thur; 11am-midnight Fri; 10am-midnight Sat; 10am-11pm Sun. Main courses $12-$21; $6 children's menu.

Crema

Among the many child-friendly offerings to be found at Julieta Ballesteros's upscale Mexican restaurant are quesadillas. The versions here are grilled flour tortillas laced with chihuahua cheese and accented with black beans, shrimp, grilled chicken breast or steak. Tropical-flavoured lemonade, ice-cream and sorbet round out the à la carte offerings.
111 W 17th Street, between Sixth & Seventh Avenues, Chelsea (1-212 691 4477, www.cremarestaurante.com). Subway F, M, 1, 2, 3 to 14th Street; L to Sixth Avenue. Open noon-10.30pm Mon-Wed; noon-11pm Thur; noon-midnight Fri; 11.30am-midnight Sat; 11.30am-10pm Sun. Main courses $11-$28.

Ditch Plains

This New England-style fish shack, named for chef-owner Marc Murphy's favourite surfing spot in Montauk, Long Island, is sophisticated and sleek. It's perfect for families at all times of day, as it excels at simple but upscale fare such as lobster roll, ceviche and soft tacos. The place offers kids a stellar menu of their own, packed with an array of hot dogs and wholewheat quesadillas.
29 Bedford Street, at Downing Street, Greenwich Village (1-212 633 0202, www.ditch-plains.com). Subway A, B, C, D, E, F, M to W 4th Street; 1 to Houston Street. Open 11am-2am daily. Main courses $10-$29; $5-$12 children's menu. Other locations 100 W 82nd Street, at Columbus Avenue, Upper West Side (1-212 362 4815).

S'MAC

A dozen varieties of mac and cheese range from simple all-American to a more complex dish with brie, roasted figs and shiitake mushrooms. There's a size for everyone, from 'nosh' (great for kids) to 'partay' (which serves eight to 12).
345 E 12th Street, between First & Second Avenues, East Village (1-212 358 7912, www.smacnyc.com). Subway L to First Avenue. Open 11am-11pm Mon-Thur, Sun; 11am-1am Fri, Sat. Main courses $8-$20. Other locations 157 E 33rd Street, between Lexington & Third Avenues, Midtown East (1-212 383 3900).

Film

Cinema Village

Film Forum

Critic's choice

1 **Film Forum** The well-loved nonprofit cinema is a cult classic. *See below.*

2 **IFC Center** Cinephiles flock to its director-hosted screenings. *See below.*

3 **Nitehawk Cinema** Get dinner *and* a movie (and cocktails!) without leaving your seat. *See p90.*

4 **Ziegfeld Theater** Experience the golden age of moviegoing at this glam picture palace. *See p90.*

5 **Film Society of Lincoln Center** Home of the prestigious New York Film Festival. *See p90.*

Film

Bright lights, big screen

Get in the picture – film lovers will be in their element in this highly cinematic city.

Woody, Marty, Spike: by now the whole world is on first-name terms with New York's canonical legends. Even if this is your first visit to NYC, the cityscape will feel familiar; every corner has been immortalised on celluloid. It's easy to feel as if you've walked on to a massive movie set, especially when photogenic landmarks such as the Empire State Building pan into view. And you might even stumble upon an actual shoot – the thriving local film industry is based in Queens.

Cinemas

Angelika Film Center
When it opened in 1989, the Angelika immediately became a player in the then-booming Amerindie scene, and the six-screen cinema still puts the emphasis on edgier fare, both domestic and foreign. The complex is packed at weekends, so buy tickets in advance. *18 W Houston Street, at Mercer Street, Greenwich Village (1-212 995 2570,* *www.angelikafilmcenter.com). Subway B, D, F, M to Broadway-Lafayette Street; 6 to Bleecker Street. Tickets $14; $11 reductions.*

Anthology Film Archives
This red-brick building feels a bit like a fortress – and, in a sense, it is one, protecting the legacy of NYC's fiercest film experimenters. Dedicated to the preservation, study and exhibition of independent, avant-garde and artist-made work, Anthology houses two screens and a film museum. *32 Second Avenue, at 2nd Street, East Village (1-212 505 5181, www.anthologyfilmarchives.org). Subway F to Lower East Side-Second Avenue; 6 to Bleecker Street. Tickets $10; $8 reductions.*

BAM Rose Cinemas
Brooklyn's premier art-film venue does double duty as a rep house for well-programmed classics on 35mm and as a first-run multiplex for indie films. June's annual BAMcinemaFest is an excellent showcase of new American work.

Brooklyn Academy of Music, 30 Lafayette Avenue, between Ashland Place & St Felix Street, Fort Greene, Brooklyn (1-718 636 4100, www.bam.org). Subway B, D, N, Q, R, 2, 3, 4, 5 to Atlantic Avenue-Barclays Center; C to Lafayette Avenue; G to Fulton Street. Tickets $13; $9 reductions.

Cinema Village
A classic marquee that charmed Noah Baumbach long before he made *The Squid and the Whale*, this three-screener specialises in indie flicks, cutting-edge documentaries and foreign films. *22 E 12th Street, between Fifth Avenue & University Place, Greenwich Village (1-212 924 3363, www.cinema village.com). Subway L, N, Q, R, 4, 5, 6 to 14th Street-Union Square. Tickets $11; $6-$8 reductions.*

Film Forum
The city's leading tastemaking venue for independent new releases and classic movies, Film Forum is programmed by festival-scouring staff who take their duties as seriously as a

Kurosawa samurai. Born in 1970 as a makeshift screening space with folding chairs, it is one of the few nonprofit cinemas in the United States – but thankfully its three screens are now furnished with comfortable seats. *209 W Houston Street, between Sixth Avenue & Varick Street, Soho (1-212 727 8110, www.filmforum.org). Subway 1 to Houston Street. Tickets $13; $7.50 reductions. No credit cards (except for online purchases).*

IFC Center
The long-darkened 1930s Waverly was once again illuminated back in 2005 when it was reborn as a modern five-screen arthouse cinema, showing the latest indie hits, along with choice midnight cult items and occasional foreign classics. You may come face to face with the directors or the actors on the screen, as many introduce their work on opening night. *323 Sixth Avenue, at W 3rd Street, Greenwich Village (1-212 924 7771, www.ifccenter.com). Subway A, B, C, D, E, F, M to W 4th Street. Tickets $13.50; $9.50 reductions.*

Landmark Sunshine Cinema

Once a renowned Yiddish theatre, this comfortable, date-friendly venue has snazz and chutzpah to spare. Intimate cinemas and excellent sound are a beautiful complement to the indie films; it also hosts New York's most consistently excellent midnight series on Fridays and Saturdays.
141-143 E Houston Street, between First & Second Avenues, East Village (1-212 260 7289, www.landmark theatres.com). Subway F to Lower East Side-Second Avenue. Tickets $13.50; $10 reductions.

Leonard Nimoy Thalia

The Thalia arthouse, which featured in *Annie Hall* (when it was screening *The Sorrow and the Pity*), has since undergone an upgrade. The cinematic fare is an eclectic mix of international, arthouse and documentary films, plus HD screenings of plays and operas.
Symphony Space, 2537 Broadway, at 95th Street, Upper West Side (1-212 864 5400, www.symphonyspace.org). Subway 1, 2, 3 to 96th Street. Tickets $14; $12 reductions.

Maysles Documentary Center

Harlem keeps it 'reel' with this intimate screening venue, run by cinema vérité legend Albert Maysles and his extended family. Socially conscious documentaries, naturally, make up the bulk of the programming, but you're also likely to catch funky series of hip hop and jazz films, critics presenting personal esoteric favourites and plenty of uptown-centric flicks.
343 Malcolm X Boulevard (Lenox Avenue), between 127th & 128th Streets, Harlem (1-212 582 6843, www.maysles.org/mdc). Subway A, B, C, D, 2, 3 to 125th Street. Tickets Suggested donation $10.

Nitehawk Cinema

See right **Dinner at the movies**.
136 Metropolitan Avenue, between Berry Street & Wythe Avenue, Williamsburg, Brooklyn (1-718 384 3980, www.nitehawkcinema. com). Subway L to Bedford Avenue. Tickets $11; $9 reductions.

Paris Theatre

Founded in 1948, the elegant, single-screen Paris is one of the oldest continually operating movie houses in the country. Its plush carpets and seats and tiny lobby have plenty of retro appeal.
4 W 58th Street, between Fifth & Sixth Avenues, Midtown (1-212 688 3800, www.theparis theatre.com). Subway N, Q, R to Fifth Avenue-59th Street. Tickets $14; $11 reductions.

Quad Cinema

The Quad's four small screens show a wide range of foreign and American indie films. But the real standout fare at this Greenwich Village operation

DINNER AT THE MOVIES
Gastro-cinemas are breaking free of the popcorn box.

Nitehawk Cinema

After the **Film Society of Lincoln Center** (*see below*) opened its stunning new Elinor Bunin Munroe Film Center, restaurateur Jason Denton premiered his smart and casual on-site street-level café attached to the cinema: Indie Food & Wine (1-212 875 5456, www.indie foodandwine.com). Movie-goers can stop in for Mediterranean-inflected fare such as salads and a milk-braised pork belly sandwich or pick up upgraded concession-stand snacks like organic hot dogs and parmesan-truffle popcorn – it's a far cry from the old spartan arthouse image.

The **Nitehawk Cinema** (*see left*) in Williamsburg, Brooklyn, goes one better by serving food in the cinema itself. Seats are arranged in pairs with sturdy tables, and viewers order from a menu created by Michelin-starred chef Saul Bolton. Just write down your order at any point during the movie on a piece of paper for a server to pick up and ferry to the kitchen. The comfort-food grub includes meaty fish tacos and a tasty burger, but the real highlights are the chef's variations on concession-stand snacks, such as popcorn tossed with parmesan, black pepper and garlic butter. Best of all, you can sip cocktails, beer or wine in your seat.

Amid these shiny competitors, trailblazer **reRun Gastropub Theater** (147 Front Street, between Jay & Pearl Streets, Dumbo, Brooklyn, 1-718 766 9110, www.reruntheater.com) still feels original – both food and booze are served from a bar inside the theatre, and guests sit in repurposed minivan seats. The bar closes when the lights go down, but food orders placed beforehand – creative riffs on junk food such as mashed potato-stuffed pretzels and duck fat- and herb-tossed popcorn – will be delivered to your seat, and you can load up on discounted buckets of beer or carafes of wine to tide you over through the show.

are the latest offerings related to gay sexuality and politics.
34 W 13th Street, between Fifth & Sixth Avenues, Greenwich Village (1-212 255 8800, www.quadcinema.com). Subway F, M to 14th Street; L to Sixth Avenue. Tickets $11; $8 reductions.

TOP TIP!
Alfresco films
In summer, you can catch screenings in Bryant Park (www.bryantpark.org) and Central Park (www. centralparknyc.org), among other green spaces.

Ziegfeld Theater

Despite its Jazz Age moniker, this movie palace actually opened in 1969; since then, its red carpets and gilded staircases have served as a last stand against stadium-seated sameness.

Temporarily endangered but saved by Bow Tie Cinemas, the city's largest single-screen theatre seats 1,162 citizens under chandeliers, harking back to when going to motion pictures was an aspirational experience.
141 W 54th Street, between Sixth & Seventh Avenues, Midtown (1-212 307 1862, www.bowtiecinemas.com). Subway B, D, E to Seventh Avenue; F, N, Q, R to 57th Street; 1 to 50th Street. Tickets $14; $10.50 reductions.

Other institutions

Film Society of Lincoln Center

Founded in 1969, the FSLC hosts the prestigious New York Film Festival, among other annual fests, in addition to presenting diverse programming throughout the year. Series are usually thematic, with an international perspective or focused on a single auteur. The $40-million Elinor Bunin Munroe Film Center houses two plush cinemas that host frequent post-screening Q&As. Between these

state-of-the-art screens and the Walter Reade Theater across the street, a small multiplex has been born.
144 & 165 W 65th Street, between Broadway & Amsterdam Avenue, Upper West Side (1-212 875 5600, www.filmlinc.com). Subway 1 to 66th Street-Lincoln Center. Tickets $13; $9 reductions.

Museum of Modern Art

Renowned for its superb programming of art films and experimental work, MoMA draws from a vast vault. You have to buy tickets in person at the museum at the lobby desk or the film desk (see www.moma.org or call 1-212 708 9480 for more information). Note that while museum admission includes the day's film programme, a film ticket doesn't include admission to the galleries – although it can be applied towards the cost within 30 days.
For listings, see p31. Tickets free with museum admission, or $12; $8-$10 reductions; free under-16s.

Museum of the Moving Image

Like the rest of this Queens institution housed in the Astoria Studios complex, the museum's screening facilities have received a magnificent renovation, resulting in a state-of-the-art 267-seat cinema. Expect excellent prints and airings of the classics.
For listings, see p46. Tickets $12; $6-$9 reductions.

FOREIGN-LANGUAGE SPECIALISTS

You can catch the latest foreign-language flicks at art and revival houses, but there is a wealth of specialist venues as well, including the **French Institute Alliance Française** (22 E 60th Street, 1-212 355 6100, www.fiaf.org), the **Japan Society** (*see p32*), **Scandinavia House** (*see p32*) and the **Asia Society & Museum** (*see p36*).

Film festivals

From late September to mid October, the Film Society of Lincoln Center hosts the **New York Film Festival** (1-212 875 5050, www.filmlinc. com), more than two weeks packed with premières, features and short flicks from around the globe. Together with Lincoln Center's *Film Comment* magazine, the FSLC also offers the popular **Film Comment Selects**, showcasing films that have yet to be distributed in the United States. January brings the annual **New York Jewish Film Festival** (www.nyjff.org) to Lincoln Center's Walter Reade Theater. Each spring, the Museum of Modern Art and the Film Society of Lincoln Center sponsor the highly regarded **New Directors/New Films** series, presenting works by on-the-cusp filmmakers. And in April, Robert De Niro's **Tribeca Film Festival** (1-212 941 2400, www.tribecafilmfestival. org) draws more than 400,000 fans to screenings of independent movies and other events.

Film

LGBT

NYC LGBT Pride March

FairyTail Lounge

Critic's choice

1 **Cubbyhole** You'll find cheap drinks and a mixed crowd at this friendly lounge. *See p92.*

2 **Eagle** Get kinky at the city's finest fetish bar. *See p93.*

3 **FairyTail Lounge** And they lived happily ever after in this fanciful Hell's Kitchen hotspot. *See p93.*

4 **Atlas Social Club** The speakeasy gets sporty. *See p93.*

5 **This n' That** Eclectic fun in Brooklyn's Nightlife Central. *See p93.*

LGBT

Gay times in Gotham

Welcome to the queer capital of America.

In summer 2011, same-sex marriage became legal in New York State, marking a major civil rights victory in the birthplace of the modern gay rights movement. Two years later, New Yorker Edith Windsor was at the centre of the Supreme Court case that established same-sex marriage as a federal right. Even as gayness moves towards the mainstream, the city's queer scene is constantly finding ways to reinvent itself as an incubator of activism and innovative nightlife.

Offering much more than drag and piano bars (though, delightfully, these still thrive), today's LGBT New York has venues devoted to rock and country music and an abundance of arty, pan-queer events. Downtown cultural institutions such as Joe's Pub and Dixon Place stage performances by iconic artists like Sandra Bernhard and Justin Vivian Bond, as well as emerging stars. **NYC Pride**, New York's biggest queer event, takes place the last week of June, bringing with it a

whirl of parties and performances. Capping the weekend, the **NYC LGBT Pride March** (*see p12*), which takes five hours to wind down Fifth Avenue from midtown to the West Village, draws millions of spectators and participants. The **Urban Bear Weekend** in May and **Black Party Weekend** in March also draw hordes to NYC, visibly upping the gay quotient around town.

For the latest queer-centric parties, shows and events, consult the Gay & Lesbian section of www.timeout.com/newyork.

Where to stay

While you'd be hard-pressed to find a gay-unfriendly hotel in New York, the following establishments are either exclusively gay or geared towards a queer clientele.

Chelsea Mews Guest House

Built in 1840, this clothing-optional guesthouse caters to gay men. The rooms are comfortable and well furnished and, in most cases, share a bathroom. Bicycle tours and coffee are complimentary – as is access to a songbird aviary! An on-site massage therapist and soothing Tempur-Pedic beds in every room help to ensure a relaxing stay. New arrivals take note: the Chelsea Mews Guest House doesn't have a sign out front, so keep your eye on the building numbers.
344 W 15th Street, between Eighth & Ninth Avenues, Chelsea (1-212 255 9174, www.chelseamewsguest house.com). Subway A, C, E to 14th Street; L to Eighth Avenue. Rooms 8. No credit cards.

Chelsea Pines Inn

On the border of Chelsea and the West Village, Chelsea Pines welcomes gay guests of all persuasions. The rooms are clean and comfortable, with classic-film themes; all have private bathrooms, and are equipped with a radio, a TV with satellite channels, a refrigerator and free Wi-Fi. Breakfast is complimentary.
317 W 14th Street, between Eighth & Ninth Avenues, Chelsea (1-212 929

1023, www.chelseapinesinn.com). Subway A, C, E to 14th Street; L to Eighth Avenue. Rooms 23.

Colonial House Inn

This beautifully renovated 1850s townhouse sits on a quiet street in Chelsea. The guesthouse was founded by late dance-music legend Mel Cheren, and is still run by (and primarily for) gay men. Although some of the cheaper rooms are a bit snug, three of the deluxe rooms have fireplaces. Nude sunbathing is allowed on the rooftop deck.
318 W 22nd Street, between Eighth & Ninth Avenues, Chelsea (1-212 243 9669, 1-800 689 3779, www. colonialhouseinn.com). Subway C, E to 23rd Street. Rooms 22.

Incentra Village House

Two cute 1841 townhouses make up this nicely restored and gay-run guesthouse in the West Village. The spacious quarters are equipped with private bathrooms and kitchenettes, and some also have fireplaces. A 1939 Steinway baby

grand graces the parlour, setting a tone of easy sophistication.
32 Eighth Avenue, between Jane & W 12th Streets, West Village (1-212 206 0007, www.incentravillage.com). Subway A, C, E to 14th Street; L to Eighth Avenue. Rooms 11.

The Out NYC
This all-gay megacomplex is located just a few blocks from Times Square and the Theater District, and in convenient proximity to the Hell's Kitchen strip of gay bars. But there's actually no need to leave – the Out also houses BPM nightclub and the unremarkable but serviceable KTCHN restaurant, as well as a spa, gym and the Rosebud NYC cocktail bar.
510 W 42nd Street, between Tenth & Eleventh Avenues (1-212 947 2999, www.theoutnyc.com). Subway A, C, E to 42nd Street-Port Authority. Rooms 103.

Restaurants & cafés

The sight of same-sex couples holding hands across a candlelit table is a pretty commonplace one in New York City. But if you want to increase the chances of being part of the majority when you dine, check out the following gay-friendly places.

Bamboo 52
This sushi restaurant (with a bamboo garden to boot) feels more like a gay bar with an extended raw fish menu. There's loungey seating (patrons nestle on low banquettes and nibble off knee-high tables), a DJ and free-flowing drinks. The fun menu features such unorthodox combinations as buffalo chicken speciality rolls and a spicy sushi sandwich – a tasty triangle of seasoned rice layered with spicy tuna, avocado, eel and American cheese.
344 W 52nd Street, between Eighth & Ninth Avenues, Hell's Kitchen (1-212 315 2777, www.bamboo52nyc.com). Subway C, E to 50th Street. Open 11am-2am daily. Sushi rolls $7-$14.

Elmo
The main attraction at this spacious, brightly decorated eaterie is the good, reasonably priced American comfort food which changes seasonally. Then there's the bar, which provides a view of the dining room jammed with guys in clingy tank tops. During warmer months, the sidewalk café is constantly bustling.
156 Seventh Avenue, between 19th & 20th Streets, Chelsea (1-212 337 8000, www.elmorestaurant.com). Subway 1 to 18th Street. Open 11am-11pm Mon-Thur; 11am-midnight Fri; 10am-midnight Sat; 10am-11pm Sun. Main courses $17-$23.

Empanada Mama
Massive flavours are crammed into tiny packages at this cute spot, right in the middle of Hell's Kitchen's boy-bar crawl. Savoury and sweet empanadas (both flour and corn varieties) make great on-the-go snacks, or combine several for a full meal. The joint tends to be packed from dinner time until the wee hours.
763 Ninth Avenue, between 51st & 52nd Streets, Hell's Kitchen (1-212 698 9008, www.empmamanyc.com). Subway C, E to 50th Street. Open 24hrs daily. Empanadas $3.

Manatus
Manatus both is and isn't your typical greasy-spoon diner. There are the standard plastic-coated menus listing dozens of fried food items, but distinguishing the place is a full bar, flattering lighting and a very gay clientele, especially late at night when tipsy bar-goers pile in.
340 Bleecker Street, between Christopher & 10th Streets, West Village (1-212 989 7042, www.manatusnyc.com). Subway 1 to Christopher Street-Sheridan Square. Open 7am-2am Sun-Thur; 24hrs Fri, Sat. Main courses $9-$25.

Rocking Horse Café
Eclectic Mexican cuisine is what originally established the Rocking Horse Café as a unique place to eat in Chelsea, but the bar now holds a distinguished reputation for its tongue-numbingly stiff frozen margaritas (the Two Fruit version features prickly pear and mango).
182 Eighth Avenue, between 19th & 20th Streets, Chelsea (1-212 463 9511, www.rockinghorsecafe.com). Subway C, E to 23rd Street. Open noon-11pm Mon-Thur; noon-midnight Fri; 11am-midnight Sat; 11am-11pm Sun. Main courses $17-$23.

Superfine
Owned by a couple of super-cool lesbians, this eaterie, bar and gallery serves Mediterranean cuisine in a massive, hip space. The mellow vibe and pool table draw a mixed local crowd. The Sunday brunch is justifiably popular.
126 Front Street, between Jay & Pearl Streets, Dumbo, Brooklyn (1-718 243 9005). Subway A, C to High Street; F to York Street. Open 11.30am-3pm, 6-11pm Mon-Sat; 11.30am-3pm, 6-10pm Sun. Main courses $18-$30.

Vynl
The boys love this pop music-themed eaterie, where old albums adorn the walls above the cosy booths and mirrorballs are shoved into every available space. Menu items are an odd mishmash of comfort food (burgers, turkey meatloaf) and Asian cuisine (massaman curry, veggie-basil stir-fry). Cocktails are named after pop icons and the vibe is all-around fun.
754 Ninth Avenue, between 50th & 51st Streets, Hell's Kitchen (1-212 974 2003, www.vynl-nyc.com). Subway C, E to 50th Street. Open 11am-11pm Mon-Wed; 11am-midnight Thur, Fri; 9.30am-midnight Sat; 9.30am-11pm Sun. Main courses $14-$19.

Bars & clubs

BPM at the **Out NYC** and club nights such as **Viva Saturdays** at Stage 48 (605 W 48th Street, between Eleventh & Twelfth Avenues, www.vivasaturdays.com) draw crowds of hot guys looking to dance to tunes from big-name DJs and even the occasional slumming pop star. But for serious dance music fans, the real action is at smaller venues. The basement disco at the **Monster** features reliably sweaty (in a good way) parties most nights, and MEN's JD Samson hosts **Scissor Sundays** at the Rusty Knot (425 West Street, West Village, 1-212 645 5668), a top-notch tea dance that assembles an eclectic crowd.

TOP TIP!
Queer culture
Check out Soho's Leslie-Lohman Museum of Gay & Lesbian Art (26 Wooster Street, between Canal & Grand Streets, 1-212 431 2609, www.leslie lohman.org).

EAST VILLAGE

The Cock
This grungy hole-in-the-wall still holds the title of New York's sleaziest gay hangout, but nowadays it's hit-and-miss. At weekends, it's a packed grind-fest, but on other nights the place can often be depressingly under-populated. It's best to go very late when the cruising is at its peak.
29 Second Avenue, between 2nd & 3rd Streets (no phone, www.the cockbar.com). Subway F to Lower East Side-Second Avenue. Open 11pm-4am daily. Admission free-$10. No credit cards.

Eastern Bloc
This cool little space has mostly shed its commie revolutionary decor for a funky living-room feel. The bartenders are cuties, and there are nightly themes, DJs and happy hours to get the ball rolling.
505 E 6th Street, between Avenues A & B (1-212 777 2555, www.eastern blocnyc.com). Subway F to Lower East-Side-Second Avenue. Open 7pm-4am daily. No credit cards.

Nowhere
Low ceilings and dim lighting help to create a speakeasy vibe at this subterranean bar. The place attracts everyone from young lesbians to bears, thanks to an entertaining line-up of theme nights. Tuesdays are especially fun, when DJ Damian's long-running Buddies party takes over. The pool table is another big draw.
322 E 14th Street, at First Avenue (1-212 477 4744, www.nowherebar nyc.com). Subway L to First Avenue. Open 3pm-4am daily. No credit cards.

WEST VILLAGE

Cubbyhole
This minuscule spot is filled with flirtatious girls, with the standard set of Melissa Etheridge or kd lang blaring. Chinese lanterns, tissue-paper fish and old holiday decorations add to the festive, homespun charm.

281 W 12th Street, between 4th Street & Greenwich Avenue (1-212 243 9041, www.cubbyholebar.com). Subway A, C, E to 14th Street; L to Eighth Avenue. Open 4pm-4am Mon-Fri; 2pm-4am Sat, Sun. No credit cards.

Henrietta Hudson
A much-loved lesbian hangout, this glam lounge attracts women from all over the New York area. Every night is different, with hip hop, pop, rock and live shows among the musical offerings.
438 Hudson Street, at Morton Street (1-212 924 3347, www.henrietta hudson.com). Subway 1 to Houston Street. Open 5pm-2am Mon, Tue; 4pm-4am Wed-Fri; 2pm-4am Sat; 2pm-2am Sun. Admission free-$10.

The Monster
Upstairs, locals gather to sing showtunes in the piano lounge, which is adorned with strings of lights and rainbow paraphernalia. The downstairs dancefloor has seen something of a renaissance lately, hosting top-notch house and disco events.
80 Grove Street, at Sheridan Square (1-212 924 3558, www.manhattan-monster.com). Subway 1 to Christopher Street-Sheridan Square. Open 4pm-4am Mon-Fri; 2pm-4am Sat, Sun. No credit cards

Rockbar
A burly, bearish crowd tends to congregate at this far-west dive with a rock 'n' roll theme. Various events include dance parties, game nights, comedy showcases and musical performances.
185 Christopher Street, at Weehawken Street (1-212 675 1864, www.rock barnyc.com). Subway 1 to Christopher Street-Sheridan Square. Open 6pm-2am Mon-Wed; 4pm-2am Thur; 4pm-4am Fri, Sat; 1pm-2am Sun.

Stonewall Inn
This gay landmark is the site of the 1969 gay rebellion against police harassment (though back then it also included the building next door). Special nights range from dance soirées and drag shows to burlesque performances and bingo gatherings.
53 Christopher Street, at Waverly Place (1-212 488 2705, www.the stonewallinnnyc.com). Subway 1 to Christopher Street-Sheridan Square. Open 2pm-4am Mon-Sat; noon-4am Sun.

CHELSEA & FLATIRON DISTRICT

Barracuda
This much beloved, slightly divey Chelsea institution is one of the most reliably bustling spots in the neighbourhood. Some of the city's most talented drag queens perform here nightly. Drinks are on the pricey

side, but you'll often get a great show with no cover, so it balances out.
275 W 22nd Street, between Seventh & Eighth Avenues (1-212 645 8613, www.facebook.com/barracudalounge). Subway C, E, 1 to 23rd Street. Open 4pm-4am daily. No credit cards.

Eagle
You don't have to be a kinky leather daddy to enjoy this manly spot, but it definitely doesn't hurt. The fetish bar is home to an array of beer blasts, foot-worship fêtes and leather soirées, plus simple pool playing and cruising nights. Thursday is gear night, so be sure to dress the part or you might not get past the doorman. In summer, the rooftop is a surprising oasis.
554 W 28th Street, at Eleventh Avenue (1-646 473 1866, www.eaglenyc.com). Subway C, E to 23rd Street. Open 9pm-4am Mon-Sat; 5pm-4am Sun (extended hrs in summer). No credit cards.

G Lounge
The neighbourhood's original slick boy lounge – a moodily lit cave with a cool brick-and-glass arched entrance – wouldn't look out of place in a boutique hotel. It's a favourite after-work cocktail spot, where a roster of DJs stays on top of the mood.
225 W 19th Street, at Seventh Avenue (1-212 929 1085, www.glounge.com). Subway 1 to 18th Street. Open 4pm-4am daily. No credit cards.

Gym Sports Bar
This popular hangout is all about games – of the actual sporting variety. Catch theme parties that revolve around gay sports leagues, play at the pool tables and video games, or watch the pro events from rodeo competitions to figure skating shown on big-screen TVs.
167 Eighth Avenue, between 18th & 19th Streets (1-212 337 2439, www.gymsportsbar.com). Subway A, C, E to 14th Street; L to Eighth Avenue. Open 4pm-2am Mon-Thur; 4pm-4am Fri; 1pm-4am Sat; 1pm-2am Sun.

HELL'S KITCHEN & THEATER DISTRICT

Atlas Social Club
This drinkery, designed to look like a cross between an old-school athletic club and a speakeasy, is one of the more relaxed options on the HK strip – at least when it's not packed to the gills, which it can be on weekends. Be sure to check out the bathrooms, which are brightly papered with vintage beefcake and sports magazines.
753 Ninth Avenue, between 50th & 51st Streets (1-212 762 8527, www.atlassocialclub.com). Subway C, E to 50th Street. Open 4pm-4am Mon-Sat; 3pm-4am Sun.

FairyTail Lounge
An easy-to-miss entrance belies the psychedelic, pseudo-Victorian enchanted forest inside this friendly watering hole. Whether you find a mellow happy-hour crowd or a hyper dance party, the vibe is more arty than you'd expect in pretty-boy central.

HOT AS HELL'S KITCHEN
Once again, NYC's gay scene has migrated north.

Atlas Social Club

In the 1990s, Chelsea was the city's – perhaps the world's – queerest zone. The Village had the history (and still does), but Chelsea had cheaper rents and empty storefronts begging to be filled with bars and shops that specialised in colourful underwear favoured by the waxed, buff 'Chelsea boys', whose aesthetic defined the era in gay New York. But then history repeated itself. Like the Village, Chelsea became overpriced and clogged with wealthy straight people. Soon, seemingly immortal queer businesses like the rough-and-tumble dive Rawhide and pioneering dance club Splash lost their leases. The area became a nightlife ghost town, and once again, things moved north.

Today, Hell's Kitchen reigns as the city's gayest gaybourhood, though it hasn't quite earned Chelsea's reputation outside of the five boroughs. Take a stroll through the area any night, and you'll see cute boys (and some girls) spilling out of bars, clubs and restaurants with rainbow flags proudly flapping outside. HK is even home to the city's first luxury gay hotel, the **Out NYC** (*see p92*), a sort of gay megaplex, which includes rooms arranged around a variety of themed courtyards, a 5,000-square-foot spa, the Rosebud NYC cocktail bar and BPM nightclub, which draws big-name DJs from around the world.

Unlike the intimidatingly fitness-focused '90s Chelsea scene, Hell's Kitchen is relaxed and diverse. You'll find well-dressed businessmen drinking next to fanny-packed Midwestern tourists and bearded Brooklyn boys, and most venues welcome female patrons (gay and straight). Your hetero friends will feel right at home at bars like **Atlas Social Club** (*see left*) and **Industry** (*see below*) since HK bars rarely get overly cruisy or sexual – for that, you'll still have to head downtown.

500 W 48th Street, at Tenth Avenue (1-646 684 3897, www.fairytail nyc.com). Subway C, E to 50th Street. Open 5pm-2am Mon, Tue; 5pm-3am Thur-Sun.

Flaming Saddles
City guys can party honky-tonk-style at this country and western gay bar. It's outfitted to look like a Wild West bordello, with red velvet drapes, antler sconces and rococo wallpaper. Dancing bartenders in cowboy boots add to the raucous vibe.
793 Ninth Avenue, at 53rd Street (1-212 713 0481, www.flamingsaddles.com). Subway C, E to 50th Street. Open 3pm-3am Mon-Thur, Sun; 3pm-4am Fri, Sat. No credit cards.

Industry
Pretty boys flock to this appropriately named garage-like industrial-chic *boite*, which features a stage for

regular drag shows and other performances, a pool table, and couches for lounging. DJs spin nightly to a sexy, fashionable crowd.
355 W 52nd Street, between Eighth & Ninth Avenues (1-646 476 2747, www.industrybar.com). Subway C, E to 50th Street. Open 4pm-4am daily. No credit cards.

InFuse 51
Formerly Vlada, this vodka-focused drinkery has more than a dozen infused versions of the spirit. Drag shows take over the space Sunday to Wednesday, and skew more towards quirky and scary than campy.
331 W 51st Street, between Eighth & Ninth Avenues (1-212 974 8030, www.infuse51.com). Subway C, E to 50th Street. Open 4pm-4am daily.

Therapy
Therapy is just what your analyst ordered. The dramatic two-level space offers comedy and musical performances, some clever cocktails (including the Freudian Sip) and a crowd of well-scrubbed boys. You'll find good food and a cosy fireplace to boot.
348 W 52nd Street, between Eighth & Ninth Avenues (1-212 397 1700, www.therapy-nyc.com). Subway C, E to 50th Street. Open 5pm-2am Mon-Wed, Sun; 5pm-4am Thur-Sat.

BROOKLYN

Excelsior
Homey Excelsior has a friendly neighbourhood crowd, an eclectic jukebox and plenty of beers on tap. This straight-friendly spot attracts gay men, lesbians and their hetero pals looking to catch up without the fuss found in trendy lounge bars.
390 Fifth Avenue, between 6th & 7th Streets, Park Slope (1-718 832 1599, www.excelsiorbrooklyn.com). Subway F, R to Fourth Avenue-9th Street. Open 6pm-4am Mon-Fri; 2pm-4am Sat, Sun. No credit cards.

Ginger's Bar
The front room of Ginger's, with its dark-wood bar, looks out on to a bustling street. The back, with an always-busy pool table, evokes a rec room, while the patio feels like a friend's yard. This local hangout is full of all sorts of dykes, many with their dogs – or favourite gay boys – in tow.
363 Fifth Avenue, between 5th & 6th Streets, Park Slope (1-718 788 0924, www.gingersbarbklyn.com). Subway F, R to Fourth Avenue-9th Street. Open 5pm-4am Mon-Fri; 2pm-4am Sat, Sun. No credit cards.

Metropolitan
Some Williamsburg spots are a little pretentious, but not this refreshingly unfancy bar, which resembles a 1960s ski lodge, complete with a fireplace. Guys dominate, but there's always a female contingent, and even some straight folks. Barbecues are held on the patio on summer weekends.
559 Lorimer Street, at Metropolitan Avenue, Williamsburg (1-718 599 4444, www.metropolitanbarny.com). Subway G to Metropolitan Avenue; L to Lorimer Street. Open 3pm-4am daily.

This n' That (TNT)
This cavernous boite is parked in the middle of the most hipstery block of the city's most hipstery neighbourhood. Still, most nights you'll find a surprisingly unpretentious crowd here, enjoying various parties (trivia, movie nights, sweaty dance fests).
108 North 6th Street, between Berry Street & Wythe Avenue, Williamsburg (1-718 599 5959, www.thisnthat brooklyn.com). Subway L to Bedford Avenue. Open 4pm-4am daily.

TOP TIP!
News and views
A number of sites feature attitude-filled thoughts on the scene, including Queerty (www.queerty.com) and Towleroad (www.towleroad.com).

LGBT

Nightlife

Output

The late shift

Whether you're a club kid or a comedy nut, the city dazzles after dark.

New York nightlife has an amazing history, and although the city can no longer claim to be the world's clubbing capital, there's fun to be had here still. Roving parties are revitalising the after-dark landscape, and now that the **Verboten** gang has chosen North 11th Street as the site of their eponymous venue, Williamsburg has officially become New York's clubland paradise.

The newest major music venue, the **Barclays Center** (*see p96*) in Brooklyn, has attracted an unexpectedly cool list of acts. For smaller rock gigs, hit the Lower East Side or Williamsburg, which have numerous venues; the latter is the epicentre of the indie rock scene.

Classic cabaret took a hit in 2012 with the closure of the iconic Oak Room, but **54 Below** (*see p100*) stepped into the spotlight, and a boundary-pushing generation of performers is reinvigorating the genre. Comedy, meanwhile, is enjoying a moment, with thriving clubs and theatres across the city.

Clubs

Hallowed halls such as the Loft, Studio 54, the Paradise Garage and Area are embedded in nightlife's collective consciousness as near-mythic ideals. But in this millennium the balance of power has shifted eastward to cities like London and Berlin. Still, New York nightlife can never be counted out – and the scene today is as strong as it's been in years. This is largely thanks to a burst of nomadic shindigs, often held in out-of-the-way warehouses. Some of the best – particularly if you're a fan of underground house, techno or bass music – are run by the teams at **Blkmarket Membership** (www.blkmarketmembership.com), **Mister Saturday Night** (www.mister saturdaynight.com), and **Verboten** (www.verbotennewyork.com), which was preparing to open a permanent 750-capacity club in Williamsburg, Brooklyn at time of writing. A visit to www.timeout.com/newyork should help to clue you in.

A visit to www.timeout.com/newyork should help to clue you in.

DANCE CLUBS

Cielo
You'd never guess from the Kardashian wannabes in the neighbourhood that the attitude at this exclusive club is close to zero – at least once you get past the bouncers on the door. On the sunken dancefloor, hip-to-hip crowds gyrate to deep beats from top DJs, including NYC old-schoolers François K, Tedd Patterson and Louie Vega. Cielo, which features a crystal-clear sound system (by the legendary Funktion One), has won a bevy of 'best club' awards. *18 Little W 12th Street, at Ninth Avenue, Meatpacking District (1-212 645 5700, www.cieloclub.com). Subway A, C, E to 14th Street; L to Eighth Avenue. Open 10pm-4am Mon, Wed-Sat. Admission $12-$25.*

Marquee
After shutting down for major renovations, the one-time models-and-bottles clubs Marquee has re-emerged…as a models-and-bottles club! In fairness, Marquee 2.0 is an entirely different – and in our opinion, far better – beast than it was in its original incarnation, with more open space, all manner of disco lights (including an impressive LCD screen behind the booth) and enough general razzle-dazzle to make your head spin. Most importantly, the Friday-night bookings have been taken over by NYC power couple Sleepy & Boo, who have been bringing in the world's house-and-techo elite – Slam, Marco Carola, Damian Lazarus, the Martinez Brothers and the like – to work their four-to-the-floor magic. *289 Tenth Avenue, between 26th & 27th Streets, Chelsea (1-646 473 0202, www.marqueeny.com). Subway C, E to 23rd Street. Open 11pm-4am Wed-Sat. Admission varies.*

Output
With the opening of Output in early 2013, New York nightlife's centre of gravity continues its eastward push into Brooklyn. Akin in ethos to such underground-music headquarters as Berlin's Berghain/Panorama Bar complex or London's Fabric, the club boasts a warehouse-party vibe and a killer sound system. Top-shelf DJs (both international hotshots and local heroes) spin the kind of left-field house, techno and bass music you rarely hear in more commercially oriented spots. Head to the rooftop bar – the view of the Manhattan skyline is a stunner. *74 Wythe Avenue, at North 12th Street, Williamsburg (no phone, www.outputclub.com). Subway L to Bedford Avenue. Open 10pm-4am Wed, Thur; 10pm-6am Fri, Sat. Admission varies.*

Pacha
The worldwide glam-club chain Pacha, with outposts in nightlife capitals such as Ibiza, London and Buenos Aires, hit the US market back in 2005 with this swanky joint helmed by superstar spinner Erick Morillo. The spot attracts heavyweights ranging from local hero Danny Tenaglia to international crowd-pleasers such as Fedde Le Grande and Benny Benassi. Like most big clubs, it pays to check the line-up in advance if you're into underground (as opposed to lowest-common-denominator) beats. *618 W 46th Street, between Eleventh & Twelfth Avenues, Hell's Kitchen (1-212 209 7500, www.pachanyc.com). Subway C, E to 50th Street. Open 10pm-6am Fri; 10pm-8am Sat. Admission $10-$40. No credit cards (online purchases and bar only).*

Santos Party House
Launched by a team that includes rocker Andrew WK, Santos Party House – two black, square rooms done out in a bare-bones, generic club

tyle – was initially hailed as a
cene game-changer. While those
oo-high expectations didn't exactly
an out, it's still a rock-solid choice,
articularly when Danny Krivit takes
he spot over for the soulful house and
lassics-oriented 718 Sessions
www.dannykrivit.net).
6 Lafayette Street, between Walker
& White Streets, Tribeca (1-212 584
492, www.santospartyhouse.com).
Subway J, N, Q, R, Z, 6 to Canal Street.
Open varies. Admission $10-$25.
No credit cards (online purchases
nd bar only).

Sapphire
apphire's bare walls and minimal
ecor are as raw as it gets, yet the
nergetic, unpretentious clientele is
blivious to the (lack of) aesthetic. A
ance crowd packs the place all week –
arious nights feature house, hip hop,
eggae and disco. Admission is usually
ree, except for a small cover charge
fter 11pm on weekend nights.
49 Eldridge Street, between Houston
& Stanton Streets, Lower East Side
1-212 777 5153, www.sapphirenyc.
om). Subway F to Lower East Side-
Second Avenue. Open 7pm-4am daily.
Admission free-$10. No credit cards
bar only).

Webster Hall
The grand Webster Hall isn't exactly
n clubland's A-list, due to a populist
DJ policy and a crowd that favours
nuscle shirts and gelled hair. But hey,

it's been open, on and off, since 1866,
so it must be doing something right.
Friday night's Girls & Boys bash
attracts music makers of the stature of
Grandmaster Flash and dubstep duo
Nero. Concerts here are booked by
Bowery Presents, the folks who run
Bowery Ballroom and Mercury
Lounge. Expect to find high-calibre
indie acts (Black Lips, Battles, Tune-
Yards), but be sure to arrive early if
you want a decent view. A smaller
space downstairs, the Studio, hosts
cheaper shows, mainly by local bands.
125 E 11th Street, at Third Avenue,
East Village (1-212 353 1600,
www.websterhall.com). Subway L to
Third Avenue; L, N, Q, R, 4, 5, 6 to
14th Street-Union Square. Open
10pm-4am Thur-Sat. Admission
free-$50. No credit cards (online
purchases & bar only).

BURLESQUE CLUBS
New York's burlesque scene is a
winking throwback to the days when
the tease was as important as the
strip. Much of the scene tends to
revolve around specific revues rather
than dedicated venues; good bets
include **Wasabassco Burlesque**
(www.wasabassco.com) at the **Bell
House** (see p97) and the Saturday-
night Floating Kabarette at
Galapagos Art Space (see p97) in
Dumbo, Brooklyn. Some of the best
producers and performers – they
often cross over – are Shien Lee
(www.dancesofvice.com), Jen
Gapay's Thirsty Girl Productions
(www.thirstygirlproductions.com),
Angie Pontani of the World Famous
Pontani Sisters (www.angiepontani.
com) and Calamity Chang, 'the Asian
Sexation'(www.calamitychang.com).

Duane Park
Formerly the Bowery Poetry Club,
the venue now operates as Southern-
inflected supper club Duane Park from
Tuesday to Saturday, but Bowery
Poetry (www.bowerypoetry.com)
still holds events on Sundays and
Mondays. Get dinner and a show –
burlesque, jazz, vaudeville or magic –
in decadent surroundings featuring
crystal chandeliers and Corinthian-
topped columns.
308 Bowery, between Bleecker & E
Houston Streets (1-212 732 5555,
www.duaneparknyc.com). Subway F
to Lower East Side-Second Avenue;
6 to Astor Place. Shows 8pm Tue;
9pm Wed, Thur; 10pm Fri; 8pm,
10.30pm Sat. Admission varies.

Nurse Bettie
The '50s-pinup-inspired venue – named
after Bettie Page, one of the 20th
century's premier hotsy-totsies – is a
natural setting for burlesque. Weekly
shows include Spanking of the Lower
East Side, produced by Calamity
Chang, which usually includes six or
seven acts, as well as pre-show go-go
dancers. Prepare to get up close and
personal in the intimate space.
106 Norfolk Street, between Delancey
& Rivington Streets, Lower East Side
(1-212 477 7515, www.nursebettie.

com). Subway F to Delancey Street;
J, Z to Delancey-Essex Streets. Open
6pm-4am daily. Admission free.

Slipper Room
After being rebuilt from the ground
up (which took a little more than two
years), the Slipper Room reopened
with a better sound system, new
lighting and a mezzanine, among other
swank touches, and reclaimed its place
as the city's premier burlesque venue.
Many of the shows that once called it
home, including Mr. Choade's Upstairs
Downstairs (which began in 1999),
have returned, and the setting is as
intimate and fun as ever – but with
upgrades that make the experience
better than before.
167 Orchard Street, at Stanton Street,
Lower East Side (1-212 253 7246,
www.slipperroom.com). Subway F
to Lower East Side-Second Avenue.
Open varies Mon, Sun; 7pm-3am
Tue-Thur; 8.30pm-4am Fri, Sat.
Admission $10-$20. No credit cards
(online purchases & bar only).

Comedy

Beyond the dedicated venues, you'll
find many worthwhile shows in the
back rooms of pubs and other
venues. Look out for **Big Terrific**,
hosted by Max Silvestri, at Cameo
(www.cameony.com) and **Comedy
at the Knitting Factory** (see p98)
with Hannibal Buress.

COMEDY VENUES
Carolines on Broadway
Carolines is a New York City
institution. It's attained that status
in part because of its long-term
relationships with national headliners,
sitcom stars and cable-special pros,
which ensures that its stage always
features marquee names. Although the
majority of bookings skew towards
mainstream, the club also makes time
for undisputedly darker and edgier fare,
such as Paul Mooney and Louis CK.
1626 Broadway, between 49th & 50th
Streets, Theater District (1-212 757
4100, www.carolines.com). Subway

N, Q, R to 49th Street; 1 to 50th Street.
Shows vary. Admission varies
(2-drink min).

Comedy Cellar
Despite being dubbed one of the
best stand-up clubs in the city year
after year, the Comedy Cellar has
maintained a hip, underground feel.
It gets incredibly crowded, but the
bookings, which typically include
no-nonsense comics Dave Chapelle,
Jim Norton and Marina Franklin,
are enough to distract you from your
bachelorette party neighbours.
117 MacDougal Street, between
Bleecker & 3rd Streets, Greenwich
Village (1-212 254 3480, www.comedy
cellar.com). Subway A, B, C, D, E, F,
M to W 4th Street. Shows 8pm, 10pm
Mon, Tue; 8pm, 9.45pm, 11.30pm
Wed; 8pm, 10pm, midnight Thur;
7pm, 8.45pm, 10.30pm, 12.15am Fri;
7.30pm, 9.15pm, 11pm, 12.45am Sat.
Admission $12-$24 (2-item min).
Other location Comedy Cellar at the
Village Underground, 130 W 3rd
Street, between Sixth Avenue &
MacDougal Street, Greenwich Village
(1-212 254 3480).

The Creek & the Cave
This hardworking Long Island City
venue offers all the things comedians
and their fans need to survive: multiple
performance spaces, convivial
environs, a fully stocked bar, cheap
Mexican food and a patio on which to
rant and laugh late into the night. As
if this weren't enough, owner Rebecca
Trent also shows her appreciation for
all who make the trek to Queens by
making nearly every show free.
10-93 Jackson Avenue, at 11th Street,
Long Island City, Queens (1-718
706 8783, www.creeklic.com).
Subway 7 to Vernon Boulevard-
Jackson Avenue. Shows daily, times
vary. Admission free-$5.

Gotham Comedy Club
Chris Mazzilli's vision for his club
involves elegant surroundings,
professional behaviour and mutual
respect. That's why the talents
he fosters, such as Jim Gaffigan,

Tribeca Comedy Lounge.
See p96.

Radio City Music Hall

Critic's choice

1 **Output** An underground
vibe and a killer sound
system. See p94.

2 **Upright Citizens Brigade
Theatre** Top-flight funny
people and long-running
free shows. See p96.

3 **Le Poisson Rouge** A
thrillingly varied
programme in a storied
Village space. See p98.

4 **Radio City Music Hall** The
glitzy setting turns a show
into an event. See p98.

5 **Smalls** The authentic jazz
joint you've been looking
for. See p100.

Nightlife

Tom Papa and Ted Alexandro, keep coming back here after they've found national fame.
208 W 23rd Street, between Seventh & Eighth Avenues, Chelsea (1-212 367 9000, www.gothamcomedyclub.com). Subway F, M, N, R to 23rd Street. Shows vary Mon-Thur, Sun; 8.30pm, 10.30pm Fri; 8pm, 10pm, 11.45pm Sat. Admission $10-$30 (2-drink min).

Magnet Theater
This comedy theatre exudes a distinctly Chicago vibe, from its DIY aesthetic to its performers, some of whom are from the Windy City. Even the local players here prefer theatrical to premise-based improvisation, and their shows give the impression they're not just seeking fame or commercial exposure, but pursue the craft simply for the joy of being on stage.
254 W 29th Street, between Seventh & Eighth Avenues, Chelsea (1-212 244 8824, www.magnettheater.com). Subway A, C, E to 34th Street-Penn Station; 1 to 28th Street. Shows vary. Admission free-$10.

Peoples Improv Theater
After inhabiting a black box in Chelsea for eight years, the PIT leapt across town into the former Algonquin Theatre space, where the improv and sketch venue has upgraded to a beautiful proscenium stage, an additional basement space for experimental shows or stand-up, and an elegant (if cluttered) full-service bar.
123 E 24th Street, between Park & Lexington Avenues, Flatiron District (1 212 563 7188, www.thepit nyc. com). Subway 6 to 23rd Street. Shows daily, times vary. Admission free-$20.

The Stand
After producing popular stand-up shows for years, the four partners behind Cringe Humor (www.cringe humor.net) founded a venue in which to promote their favourite comics – think bawdy, raw and dark acts like Jim Norton and Dave Attell. The bi-level Gramercy spot offers cocktails and embellished comfort food upstairs, while shows take place seven nights a week in its long, narrow basement. The snug 80-seat room places the audience of frat guys and young professionals in close proximity to the performers, and they get pumped when one of their idols (Dane Cook, for instance) drops by.
239 Third Avenue, between 19th & 20th Streets, Gramercy Park (1-212 677 2600, www.thestandnyc.com). Subway L, N, Q, R, 4, 5, 6 to 14th Street-Union Square. Open 5.30pm-midnight Mon, Tue, Sun; 5.30pm-2am Wed-Sat. Shows 8.30pm Mon-Thur; 8.30pm, 10.30pm, midnight Fri, Sat; 7pm, 9pm Sun. Admission $5-$40.

Stand-up NY
After some managerial shifts, this musty uptown spot has begun to garner attention again. The line-ups (including stalwart club denizens such as Jay Oakerson and Godfrey) keep things pretty simple, but there's

NYC COMEDY 101
A few tips from Time Out New York's comedy editor, Matthew Love.

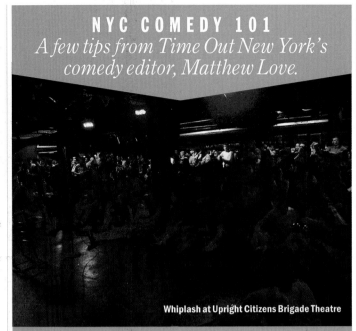

Whiplash at Upright Citizens Brigade Theatre

Fall in line
NYC's reputation as a stand-up hub is unquestioned, but it also boasts a strong long-form improv scene. Start with the best – the **Upright Citizens Brigade Theatre** (*see below*). Its **ASSSSCAT 3000** on Sundays features a rotating cast making up scenes based on the stories of a celebrity monologuist. Tickets to the 7.30pm show are $10, and tend to sell out weeks in advance. The one at 9.30pm, however, is always free, and tickets are distributed at 8.15pm outside the theatre. (Psst, the line forms around 7pm.)

Stay up late
Keep caffeinated – some of the top gigs go down way past bedtime. On Mondays at 11pm, the UCB throws **Whiplash**, a free show that speeds through up-and-coming and big-name comics. Reservations can be made online, but get there at least 15 minutes early. Stop by **Gotham Comedy**

Club (*see p95*) on a Tuesday night at 9.30pm for **ComedyJuice**, in which national headliners practise new jokes. Tickets are $15 (plus a two-item minimum).

Explore Brooklyn
Head to Park Slope and Gowanus, where the **Bell House** (*see p97*), **Union Hall** (*see p98*) and art/performance space **Littlefield** (622 DeGraw Street, between Third & Fourth Avenues, Gowanus, Brooklyn, www.littlefieldnyc.com) are within a square mile of one another, and regularly host great events. Bonus: they all have cool bars and reasonable entry fees.

Look for surprises
Watch for the phrase 'and special guests'. Famous comics often try out their material on unsuspecting crowds. It's not uncommon to see Jim Gaffigan or Mike Birbiglia drop in unannounced – or even Louis CK, Aziz Ansari, Chris Rock or a visiting Zach Galifianakis.

almost always one performer on the bill that makes it worth the trip.
236 W 78th Street, at Broadway, Upper West Side (1-212 595 0850, www.standupny.com). Subway 1 to 79th Street. Shows 8pm, 10pm Mon-Thur; 7pm, 9pm, 11pm Fri; 5pm, 7pm, 11pm Sat; 8pm, 10pm Sun. Admission $15-$20 (2-drink min).

Tribeca Comedy Lounge
The brick walls and makeshift stage in this congenial spot remind you that you're in a basement, but the doting waitstaff, haute Italian menu from Brick NYC upstairs and roomy layout will please fans of creature comforts. Adam Strauss, the owner-booker and a burgeoning comic himself, makes sure that his programming is packed with next-wave talent (young, funny stars such as Sara Schaefer, Dan St Germain

and Kevin Barnett) while also saving stage time for himself.
22 Warren Street, between Broadway & Church Street, Tribeca (1-646 504 5653, www.tribecacomedylounge. com). Subway A, C, 1, 2, 3 to Chambers Street; N, R to City Hall. Shows 8pm Tue-Thur; 8pm, 10pm Fri, Sat. Admission $20 (2-drink min).

Upright Citizens Brigade Theatre
The most visible catalyst in New York's current alternative comedy boom. The improv troupes and sketch groups here are some of the best in the city. Stars of *Saturday Night Live* and writers for late-night talk-shows gather on Sunday nights to wow crowds in the long-running ASSSSCAT 3000. Other premier teams include the Stepfathers (Friday) and Death by Roo Roo (Saturday).

Arrive early for a good seat – the venue has challenging sightlines.

UCBEast (153 E Third Street, East Village, 1-212 366 9231), which opened in 2011, gave the enormous community another space – and a bar. The warm lighting and low, rounded ceiling of the ex-arthouse cinema create immediate intimacy, whether the fare is improv or stand-up, and the venue snapped up some of the fledgling comedy variety shows that were scattered in East Side venues.
307 W 26th Street, at Eighth Avenue, Chelsea (1-212 366 9176, www.ucb theatre.com). Subway C, E to 23rd Street; 1 to 28th Street. Shows daily, times vary. Admission free-$10. No credit cards.

Music
Rock, pop & soul

Not only are venues offering increasingly eclectic fare, but gigs are also busting out of their usual club and concert hall confines: the **City Winery** (*see p97*) crushes and ferments grapes as well as staging shows, while bowling alley-music venue hybrid **Brooklyn Bowl** (61 Wythe Avenue, between North 11th & 12th Streets, Williamsburg, Brooklyn, 1-718 963 3369, www.brooklynbowl.com) has a 600-capacity space that features small acts for tiny cover charges, as well as a smattering of larger concerts (Art Brut, Sharon Jones & the Dap-Kings).

MAJOR ARENAS & STADIUMS

Barclays Center
The city's newest arena, home of the rechristened Brooklyn Nets basketball team, opened in autumn 2012 with a series of concerts by native son and Nets investor Jay-Z. Though its mere existence remains a point of contention for some Brooklynites, the arena has already been a success. The staff is efficient and amiable, the acoustics are excellent, and there's a top-notch view from nearly every one of the 19,000 seats. And since it opened, it has attracted an unexpectedly cool list of acts, with local luminaries like Vampire Weekend, Yeah Yeah Yeahs and MGMT gracing its stage.
620 Atlantic Avenue, at Flatbush Avenue, Prospect Heights, Brooklyn (1-917 618 6700, www.barclayscenter com) Subway B, D, N, Q, R, 2, 3, 4, 5 to Atlantic Avenue-Barclays Center. Box office noon-6pm Mon-Fri; noon-2pm Sat (varies on event days). Tickets vary

Madison Square Garden
Some of music's biggest acts – Jay-Z, Lady Gaga, Rush – come out to play at the world's most famous basketball arena, home to the Knicks and also hockey's Rangers. Whether you'll actually be able to get a look at them depends on your seat number or the quality of your binoculars. While it is undoubtedly a part of the fabric of New York, the storied venue is too vast

or a rich concert experience, but it has been improved by a major renovation. The three-year revamp brought new seating and food from top New York City chefs, among other improvements, while respecting the Garden's history. The striking circular ceiling has been restored, while the north and south corridors on the entry level have been returned to their original appearance, including advertisements and event posters from 1968.
Seventh Avenue, between 31st & 33rd Streets, Garment District (1-212 465 6741, www.thegarden.com). Subway A, C, E, 1, 2, 3 to 34th Street-Penn Station. Box office 10am-6pm Mon-Sat; noon-6pm Sun (plus 1 hr after show starts). Tickets vary.

VENUES

Apollo Theater
This 100-year-old former burlesque theatre has been a hub for African-American artists for decades, and launched the careers of Ella Fitzgerald and D'Angelo, among many others. The now-legendary Amateur Night showcase has been running since 1934. The venue, known for jazz, R&B and soul music, mixes veteran talents such as Dianne Reeves with younger artists such as John Legend.
253 W 125th Street, between Adam Clayton Powell Jr Boulevard (Seventh Avenue) & Frederick Douglass Boulevard (Eighth Avenue), Harlem (1-212 531 5300, www.apollotheater. org). Subway A, B, C, D, 1 to 125th Street. Box office 10am-6pm Mon-Fri; noon-5pm Sat. Tickets vary.

Barbès
Show up early if you want to get into Park Slope's global-bohemian club – it's tiny. Run by musically inclined French expats, this venue brings in traditional swing and jazz of more daring stripes – depending on the night, you could catch Colombian, Brazilian, African or French music or acts that often defy categorisation. Chicha Libre, a Brooklyn band reviving psychedelic Peruvian music, holds down Mondays.
376 9th Street, between Sixth & Seventh Avenues, Park Slope, Brooklyn (1-347 422 0248, www.barbes brooklyn.com). Open 5pm-2am Mon-Thur; 2pm-4am Fri, Sat; 2pm-2am Sun. Tickets free-$10.

Beacon Theatre
This spacious former vaudeville theatre hosts a variety of popular acts, from Aziz Ansari to ZZ Top; once a year, the Allman Brothers take over for a lengthy residency. While the vastness can be daunting to performers and audience alike, the baroque, gilded interior makes you feel like you're having a real night out on the town.
2124 Broadway, between 74th & 75th Streets, Upper West Side (1-212 465 6500, www.beacontheatrenyc.com). Subway 1, 2, 3 to 72nd Street. Box office 11am-7pm Mon-Sat (varies on event days). Tickets vary.

The Bell House
The pioneering venue offers a plethora of cool events each week, including concerts, nerdy lectures and dance parties. Fixtures on the schedule include Wasabassco Burlesque, off-the-cuff storytelling slam the Moth, trivia show Ask Me Another and the Rub, a funky long-running affair tossed by DJs Ayres and Eleven.
149 7th Street, between Second & Third Avenues, Gowanus, Brooklyn (1-718 643 6510, www.thebell houseny.com). Subway F, G, R to Fourth Avenue-9th Street. Shows vary. Tickets free-$27.

Best Buy Theater
This large, corporate club begs for character but finds redemption in its creature comforts. The sound and sightlines are both good, and there's even edible food. Those who wish to look into a musician's eyes can stand in the ample front section; foot-weary fans can sit in the cinema-like section at the back. It's a comfortable place to see a well-known band that hasn't (yet) reached stadium-filling fame.
1515 Broadway, at 44th Street, Theater District (1-212 930 1950, www.bestbuytheater.com). Subway N, Q, R, S, 1, 2, 3, 7 to 42nd Street-Times Square. Box office noon-6pm Mon-Sat. Tickets $20-$70.

Bowery Ballroom
Bowery Ballroom is probably the best venue in the city for seeing indie bands, either on the way up or holding their own. But it also brings in a diverse range of artists from home and abroad, and you can expect a clear view and bright sound from any spot in the venue. The spacious downstairs lounge is a great place to hang out between sets.
6 Delancey Street, between Bowery & Chrystie Street, Lower East Side (1-212 533 2111, www.bowery ballroom.com). Subway B, D to Grand Street; J, Z to Bowery; 6 to Spring Street. Box office at Mercury Lounge (see p98). Tickets $15-$35.

Cake Shop
It can be difficult to see the stage in this narrow, stuffy basement space, but Cake Shop gets big points for its keen indie and underground-rock bookings, among the best and most adventurous in the city. The venue lives up to its name, selling vegan pastries and coffee upstairs, while the back room at street level sells record-store ephemera.
152 Ludlow Street, between Rivington & Stanton Streets, Lower East Side (1-212 253 0036, www.cake-shop. com). Subway F to Lower East Side-Second Avenue. Open 10am-4am daily. Tickets free-$12.

City Winery
Unabashedly grown-up and yuppie-friendly, this slick, spacious club launched by oenophile Michael Dorf

is New York's only fully functioning winery – as well as a 300-seat concert space. Acts tend to be on the quiet side – this is, after all, a wine bar – but that doesn't mean the shows lack bite. Younger singer-songwriters such as Laura Marling and Keren Ann have appeared, but the place is dominated by older artists (Steve Earle, Los Lobos).
155 Varick Street, at Vandam Street, Soho (1-212 608 0555, www.city winery.com). Subway 1 to Houston Street. Open 11.30am-3pm, 5.30pm-midnight Mon-Fri; 5pm-midnight Sat; 10am-3pm, 5.30pm-midnight Sun. Box office 11am-6pm Mon-Fri. Tickets vary.

Galapagos Art Space
Galapagos established itself in Williamsburg years before the neighbourhood's renaissance – and, like many colonisers, got squeezed out of the scene it had helped to create. The much larger space in Dumbo offers a grander mix of the cultural offerings for which Galapagos is known and loved: music, performance art, burlesque, drag queens and other weird stuff. Just be careful not to fall into the pools of water strategically placed throughout the club.
16 Main Street, at Water Street, Dumbo, Brooklyn (1-718 222 8500, www.galapagos artspace.com). Subway A, C to High Street; F to York Street. Shows vary. Tickets free-$25.

Glasslands Gallery
If you're looking to catch a Brooklyn buzz band before it breaks, look here. Marvel at the cool DIY decor while nodding to sets from local indie faves such as Ducktails and Cults. The music/burlesque/party destination spotlights less-hyped acts; metal band Liturgy has rocked the house, and Canadian electro-rock crew Suuns have played here.
289 Kent Avenue, between South 1st & 2nd Streets, Williamsburg, Brooklyn (no phone, www.theglasslands.com). Subway L to Bedford Avenue. Shows vary (usually 8.30pm daily). Tickets free-$15. No credit cards.

Goodbye Blue Monday
Relax while taking in this cult Bushwick drinkery's distinct junkyard aesthetic (the walls are lined with old books, random lamps and retro radios). The acts that play here are pretty eclectic, ranging from anti-folk to experimental jazz, and, best of all, gigs are always free.
1087 Broadway, at Dodworth Street, Bushwick, Brooklyn (1-718 453 6343, www.goodbye-blue-monday.com). Open 11am-2am Mon-Thur, Sun; 11am-3am Fri, Sat. Admission free.

Gramercy Theatre
The Gramercy Theatre looks exactly like what it is, a run-down former movie theatre; yet it has a decent sound system and good sightlines.

Concert-goers can lounge in raised seats on the top level or get closer to the stage. Bookings have included such Baby Boom underdogs as Loudon Wainwright III and Todd Rundgren, and the occasional niche hip hop show, but tilt towards niche metal and emo.
127 E 23rd Street, between Park & Lexington Avenues, Gramercy Park (1-212 614 6932, www.thegramercy theatre.com). Subway N, R, 6 to 23rd Street. Box office noon-6.30pm Mon-Fri (and 1 hr before weekend shows). Tickets $10-$100.

Hammerstein Ballroom
Queues can wind across the block, drinks prices are high, and those seated in the balcony should bring binoculars if they want a clear view of the band. Still, this cavernous space regularly draws big performers in the limbo between club and arena shows, and it's ideal for theatrical blow-outs; Kylie, the Pet Shop Boys and Grace Jones have all wowed here.
Manhattan Center, 311 W 34th Street, between Eighth & Ninth Avenues, Garment District (1-212 279 7740, Ticketmaster 1-800 745 3000, www. mcstudios.com). Subway A, C, E to 34th Street-Penn Station. Tickets vary.

Highline Ballroom
This West Side club is LA-slick and bland, in a corporate sense, but it has a lot to recommend it: the sound is top-of-the-heap and sightlines are pretty good. The bookings are also impressive, ranging from hip hop heatseekers such as Yelawolf and Wiz Khalifa, to singer-songwriter pop, world music and burlesque.
431 W 16th Street, between Ninth & Tenth Avenues, Chelsea (1-212 414 5994, www.highlineballroom.com). Subway A, C, E to 14th Street; L to Eighth Avenue. Box office 11am-end of show. Tickets free-$100 ($10 food/drink min at tables).

Irving Plaza
Lying just east of Union Square, this midsize rock venue has served as a Democratic Party lecture hall (in the 19th century), a Yiddish theatre and a burlesque house (Gypsy Rose Lee made an appearance). Most importantly, it's a great place to see big stars keeping a low profile (Jeff Beck, Jane's Addiction and Lenny Kravitz) and medium heavies on their way up.
17 Irving Place, at 15th Street, Gramercy & Flatiron (1-212 777 6800, www.irvingplaza.com). Subway L, N, Q, R, 4, 5, 6 to 14th Street-Union Square. Box office noon-6.30pm Mon-Fri; 1-5pm Sat. Tickets $15-$75.

Joe's Pub
One of the city's premier small spots for sit-down audiences, the recently refurbished Joe's Pub brings in impeccable talent of all genres and origins. While some well-established names play here, Joe's also lends its stage to up-and-comers (this is where Amy Winehouse made her debut in the United States), drag acts and cabaret performers (Justin Vivian

TOP TIP!
Prove yourself
Most clubs operate an over-21 door policy. Even if you're in the running for the World's Oldest Clubber award, you'll need ID, such as a passport or driving licence.

Nightlife

Bond is a mainstay). The food menu – a mix of snacks, shareable plates and main courses – has been revitalised by hot chef Andrew Carmellini.
Public Theater, 425 Lafayette Street, between Astor Place & E 4th Street, East Village (1-212 967 7555, www.joespub.com). Subway N, R to 8th Street-NYU; 6 to Astor Place. Box office 1-6pm Mon, Sun; 1-7.30pm Tue-Sat. Tickets ($12 food or 2-drink minimum) $12-$30.

Knitting Factory Brooklyn
Once a downtown Manhattan incubator of experimental music, Knitting Factory now has outposts across the country. Its New York base, which relocated to Williamsburg in 2009, is a professional, well-managed club, with a happening front-room bar, and solid indie-rock and hip hop bills (Zola Jesus, Black Milk) designed to suit its hipster clientele.
361 Metropolitan Avenue, at Havemeyer Street, Williamsburg, Brooklyn (1-347 529 6696, www.knittingfactory.com). Subway L to Lorimer Street; G to Metropolitan Avenue. Open 5pm-3.30am Mon-Fri; 3pm-3.30am Sat, Sun. Tickets free-$25.

Mercury Lounge
The unassuming, boxy Mercury Lounge is an old standby, with solid sound and sightlines (and a cramped bar in the front room). There are four-band bills most nights, although they can seem stylistically haphazard and set times are often later than advertised. (It's a good rule of thumb to show up half an hour later than you think you should.) Some of the bigger shows sell out in advance, and the club thrives during autumn's CMJ Music Marathon; young hopefuls from years gone by include Mumford & Sons.
217 E Houston Street, between Essex & Ludlow Streets, Lower East Side (1-212 260 4700, www.mercuryloungenyc.com). Subway F to Lower East Side-Second Avenue. Box office noon-7pm Mon-Sat. Tickets $8-$20. No credit cards (online purchases & bar only).

Music Hall of Williamsburg
When, in 2007, the local promoter Bowery Presents found itself in need of a Williamsburg outpost, it gave the former Northsix a facelift and took over the bookings. It's basically a Bowery Ballroom in Brooklyn – and bands such as Sonic Youth, Hot Chip and Real Estate headline, often on the day after they've played Bowery Ballroom or Terminal 5.
66 North 6th Street, between Kent & Wythe Avenues, Williamsburg, Brooklyn (1-718 486 5400, www.musichallofwilliamsburg.com). Subway L to Bedford Avenue. Box office 11am-6pm Sat. Tickets $15-$35.

Pete's Candy Store
An overlooked gem tucked away in an old candy shop, Pete's is beautifully ramshackle, tiny and almost always free. The performers are generally unknown and crowds can be thin, but

it can be a charming place to catch a singer-songwriter. Worthy underdogs may stop by for casual sets.
709 Lorimer Street, between Frost & Richardson Streets, Williamsburg, Brooklyn (1-718 302 3770, www.petescandystore.com). Subway L to Lorimer Street. Open 5pm-2am Mon-Wed; 5pm-4am Thur; 4pm-4am Fri, Sat; 4pm-2am Sun. Admission free.

Pianos
In recent years, a lot of the cooler bookings have moved down the block to venues such as Cake Shop or to Brooklyn. But while the sound is often lousy and the room can get uncomfortably mobbed, there are always good reasons to go back to Pianos – very often the under-the-radar, emerging rock bands that make local music scenes tick.
158 Ludlow Street, between Rivington & Stanton Streets, Lower East Side (1-212 505 3733, www.pianosnyc.com). Subway F to Delancey Street; J, M, Z to Delancey-Essex treets. Open 2pm-4am daily. Admission free-$12.

Le Poisson Rouge
Tucked into the basement of the long-gone Village Gate – a legendary performance space that hosted everyone from Miles Davis to Jimi Hendrix – Le Poisson Rouge was opened in 2008 by a group of young music enthusiasts with ties to both the classical and the indie rock worlds. The booking policy reflects both camps, often on a single bill. No other joint in town books such a wide range of great music, whether from a feverish Malian band (Toumani Diabaté's Symmetric Orchestra), rising indie stars (Zola Jesus) or young classical luminaries (pianist Simone Dinnerstein).
158 Bleecker Street, at Thompson Street, Greenwich Village

(1-212 505 3474, www.lepoissonrouge.com). Subway A, B, C, D, E, F, M to W 4th Street. Open 5pm-2am Mon-Wed, Sun; 5pm-4am Thur-Sat. Box office 5pm-close daily. Tickets free-$30.

Radio City Music Hall
Few rooms scream 'New York City!' more than this gilded hall, which in recent years has drawn Leonard Cohen, Drake and Bon Iver as headliners. The greatest challenge for any performer is to not be upstaged by the awe-inspiring art deco surroundings, although those same surroundings lend historic heft to even the flimsiest showing. Bookings are all over the map – expect everything from seasonal staples like the Rockettes to lectures with the Dalai Lama.
1260 Sixth Avenue, at 50th Street, Midtown (1-212 247 4777, www.radiocity.com). Subway B, D, F, M to 47th-50th Streets-Rockefeller Center. Box office 10am-8pm Mon-Sat. Tickets vary.

Rockwood Music Hall
The cramped quarters are part of this club's appeal: there are no bad seats (or standing spots) in the house. You can catch multiple acts every night of the week on three separate stages, and it's likely that many of those performers will soon be appearing in much bigger halls. Multi-genre polymath Gabriel Kahane is a regular, as is bluegrass great Michael Daves.
196 Allen Street, between E Houston & Stanton Streets, Lower East Side (1-212 477 4155, www.rockwoodmusichall.com). Subway F to Lower East Side-Second Avenue. Open 5.30pm-3am Mon-Fri; 2.30pm-3am Sat, Sun. Tickets free-$20 (1-drink min per set). No credit cards (online purchases & bar only).

Highline Ballroom. See p97.

Sidewalk Café
Despite its cramped, awkward layout, the Sidewalk Café is the focal point of the city's anti-folk scene – although that category means just about anything from piano pop to wry folk. Nellie McKay, Regina Spektor and the Moldy Peaches all started here.
94 Avenue A, at 6th Street, East Village (1-212 473 7373, www.sidewalkny.com). Subway 6 to Astor Place. Open 5pm-3am Mon-Thur; 11am-4am Fri, Sat; 11am-2am Sun. Shows usually 7pm daily. Admission free (1-drink min).

SOB's
The titular Sounds of Brazil (SOB, geddit?) are just some of the many global genres that keep this venue hopping. Soul, hip hop, reggae and Latin beats figure in the mix, with Raphael Saadiq, Maceo Parker and Eddie Palmieri each appearing in recent years. The drinks are expensive, but the sharp-looking clientele doesn't seem to mind.
204 Varick Street, at Houston Street, Soho (1-212 243 4940, www.sobs.com). Subway 1 to Houston Street. Box office 11am-6pm Mon-Fri. Tickets $5-$40. No credit cards (online purchases, food & bar only).

Terminal 5
Opened by Bowery Presents, this three floor, 3,000-capacity place is the largest midtown venue to set up shop in more than a decade. Bookings include bands that only a short time ago were playing in the smaller Bowery confines (Odd Future), plus bigger stars (Florence and the Machine) and veterans with their loyal fan bases (Morrissey, Jane's Addiction). It's great for dancey acts (Chromeo, Matt & Kim), but be warned: sightlines from the T5 balconies are among the worst in the city.
610 W 56th Street, between 11th & 12th Avenues, Hell's Kitchen (1-212 582 6600, www.terminal5nyc.com). Subway A, B, C, D, 1 to 59th Street-Columbus Circle. Box office at Mercury Lounge (see left). Tickets $15-$90.

Town Hall
Acoustics at the 1921 'people's auditorium' are superb, and there's no doubting the gravitas of the surroundings – the building was designed by illustrious architects McKim, Mead & White as a meeting house for a suffragist organisation. George Benson, Grizzly Bear and Lindsey Buckingham have performed here, and smart indie songwriters such as the Magnetic Fields have set up shop for a number of nights.
123 W 43rd Street, between Sixth Avenue & Broadway, Theater District (1-212 840 2824, www.thetownhallnyc.org). Subway B, D, F, M to 42nd Street-Bryant Park; N, Q, R, S, 1, 2, 3, 7 to 42nd Street-Times Square; 7 to Fifth Avenue. Box office noon-6pm Mon-Sat. Tickets vary.

Union Hall
The spacious main floor of this Brooklyn bar has a garden, food

ervice and a bocce ball court. Tucked
 the basement is a comfortable space
ominated by the more delicate side
 indie rock, with infrequent sets by
dic comics such as Mike Birbiglia
nd Eugene Mirman.
02 Union Street, between Fifth &
ixth Avenues, Park Slope, Brooklyn
1-718 638 4400, www.unionhallny.
om). Subway R to Union Street. Open
pm-4am Mon-Fri; 1pm-4am Sat,
un. Tickets $5-$20.

nion Pool
Wind through the kitschy backyard
pace of this modest but super-cool
Williamsburg bar (which featured in
he movie *Nick and Norah's Infinite
Playlist*) and you'll find yourself back
indoors, facing a small stage. Local
tars check in from time to time
members of Yeah Yeah Yeahs have
howed off their side projects here),
ut it's dominated by well-plucked
maller indie acts. For a rowdy,
musing Monday night, check out
everend Vince Anderson and his
ove Choir.
84 Union Avenue, at Meeker
venue, Williamsburg, Brooklyn
1-718 609 0484, www.union-
ool.com). Subway L to Lorimer
treet; G to Metropolitan Avenue.
pen 5pm-4am Mon-Fri; 1pm-4am
at, Sun. Tickets free-$12. No credit
ards (online purchases & bar only).

World, country
& roots

mong the cornucopia of live
ntertainment programmes at the
rooklyn Academy of Music (*see
101*), the BAMcafé above the lobby
omes to life on weekend nights with
orld music and other genres. *See
lso p98* **SOB's**, *p97* **Barbès** *and
ight* **BB King Blues Club & Grill**.

Nublu
Nublu's prominence on the local
lobalist club scene has been inversely
roportional to its size. A pressure-
ooker of creativity, it gave rise to the
razilian Girls, who started jamming
t one late-night session and still
ccasionally bring their loungy
lectronic sounds back to the club.
However, at time of writing, Nublu
vas looking for a new venue – call or
ee website for updates.
2 Avenue C, between 4th & 5th
treets, East Village (no phone,
ww.nublu.net). Open 9pm-4am
aily. Admission $5-$10.

Rodeo Bar & Grill
The unpretentious, if sometimes
aucous crowd, roadhouse atmosphere
nd absence of a cover charge help to
nake the Rodeo the city's best roots
lub, with a steady stream of rockabilly,
ountry and related sounds. Kick back
vith a beer from the bar – a funked-up
railer in the middle of the room.
375 Third Avenue, at 27th Street,
Gramercy Park (1-212 683 6500,
ww.rodeobar.com). Subway 6 to 28th

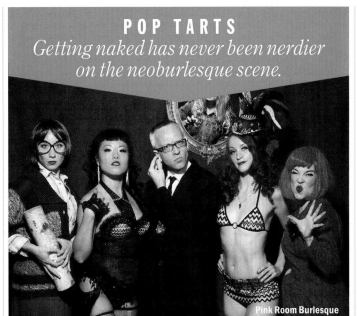

POP TARTS
*Getting naked has never been nerdier
on the neoburlesque scene.*

Pink Room Burlesque

Pop culture permeates every aspect of American life – and NYC's
neoburlesque circuit is no exception. Often referred to as
'nerdlesque', the subgenre emerged a few years ago with racy
tributes to longtime mainstream fan favourites like *Star Trek*, *Star Wars*
and superheroes featuring meticulously recreated costumes and in-the-
know references. These days the scene also offers more obscure
themes (horror author HP Lovecraft, children's edutainment TV series
Reading Rainbow) and sexy send-ups of sitcoms and reality shows.
Practitioners say the combination allows them to attract audiences
who might not go to a straight-up burlesque show. 'We really started
packing 'em in when we embraced our nerdy nakedness,' says Ruby
Solitaire, co-producer of **Excelsior Burlesque** (www.excelsiorburlesque.
com). 'We create shows that are not only accessible to pop-culture
audiences, but also offer a wink and a nod for people familiar with the
more esoteric, deep tracks of geekdom.' Upcoming themes include the
work of Alan *Watchmen* Moore and cult BBC TV shows.
Francine 'the Lucid Dream' has a singular obsession: the oeuvre of
surreal auteur David Lynch. Since mounting her first *Twin Peaks*-themed
Pink Room Burlesque show in 2011, she's gone on to 'sexplore' *Blue
Velvet*, *Wild at Heart*, *Mulholland Drive* and even his infamous flop-
turned-cult epic *Dune*. The quarterly performances include the annual
Miss Twin Peaks Pageant. Visit www.francineburlesque.com for info.
Also Look out for **RAWR! Burlesque** (www.rawrnyc.com), co-produced
by renowned cosplayer Stella Chuu; video game enthusiast Anja
Keister's **D20 Burlesque** (www.d20burlesque.com); and poplesque
pioneers **Hotsy Totsy Burlesque** (www.hotsytotsyburlesque.com),
who will put their unique, scripted strip-tease spin on *Game of Thrones*,
Harry Potter and *Mad Men* in the coming months.

Street. Shows 9pm-midnight Mon-
Wed, Sun; 9.30pm-12.30am Thur;
11pm-2am Fri, Sat. Admission free.

Jazz, blues &
experimental

Ever since Duke Ellington urged
folks to take the A train up to Harlem,
New York has been a hotbed of
improvisational talent. While Harlem
is no longer the centre of the jazz
scene, in the Village, you can soak
up the vibe at clubs that once
provided a platform for the virtuoso
experimentations of Miles Davis,
John Coltrane and Thelonious Monk.
Boundaries are still being pushed
in eclectic avant-garde venues like
Roulette, **Spectrum** (for both, *see*

p103) and the **Stone** (*see p100*). For
well-known jazz joints such as the
Village Vanguard (*see p100*) and
Birdland (*see right*), booking ahead
is recommended.

55 Bar
This tiny Prohibition-era dive is one
of New York's most artist-friendly
rooms, thanks to its knowledgeable,
appreciative audience. You can catch
emerging talent almost every night at
the free early shows; late sets regularly
feature established artists such as Mike
Stern, Wayne Krantz and David Binney.
*55 Christopher Street, between
Seventh Avenue South & Waverly
Place, West Village (1-212 929 9883,
www.55bar.com). Subway 1 to
Christopher Street-Sheridan Square.
Open 3pm-4am daily. Tickets free-$15.
No credit cards.*

92nd Street Y
Best known for the series Jazz in July
and spring's Lyrics & Lyricists, this
multidisciplinary cultural centre also
offers cabaret, mainstream jazz and
singer-songwriters. The small,
handsome theatre provides a fine
setting for the sophisticated fare.
For listings, see p102.

BB King Blues Club & Grill
BB's Times Square joint hosts one of the
most varied music schedules in town.
Cover bands and tributes fill the gaps
between big-name bookings such as
George Clinton and Buddy Guy, but the
venue also regularly hosts hip hop and
the odd extreme-metal blowout. The
best seats are often at the dinner tables
in front, but the menu prices are steep
(and watch out for drink minimums).
The Harlem Gospel Choir's buffet
brunch ($47, $44 booked in advance,
12.30pm Sun) raises the roof.
*237 W 42nd Street, between Seventh
& Eighth Avenues, Theater District (1-
212 997 4144, www.bbkingblues.com).
Subway A, C, E to 42nd Street-Port
Authority; N, Q, R, S, 1, 2, 3, 7 to 42nd
Street-Times Square. Box office 11am-
midnight daily. Tickets $12-$150.*

Birdland
The flagship venue for midtown's jazz
resurgence, Birdland takes its place
among the neon lights of Times Square
seriously. That means it's a haven for
great jazz musicians (Joe Lovano, Kurt
Elling) as well as performers like John
Pizzarelli and Aaron Neville. The club is
also notable for its roster of bands-in-
residence. Sundays belong to the Arturo
O'Farrill Afro Latin Jazz Orchestra.
*315 W 44th Street, between Eighth
& Ninth Avenues, Theater District
(1-212 581 3080, www.birdlandjazz.
com). Subway A, C, E to 42nd Street-
Port Authority. Open 5pm-1am daily.
Tickets $20-$50 ($10 food/drink min).*

Blue Note
The Blue Note prides itself on being
'the jazz capital of the world'. Bona fide
musical titans (Jimmy Heath, Lee
Konitz) rub against contemporary
heavyweights (the Bad Plus), while the
close-set tables in the club get patrons
rubbing up against each other. The
edgy Friday Late Night Groove series
and the Sunday brunches (10.30am-
3pm; $29.50) are the best bargain bets.
*131 W 3rd Street, between MacDougal
Street & Sixth Avenue, Greenwich
Village (1-212 475 8592, www.blue
note.net). Subway A, B, C, D, E, F, M
to W 4th Street. Shows 8pm, 10.30pm
Mon-Thur, Sun; 8pm, 10.30pm,
12.30am Fri, Sat. Tickets $10-$75
($5 food/drink min).*

Carnegie Hall
Carnegie Hall means the big time. In
recent years, though, the 599-seat,
state-of-the-art Zankel Hall has greatly
augmented the venue's pop, jazz and
world music offerings. The complex
has welcomed Keith Jarrett, Randy
Newman and Bobby McFerrin, among
other high-wattage names.
For listings, see p101.

Nightlife

Cornelia Street Café

Upstairs at the Cornelia Street Café is a cosy eaterie. Downstairs is an even cosier music space hosting adventurous jazz, poetry, world music and folk. Regular mini-festivals spotlight blues and songwriters. It's a good idea to arrive when the doors open for shows (5.45pm, 8.30pm or 10.15pm) because reservations are only held for 15 minutes after the set starts.
29 Cornelia Street, between Bleecker & 4th Streets, Greenwich Village (1-212 989 9319, www.corneliastreetcafe. com). Subway A, B, C, D, E, F, M to W 4th Street. Open 10am-midnight Mon-Thur, Sun; 10am-1am Fri, Sat. Shows 6pm, 8.30pm Mon-Thur, Sun; 6pm, 9pm, 10.30pm Fri, Sat. Tickets $10-$15 ($10 food/drink min). No credit cards (food & bar only).

Iridium

Iridium lures upscale crowds with a line-up that's split between household names and those known only to the jazz-savvy. The sight lines and sound system are truly worthy of celebration. Long the site of a Monday-night residency by guitar icon Les Paul, the club now hosts a stream of veteran pickers who perform in his honour.
1650 Broadway, at 51st Street, Theater District (1-212 582 2121, www.iridiumjazzclub.com). Subway 1 to 50th Street; N, R to 49th Street. Shows 8pm, 10pm daily. Tickets $25-$40 ($15 food/drink min).

Jazz Gallery

This beloved haunt, one of the city's premier incubators for progressive-jazz talent, relocated from its former Soho digs to a gallery-like space near the Flatiron Building. It's a place to witness true works of art from sometimes obscure but always interesting jazzers (Henry Threadgill and Vijay Iyer, to name a couple).
5th floor, 1160 Broadway, between 27th and 28th Streets, Flatiron District (1-646 494 3625, www.jazz gallery.org). Subway N, R to 28th Street. Shows 9pm, 11pm Tue-Sat. Tickets $10-$35. No credit cards (online purchases only).

Jazz at Lincoln Center

The jazz arm of Lincoln Center is located several blocks away from the main campus, high atop the Time Warner Center. It includes three rooms: the Rose Theater is a traditional mid-size space, but the crown jewels are the Allen Room and the smaller Dizzy's Club Coca-Cola, with stages that are framed by enormous windows looking on to Columbus Circle and Central Park. The venues feel like a Hollywood cinematographer's vision of a Manhattan jazz club. Some of the best players in the business regularly grace the spot; among them is Wynton Marsalis, Jazz at Lincoln Center's famed artistic director.
Frederick P Rose Hall *Broadway, at 60th Street, Upper West Side (1-212 258 9800, www.jalc.org). Subway A, B, C, D, 1 to 59th Street-Columbus Circle.*

Rose Theater & the Allen Room

CenterCharge 1-212 721 6500. Shows vary. Box office 10am-6pm Mon-Sat; noon-6pm Sun. Tickets Rose Theater $30-$120. The Allen Room $55-$65.
Dizzy's Club Coca-Cola *1-212 258 9595. Shows 7.30pm, 9.30pm Mon-Thur, Sun; 7.30pm, 9.30pm, 11.30pm Fri, Sat. Tickets $10-$35 ($5-$10 food/drink min).*

Jazz Standard

Renovation was just what the doctor ordered for the jazz den below restaurateur Danny Meyer's Blue Smoke barbecue joint. Now the room's marvellous sound matches its already splendid sight lines. The jazz is of the groovy, hard-swinging variety, featuring such musicians as organist Dr Lonnie Smith, Larry Goldings and Cedar Walton.
116 E 27th Street, between Park Avenue South & Lexington Avenue, Flatiron District (1-212 576 2232, www.jazzstandard.com). Subway 6 to 28th Street. Shows 7.30pm, 9.30pm Mon-Thur; 7.30pm, 9.30pm, 11.30pm Fri, Sat. Tickets $20-$35.

Merkin Concert Hall

The Merkin provides a polished platform for classical and jazz composers, with chamber music, jazz, folk, cabaret and experimental music performers taking the stage at the intimate venue. Popular annual series include the New York Guitar Festival, WNYC's New Sounds Live (part of the Ecstatic Music Festival) and Broadway Close Up.
For listings, see p102.

Smalls

For those looking for an authentic jazz club experience – rather than the cheesy dinner-club vibe that prevails at too many other spots around town – Smalls is a must. The cosy basement space feels like a speakeasy, or more specifically, one of those hole-in-the-wall NYC jazz haunts of yore over which fans obsess. Best of all, the booking skews retro, yet not stubbornly so. You'll hear classic hardbop as well as more adventurous, contemporary approaches.
183 W 10th Street, between Seventh Avenue South & W 4th Street, West Village (1-212 252 5091, www.smallsjazzclub.com). Subway 1 to Christopher Street-Sheridan Square. Open 6pm-3am Mon-Wed; 4pm-4am Thur-Sun. Admission $10-$20. No credit cards.

Smoke

Not unlike a swanky living room, Smoke is a classy little joint that acts as a haven for local jazz legends and touring artists looking to play an intimate space. Early in the week, evenings are themed: on Monday, it's big band; Tuesday, organ jazz; Wednesday, jazz-soul. On weekends, renowned jazzers hit the stage, relishing the chance to play informal gigs uptown.
2751 Broadway, between 105th & 106th Streets, Upper West Side

(1-212 864 6662, www.smoke jazz.com). Subway 1 to 103rd Street. Shows 7pm, 9pm, 10.30pm, midnight daily. Admission free ($10-$30 food/drink min).

The Stone

Don't call sax star John Zorn's not-for-profit venture a 'club'. You'll find no food or drinks here, and no nonsense, either: the Stone is an art space dedicated to 'the experimental and the avant-garde'. If you're down for some rigorously adventurous sounds (intense improvisers like Tim Berne and Okkyung Lee, or moonlighting rock mavericks such as Thurston Moore), Zorn has made it easy: no advance sales, and all ages admitted (under-19s get discounts, under-12s get in free). The bookings are left to a different artist-curator each month.
Avenue C, at 2nd Street, East Village (no phone, www.thestonenyc.com). Subway F to Lower East Side-Second Avenue. Shows 8pm, 10pm daily. Admission $15. No credit cards.

Village Vanguard

Going strong for more than three-quarters of a century, the Village Vanguard is one of New York's legendary jazz centres. History surrounds you: the likes of John Coltrane, Miles Davis and Bill Evans have all grooved in this hallowed basement haunt. Big names – both old and new – continue to fill the schedule here, and the Grammy Award-winning Vanguard Jazz Orchestra has been the Monday-night regular here for almost 50 years. Reservations are recommended.
178 Seventh Avenue South, at Perry Street, West Village (1-212 255 4037, www.villagevanguard.com). Subway A, C, E, 1, 2, 3 to 14th Street; L to Eighth Avenue. Shows 9pm, 11pm daily. Tickets $25 (1-drink min).

Cabaret

In an age of globalism, cabaret is a fundamentally local art: a private party in a cosy club, where music gets stripped down to its bare essence. The intense intimacy of the experience can make it transformative if you're lucky, or mortifying if you're not. Expect consistently high-grade entertainment at Manhattan's fanciest venues, the **Café Carlyle** and the more theatre-oriented **54 Below**. Local clubs such as **Don't Tell Mama** and the **Duplex** are cheaper and more casual, but the talent is sometimes entry-level. The **Metropolitan Room** falls between these two poles.

54 Below

A team of Broadway producers is behind this swank supper club in the bowels of the legendary Studio 54 space. The schedule is dominated by big Broadway talent – such as Patti LuPone, Ben Vereen and Sherie Rene Scott – but there's also room for edgier

talents like Justin Vivian Bond and Jackie Hoffman.
254 W 54th Street, between Broadway & Eighth Avenue, Theater District (1-646 476 3551, www.54below.com). Subway B, D, E to Seventh Avenue; C, E, 1 to 50th Street; R to 57th Street. Shows vary. Admission $15-$95 ($25 food/drink min).

Café Carlyle

With its airy murals by Marcel Vertes, this elegant boîte in the Carlyle hotel remains the epitome of New York class, attracting such top-level singers as folk legend Judy Collins, Broadway star Sutton Foster and soul queen Bettye LaVette. Woody Allen often plays clarinet with Eddie Davis and his New Orleans Jazz Band on Monday nights.
Carlyle, 35 E 76th Street, at Madison Avenue, Upper East Side (1-212 744 1600, www.thecarlyle.com). Subway 6 to 77th Street. Shows vary. Admission $65-$185 (dinner or $25 food/drink min required).

Don't Tell Mama

Showbiz pros and piano-bar buffs adore this dank but homey Theater District stalwart, where acts range from the strictly amateur to potential stars of tomorrow. The line-up may include pop, jazz and musical-theatre singers, as well as comedians and drag artists.
343 W 46th Street, between Eighth & Ninth Avenues, Theater District (1-212 757 0788, www.donttellmam-nyc.com). Subway A, C, E to 42nd Street-Port Authority. Open Piano bar 9pm-2.30am Mon-Thur, Sun; 9pm-4am Fri, Sat. Shows vary; 2-4 shows per night. Admission $10-$25 (2-drink min). Piano bar free (2-drink min). No credit cards.

The Duplex

This cosy, brick-lined room, located in the heart of the West Village, is a good natured testing ground for new talent. The eclectic offerings often come served with a generous dollop of good, old-fashioned camp. The no-cover downstairs piano bar provides an open mic until the wee hours of the morning
61 Christopher Street, at Seventh Avenue South, West Village (1-212 255 5438, www.theduplex.com). Subway 1 to Christopher Street-Sheridan Square. Open Piano bar 9pm-4am daily. Shows vary. Admission varies (2-drink min).

Metropolitan Room

The Metropolitan Room occupies a comfortable middle zone on the city's cabaret spectrum, being less expensive than the fancier supper clubs and more polished than the cheaper spots. Regular performers range from rising jazz artists to established cabaret acts such as Baby Jane Dexter and Annie Ross.
34 W 22nd Street, between Fifth & Sixth Avenues, Flatiron District (1-212 206 0440, www.metropolitan room.com). Subway F, M, N, R to 23rd Street. Shows vary. Admission $15-$35 (2-drink min).

Performing Arts

New York Philharmonic in Central Park

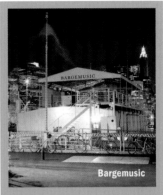

Bargemusic

Critic's choice

1 **Brooklyn Academy of Music** For star-studded plays and the adventurous Next Wave Festival. *See below*.

2 **Lincoln Center** Home of the Metropolitan Opera, New York City Ballet and New York Phil. *See p102*.

3 **Bargemusic** A magical setting for chamber concerts. *See p102*.

4 **The Kitchen** Some of the most provocative dance in the city. *See p105*.

5 **Public Theater** Ambitious works at an East Village landmark. *See p109*.

Live from New York…

From innovative classical to the best of Broadway, the cultural scene is thriving.

An omnivorous approach to the arts is increasingly common on New York's cultural scene. The city is continuing to enjoy a classical music renaissance, with small genre-crossing venues in downtown Manhattan and Brooklyn serving as laboratories for exciting new sounds.

Dance is also stepping beyond traditional boundaries, into venues such as the Museum of Modern Art, while, in theatre, an Off-Broadway boom has resulted in several lower-priced offshoots of established venues, including Lincoln Center's Claire Tow Theater and Brooklyn Academy of Music's Richard B Fisher Building. The latter, a seven-storey performing-arts centre, provides a space not only for theatre, but also dance, music and performance art. The surrounding area has evolved into a thriving arts district with the opening of several new venues.

Check out www.timeout.com/newyork for current cultural listings.

Classical music & opera

At the big institutions such as the **New York Philharmonic**, the **Metropolitan Opera** and **Carnegie Hall**, confident artistic leaders such as Alan Gilbert, Peter Gelb and Clive Gillinson are embracing new productions, living composers and innovative approaches to concert programming.

Meanwhile, some of the most exciting work is happening outside of Lincoln Center and Carnegie Hall. New-music groups like the International Contemporary Ensemble, Alarm Will Sound and So Percussion have grown from promising upstarts to become influential pillars of the artistic community. Genre-blind venues, including **Le Poisson Rouge** (*see p98*), **Roulette** (*see p103*), **Spectrum** (*see p103*) and the **Stone** (*see p100*) are happy to give them space to do their thing.

The standard New York concert season lasts from September to June, but there are plenty of outdoor festivals and musical events in summer, including performances by the New York Philharmonic and the Metropolitan Opera in Central Park among other green spaces. Box office hours may change in summer, so phone ahead or check venue websites for times.

Major concert halls

Brooklyn Academy of Music

America's oldest performing-arts academy continues to present some of the freshest programming in the city. Every year from September through December, the Next Wave Festival brings avant-garde music, dance and theatre. The nearby BAM Harvey Theater (651 Fulton Street, at Rockwell Place) offers a smaller and more atmospheric setting for multimedia creations by composers and performers such as Tan Dun, So Percussion and Meredith Monk. The newest facility, BAM Fisher (321 Ashland Place, between Ashland Place & Lafayette Avenue), houses an intimate performance space in addition to studios.

Peter Jay Sharp Building, 30 Lafayette Avenue, between Ashland Place & St Felix Street, Fort Greene, Brooklyn (1-718 636 4100, www.bam.org). Subway B, D, N, Q, R, 2, 3, 4, 5 to Atlantic Avenue-Barclays Center; C to Lafayette Avenue; G to Fulton Street. Box office noon-6pm Mon-Sat. Phone bookings 10am-6pm Mon-Fri; noon-6pm Sat; noon-4pm Sun (show days). Tickets vary.

Carnegie Hall

Artistic director Clive Gillinson continues to put his stamp on Carnegie Hall. The stars – both soloists and orchestras – still shine brightly inside this renowned concert hall in the Isaac Stern Auditorium. But it's the spunky upstart Zankel Hall that has generated the most buzz, offering an eclectic mix of classical, contemporary, jazz, pop and world music. Next door, the Weill Recital Hall hosts intimate concerts and chamber music programmes. Keep an eye out for Ensemble ACJW, which is comprised of some of the city's most exciting young musicians and also performs at the Juilliard School of music, and the annual Spring for Music (a festival which features eclectic programmes from North America's most innovative regional orchestras, held at Carnegie Hall). *154 W 57th Street, at Seventh Avenue, Midtown (1-212 247 7800, www.carnegiehall.org). Subway N, Q, R to 57th Street. Box office 11am-6pm Mon-Sat; noon-6pm Sun. Phone bookings 8am-8pm daily. Tickets vary.*

LINCOLN CENTER

Built in the early 1960s, this massive complex is the nexus of Manhattan's – in fact, probably the whole country's – performing arts scene. The campus has undergone a major revamp, providing new performance facilities as well as more inviting public gathering spaces and restaurants. Also here are the **Juilliard School** (www.juilliard.edu) and the **Fiorello H LaGuardia High School of Music & Art and Performing Arts** (www.laguardiahs.org), which frequently host performances by professional ensembles as well as students who may go on to be the stars of tomorrow.

The main entry point for Lincoln Center is from Columbus Avenue, at 65th Street, but the venues that follow are spread out across the square of blocks from 62nd to 66th Streets, between Amsterdam and Columbus Avenues. Tickets to most performances at Lincoln Center are sold through **Centercharge** (1-212 721 6500, 10am-9pm daily). There is now a central box office selling discounted tickets to same-day performances at the **David Rubenstein Atrium** (between W 62nd & W 63rd Streets, Broadway & Columbus Avenues). *Columbus Avenue, between 62nd & 65th Streets, Upper West Side (1-212 546 2656, www.lincoln center.org). Subway 1 to 66th Street-Lincoln Center.*

Alice Tully Hall

An 18-month renovation turned the cosy home of the Chamber Music Society of Lincoln Center (www.chambermusicsociety.org) into a world-class, 1,096-seat theatre. A new contemporary foyer with an elegant (if a bit pricey) café is immediately striking, but, more importantly, the revamp also brought dramatic acoustic improvements. *1-212 875 5050. Box office 10am-6pm Mon-Sat; noon-6pm Sun. Tickets vary.*

Polonsky Shakespeare Center

In the 1950s and '60s, city planner Robert Moses transformed a run-down portion of the Upper West Side into an artistic hub when he spearheaded the construction of Lincoln Center. Today, a portion of Brooklyn is undergoing a similar metamorphosis, as funds and support from the city are pouring in to build arts-centric spaces in a once-industrial patch at the nexus of Fort Greene, Boerum Hill and Downtown Brooklyn. Plans have been afoot since 2004, but it's only in the past few years that the so-called Downtown Brooklyn Cultural District, which will also include apartments, restaurants and retail, has truly come into its own. The developments are centred on the **Brooklyn Academy of Music** (*see p101*), the oldest performing arts institution in America, which has been operating in one form or another since 1861.

Longtime downtown Manhattan arts organisation **Roulette** (*see p103*) moved further south to Kings County in 2011, setting up shop in a retooled art deco theatre. Here, you can see a variety of affordable performances in dance, music and more; in particular, it's become a haven for NYC's thriving new music scene. A few blocks away is the **Theatre for a New Audience** at the **Polonsky Shakespeare Center** (*see p109*). After 34 years of vagabonding, the powerhouse classical-theatre company opened this permanent home in 2013. Inside the striking modernist structure, audiences can see works by the Bard and others mounted by heavyweights such as *The Lion King* director Julie Taymor.

The other new kid on the block is multi-use arts centre **BRIC House** (647 Fulton Street, at Rockwell Place, Fort Greene, 1-718 683 5600, www.bricartsmedia.org), housed in the Strand Theatre, once a vaudeville venue. It has a theatre, a TV studio and a café overlooking an art gallery.

Avery Fisher Hall

This handsome, comfortable, 2,700-seat hall is the headquarters of the New York Philharmonic (1-212 875 5656, www.nyphil.org), the country's oldest symphony orchestra (founded in 1842) – and one of its finest. Depending on who you ask, the sound ranges from good to atrocious. A future renovation is planned, though the date hasn't been set. The ongoing Great Performers series – which also takes place at Alice Tully Hall and other Lincoln Center venues – features top international soloists and ensembles. *1-212 875 5030. Box office 10am-6pm Mon-Sat; noon-6pm Sun; closes 30mins after performance time. Tickets vary.*

Metropolitan Opera House

The grandest of the Lincoln Center buildings, the Met is a spectacular place to see and hear opera. It hosts the Metropolitan Opera from September to May, with major visiting companies appearing in summer. Audiences are knowledgeable and fiercely devoted, with subscriptions remaining in families for generations. Opera's biggest stars appear here regularly, and music director James Levine has turned the orchestra into a true symphonic force. The Met had already started becoming more inclusive before current impresario Peter Gelb took the reins in 2006. Now, the company is placing a priority on creating novel theatrical experiences with visionary directors (Robert Lepage, Bartlett Sher, Michael Grandage, David McVicar) and assembling a new company of physically graceful, telegenic stars (Anna Netrebko, Danielle de Niese, Jonas Kaufmann, Erwin Schrott). Its high-definition movie-theatre broadcasts continue to reign supreme

outside the opera house. Although most tickets are expensive, 200 prime seats (50 of which are reserved for over-65s) for all are sold for a mere $20 apiece from Monday to Thursday, two hours before curtain up. *1-212 362 6000, www.metopera family.org. Box office 10am-8pm Mon-Sat; noon-6pm Sun. Tickets $25-$400.*

Other venues

92nd Street Y

The Y has always stood for solidly traditional orchestral, solo and chamber masterpieces. But the organisation also fosters the careers of young musicians and explores European and Jewish-American music traditions, with innovative results. In addition to showcasing several master classes (such as guitarist Eliot Fisk), the Y has recently lent its stage to the Takács Quartet and pianist Paul Lewis. And in an effort to make its concerts more affordable, $25 tickets to premium programmes are available to everyone age 35 and younger. *1395 Lexington Avenue, at 92nd Street, Upper East Side (1-212 415 5500, www.92y.org). Subway 6 to 96th Street. Box office noon-8pm Mon-Thur, Sun; noon-5pm Fri. Tickets $25-$62.*

Bargemusic

This former coffee bean barge usually presents four chamber concerts a week set against a panoramic view of lower Manhattan. It's a magical experience (and the programming has recently grown more ambitious), but be sure to dress warmly in the winter. In the less chilly months, admire the view from the upper deck during the interval. *Fulton Ferry Landing, between Old Fulton & Water Streets, Dumbo, Brooklyn (1-718 624 4924, www.bargemusic.org). Subway A, C to High Street; F to York Street; 2, 3 to Clark Street. Tickets $35; $15-$30 reductions. No credit cards at venue.*

Frick Collection

Concerts in the Frick's elegantly appointed concert hall are a rare treat, generally featuring both promising debutants and lesser-known but world-class performers. Concerts are broadcast live in the Garden Court, where tickets aren't required. *For listings, see p36. Tickets $35.*

Gilder Lehrman Hall

This elegant, 264-seat gem of a concert hall is a perfect venue for song recitals and chamber groups. The St Luke's Chamber Ensemble was quick to establish a presence here. *The Morgan Library & Museum, 225 Madison Avenue, at 36th Street, Murray Hill (1-212 685 0008, www.themorgan.org). Subway 6 to 33rd Street. Tickets vary.*

Merkin Concert Hall

On a side street in the shadow of Lincoln Center, this 449-seat treasure offers a robust mix of early music and

Performing Arts

avant-garde programming, plus a healthy amount of jazz, folk and some more eclectic fare. The Ecstatic Music Festival, featuring the latest generation of composers and performers, heats up the space each January through March, and the New York Festival of Song regularly presents outstanding singers in appealingly quirky thematic programmes.
Kaufman Music Center, 129 W 67th Street, between Amsterdam Avenue & Broadway, Upper West Side (1-212 501 3330, www.kaufman-center.org). Subway 1 to 66th Street-Lincoln Center. Box office noon-7pm Mon-Thur, Sun; noon-4pm (until 8pm Nov-Jan) Fri. Tickets $15-$60.

Metropolitan Museum of Art
When it comes to established virtuosos and revered chamber ensembles, the Met's year-round programming is rich and full (and ticket prices can be correspondingly high). Under the leadership of Limor Tomer, the museum's programming has recently taken a sharp turn towards genre-flouting performers and intriguing artistic juxtapositions. Lately, performances by Alarm Will Sound and the Estonian Philharmonic Chamber Choir have transformed the museum's famous Temple of Dendur into an atmospheric spot to hear some mystical music. At Christmas and Easter, early music concerts are held in the Fuentidueña Chapel at the Cloisters; see p41.
For listings, see p37. Tickets $35-$60.

Miller Theatre at Columbia University
Columbia University's Miller Theatre is at the forefront of making contemporary classical music sexy in New York City. The credit belongs to former executive director George Steel, who has proved that presenting challenging fare in a casual, unaffected setting can attract young audiences – and hang on to them. Director Melissa Smey seems to be continuing the tradition with programmes ranging from early music to contemporary, highlighted by musical upstarts such as Ensemble Signal and violinist Jennifer Koh.
2960 Broadway, at 116th Street, Morningside Heights (1-212 854 7799, www.millertheatre.com). Subway 1 to 116th Street-Columbia University. Box office noon-6pm Mon-Fri (also 2hrs before performance on show days). Tickets $25-$40.

Roulette
This legendary experimental music institution recently moved from dingy Soho digs to a spectacularly redesigned art deco theatre in Brooklyn. The setting may have changed, but Roulette continues to offer a gold mine of far-out programming that could include

anything from a John Cage Musicircus, where the audience is invited to wander through a forest of musical acts all playing at once, to a four-day festival of genre-defying fare from Anthony Braxton.
509 Atlantic Avenue, at Third Avenue, Boerum Hill, Brooklyn (1-917 267 0363, www.roulette.org). Subway B, D, N, Q, R, 2, 3, 4, 5 to Atlantic Avenue-Barclays Center. Box office 1-4pm Mon-Fri (also 1hr before performances and during performances). Tickets vary.

TOP TIP!
Backstage passes
From October to May, you can go behind the scenes on tours of the Met Opera House (1-212 769 7028, $18-$22) and Carnegie Hall (1-212 903 9765, $5-$15).

Spectrum
New York's newest contemporary-classical laboratory harks back to the days when the city's most innovative work was done in private lofts and similar spaces. Housed in a cosy Lower East Side walk-up, this busy venue largely relies on word of mouth and social media to publicise its ambitious chamber music, progressive jazz and avant-garde rock events.
2nd Floor, 121 Ludlow Street, between Delancey & Rivington Streets, Lower East Side (no phone, www.spectrumnyc.com). Subway F to Lower East Side-Second Ave or Delancey Street; J, M, Z to Delancey-Essex Streets. Tickets $15; $10 reductions. No credit cards.

Symphony Space
Despite the name, programming at Symphony Space is anything but orchestra-centric: recent seasons have featured sax quartets, Indian classical music, a cappella ensembles and HD opera simulcasts from Europe. The annual Wall to Wall marathons (usually held in spring) provide a full day of music free of charge, all focused on a particular theme (for instance, a composer or period).
2537 Broadway, at 95th Street, Upper West Side (1-212 864 5400, www.symphonyspace.org). Subway

1, 2, 3 to 96th Street. Box office Mon (times vary, show days only); 1-6pm Tue-Sun. Tickets vary.

Opera companies

The Metropolitan Opera may be the leader of the pack, but it's not the only game in town. Contact the organisations or check their websites for information and prices, schedules and venues.

American Opera Projects
AOP is not so much an opera company as a living, breathing workshop that lets you follow a new work from gestation to completion. Shows, which can be anything from a table reading of a libretto to a complete orchestral production, are staged around the city and beyond.
South Oxford Space, 138 S Oxford Street, between Atlantic Avenue & Hanson Place, Fort Greene, Brooklyn (1-718 398 4024, www.operaprojects.org). Subway B, D, N, Q, R, 2, 3, 4, 5 to Atlantic Avenue-Barclays Center; C to Lafayette Avenue; G to Fulton Street. Tickets vary (average $20).

Amore Opera Company
One of two successors to the late, great Amato Opera Company, the Amore has literally inherited the beloved former company's sets and costumes. Many of the cast members have migrated as well to keep the feisty Amato spirit alive. In previous seasons, they have presented US premières of lesser known or forgotten works – for example, Mercadante's 1835 opera *I due Figaro* in combination with two more famous Figaro incarnations, Mozart's *The Marriage of Figaro* and Rossini's *The Barber of Seville*.
Connelly Theatre, 220 E 4th Street, between Avenues A & B, Lower East Side (Ovation Tix 1-866 811 4111,

www.amoreopera.org). Subway F to Lower East Side-Second Avenue. Tickets $20-$40.

Dicapo Opera Theatre
This top-notch chamber opera troupe features high-quality singers performing in a delightfully intimate setting in the basement of St Jean Baptiste Church. Dicapo has recently augmented its diet of standard classics with a healthy dose of offbeat works and even premières.
184 E 76th Street, between Lexington & Third Avenues, Upper East Side (1-212 759 7652, Smarttix 1-212 868 4444, www.dicapo.com). Subway 6 to 77th Street. Box office 11am-4pm Mon-Fri. Tickets $50.

Gotham Chamber Opera
Although they perform in a variety of venues in the city – such as the Hayden Planetarium for a highly imaginative production of Haydn's *Il Mondo della Luna* – this fine young company often appears at John Jay College's Gerald W Lynch Theater on the Upper West Side. Expect a treasure trove of rarely staged shows (directed by the likes of Mark Morris and Tony-winner Diane Paulus) and new fare.
1-212 868 4460, Ticket Central 1-212 279 4200, www.gothamchamber opera.org. Tickets $30-$175.

Dance

With its uptown and downtown divide, New York dance includes both luminous tradition and daring experimentation. While Lincoln Center remains the hub for traditional balletic offerings, with annual seasons by American Ballet Theatre and New York City Ballet, the deeper downtown you travel, the more you will encounter more subversive, modern voices – and it's not limited to Manhattan. In Brooklyn, Williamsburg, Bushwick and Bedford-Stuyvesant have

Lincoln Center

sparked a new generation of dancers and choreographers, and Long Island City, Queens, is also pulsing with movement.

Multidisciplinary festivals such as **Crossing the Line** in autumn, presented by the French Institute Alliance Française (22 E 60th Street, between Madison & Park Avenues, 1-212 355 6100, www.fiaf.org), and **Performa** (1-212 366 5700, www.performaarts.org), a November biennial, showcase the latest developments in dance and performance. Autumn also brings **Fall for Dance** at New York City Center, which focuses on eclectic mixed bills.

Major venues

Baryshnikov Arts Center

Mikhail Baryshnikov, former artistic director of American Ballet Theatre, is something of an impresario. His home base, on a stark overpass near the Lincoln Tunnel, includes several studios, the Howard Gilman Performance Space – a 136-seat theatre – and superb facilities for rehearsals and workshops. With 238 seats, the recently renovated Jerome Robbins Theatre is both intimate and refined. *450 W 37th Street, between Ninth & Tenth Avenues, Hell's Kitchen (1-646 731 3200, www.bacnyc.org). Subway A, C, E to 34th Street-Penn Station. Tickets free-$35.*

Brooklyn Academy of Music

With its Federal-style columns and carved marble, the 2,100-seat Howard Gilman Opera House is the Brooklyn Academy of Music's most regal dance venue, and has showcased the talents of Mark Morris and William Forsythe. The 1904 Harvey Theater hosts contemporary choreographers – past artists have included Wally Cardona, John Jasperse and Sarah Michelson. Annual events include the DanceAfrica Festival, held in late May, and the Next Wave Festival, which features established groups from New York and abroad in autumn. *For listings, see p101.*

David H Koch Theater

The neoclassical New York City Ballet headlines at this opulent theatre, which Philip Johnson designed to resemble a jewellery box. During its spring, autumn and winter seasons, ballets by George Balanchine are performed by a wonderful crop of young dancers; there are also works by Jerome Robbins, Peter Martins (the company's ballet master in chief) and former resident choreographer Christopher Wheeldon. The popular *Nutcracker* runs from the end of November, just into the new year. In the early spring, look for performances by the revered Paul Taylor Dance Company. *Lincoln Center, 63rd Street and Columbus Avenue, Upper West Side (1-212 870 5570, www.davidkoch theater.com). Subway 1 to 66th Street-Lincoln Center. Tickets $10-$200.*

Joyce Theater

This intimate space houses one of the finest theatres – we're talking about sightlines – in town. Companies and choreographers that present work here, among them Ballet Hispanico, Pilobolus Dance Theater and Doug Varone, tend to be somewhat traditional. Regional ballet troupes, such as the Houston Ballet or Pacific Northwest Ballet, appear here too. The Joyce hosts dance throughout much of the year – Pilobolus is a summer staple. *175 Eighth Avenue, at 19th Street, Chelsea (1-212 242 0800, www.joyce.org). Subway A, C, E to 14th Street; 1 to 18th Street; L to Eighth Avenue. Tickets $10-$59.*

Metropolitan Opera House

A range of international companies, from the Paris Opera Ballet to the Kirov, performs here. In spring, the majestic space is home to American Ballet Theatre, which presents full-length traditional story ballets, contemporary classics by Frederick Ashton and Antony Tudor, and the occasional world première by the likes of Twyla Tharp. The acoustics are wonderful, but the theatre is immense: get as close to the stage as you can afford. *For listings, see p102.*

New York City Center

Before Lincoln Center changed the city's cultural geography, this was the home of the American Ballet Theatre, the Joffrey Ballet and the New York City Ballet. City Center's lavish decor is golden the theatre has recently been renovated – as are the companies that pass through here. Regular events include Alvin Ailey American Dance

Theater in December and the popular Fall for Dance Festival, in autumn, which features mixed bills for just $15. *131 W 55th Street, between Sixth & Seventh Avenues, Midtown (1-212 581 1212, www.nycitycenter.org). Subway B, D, E to Seventh Avenue; F, N, Q, R to 57th Street. Tickets $10-$150.*

Other venues

Abrons Arts Center

This venue, which features a beautiful proscenium theatre, focuses on a wealth of contemporary dance, courtesy of artistic director Jay Wegman; past artists have included Miguel Gutierrez, Jonah Bokaer, Ann Liv Young and Fitzgerald & Stapleton. *466 Grand Street, at Pitt Street, Lower East Side (1-212 598 0400, www.henrystreet.org/arts). Subway B, D to Grand Street; F to Delancey Street; J, M, Z to Delancey-Essex Streets. Tickets $15-$25.*

Ailey Citigroup Theater

The elegant home of Alvin Ailey American Theater contains this flexible downstairs venue; when not in use as rehearsal space by the company or for the home seasons of Ailey II, its junior ensemble, it is rented out to a range of groups of varying quality. *Joan Weill Center for Dance, 405 W 55th Street, at Ninth Avenue, Hell's Kitchen (1-212 405 9000, www.alvinailey.org). Subway A, B, C, D, 1 to 59th Street-Columbus Circle; N, Q, R to 57th Street. Tickets vary.*

Brooklyn Arts Exchange

Brooklyn Arts Exchange holds classes and performances in its intimate

theatre; the space hosts more than 50 performance evenings each season. Artists in residence have included choreographers Yasuko Yokoshi, Dean Moss and Jillian Peña; it's a great place to witness the creative process up close. *421 Fifth Avenue, between 7th & 8th Streets, Park Slope, Brooklyn (1-718 832 0018, www.bax.org). Subway F, G, R to Fourth Avenue-9th Street. Tickets $8-$15.*

Center for Performance Research

Founded by choreographers Jonah Bokaer and John Jasperse, Performance Research represents a new trend of artists taking control of the means of production. It's based in an LEED-certified eco-conscious building with a performance space of approximately 40ft by 40ft. Presentations are sporadic. *Unit 1, 361 Manhattan Avenue, at Jackson Street, Williamsburg, Brooklyn (1-718 349 1210, www.cprnyc.org). Subway L to Graham Avenue. Tickets $10-$20.*

Chocolate Factory Theater

Brian Rogers and Sheila Lewandowski founded this 5,000sq ft performance venue in Long Island City in 2005, converting a one-time hardware store into two spaces: a low-ceilinged downstairs room and a loftier, brighter upstairs white box that caters to the interdisciplinary and the avant-garde. Past choreographers include Beth Gill, Jillian Peña, Big Dance Theater and Tere O'Connor. Rogers, an artist in his own right, also presents work here. *5-49 49th Avenue, at Vernon Boulevard, Long Island City, Queens (1-718 482 7069, www.chocolate factorytheater.org). Subway G to 21st Street; 7 to Vernon Boulevard-Jackson Avenue. Tickets $15.*

Danspace Project

A space is only as good as its executive director, and Judy Hussie-Taylor has injected new life into Danspace's programming by creating the Platform series, in which artists curate seasons based on a particular idea. Moreover, the space itself – a high-ceilinged sanctuary – is very handsome. Ticket prices are reasonable, making it easy to take a chance on unknown work. *St Mark's Church in-the-Bowery, 131 E 10th Street, at Second Avenue, East Village (1-212 674 8112 information, 1-866 811 4111 reservations, www.danspaceproject.org). Subway L to Third Avenue; 6 to Astor Place. Tickets free-$20.*

Dixon Place

Ellie Covan started hosting experimental performances in her living room in the mid 1980s; two decades later, this plucky organisation finally opened a state-of-the-art space on the Lower East Side. Along with a mainstage theatre, there is a cocktail lounge – perfect for post-show discussions. Dixon Place supports emerging artists and works in

Chocolate Factory Theater

progress; summer events include the annual Hot! festival of queer arts.
161 Chrystie Street, at Delancey Street, Lower East Side (1-212 219 0736, www.dixonplace.org). Subway F to Lower East Side-Second Avenue; J, Z to Bowery. Tickets free-$20.

Flea Theater
The two stages here host a variety of offerings including the free June festival, Dance Conversations, with more than 30 performance pieces from both established and emerging choreographers.
For listings, see p109.

Harlem Stage at the Gatehouse
Performances at this theatre, formerly an operations centre for the Croton Aqueduct water system, celebrate African-American life and culture. Companies that have graced this flexible space, designed by Frederick S Cook and now designated a New York City landmark, include the Bill T Jones/Arnie Zane Dance Company and Kyle Abraham. Each spring, the space hosts the E-Moves Festival.
150 Convent Avenue, at W 135th Street, Harlem (1-212 281 9240 ext.19, www.harlemstage.org). Subway 1 to 137th Street-City College. Tickets free-$45.

The Kitchen
The Kitchen, led by Tim Griffin, offers some of the best experimental dance around: inventive, provocative and rigorous. Some of the artists who have presented work here are the finest in New York, such as Sarah Michelson (who has served as a guest curator for specific programmes), Dean Moss, Ann Liv Young and Jodi Melnick.
512 W 19th Street, between Tenth & Eleventh Avenues, Chelsea (1-212 255 5793, www.thekitchen.org). Subway A, C, E to 14th Street; L to Eighth Avenue. Tickets free-$25.

La MaMa ETC
This experimental theatre hosts the La MaMa Moves dance festival every spring, featuring a variety of up-and-coming artists, and presents international troupes throughout the year. While shows can be worthwhile, some of the programming is marginal.
74A E 4th Street, between Bowery & Second Avenue, East Village (1-212 475 7710, www.lamama.org). Subway F to Lower East Side-Second Avenue; 6 to Astor Place. Tickets $10-$25.

Movement Research at the Judson Church
This free performance series is a great place to check out experimental works and up-and-coming artists. Performances are held roughly every Monday evening at 8pm, from September to June, but it's best to check the website. The group's festivals, in December and May, feature a week-long series of performances held in venues across the city. Movement Research also offers a variety of classes and other events around town.

After Midnight

Evoking Harlem and the legendary Cotton Club, this raucous, joyous, white-hot revue features an array of fiercely talented dancers, singers and musicians (the latter handpicked by Wynton Marsalis). Warren Carlyle directs and choreographs this jazz phantasmagoria of tap, scatting and Duke Ellington classics.
Brooks Atkinson Theatre, 256 W 47th Street, between Broadway & Eighth Avenues, Theater District (Telecharge 1-212 239 6200, www.aftermidnight broadway.com). Subway C, E, 1 to 50th Street; N, R to 49th Street. Box office 10am-8pm Mon-Sat. Tickets $60-$142.

---

55 Washington Square South, at Thompson Street, Greenwich Village (1-212 598 0551, www.movement research.org). Subway A, B, C, D, E, F, M to W 4th Street. Tickets free.

New York Live Arts
In 2010, the Dance Theater Workshop and the Bill T Jones/Arnie Zane Dance Company merged to form New York Live Arts, which is dedicated to contemporary dance under Mr Jones and Carla Peterson. The company performs here regularly, along with local and international choreographers.
219 W 19th Street, between Seventh & Eighth Avenues, Chelsea (1-212 924 0077, www.newyorklivearts. org). Subway 1 to 18th Street. Tickets from $15.

Symphony Space
The World Music Institute hosts traditional dancers from around the globe at this multidisciplinary performing arts centre, but Symphony Space also stages works by contemporary choreographers.
For listings, see p103.

Theatre

Tom Hanks, Scarlett Johansson, Denzel Washington, Daniel Craig and Jessica Chastain are among the many boldface names that have shone on Broadway marquees lately. Major musicals tend not to have big stars above the title, but favour the familiar in a different way. In recent years, many of them have been adapted from pop-culture sources (such as *Once* and *The Lion King*) or have been built around existing catalogues of popular songs (such as *Jersey Boys* and *Motown – The Musical*).

Nearly all Broadway and Off Broadway shows are served by one of the 24-hour ticketing agencies. For cheap seats, your best bet is one of the Theatre Development Fund's **TKTS** discount booths.

TKTS
At Times Square's architecturally striking TKTS base, you can get tickets on the day of the performance (or the evening before, in the case of matinées) for as much as 50% off face value. Although there is often a queue when it opens for business, this has usually dispersed one to two hours later, so it's worth trying your luck an hour or two before the show. The downtown and Brooklyn branches, which are much less busy and open earlier (so you can secure your tickets on the morning of the show), also sell matinée tickets the day before a show. *Father Duffy Square, Broadway & 47th Street, Theater District (www.tdf.org). Subway N, Q, R, S, 1, 2, 3, 7 to 42nd Street-Times Square. Open for evening tickets 3-8pm Mon, Wed-Sun; 2-8pm Tue. For same-day matinée tickets 10am-2pm Wed, Sat; 11am-3pm Sun.*

Other locations corner of Front and John Streets, South Street Seaport; 1 Metrotech Center, corner of Jay Street & Myrtle Avenue Promenade, Downtown Brooklyn.

Broadway

Technically speaking, 'Broadway' is the theatre district that surrounds Times Square on either side of Broadway (the actual avenue), between 41st and 54th Streets (plus the Vivian Beaumont Theater, uptown at Lincoln Center). This is where you'll find the grandest theatres in town: wood-panelled, frescoed jewel boxes, mostly built between 1900 and 1930. Officially, 40 of them – those with more than 500 seats – are designated as being part of Broadway. Full-price tickets can easily set you back more than $100; the very best (so-called 'premium') seats can sell for almost $500 at the most popular shows.

The big musicals are still there, and hard to miss. At any given point, however, there are also a handful of new plays, as well as serious revivals of classic dramas ranging from William Shakespeare through Tennessee Williams and David Mamet. Each season also usually includes several small, artistically adventurous musicals to balance out the rafter-rattlers.

Straight plays can provide some of Broadway's most stirring experiences, but they're less likely than musicals to enjoy long runs. Check www.timeout.com/newyork for current listings and reviews; bear in mind that the shows listed below are subject to change.

The Book of Mormon
This gleefully obscene and subversive satire may be the funniest show to grace the Great White Way since *The Producers* and *Urinetown*. Writers Trey Parker and Matt Stone of *South Park*, along with composer Robert Lopez (*Avenue Q*), find the perfect blend of sweet and nasty for this tale of mismatched Mormon proselytisers in Uganda.
Eugene O'Neill Theatre, 230 W 49th Street, between Broadway & Eighth Avenue, Theater District (Telecharge 1-212 239 6200, www.bookofmormon broadway.com). Subway C, E to 50th Street; N, Q, R, S, 1, 2, 3, 7 to 42nd Street-Times Square; N, R to 49th Street. Box office 10am-8pm Mon-Sat; noon-6pm Sun. Tickets $69-$477.

Chicago
This John Kander-Fred Ebb-Bob Fosse hit – revived by director Walter Bobbie and choreographer Ann Reinking – tells the saga of chorus girl Roxie Hart, who murders her lover and, with the help of a huckster lawyer, becomes a vaudeville star. New headliners, sometimes including celebrities, rotate into the cast on a regular basis.

Performing Arts

Ambassador Theater, 219 W 49th Street, between Broadway and Eighth Avenue, Theater District (Telecharge 1-212 239 6200, www.chicagothemusical.com). Subway C, E, 1 to 50th Street; N, R to 49th Street. Box office 10am-8pm Mon-Sat; noon-7pm Sun. Tickets $69-$200.

Jersey Boys

The Broadway musical finally does right by the jukebox with this nostalgic behind-the-music tale, presenting the Four Seasons' infectiously energetic 1960s tunes (including 'Walk Like a Man' and 'Big Girls Don't Cry') as they were intended to be performed. Sleek direction by Des McAnuff ensures that Marshall Brickman and Rick Elice's script feels canny instead of canned. August Wilson Theatre, 245 W 52nd Street, between Broadway & Eighth Avenue, Theater District (Telecharge 1-212 239 6200, www.jerseyboysinfo.com/broadway). Subway C, E, 1 to 50th Street. Box office 10am-8pm Mon-Sat; noon-6pm Sun. Tickets $47-$297.

Kinky Boots

Harvey Fierstein and Cyndi Lauper's fizzy crowd-pleaser, in which a sassy-dignified drag queen kicks an English shoe factory into gear, feels familiar at every step. But it has been manufactured with solid craftsmanship and care (Lauper is a musical-theatre natural), and is boosted by a heart-strong cast. The overall effect is nigh irresistible. Al Hirschfeld Theatre, 302 W 45th Street, between Eighth & Ninth Avenues, Theater District (Telecharge 1-212 239 6200, kinkybootsthemusical.com). Subway A, C, E to 42nd Street-Port Authority; N, Q, R, S, 1, 2, 3, 7 to 42nd Street-Times Square. Box office 10am-8pm Mon-Sat; noon-6pm Sun. Tickets $87-$399.

The Lion King

Director-designer Julie Taymor surrounds the Disney movie's mythic plot and Elton John-Tim Rice score with African rhythm and music. Through elegant puppetry, Taymor populates the stage with a menagerie of African beasts; her staging has expanded a simple cub into the pride of Broadway. Minskoff Theatre, 200 W 45th Street, between Broadway & Eighth Avenue, Theater District (Ticketmaster 1-866 870 2717, www.lionking.com). Subway A, C, E to 42nd Street-Port Authority; N, Q, R, S, 1, 2, 3, 7 to 42nd Street-Times Square. Box office 10am-8pm Mon-Sat; noon-6pm Sun. Tickets $89-$299.

Matilda

Based on Roald Dahl's book about a child prodigy who must outwit horrid parents and a sadistic headmistress, this English musical delivers mischievous fun while hitting the requisite sentimental notes and smuggling in an anti-authoritarian message. Tim Minchin's cheeky

Britpop score and Matthew Warchus's cartoonish staging offer sheer delight. Shubert Theatre, 225 W 44th Street, between Broadway & Eighth Avenue, Theater District (Telecharge 1-212 239 6200, http://us.matildathemusical.com). Subway A, C, E to 42nd Street-Port Authority; N, Q, R, S, 1, 2, 3, 7 to 42nd Street-Times Square. Box office 10am-8pm Mon-Sat; noon-6pm Sun. Tickets $37-$167.

Newsies

Not since Wicked has there been a big-tent, family-friendly Broadway musical that gets so much so right. Disney's barnstorming, four-alarm delight focuses on the newsboy strike of 1899, in which spunky (and high-kicking) newspaper hawkers stand up to the media magnates of their day. The Alan Menken tunes are pleasing, the book is sharp, and the dances are simply spectacular. Nederlander Theatre, 208 W 41st Street, between Broadway & Eighth Avenue (Ticketmaster 1-866 870 2717, www.newsiesthemusical.com). Subway A, C, E to 42nd Street-Port Authority; N, Q, R, S, 1, 2, 3, 7 to 42nd Street-Times Square. Box office 10am-8pm Mon-Sat. Tickets $67-$189.

Once

Known for big, splashy spectacles, Broadway also has room for more sincere and understated musicals. This touching hit, adapted from the 2006 indie flick about an Irish songwriter and the Czech immigrant who inspires and enchants him, has a brooding emo-folk score and a bittersweet sense of longing that make it an ideal choice for a romantic evening out. Bernard B Jacobs Theatre, 242 W 45th Street, between Broadway & Eighth Avenue (Telecharge 1-212 239 6200, www.oncemusical.com). Subway A, C, E to 42nd Street-Port Authority; N, Q, R, S, 1, 2, 3, 7 to 42nd Street-Times Square. Box office 10am-8pm Mon-Sat; noon-6pm Sun. Tickets $60-$252.

Wicked

Based on novelist Gregory Maguire's 1995 riff on The Wizard of Oz, Wicked is a witty prequel to the classic children's book and movie. The show's combination of pop dynamism and sumptuous spectacle has made it the most popular show on Broadway. Teenage girls, especially, have responded to the story of how a green girl named Elphaba comes to be known as the Wicked Witch of the West. Gershwin Theatre, 222 W 51st Street, between Broadway & Eighth Avenue, Theater District (Ticketmaster 1-800 982 2787, www.wickedthemusical.com). Subway C, E, 1 to 50th Street. Box office 10am-8pm Mon-Sat; noon-6pm Sun. Tickets $65-$301

Off Broadway

As the cost of mounting shows on Broadway continues to soar, many serious playwrights (including major

Matilda

ones such as Edward Albee and Tony Kushner) are opening their shows in the less financially arduous world of Off Broadway, where many of the theatres are not-for-profit enterprises. The venues here have between 100 and 499 seats; tickets usually run from $30 to $80. Here, we've listed some reliable long-running shows, plus some of the best theatres and repertory companies.

LONG-RUNNING SHOWS

Avenue Q

After many years, which have included a Broadway run followed by a return to its Off Broadway roots, the sassy and clever puppet musical doesn't show its age. Robert Lopez and Jeff Marx's deft Sesame Street-esque novelty tunes about porn and racism still earn their laughs, and Avenue Q remains a sly and winning piece of metamusical tomfoolery. New World Stages, 340 W 50th Street, between Eighth & Ninth Avenues, Theater District (Telecharge 1-212 239 6200, www.avenueq.com). Subway C, E, 1 to 50th Street. Box office 1-8pm Mon, Thur, Fri; 1-7pm Tue; 10am-8pm Wed, Sat; 10am-7.30pm Sun. Tickets $72.50-$126.50.

Blue Man Group

Three deadpan men with extraterrestrial imaginations (and head-to-toe blue body paint) carry this long-time favourite, which may be the world's most accessible piece of multimedia performance art. A weird, exuberant trip through the trappings of modern culture, the show is as smart as it is ridiculous. Astor Place Theatre, 434 Lafayette Street, between Astor Place & 4th

Street, East Village (1-800 258 3626, www.blueman.com). Subway N, R to 8th Street-NYU; 6 to Astor Place. Box office noon-7.45pm daily. Tickets $82-$106.

Sleep No More

A multitude of searing sights awaits at this bedazzling and uncanny installation by the English company Punchdrunk. Your sense of space is blurred as you wend through more than 90 discrete spaces, from a cloistral chapel to a ballroom floor. A Shakespearean can check off allusions to Macbeth; others can just revel in the haunted-house vibe. McKittrick Hotel, 530 W 27th Street, between Tenth & Eleventh Avenues, Chelsea (Ovationtix 1-866 811 4111, www.sleepnomorenyc.com). Subway 1 to 28th Street; C, E to 23rd Street. Tickets $75-$162.50.

REPERTORY COMPANIES & VENUES

59E59 Theaters

This chic, state-of-the-art venue, which comprises an Off Broadway space and two smaller theatres, is home to the Primary Stages company. It's also where you'll find the annual Brits Off Broadway festival (www.britsoffbroadway.com), which imports some of the UK's best work for brief runs, and its newer offshoot, Americas Off Broadway. 59 E 59th Street, between Madison & Park Avenues, Upper East Side (1-212 753 5959, Ticket Central 1-212 279 4200, www.59e59.org). Subway N, Q, R to Lexington Avenue-59th Street; 4, 5, 6 to 59th Street. Box office noon-6pm Mon; noon-7.30pm Tue-Thur; noon-8.30pm Fri, Sat; noon-3.30pm Sun. Tickets $18-$60.

Bags packed, milk cancelled, house raised on stilts.

You've packed the suntan lotion, the snorkel set, the stay-pressed shirts. Just one more thing left to do – your bit for climate change. In some of the world's poorest countries, changing weather patterns are destroying lives.

You can help people to deal with the extreme effects of climate change. Raising houses in flood-prone regions is just one life-saving solution.

Climate change costs lives.
Give £5 and let's sort it *Here & Now*

www.oxfam.org.uk/climate-change

Be Humankind Oxfam

Ars Nova

Committed to presenting innovative new theatre, music and comedy, this offbeat Hell's Kitchen space has been a boon to developing artists since it opened in 2002. Along with full productions, Ars Nova also presents an eclectic monthly special called Showgasm and the annual ANT Fest for emerging talents.
511 W 54th Street, between Tenth & Eleventh Avenues, Hell's Kitchen (1-212 489 9800, Ovationtix 1-866 811 4111, www.arsnovanyc.com). Subway C, E, 1 to 50th Street. Box office 30mins before show. Tickets $15-$35.

Atlantic Theater Company

Created in 1985 as an offshoot of acting workshops led by playwright David Mamet and actor William H Macy, the dynamic Atlantic Theater Company has presented dozens of new plays, including Steven Sater and Duncan Sheik's rock musical *Spring Awakening*, and Conor McPherson's *The Night Alive*. The Atlantic also has a smaller second stage deep underground at 330 W 16th Street.
336 W 20th Street, between Eighth & Ninth Avenues, Chelsea (1-212 691 5919, Ticket Central 1-212 279 4200, www.atlantictheater.org). Subway C, E to 23rd Street. Box office noon-6pm Mon-Fri. Tickets $35-$70.

Brooklyn Academy of Music

BAM's beautifully distressed Harvey Theater – along with its grand old opera house in the Peter Jay Sharp Building – is the site of the Next Wave Festival (*see p13*) and other international events. The spring season usually features high-profile productions of classics by the likes of Chekhov and Shakespeare, often shipped from England with major actors attached.
For listings, see p101.

Classic Stage Company

With a purview that runs from medieval mystery plays and Elizabethan standards to early modern drama and original period pieces, Classic Stage Company is committed to making the old new again. Under artistic director Brian Kulick, the company has a knack for attracting major stars, as recent productions of Chekhov plays with Maggie Gyllenhaal and Dianne Wiest attest.
136 E 13th Street, between Third & Fourth Avenues, East Village (1-212 677 4210, www.classicstage.org). Subway L, N, Q, R, 4, 5, 6 to 14th Street-Union Square. Box office noon-6pm Mon-Fri. Tickets $55-$125.

Flea Theater

Founded in 1997, Jim Simpson's versatile and well-appointed venue has presented avant-garde experimentation and politically provocative satires. A second, basement theatre hosts the Flea's resident young acting company, the Bats. Construction recently started on a new theatre complex nearby, expected to open in 2015.
41 White Street, between Broadway & Church Street, Tribeca (1-212 226 2407, Ovationtix 1-866 811 4111, www.theflea.org). Subway A, C, E, J, M, N, Q, R, Z, 6 to Canal Street; 1 to Franklin Street. Box office noon-6pm Mon-Sat. Tickets $15-$60.

Irish Repertory Theatre

Set in a cosily odd, L-shaped venue, the Irish Repertory Theatre puts on compelling shows by Irish and Irish-American playwrights. Fine revivals of classics by the likes of Oscar Wilde and George Bernard Shaw alternate with plays by lesser-known modern authors.
132 W 22nd Street, between Sixth & Seventh Avenues, Chelsea (1-212 727 2737, www.irishrep.org). Subway F, M, 1 to 23rd Street. Box office 10am-6pm Mon; 10am-8pm Tue-Fri; 11am-8pm Sat; 11am-6pm Sun. Tickets $55-$65.

Lincoln Center Theater

The majestic and prestigious Lincoln Center Theater complex has a pair of amphitheatre-style drama venues. The Broadway house, the 1,080-seat Vivian Beaumont Theater, is home to star-studded and elegant major productions. Downstairs is the 299-seat Mitzi E Newhouse Theater, an Off Broadway space devoted to new work by the upper layer of American playwrights. In 2008, in an effort to shake off its reputation for stodginess, Lincoln Center launched LCT3, which now presents the work of emerging playwrights and directors at the new Claire Tow Theater, built on top of the Beaumont.
Lincoln Center, 150 W 65th Street, at Broadway, Upper West Side (Telecharge 1-212 239 6200, www.lct.org). Subway 1 to 66th Street-Lincoln Center. Box office 10am-8pm Mon-Sat; noon-7pm Sun. Tickets $20-$200.

Manhattan Theatre Club

One of the city's most important non-profit companies, Manhattan Theatre Club spent decades as an Off Broadway outfit before moving into the 622-seat Friedman Theatre in 2003. But it still maintains two smaller spaces at New York City Center (*see p104*), where it presents some of its best material – such as Lynn Nottage's 2009 Pulitzer Prize winner, *Ruined*. Twentysomethings and teens can sign up for the 30 Under 30 Club to get tickets at both theatres for $30.
Samuel J Friedman Theatre, 261 W 47th Street, between Broadway & Eighth Avenue, Theater District (Telecharge 1-212 239 6200, www.manhattantheatreclub.com). Subway N, Q, R, S, 1, 2, 3, 7 to 42nd Street-Times Square. Box office noon-6pm Tue-Sun. Tickets $30-$120.

New Victory Theater

The New Victory Theater is a perfect symbol of the transformation that has occurred in Times Square. Built in 1900, Manhattan's oldest surviving theatre became a strip club and adult cinema in the sleazy days of the 1970s and '80s. Renovated by the city in 1995, the building now functions as a kind of kiddie version of the Brooklyn Academy of Music, offering a full season of smart, adventurous, reasonably priced and family-friendly plays (including many international productions). *See also p87.*
209 W 42nd Street, between Seventh & Eighth Avenues, Theater District (1-646 223 3010, www.newvictory.org). Subway N, Q, R, S, 1, 2, 3, 7 to 42nd Street-Times Square. Box office 11am-5pm Mon, Sun; noon-7pm Tue-Sat. Tickets $14-$38.

New World Stages

Formerly a movie multiplex, this centre – one of the last bastions of commercial Off Broadway in New York – boasts a shiny, space-age interior and five stages, presenting everything from family-friendly spectacles (like *Gazillion Bubble Show*) to downsized transfers of Broadway musicals (including the long-running *Avenue Q*).
340 W 50th Street, between Eighth & Ninth Avenues, Theater District (1-646 871 1730, Telecharge 1-212 239 6200, www.newworldstages.com). Subway C, E, 1 to 50th Street. Box office 1-8pm Mon, Thur, Fri; 1-7pm Tue; 10am-8pm Wed, Sat; 10am-7.30pm Sun. Tickets $40-$150.

New York Theatre Workshop

Founded in 1979, the New York Theatre Workshop works with emerging directors eager to take on challenging pieces. Besides presenting plays by world-class artists such as Caryl Churchill and Tony Kushner, this company also premièred *Rent*, Jonathan Larson's seminal 1990s musical. The iconoclastic Flemish director Ivo van Hove has made the NYTW his New York pied-à-terre.
79 E 4th Street, between Bowery & Second Avenue, East Village (1-212 460 5475, www.nytw.org). Subway F to Lower East Side-Second Avenue; 6 to Astor Place. Box office 1-6pm Tue-Sun. Tickets $45-$85.

Pershing Square Signature Center

The award-winning Signature Theatre Company, founded by James Houghton in 1991, focuses on exploring and celebrating playwrights in depth, with whole seasons devoted to works by individual living writers. Over the years, the company has delved into the oeuvres of August Wilson, John Guare, Horton Foote and many more. Special programmes are designed to keep prices low. In 2012 the troupe expanded hugely into a new home – a theatre complex designed by Frank Gehry, with three major spaces and ambitious long-term commission programmes, cementing it as one of the city's key cultural institutions.
480 W 42nd Street, at Tenth Avenue, Hell's Kitchen (1-212 244 7529,

TOP TIP!
Free lunch music
Stately sanctuary Trinity Wall Street (*see p18*) offers gratis Thursday afternoon recitals in its Concerts at One series (Mar-June, Sept-Dec).

www.signaturetheatre.org). Subway A, C, E to 42nd Street-Port Authority. Box office 11am-6pm Tue-Sun. Tickets $25-$65.

Playwrights Horizons

More than 300 important contemporary plays have had their première here, including dramas (*Driving Miss Daisy, The Heidi Chronicles*) and musicals (Stephen Sondheim's *Assassins* and *Sunday in the Park with George*). More recent seasons have included new works by Edward Albee and Craig Lucas, as well as Bruce Norris's Pulitzer Prize-winning *Clybourne Park*.
416 W 42nd Street, between Ninth & Tenth Avenues, Theater District (1-212 564 1235, Ticket Central 1-212 279 4200, www.playwrights horizons.org). Subway A, C, E to 42nd Street-Port Authority. Box office noon-8pm daily. Tickets $50-$90.

Polonsky Shakespeare Center

Founded in 1979, Theatre for a New Audience has grown steadily to become New York's most prominent classical-theatre company. Now, finally, it has a home of its own: the Polonsky Shakespeare Center (near BAM, in Brooklyn's cultural district). This flashy, glass-fronted 299-seat venue, designed by Hugh Hardy, opened its doors in 2013 with Julie Taymor's production of *A Midsummer Night's Dream*.
262 Ashland Place, between Fulton Street & Lafayette Avenue, Fort Greene, Brooklyn (Ovationtix 1-866 811 4111, www.tfana.org). Subway B, D, N, Q, R, 2, 3, 4, 5 to Atlantic Avenue-Barclays Center; C to Lafayette Avenue; G to Fulton Street. Box office 1-6pm Tue-Sat. Tickets $60-$85.

Public Theater

Under the guidance of the civic-minded Oskar Eustis, this local institution – dedicated to producing the work of new American playwrights, but also known for its Shakespeare in the Park productions – has regained its place at the forefront of the Off Broadway world. The ambitious, multicultural programming ranges from new works by major playwrights to the annual Under the Radar festival for emerging artists. The company's home building, an Astor Place landmark, has five stages and has recently been extensively renovated.
425 Lafayette Street, between Astor Place & 4th Street, East Village (1-212 539 8500, tickets 1-212 967 7555, www.publictheater.org). Subway N, R to 8th Street-NYU; 6 to Astor Place. Box office 1-6pm Mon, Sun; 1-7.30pm Tue-Sat. Tickets $15-$95.

Roundabout Theatre Company

Devoted mostly to revivals, the Roundabout often pairs beloved old chestnuts with celebrity casts.

In addition to its Broadway flagship, the company also mounts shows at Studio 54 (254 W 54th Street, between Broadway & Eighth Avenue), the Stephen Sondheim Theatre (124 West 43rd Street, between Sixth & Seventh Avenues) and Off Broadway's Laura Pels Theatre (111 W 46th Street, between Sixth & Seventh Avenues). *American Airlines Theatre, 227 W 42nd Street, between Seventh & Eighth Avenues, Theater District (1-212 719 1300, www. roundabouttheatre. org). Subway N, Q, R, S, 1, 2, 3, 7 to 42nd Street-Times Square. Box office 10am-6pm Mon, Sun; 10am-8pm Tue-Sat. Tickets $20-$147.*

St Ann's Warehouse
The adventurous theatregoer's alternative to Brooklyn Academy of Music, St Ann's Warehouse offers an eclectic line-up of drama and music. The company recently left its longtime digs on Water Street for a nearby Dumbo location but is scheduled to move again in late 2015 to a converted space within Brooklyn Bridge Park's 1870s Tobacco Warehouse. Recent shows have included high-level work by the Wooster Group, Daniel Kitson and the National Theatre of Scotland. *29 Jay Street, between John & Plymouth Streets, Dumbo, Brooklyn (1-718 254 8779, www.stanns warehouse.org). Subway A, C to High Street; F to York Street. Box office 1-7pm Tue-Sat. Tickets $25-$75.*

Second Stage Theatre
Occupying a beautiful Rem Koolhaas-designed space near Times Square, Second Stage Theatre specialises in American playwrights, and hosted the New York première of Edward Albee's *Peter and Jerry*. It also provides a stage for serious new musicals, such as the Pulitzer Prize-winning *Next to Normal*. *307 W 43rd Street, at Eighth Avenue, Theater District (1-212 246 4422, www.2st.com). Subway A, C, E to 42nd Street-Port Authority. Box office 10am-6pm Mon-Sat; 10am-3pm Sun. Tickets $75-$125.*

Shakespeare in the Park at the Delacorte Theater
The Delacorte Theater in Central Park is the fair-weather sister of the Public Theater (*see p109*). When not producing Shakespeare in the East Village, the Public offers the best of the Bard outdoors during Shakespeare in the Park (June-Aug). Free tickets (two per person) are distributed at the Delacorte at noon on the day of the performance. Around 8am is usually a good time to begin waiting, although the queue can start forming as early as 6am when big-name stars are on the bill. There is also an online lottery for tickets. *Park entrance on Central Park West, at 81st Street, then follow the signs (1-212 539 8750, www.shakespeare*

inthepark.org). Subway B, C to 81st Street-Museum of Natural History. Tickets free.

Soho Rep
A few years ago, this Off-Off mainstay moved to an Off Broadway contract, but tickets for most shows have remained cheap. Artistic director Sarah Benson's programming is diverse and audacious: recent productions include works by Young Jean Lee, Sarah Kane and the Nature Theater of Oklahoma. *46 Walker Street, between Broadway & Church Street, Tribeca (TheaterMania 1-212 352 3101, www. sohorep.org). Subway A, C, E, N, R, 6 to Canal Street; 1 to Franklin Street. Box office 9am-9pm Mon-Fri; 10am-9pm Sat, Sun. Tickets 99¢-$35.*

Theatre Row
Comprising five main venues of various sizes, Theatre Row hosts new plays and revivals by the trendy and celebrity-friendly New Group (Ethan Hawke, Ed Harris, Bill Pullman and Matthew Broderick are among the recent stars), as well as scores of other productions by assorted theatre companies. *410 W 42nd Street, between Ninth & Tenth Avenues, Hell's Kitchen (1-212 714 2442, Telecharge 1-212 239 6200, www.theatrerow.org). Subway A, C, E to 42nd Street-Port Authority. Box office noon-6pm daily. Tickets $18-$95.*

Vineyard Theatre
The Vineyard Theatre produces some excellent new plays and musicals, including *The Scottsboro Boys*, the

wittily named *[title of show]* and the Tony Award-winning *Avenue Q*, all of which transferred to Broadway. *108 E 15th Street, at Union Square East, Union Square (1-212 353 0303, www.vineyardtheatre.org). Subway L, N, Q, R, 4, 5, 6 to 14th Street-Union Square. Box office 1-6pm Mon-Fri. Tickets $45-$100.*

Off-Off Broadway

Technically, Off-Off Broadway denotes a show that is presented at a theatre with fewer than 100 seats, usually for less than $25. It's where some of the most daring writers and performers – who aren't necessarily card-carrying union professionals – create their edgiest work: **Radiohole** (www.radiohole.com), the **Debate Society** (www.thedebatesociety.org) and **Nature Theater of Oklahoma** (www.oktheater.org) are among many troupes in the city that offer inspired theatre.

The **New York International Fringe Festival** (1-212 279 4488, www.fringenyc.org), held every August, provides a wide opportunity to see the wacky side of the stage, and the **New York Musical Theatre Festival** (www.nymf.org) in July has become an important testing ground for composers and lyricists.

REPERTORY COMPANIES & VENUES

For multidisciplinary venue **Dixon Place**, see p104.

The Brick
This spunky, brick-lined venue presents a variety of boundary-pushing work. Its tongue-in-cheek themed summer series have included

Moral Values, Hell, Pretentious and Antidepressant Festivals. *575 Metropolitan Avenue, between Lorimer Street & Union Avenue, Williamsburg, Brooklyn (1-718 907 6189, Ovationtix 1-866 811 4111, www.bricktheater.com). Subway G to Metropolitan Avenue; L to Lorimer Street. Box office opens 15mins before curtain. Tickets $15-$20. No credit cards.*

The Bushwick Starr
As small companies continue to be priced out of Manhattan, everyone's looking to Brooklyn to pick up the slack. This funky black box is one good option: some of the city's fiercest experimental troupes – Half Straddle, the TEAM and others – have made the Starr shine brightly. *207 Starr Street, between Irving & Wyckoff Avenues, Bushwick, Brooklyn (Ovationtix 1-866 811 4111, www.thebushwickstarr.org). Subway L to Jefferson Street. Box office opens 30mins before curtain. Tickets $15-$25.*

HERE
Dedicated to not-for-profit arts enterprises, this theatre complex has been the launch pad for such well-known shows as Eve Ensler's *The Vagina Monologues*. More recently, HERE has showcased the talents of the brilliantly freaky playwright-performer Taylor Mac. *145 Sixth Avenue, between Broome & Spring Streets, Soho (1-212 647 0202, TheaterMania 1-212 352 3101, www.here.org). Subway C, E to Spring Street. Box office 5-10pm daily. Tickets $20-$50.*

Incubator Arts Center
Located upstairs at the historic St Mark's Church-in-the-Bowery, this adventurous developmental venue has an eye for the best in local avant-garde theatre. Dave Malloy, Tina Satter and Julia Jarcho have staged pieces there recently, negotiating the space's asymmetrical shape and weirdly placed columns to create exciting work; Incubator also produces the Other Forces festival each January. *131 E 10th Street, at Second Avenue, East Village (TheaterMania 1-212 352 3101, www.incubatorarts.org). Subway L to First or Third Ave; 6 to Astor Place. Box office opens 45mins before curtain. Tickets $15-$25.*

La MaMa ETC
Founded by the late Ellen Stewart, La MaMa has been a bastion of the Off-Off scene for more than half a century. The complex has helped to nurture such innovators as Sam Shepard, Charles Ludlam, Lanford Wilson and Ping Chong, and it continues to be an important rung in many rising artists' ladders. *74A E Fourth Street, between Bowery & Second Avenue, East Village (1-212 475 7710, www.lamama.org). Subway 6 to Bleecker Street. Box office noon-6pm Mon-Sun. Tickets $10-$25.*

Kinky Boots. See p107.

Hotels

New York's best beds: budget, boutique and blowout

Hotels

Chambers Hotel. *See p118*.

Checking in

Where to get a room in the city that never sleeps.

New York's hotel business is booming. The citywide room count is nearly 100,000, an increase of nearly 25 per cent over the past five years. And despite an average rate of more than $300 a night in the autumn high season, most of them are full year-round.

There is now more boutique choice in popular areas like Chelsea and Greenwich Village with the arrival of the **High Line Hotel** (*see p116*) and the **Marlton** (*see p115*). But perhaps the strongest indication of the economic recovery is a cluster of new development on, or around, midtown's West 57th Street (*see p119* **The New 57**). It's also worth looking to the outer boroughs for competitive pricing – Brooklyn, especially, is an increasingly desirable place to stay.

Accommodation in this chapter has been organised by price level to give you an idea of what you can expect to pay at a given hotel, but note that rates can vary wildly according to the season or the room category within a single property. As a guide, you can expect to pay $500 or more per night in the deluxe category, $300-$500 for expensive hotels, $150-$300 for moderate accommodation and under $150 for properties listed as budget. Don't forget to factor in the hefty 14.75 per cent tax, plus an extra $3.50 per night for most rooms. For gay-oriented lodging, *see pp91-92*.

Financial District

EXPENSIVE

Andaz Wall Street

Hyatt subsidiary Andaz prides itself on giving each property a local flavour. The first New York outpost occupies 13 floors of a former Barclays bank building, outfitted by David Rockwell. The vibe inside is anything but corporate: upon entering the spacious, bamboo-panelled lobby-lounge, you're greeted by a free-range 'host', who acts as combination check-in clerk and concierge. The chic, loft-style rooms (starting at 350sq ft) are equally casual and user-friendly. A long, blond-wood unit doubles as desk, entertainment console and dressing table; remote-controlled blackout blinds descend to cover the seven-foot-high windows; and Wi-Fi and non-alcoholic drinks and snacks are free. The local-centric restaurant (Wall & Water), bar and spa are welcome attributes in an area with little action at weekends. *75 Wall Street, between Water Street & Pearl Street, New York, NY 10005 (1-212 590 1234, www.wallstreet andaz.com). Subway 2, 3, 4, 5 to Wall Street. Rooms 253.*

Conrad New York

This sophisticated Hilton offshoot fronts Battery Park City's riverside Nelson A Rockefeller Park. West-facing guest quarters have views of the Hudson, but there's also plenty to see within the all-suite property. Sol LeWitt's vivid 100ft by 80ft painting Loopy Doopy (Blue and Purple) graces the 15-storey, glass-ceilinged, marble-floored lobby, and coolly understated suites are adorned with pieces by the likes of Elizabeth Peyton and Mary Heilmann. Nespresso machines and Aromatherapy Associates bath products are indulgent touches. The rooftop bar (open May-Oct) offers Statue of Liberty views. *102 North End Avenue, at Vesey Street, New York, NY 10282 (1-212 945 0100, www.conradnewyork. com). Subway A, C, 1, 2, 3 to Chambers Street; E to World Trade Center; R to Cortlandt Street; 2, 3 to Park Place. Rooms 88.*

Tribeca & Soho

DELUXE

Crosby Street Hotel

In 2009, Britain's hospitality power couple, Tim and Kit Kemp, brought

their super-successful Firmdale formula across the Atlantic with the 11-storey, warehouse-style Crosby Street Hotel – their first outside London. Design director Kit Kemp's signature style – a contemporary take on classic English decor characterised by an often audacious mix of patterns, bold colours and well-chosen antiques – is instantly recognisable. Other Firmdale imports include a carefully selected art collection, a guests-only drawing room as well as a public restaurant and bar, a slick, 99-seat screening room and a private garden.
79 Crosby Street, between Prince & Spring Streets, New York, NY 10012 (1-212 226 6400, www.firmdalehotels. com). Subway N, R to Prince Street; 6 to Spring Street. Rooms 86.

Greenwich Hotel
The design inspiration at this Tribeca retreat, co-owned by Robert De Niro, is as international as the jet-set clientele. Individually decorated rooms combine custom-made English leather seating, Tibetan rugs and gorgeous Moroccan or Carrara marble-tiled bathrooms, most outfitted with capacious tubs that fill up in a minute flat. Breaststroke meditatively beneath the frame of a 250-year-old Kyoto farmhouse in the Shibui Spa's underground pool, then unwind with a bottle of wine by the water's edge. For dinner, there's no need to rub shoulders with the masses at the always-mobbed house restaurant, Locanda Verde. Have your meal delivered to the cloistered courtyard, where travertine floors and terracotta pots evoke a Florentine villa.
377 Greenwich Street, between Franklin & North Moore Streets, New York, NY 10013 (1-212 941 8900, www.thegreenwichhotel.com). Subway 1 to Franklin Street. Rooms 88.

The Mercer
Opened in 2001 by trendsetting hotelier André Balazs, this pioneering boutique hotel still has ample attractions that appeal to a celebrity-heavy clientele. The lobby, decked out with a range of oversized couches and chairs, acts as a bar, library and lounge. The loft-like rooms are large by NYC standards and feature furniture by Christian Liaigre, enormous washrooms and Face Stockholm products. The restaurant, the Mercer Kitchen, serves Jean-Georges Vongerichten's stylish version of casual American cuisine.
147 Mercer Street, at Prince Street, New York, NY 10012 (1-212 966 6060, www.mercerhotel.com). Subway N, R to Prince Street. Rooms 75.

EXPENSIVE

60 Thompson
The first property of boutique chain Thompson has been luring film, fashion and media elites since it opened in 2001. British designer Tara Bernerd, who created the classy contemporary interiors for the group's London hotel, Belgraves, and the new Thompson Chicago, is behind a redesign that

should be completed by summer 2014. Indulgent details in the guest rooms include Sferra linens and REN products. The hotel's acclaimed restaurant, Kittichai, serves creative Thai cuisine beside a pool filled with floating orchids, while A60, the exclusive guests-only rooftop bar, offers inspiring city views and a Moroccan-inspired decor.
60 Thompson Street, between Broome & Spring Streets, New York, NY 10012 (1-212 431 0400, www. thompsonhotels.com). Subway C, E to Spring Street. Rooms 100. Other locations throughout the city.

The James New York
Hotel art displays are usually limited to some eye-catching lobby installations or forgettable in-room prints. Not so at the James, which maintains a substantial showcase of local talent, selected by a house curator. Although compact, bedrooms make the most of the available space with high ceilings, wall-spanning windows and glassed-off bathrooms (modesty is preserved by an artist-embellished, remote-controlled screen). Natural materials (wooden floors, linen duvet covers) warm up the clean contemporary lines, beds are piled with eco-friendly pillows, and bathroom products are courtesy of Intelligent Nutrients. A two-level 'urban garden' (open May-Oct) houses an outdoor bar and eaterie. The rooftop bar, Jimmy, opens on to the (admittedly tiny) roof.
27 Grand Street, at Thompson Street, New York, NY 10013 (1-212 465 2000, www.jameshotels.com). Subway A, C, E to Canal Street. Rooms 114.

Mondrian Soho
An ivy-covered passageway leads to a 26-storey glass tower, set back from Crosby Street. Inspired by Jean Cocteau's *La Belle et la Bête*, designer Benjamin Noriega Ortiz has created a fanciful interior in which lobby coffee tables have talons and floor lamps are shaded with petite parasols. Trippy, saturated-blue hallways lead to rooms that combine white minimalism with

classic elements such as china blue arabesque-print upholstery and marble-topped vanity sinks that perch outside the bathroom. Floor-to-ceiling windows give rooms on higher floors spectacular vistas. Going one better than Wi-Fi, every room is equipped with an in-room iPad that also connects to hotel services. The Italian restaurant, Isola Trattoria & Crudo Bar, offers seating in an adjacent greenhouse, fitted out with crystal chandeliers, ferns and ficus trees, while the dimly lit, cushion-strewn bar, Mister H, looks like a 1930s Shanghai opium den by way of Casablanca.
9 Crosby Street, between Grand & Howard Streets, New York, NY 10013 (1-212 389 1000, www. mondriansoho.com). Subway J, N, Q, R, Z, 6 to Canal Street. Rooms 270.

Soho Grand Hotel
The Soho Grand, which pioneered the downtown hotel migration in 1996, is still fresh from a revamp that updated all the guest quarters a few years ago. The original designer, Bill Sofield, introduced new custom pieces to the elegant brown-and-beige rooms, including travel trunk-inspired minibars and natty houndstooth tuxedo chairs. Bathrooms feature charming wallpaper by the late illustrator Saul Steinberg (whose work was a longtime staple of the *New Yorker*) and CO Bigelow products. Endearingly, you can request a goldfish for the duration of your stay. Guests can also borrow old-fashioned bicycles in the warmer months to explore the city; after your exertions, claim a lounger in the hotel's seasonal outdoor bar-eaterie the Yard, or hole up with a cocktail by the fireplace in the Club Room, a glamorous year-round lounge.
310 West Broadway, between Canal & Grand Streets, New York, NY 10013 (1-212 965 3000, www.sohogrand. com). Subway A, C, E, 1 to Canal Street. Rooms 363.

MODERATE

Cosmopolitan
Open continuously since the mid 19th century, the Cosmopolitan has long been a tourist favourite for its address, clean rooms and reasonable rates. In early 2014 the hotel embarks on a floor-by-floor revamp to upgrade its guest quarters and introduce a bar and restaurant. Other convenient facilities include a small gym and a business centre with two Macs that guests can use free of charge (there's also complimentary in-room Wi-Fi). A wide range of room configurations is available, including a suite with two queen beds and a sofa bed, ideal for families.
95 West Broadway, at Chambers Street, New York, NY 10007 (1-212 566 1900, www. cosmohotel.com). Subway A, C, 1, 2, 3 to Chambers Street. Rooms 131.

TOP TIP!
Clock this
The iconic Metropolitan Life tower (*see p27*), currently being converted to an all-suite property by Edition Hotels, is tipped to welcome guests in 2015.

Duane Street Hotel
Opened on a quiet Tribeca street in 2007, this boutique property takes its cues from its well-heeled residential neighbourhood, offering loft-inspired rooms with high ceilings, oversized triple-glazed windows and hardwood floors, and a chic, monochrome colour scheme. Free Wi-Fi, Ren products in the slate-tiled bathrooms, Nespresso machines in the deluxe-category accommodation and complimentary passes to the nearby swanky Equinox gym cement the value-for-money package – a rare commodity in this part of town. The chic Asian-inspired restaurant on the ground floor is helmed by *Iron Chef* regular Jehangir Mehta.
130 Duane Street, at Church Street, New York, NY 10013 (1-212 964 4600, www.duanestreethotel.com). Subway A, C, 1, 2, 3 to Chambers Street. Rooms 45.

Nolita

EXPENSIVE

Nolitan
To make like a Nolitan, check in to this boutique hotel. The rooms feature floor-to-ceiling windows, custom-made walnut beds, wooden floors and toiletries from Prince Street spa Red Flower. The emphasis on keeping it local is reflected in numerous guest perks: the luxuriously laid-back property lends out bikes and skateboards and lays on free local calls. Complimentary wine and cheese is served Monday to Saturday in the lobby, which is stocked with tomes from nearby Phaidon Books. Admire views of Nolita and beyond from the 2,400sq ft roof deck, complete with fire pit, or your private perch – more than half the guest quarters have balconies.
30 Kenmare Street, at Elizabeth Street, New York, NY 10012 (1-212 925 2555, www.nolitanhotel.com). Subway J, Z to Bowery; 6 to Spring Street. Rooms 55.

Dream Downtown. *See p115.*

Hotels

Bowery House

Two young real-estate developers transformed a 1927 Bowery flophouse into a stylish take on a hostel. History buffs will get a kick out of the original wainscotted corridors leading to cubicles (singles are a cosy 35sq ft, and not all have windows) with latticework ceilings to allow air circulation. It might not be the best bet for light sleepers, but the place is hopping with pretty young things attracted to the hip aesthetic and the location (close to Soho and the Lower East Side). Quarters are decorated with vintage prints and historical photographs, and lit by lightbulbs encased in 1930s and '40s Mason jars; towels and robes are courtesy of Ralph Lauren. The gender-segregated communal bathrooms have rain showerheads and products from local spa Red Flower, while the lounge is outfitted with chesterfield sofas and a huge LCD TV. There's also a 3,000sq ft roof terrace, and an eaterie serving eclectic small plates. To keep out the riff-raff and the rowdy, guests must be over 21 and reserve with a credit card.
220 Bowery, between Prince & Spring Streets, New York, NY 10012 (1-212 837 2373, www.theboweryhouse.com). Subway J, Z to Bowery. Rooms 75.

Sohotel

Established as an inn in 1805, but altered considerably since then, this is the oldest hotel in the city. By the time you read this, a renovation should be complete that will introduce a more industrial look while emphasising the building's period character with exposed-brick walls, ceiling beams and hardwood floors. While the rates put it at the upper end of the budget category, the hotel offers perks that place it a rung above similarly priced establishments, including bathroom products courtesy of CO Bigelow, complimentary morning tea and coffee served in the lobby and free in-room Wi-Fi. The Superior Family rooms, which can accommodate five, are the best bargain. Guests get a 10% discount at the on-site craft-brew emporium, Randolph Beer.
341 Broome Street, between Elizabeth Street & Bowery, New York, NY 10013 (1-212 226 1482, www.thesohotel.com). Subway J, Z to Bowery; 6 to Spring Street. Rooms 98.

Lower East Side

Hotel on Rivington

When the Hotel on Rivington opened in 2005, its ultra-modern glass-covered façade was a novelty on the largely low-rise Lower East Side. Now, with condos popping up everywhere, the building (designed by NYC firm Grzywinski & Pons) seems less out of place, but it remains one of the few luxury hotels in the neighbourhood. Rooms are super-sleek and minimalist, with black and white decorative touches, Frette bedlinen and robes, and floor-to-ceiling windows with views of Manhattan and beyond. A stylish crowd congregates in the hotel's two eateries, Co-op Food & Drink, and Viktor & Spoils, a contemporary taqueria and tequila bar.
107 Rivington Street, between Essex & Ludlow Streets, New York, NY 10002 (1-212 475 2600, www.hotelon rivington.com). Subway F to Delancey Street; J, M, Z to Delancey-Essex Streets. Rooms 108.

Off Soho Suites Hotel

These no-frills suites have become all the more popular in recent years due to the Lower East Side's burgeoning bar and restaurant scene. The rates are decent value, especially as all have a sitting area and access to a kitchenette. Economy options have two twin beds and a shared kitchen or, if you're travelling in a group, book a deluxe suite; furnished with a queen bed, plus a sleeper sofa in the living area, it can accommodate four. There's also free Wi-Fi, a gym and a handy coin-operated laundry.
11 Rivington Street, between Bowery & Chrystie Street, New York, NY 10002 (1-212 979 9808, www. offsoho.com). Subway B, D to Grand Street; F to Lower East Side-Second Avenue; J, Z to Bowery. Rooms 38.

East Village

Bowery Hotel

This fanciful boutique hotel from prominent duo Eric Goode and Sean MacPherson is the capstone in the gentrification of the Bowery. Shunning minimalism, the pair have created plush rooms that combine old-world touches (oriental rugs, wood-beamed ceilings, marble washstands) with modern amenities (free Wi-Fi, flatscreen TVs, a DVD library). Tall windows offer views of historic tenements, and the property includes an antique-looking trattoria, Gemma.
335 Bowery, at 3rd Street, New York, NY 10003 (1-212 505 9100, www.theboweryhotel.com). Subway B, D, F, M to Broadway-Lafayette Street; 6 to Bleecker Street. Rooms 135.

East Village Bed & Coffee

Popular with European travellers, this B&B (minus the breakfast) embodies quirky downtown culture. Each of the nine guest rooms has a unique theme: for example, the Black and White Room or the Treehouse (not as outlandish as it sounds: it has an ivory and olive colour scheme, animal-print linens and a whitewashed brick wall). Bathrooms are shared. Owner Anne Edris encourages guests to mingle in the communal areas, which include fully equipped kitchens and three loft-like living rooms with free Wi-Fi. When the weather's nice, sip your morning java in the private garden.
110 Avenue C, between 7th & 8th Streets, New York, NY 10009 (1-917 816 0071, www.bedandcoffee.com). Subway F to Lower East Side-Second Avenue; L to First Avenue. Rooms 9.

Hotel 17

Shabby chic is the best way to describe this East Village hotel a few blocks from Union Square. Past the minuscule lobby, the rooms are a study in contrast, as antique dressers are paired with paisley bedspreads and mismatched patterned wallpaper. Bathrooms are generally shared between two to four rooms, but they're kept immaculately clean. Over the years, the building has been featured in numerous fashion mag layouts and films – including Woody Allen's *Manhattan Murder Mystery* – and has put up Madonna, and, more recently, transsexual downtown diva Amanda Lepore. Who knows who you might bump into on your way to the loo?
225 E 17th Street, between Second & Third Avenues, New York, NY 10003
(1-212 475 2845, www.hotel17ny. com). Subway L to Third Avenue; L, N, Q, R, 4, 5, 6 to 14th Street-Union Square. Rooms 125.

Greenwich Village

The Jade Hotel

With its Georgian-style portico and decorative brickwork, the Jade Hotel is indistinguishable from the pre-war apartment buildings in its Greenwich Village locale. But the sensitively conceived 18-storey structure was built from scratch as a hotel a few years ago. The rooms, designed by Andres Escobar in an art deco style, feature marble-inlaid Macassar ebony desks, chrome period lamps and champagne satin poufs – to preserve the period illusion, the TV is hidden behind a decorative cabinet. The classic black-and-white tiled bathrooms are stocked with toiletries from venerable Village pharmacy CO Bigelow. Some rooms have private terraces, floor-to-ceiling windows or cosy window seats. The bar and restaurant, Grape & Vine, evokes snug glamour through distressed mirrors and red velvet banquettes.
52 W 13th Street, between Fifth & Sixth Avenues, New York, NY 10011 (1-212 375 1300, www.thejadenyc. com). Subway F, M, 1, 2, 3 to 14th Street; L to Sixth Avenue; L, N, Q, R, 4, 5, 6 to 14th Street-Union Square. Rooms 113.

Washington Square Hotel

Opened in 1902 as the Hotel Earle, this Village fixture has sheltered the likes of Ernest Hemingway, Dylan Thomas and Bob Dylan (who lodged in room 305 in 1964). Run by the same family since 1973, it has been restored in an art deco style. The regularly updated rooms, currently sporting a cream-and-tan colour palette with black faux-leather headboards and plain, white-tiled bathrooms, may not be the height of fashion, but they offer comforts such as Keurig coffee makers, iPod docks and free Wi-Fi. Rates include continental breakfast. Many quarters have partial views of the park or picturesque Village streets from large windows.
103 Waverly Place, between MacDougal Street & Sixth Avenue, New York, NY 10011 (1-212 777 9515, www.washingtonsquarehotel. com). Subway A, B, C, D, E, F, M to W 4th Street. Rooms 152.

Larchmont Hotel

Housed in a 1910 Beaux Arts building, the Larchmont is great value for this area. The basic decor has been spruced up with new IKEA furniture and flatscreen TVs, but with prices this reasonable, you can accept less than glossy-mag style. Except for the en-suite family room, which has one double and one trundle

Bowery House

bed, bathrooms are shared, but all guest quarters come with a washbasin, toiletries, bathrobe and slippers. Continental breakfast is included in the rate and Wi-Fi is thrown in free of charge.
27 W 11th Street, between Fifth & Sixth Avenues, New York, NY 10011 (1-212 989 9333, www.larchmont hotel.com). Subway F, M to 14th Street; L to Sixth Avenue. Rooms 67.

West Village & Meatpacking District

EXPENSIVE

Gansevoort Meatpacking NYC
This Meatpacking District pioneer is known for its rooftop pool-lounge playgrounds at two NYC locations (a Park Avenue property opened in 2010). By day, you can soak up the sun, and the Hudson River panorama, on a lounger by the 45ft heated open-air pool. After dark, the wraparound terrace bar becomes a DJed outdoor party with a glittering Manhattan backdrop. If you prefer a quieter night, admire the view through ample glass in your room – many feature contemporary bay windows or mini balconies. The guest quarters are outfitted with Studio 54-inspired photography that plays on the hotel's reputation as a party hub, plush feather-bed layers atop excellent mattresses and marble bathrooms. The Exhale spa is a dimly lit subterranean sanctuary, and the house restaurant, the Chester, serves American classics like Long Island oysters and steaks.
18 Ninth Avenue, at 13th Street, New York, NY 10014 (1-212 206 6700, www.hotelgansevoort.com). Subway A, C, E to 14th Street; L to Eighth Avenue. Rooms 186. Other location 420 Park Avenue South, at 29th Street, enter on 29th Street, Flatiron District (1-212 317 2900, www.gansevoortpark.com).

Soho House
Members of this British-born network of 11 clubs enjoy a slew of perks, and for the price of a room, so can you. Chief among them is the recently revamped roof deck, which feels more Montauk than Meatpacking District – in summer, you can hang out at the beach shack-style bar or recline by the pool in the company of swimsuit-clad models, actors, and movers and shakers. (Don't be tempted to take any snaps, though: photography is strictly forbidden in the public spaces.) In the bedrooms, refined English furnishings – hand-carved beds, classic Colefax & Fowler wallpaper and vintage chandeliers – contrast with reclaimed barn-wood floors and exposed brick. You can get a bespoke pummelling in the Cowshed Spa, a diminutive version of the rural original at posh Babington House in Somerset, UK, and, if you time it right, catch a

Hip hotelier Sean MacPherson, who co-owns the Bowery (*see p114*), Maritime (*see p116*) and Jane (*see below*), has sealed the transformation of a formerly run-down Village strip with this affordable boutique hotel. The 1900 building has plenty of local history – Beat icon Jack Kerouac wrote a couple of novellas while lodging there, and the place put up would-be Andy Warhol assassin Valerie Solanas – but the lobby's deceptively lived-in-looking interior has largely been created from scratch; lounge on a broken-in leather armchair while sipping a house-roasted Ferndell coffee, and flip through tomes on NYC history or local artists. Measuring a mere 150sq ft each, the bedrooms are mini versions of a Paris grand hotel, with gilt-edged velvet headboards, crown mouldings and shaded sconces held by brass hands. The bathrooms feature petite marble sinks, brass rain showerheads and products by Provençal perfumer Côté Bastide. The classic decor is offset by midcentury touches: art by Berlin-based artist Stefano Castronovo, inspired by Abstract Expressionists like Franz Kline and Robert Motherwell, and Serge Mouille chandeliers that look like Anglepoise lamps on steroids.
5 W 8th Street, between Fifth and Sixth Avenues, New York, NY 10011 (1-212 321 0100, www.marltonhotel.com). Subway A, B, C, D, E, F, M to W 4th Street; N, R to 8th Street-NYU. Rooms 107.

pre-release screening of a hotly anticipated flick in the 44-seat cinema.
29-35 Ninth Avenue, at W 13th Street, New York, NY 10014 (1-212 627 9800, www.sohohouseny.com). Subway A, C, E to 14th Street; L to Eighth Avenue. Rooms 30.

The Standard
André Balazs's lauded West Coast mini-chain arrived in New York in early 2009. Straddling the High Line, the retro 18-storey structure has been configured to give each room an exhilarating view, of either the river or a midtown cityscape. Quarters are compact, but the combination of floor-to-ceiling windows, curving tambour wood panelling (think old-fashioned roll-top desks) and 'peekaboo' bathrooms (with Japanese-style tubs or huge showerheads and Kiss My Face products) give a sense of space. Eating and drinking options include a chop house, a beer garden and an exclusive top-floor bar with a massive jacuzzi and 180-degree views.
848 Washington Street, at 13th Street, New York, NY 10014 (1-212 645 4646, www.standardhotels. com). Subway A, C, E to 14th Street;

L to Eighth Avenue. Rooms 337. Other locations 25 Cooper Square, between 5th & 6th Streets (1-212 475 5700).

MODERATE

The Jane
Opened in 1907 as the American Seaman's Friend Society Sailors H ome, the six-storey landmark was a residential hotel when hoteliers Eric Goode and Sean MacPherson of the Bowery and the Maritime took it over. The wood-panelled, 50sq ft rooms ($99-$115) were inspired by vintage train sleeper compartments: there's a single or bunk bed with built-in storage and brass hooks for hanging up your clothes – but also iPod docks, free Wi-Fi and wall-mounted flatscreen TVs. Alternatively, opt for a more spacious, wainscoted Captain's Cabin with private facilities – many have terraces or Hudson River views. If entering the hotel feels like stepping on to a film set, there's good reason. Inspiration came from various celluloid sources, including *Barton Fink*'s Hotel Earle for the lobby. The 'ballroom', decorated with mismatched chairs, oriental rugs and a fireplace topped with a stuffed

ram, evokes an eccentric mansion, and there's also an airy faux-vintage French-Moroccan café.
113 Jane Street, at West Street, New York, NY 10014 (1-212 924 6700, www.thejanenyc.com). Subway A, C, E to 14th Street; L to Eighth Avenue. Rooms 208.

Chelsea

EXPENSIVE

Dream Downtown
Be sure to pack your totem: staying at this surreal property from hotel wunderkind Vikram Chatwal may make you wonder if you're in a dream within a Dream. The tree-shaded lobby, presided over by a nightly DJ, provides an overhead view of swimmers doing laps in the glass-bottomed pool on the terrace above. Housed in the former annex of the New York Maritime Union (now the adjacent Maritime Hotel, *see p116*), the building is riddled with round windows. In the upper-floor rooms, these frame elements of the Manhattan skyline, such as the Empire State Building, in intriguing ways and are picked up by circular mirrors and wallpaper motifs. Rooms combine classic elements (white chesterfield chairs or sofas, Tivoli radios, Turkish rugs) with futuristic touches like shiny steel bathtubs in some rooms. The hotel recreates a 'beach club' experience on its pool deck with a sandy patch and suites that lead directly on to the pool area. Also channelling the feel of a luxury resort, the rooftop PH-D bar-nightclub has a lushly planted terrace running the entire length of the building.
355 W 16th Street, between Eighth & Ninth Avenues, New York, NY 10011 (1-212 229 2559, www.dream downtown.com). Subway A, C, E to 14th Street; L to Eighth Avenue. Rooms 316.

Eventi
Managed by Kimpton, a brand that's known for its informal, friendly ethos, flamboyant decor and nice perks like its free evening wine hour, Eventi feels luxurious for the upper-mid-range rates. The spacious rooms (which seem even more open thanks to floor-to-ceiling outlooks) have either a king-size bed or two queens, outfitted with dapper grey fabric headboards and Frette linens. Cool marble bathrooms are stocked with CO Bigelow products. You can get an on-site bite at the sprawling, indoor-outdoor farm-to-table eaterie Humphrey and some pampering in the spa.
851 Sixth Avenue, between 29th & 30th Streets, New York, NY 10001 (1-212 564 4567, www.eventihotel. com). Subway B, D, F, M, N, Q, R to 34th Street-Herald Square; N, R to 28th Street. Rooms 292.

Hôtel Americano
You won't find any Talavera tiles in Grupo Habita's first property outside Mexico. Mexican architect Enrique

Hotels

Norten's sleek, mesh-encased structure stands alongside the High Line. The decor evokes classic midcentury American style, interpreted by a European (Colette designer Arnaud Montigny). The minimalist rooms have Japanese-style platform beds, iPads and, in one of several subtle nods to US culture, super-soft denim bathrobes. After a day of gallery-hopping, get an even more elevated view of the neighbourhood from the rooftop bar and grill, where a petite pool does double duty as a hot tub in winter. There's also an airy ground-floor eaterie and two subterranean bars. *518 W 27th Street, between Tenth & Eleventh Avenues, New York, NY 10001 (1-212 216 0000, www.hotel-americano.com). Subway C, E to 23rd Street. Rooms 56.*

Maritime Hotel

Steve Zissou would feel at home at this nautically themed hotel (the former headquarters of the New York Maritime Union), which is outfitted with self-consciously hip details befitting a Wes Anderson film. Standard rooms are modelled on cruise cabins; lined with teak panelling and sporting a single porthole window, they're small but thoughtfully appointed (with CO Bigelow products in the bathroom, a Booty Parlor 'pleasure kit' in the minibar, and a well-curated list of DVDs that you can order from the front desk). The hotel's busy Italian restaurant, La Bottega, also supplies room service. *363 W 16th Street, between Eighth & Ninth Avenues, New York, NY 10011 (1-212 242 4300, www.themaritimehotel.com). Subway A, C, E to 14th Street; L to Eighth Avenue. Rooms 126.*

MODERATE

The Inn on 23rd

This renovated 19th-century townhouse offers the charm of a traditional B&B with enhanced amenities (an elevator, pillow-top mattresses, private bathrooms, white-noise machines). Owners Annette and Barry Fisherman have styled each bedroom with a unique theme, such as the Asian-inspired Bamboo and the 1940s room, furnished with vintage Heywood-Wakefield pieces. The 'library', a cosy jumble of tables and chairs is open 24/7 to guests for coffee and tea, and hosts wine and cheese receptions on Friday and Saturday evenings. Another nice perk: guests receive 20% off the bill at the Guilty Goose, the owners' modern American brasserie on the ground floor. *131 W 23rd Street, between Sixth & Seventh Avenues, New York, NY 10011 (1-212 463 0330, www.innon23rd.com). Subway F, M, 1 to 23rd Street. Rooms 13.*

BUDGET

Chelsea Lodge

Situated in a landmark brownstone blocks from the Chelsea gallery district, Chelsea Lodge is a long way from any arcadian idylls. Yet the rustic name is reflected in the mishmash of Americana that adorns the pine panelling of the inn's public spaces, such as rough-hewn duck decoys and early 20th-century photos. While all of the mostly tiny wood-floored rooms have TVs, sinks, showers and air-conditioning, most share toilets, so it's not for everyone. For more privacy and space, book one of the four suites down the block at 334 West 20th Street: all are former studio apartments with kitchenettes that sleep up to four people. The two at the back have direct access to the private garden. *318 W 20th Street, between Eighth & Ninth Avenues, New York, NY 10011 (1-212 243 4499, www.chelsealodge.com). Subway C, E to 23rd Street. Rooms 26.*

Flatiron District

EXPENSIVE

Ace Hotel New York

Founded in Seattle by a pair of DJs, this cool chainlet has expanded beyond the States to London and Panama. In its New York digs, the musical influence is clear: select rooms in the 1904 building have functioning turntables, stacks of vinyl and gleaming Gibson guitars. And while you'll pay a hefty amount for the sprawling loft spaces, there are more reasonable options for those on a smaller budget. The 'medium' rooms are fitted with vintage furniture and original art; even cheaper are the snug bunk-bed set-ups. Should you find the latter lodging stifling, repair to the buzzing lobby, where the bar is set within a panelled library salvaged from a Madison Avenue apartment. Guests can score a table at chef April Bloomfield's popular Breslin Bar & Dining Room and the John Dory Oyster Bar (for both, *see p58*). There's even an outpost of Opening Ceremony if you find you haven't a thing to wear. *20 W 29th Street, at Broadway, New York, NY 10012 (1-212 679 2222, www.acehotel.com). Subway N, R to 28th Street. Rooms 265.*

The NoMad

Like nearby hipster hub the Ace Hotel, the NoMad is also a self-contained microcosm encompassing destination dining – courtesy of Daniel Humm and Will Guidara, of Michelin-three-starred Eleven Madison Park (*see p58*) – and the first stateside outpost of Parisian concept store Maison Kitsuné. Jacques Garcia, designer of Paris celeb hangout Hôtel Costes, transformed the interior of a 1903 New York office building into this convincing facsimile of a grand hotel. The chic rooms, furnished with vintage Heriz rugs and distressed-leather armchairs, are more personal – Garcia based the design on his old Paris apartment. Many feature old-fashioned claw-foot tubs for a scented soak in Côté Bastide bath salts. *1170 Broadway, at 28th Street, New York, NY 10001 (1-212 796 1500, www.thenomadhotel.com). Subway N, R to 28th Street. Rooms 168.*

Gramercy Park

DELUXE

Gramercy Park Hotel

Many NYC hotels have exclusive terraces or gardens, but only one boasts access to the city's most renowned private outdoor space: Gramercy Park. The hotel's interior resembles a baronial manor occupied by a rock star, with rustic wooden beams and a roaring fire in the lobby; a $65 million art collection, including works by Richard Prince, Damien Hirst and Andy Warhol; and studded velvet headboards and mahogany drink cabinets in the bedrooms. Get a taste of the Eternal City in the restaurant, Maialino, Danny Meyer's tribute to Roman trattorias. *2 Lexington Avenue, at 21st Street, New York, NY 10010 (1 212 920 3300, www.gramercyparkhotel.com). Subway 6 to 23rd Street. Rooms 192.*

BUDGET

Carlton Arms

The Carlton Arms Art Project started in the late 1970s, when a small group of creative types brought fresh paint and new ideas to a run-down shelter. Today, the site is a bohemian backpackers' paradise and a live-in gallery – every room, bathroom and hallway is festooned with outré artwork, including a couple of early stairwells by Banksy. Eye-popping themed quarters include the Money Room and a tribute to the traditional English cottage; new works are introduced regularly and artists return to restore their creations. Roughly half of the rooms have shared bathrooms. *160 E 25th Street, at Third Avenue, New York, NY 10010 (1-212 679 0680, www.carltonarms.com). Subway 6 to 23rd Street. Rooms 54.*

Herald Square & Garment District

EXPENSIVE

Refinery Hotel

The Garment District finally has a fittingly fashionable hotel. Stonehill & Taylor Architects, the firm behind this

---

RECOMMENDED
High Line Hotel

In the early 19th century, Chelsea was a country estate owned by Clement Clarke Moore, author of the poem 'A Visit from St Nicholas' (''Twas the Night Before Christmas'). The man of letters gifted a chunk of land to the Episcopal Church to establish the General Theological Seminary, which remains a bastion of religious study. These days, however, it's across the street from one of the city's most popular attractions: the High Line. And the railway line-turned-park lends its name to a new boutique hotel in the seminary's old guest wing. The lobby of the imposing 1895 neo-Gothic landmark is home to NYC's first outpost of Chicago's Intelligentsia Coffee. Exuding an old-fashioned residential vibe, the 60 rooms feature antique Persian rugs on hardwood floors, custom-designed wallpaper and a mix of vintage furnishings and reproductions of pieces sourced by the hotel's design firm, Roman and Williams. Many rooms retain original fireplaces – though these days the eco-friendly property is heated and cooled by a geothermal system. Rewired 1930s rotary phones and desktop embossers for customising your snail mail may seem like an antidote to the digital age, but there's also free in-room Wi-Fi, and you can connect your iPod to the retro Tivoli radio by the bed. **180 Tenth Avenue, at 20th Street, New York, NY 10011 (1-212 929 3888, www.thehighlinehotel.com). Subway C, E to 23rd Street. Rooms 60.**

Hotels

1912 neo-Gothic building's conversion and design, took inspiration from its former life as a hat-making hub. In the guest rooms, furnishings subtly reference the garment industry for a look that's more sophisticated than steampunk. Super-soft bed throws mimic burlap, coffee tables are modelled on factory carts, and desks are reproductions of vintage Singer sewing-machine tables. Luxurious touches like Frette linens and walk-in showers with room for two offset the industrial elements. Eating and drinking options include Winnie's Lobby Bar, which takes its name from Winifred McDonald, who owned a ladies' tearoom in the building in the early 20th century, and a sprawling indoor-outdoor roof bar.
63 W 38th Street, between Fifth & Sixth Avenues, New York, NY 10018 (1-646 664 0310, www.refineryhotel newyork.com). Subway B, D, F, M, N, Q, R to 34th Street-Herald Square; B, D, F, M to Bryant Park; 7 to Fifth Avenue. Rooms 197.

MODERATE

Hotel Metro

It may not be trendy, but the Metro is a solid, good-value hotel that is extremely well maintained. Every two years, the owners start renovating the rooms, floor by floor, starting at the top; by the time they're finished it's almost time to start again. So even 'old' rooms are virtually new. The stylishly contemporary quarters feature marble-topped furniture and beige leather-effect headboards; premier rooms have luxurious rain showers. Unusually for NYC, the hotel offers 18 family rooms, consisting of two adjoining bedrooms. Also rare: a generous continental breakfast buffet is offered in the guests' lounge, which is outfitted with several large TVs. The rooftop bar (open from April to October) has views of the Empire State Building.
45 W 35th Street, between Fifth & Sixth Avenues, New York, NY 10001 (1-212 947 2500, www.hotelmetro nyc.com). Subway B, D, F, M, N, Q, R to 34th Street-Herald Square. Rooms 181.

Theater District & Hell's Kitchen

DELUXE

The Chatwal New York

In a city awash with incongruous nods to the style, the Chatwal New York occupies a Stanford White building that has been given a pitch-perfect art deco interior. Hotelier Sant Chatwal entrusted the design of this 1905 Beaux Arts building (formerly the clubhouse for the Lamb's Club, America's first professional theatre organisation) to Thierry Despont, who worked on the centennial restoration of the Statue of Liberty. The glamorous lobby is adorned with

murals recalling the hotel's theatrical pedigree – past members of the Lamb's Club include Oscar Hammerstein, Charlie Chaplin, John Wayne and Fred Astaire – and the hotel's restaurant, helmed by Geoffrey Zakarian, takes its name from the club. The elegant rooms feature vintage Broadway posters as well as hand-tufted Shifman mattresses, 400-thread count Frette linens and custom Asprey toiletries, and 15 rooms have spacious terraces. Unwind in the Elizabeth Arden Red Door Spa, which boasts a small saltwater lap pool.
130 W 44th Street, between Sixth Avenue & Broadway, New York, NY 10036 (1-212 764 6200, www.the chatwalny.com). Subway N, Q, R, S, 1, 2, 3 to 42nd Street-Times Square. Rooms 76.

EXPENSIVE

The London NYC

This 54-storey high-rise was completely overhauled by David Collins and reopened as the London NYC in 2007. The designer's sleek, contemporary-British style pervades the rooms, with attractive signature touches such as limed oak parquet flooring, embossed leather travel trunks at the foot of the beds, hand-woven throws and inventive coffee tables that adjust to dining-table height. But space is perhaps the biggest luxury: the London Suites (the starting-priced accommodation) are a minimum of 500sq ft and either open-plan or divided with mirrored French doors, and bathrooms feature double rain showerheads. Upper-floor Vista suites command impressive city views. The London is, appropriately, the site of two eateries from Britain's best-known celebrity chef, the eponymous Gordon Ramsay at the London and the less formal Maze.
151 W 54th Street, between Sixth & Seventh Avenues, New York, NY 10019 (1-866 690 2029, www. thelondonnyc.com). Subway B, D, E to Seventh Avenue. Rooms 561.

MODERATE

414 Hotel

Tucked into a residential yet central neighbourhood a short walk from Times Square, this budget-friendly boutique hotel is a real find. The place is twice as big as it looks, as it consists of two walk-up buildings separated by a leafy courtyard, which in warmer months is a lovely place to eat your complimentary breakfast. Rooms are simple yet chic, with a modern colour scheme that pairs grey headboards with red accents, and equipped with fridges, flatscreen TVs and iPod docks.
414 W 46th Street, between Ninth & Tenth Avenues, New York, NY 10036 (1-212 399 0006, www.414hotel.com). Subway A, C, E to 42nd Street-Port Authority. Rooms 22.

Distrikt Hotel

Although it's on an unlovely street alongside Port Authority, this hotel has much to recommend it. Distrikt has a Manhattan theme, but it's subtle

and conceptual. Each of the 31 guest floors is named after one of the city's beloved 'hoods and a backlit photo collage created by local artist Chris Rubino adorns the hallways; smaller framed versions liven up the rooms, which are otherwise coolly neutral, with luxury features such as Frette linens and marble in the bathrooms. Request a higher floor for Hudson River or Times Square views – the rates rise accordingly. A 14ft 'living wall' representing Central Park anchors the lobby, but what really impresses are the three big iMacs equipped with free Wi-Fi for guest use.
342 W 40th Street, between Eighth & Ninth Avenues, New York, NY 10018 (1-212 706 6100, 1-888 444 5610, www.distrikt hotel.com). Subway A, C, E to 42nd Street-Port Authority. Rooms 155.

Hotel Edison

This 1931 art deco hotel retains enough original touches – such as gorgeous elevator doors and brass door handles – to evoke old New York. Its affordable rates and proximity to Broadway's theatres seal it as the ideal Gotham hotel for many guests. The no-frills rooms are standard in size, and clean, if also devoid of personality. For more upscale accommodation, the newly renovated Signature Collection quarters on the 19th to the 22nd floors feature 32in flatscreen TVs, upgraded bedding, free Wi-Fi and Times Square or river views from some suites. Café Edison, a classic diner just off the lobby, is a long-time favourite of Broadway actors – Neil Simon was so smitten that he put it in one of his plays.
228 W 47th Street, between Broadway & Eighth Avenue, New York, NY 10036 (1-212 840 5000, www.edison hotelnyc.com). Subway N, Q, R to 49th Street; 1 to 50th Street. Rooms 800.

Novotel New York Times Square

If you want to immerse yourself in the pulsing heart of Times Square, check in to this redesigned hotel, part of the European Accor group (which also includes luxury brand Sofitel). Architecture and design firm Stonehill & Taylor brought elements of the dazzling, dynamic surroundings to the interiors of the 33-storey tower. Illuminated wall and ceiling panels in the check-in area riff on the hexagonal LEDs of the New Year's Eve ball. You can get a glimpse of the famed animated billboards from the glass-walled restaurant and bar and its 5,700-square-foot wraparound terrace, which is warmed by two large fire pits. Wisely, the design team kept special effects out of the spare, contemporary guest rooms, which have a cool-beige colour scheme and sleek pear-wood-veneer furnishings. Room amenities include 46-inch flatscreen TVs, soundproof windows you can actually open and, instead of a costly minibar,

a handy fridge for storing your own drinks and snacks.
226 W 52nd Street at Broadway, New York, NY 10019 (1-212 315 0100, www.novotel.com). Subway B, D, E to Seventh Avenue; C, E to 50th Street; 1 to 50th Street; N, Q, R to 49th Street. Rooms 480.

Yotel New York

The British team behind this futuristic hotel is known for airport-based capsule accommodation that gives long-haul travellers just enough space to get horizontal between flights. Yotel New York has ditched the 75sq ft cubbies in favour of 'premium cabins' more than twice the size. Adaptable furnishings (such as motorised beds that fold up futon-style) maximise space, and the bathrooms have streamlined luxuries such as heated towel rails and monsoon showers. Some first-class 'cabins' even have private terraces with hot tubs. If you want to unload excess baggage, the 20ft tall robot (or Yobot, in the hotel's playful lingo) will stash it away for you in a lobby locker. In contrast with the compact quarters, the sprawling public spaces include an eaterie serving Latin-Asian small plates and a wraparound terrace so large it's serviced by two bars.
570 Tenth Avenue, at 42nd Street, New York, NY 10036 (1-646 449 7700, www.yotel.com). Subway A, C, E to 42nd Street-Port Authority. Rooms 669.

TOP TIP!
Best friends welcome
The Benjamin (*see p118*) and Eventi (*see p115*) are among many hotels offering pet perks – Soho Grand (*see p113*) has a dog park, compete with 'fire hydrants'.

Fifth Avenue & around

DELUXE

The Plaza

The closest thing to a palace in New York, this 1907 French Renaissance-style landmark reopened in spring 2008 after a two-year, $400-million renovation. Although 152 rooms were converted into private condo units, guests can still check into one of 282 elegantly appointed quarters with Louis XV-inspired furnishings and white-glove butler service. The opulent vibe extends to the bathrooms, which feature mosaic baths, 24-carat gold-plated sink fittings and even chandeliers. Embracing the 21st century, the hotel has equipped every room with an iPad. The legendary Oak Room and Oak Bar, both designated landmarks, are currently open only for private events, but you can still take afternoon tea in the restored Palm Court. There's also an upscale food hall conceived by celebrity chef Todd English, and an on-site Caudalie Vinothérapie Spa.
768 Fifth Avenue, at Central Park South, New York, NY 10019 (1-212 759 3000, www.theplazany.com). Subway N, Q, R to Fifth Avenue-59th Street. Rooms 282.

The Quin

See p119 The New 57.
101 W 57th Street, at Sixth Avenue, New York, NY 10019 (1-212 245 7846, www.thequinhotel.com). Subway F, N, Q, R to 57th Street. Rooms 208.

Algonquin Hotel

Alexander Woollcott and Dorothy Parker swapped bons mots in the famous Round Table Room of this 1902 landmark – and you'll still find writer types holding court in the sprawling lobby. The Algonquin certainly trades on its literary past (quotes from Parker and other Round Table members adorn the door to each guest room and vintage *New Yorker* covers hang in the hallways), but a major 2012 renovation has spruced up the grande dame. Backlit vintage photographs of NYC in the rooms are nods to old New York but the sleek quarters could be in any corporate hotel, with faux-leather headboards, Frette linens, iHome clock radios and slate-floored bathrooms. Although it's now part of the Marriott-affiliated Autograph Collection, the hotel retains some of its quirky identity in the public spaces – in the lobby bar and restaurant, original panelling and some decorative fixtures remain and the hotel car still slumbers behind the check-in desk.
59 W 44th Street, between Fifth & Sixth Avenues, New York, NY 10036 (1-212 840 6800, www.algonquin hotel.com). Subway B, D, F, M to 42nd Street-Bryant Park; 7 to Fifth Avenue. Rooms 181.

Bryant Park Hotel

When the shows and the shoots are finished, the fashion and film folk flock to this luxe landing pad (it's particularly busy during Fashion Week). In its days as the American Radiator Building, the hotel was immortalised by Georgia O'Keeffe. Although the exterior (which you can appreciate up-close in one of several balconied rooms) is gothic art deco, the inside is all clean-lined and contemporary, with soft lighting, blanched hardwood floors, Tibetan rugs and soothing conveniences such as sleep-aiding sound machines and Bose Wave radios. Room services is courtesy of the house restaurant, slick sushi destination Koi.
40 W 40th Street, between Fifth & Sixth Avenues, New York, NY 10018 (1-212 869 0100, www.bryantpark hotel.com). Subway B, D, F, M to 42nd Street-Bryant Park; 7 to Fifth Avenue. Rooms 128.

Chambers Hotel

Although it opened in 2001, Chambers has a contemporary residential style that feels utterly current. The double-height lobby, with low seating and a gas fire, exudes Zen serenity. It also showcases some of the owners' 500-piece art collection, which is scattered around the public spaces and guest quarters. Room design takes its cue from upscale loft apartments, combining designer furniture with raw concrete ceilings, exposed pipes, floor-to-ceiling windows and either polished walnut floorboards or Tibetan wool carpeting. Everything is designed to make you feel at home, from the bright terrycloth slippers to the architect's desks stocked with a roll of paper and coloured pencils should artistic inspiration hit. There's no need to leave the hotel for meals, since David Chang's Má Pêche and an outpost of his Milk Bar are on site.
15 W 56 Street, between Fifth & Sixth Avenues, New York, NY 10019 (1-212 974 5656, www.chambershotel.com). Subway E, M to Fifth Avenue-53rd Street. Rooms 77.

Viceroy New York

See p119 The New 57.
120 W 57th Street, between Sixth and Seventh Avenues, New York, NY 10019 (1-212 830 8000, www.viceroy hotelsandresorts.com/newyork). Subway F, N, Q, R to 57th Street. Rooms 240.

WestHouse

See p119 The New 57.
201 W 55th Street, at Seventh Avenue, New York, NY 10019 (1-212 707 4888, www.westhousehotelnewyork. com). Subway F, N, Q, R to 57th Street. Rooms 172.

Midtown East

The Benjamin

All rooms in this pet-friendly hotel have kitchenettes with microwaves and sinks, so it's a hit with families as well as business travellers. The decor, in restful shades of beige and cream, is unfussy, with the emphasis on comfort: choose from a menu of ten pillows from Swedish memory foam to a five-foot-long body cushion for side-slumberers. The list was devised in consultation with sleep expert Rebecca Robbins, who also advised on a selection of soothing before-bed snacks and treatments. Facilities include a gym, a hair salon and spa, and the National Bar & Dining Rooms, from *Iron Chef* Geoffrey Zakarian.
125 E 50th Street, at Lexington Avenue, New York, NY 10022 (1-212 715 2500, www.thebenjamin. com). Subway E, M to Lexington Avenue-53rd Street; 6 to 51st Street. Rooms 209.

Hotel Elysée

The former home of Tennessee Williams and Tallulah Bankhead, among other colourful figures, this small 1926 property is like a scaled-down grand hotel: rooms are furnished with antiques, gilt-framed paintings and old prints, and most of the marble-tiled bathrooms have tubs. Many suites are decked out with (non-functioning) fireplaces and crystal chandeliers. Stop by the sedate second-floor lounge for the complimentary wine and cheese, served every evening, on your way to dinner at the exclusive Monkey Bar, *Vanity Fair* editor Graydon Carter's restaurant that shares the building. A few tables at the hotspot are set aside for guests every night.
60 E 54th Street, between Madison & Park Avenues, New York, NY 10022 (1-212 753 1066, www. elyseehotel.com). Subway E, M to Fifth Avenue-53rd Street; 6 to 51st Street. Rooms 100.

Morgans

New York's original boutique hotel, Morgans opened in 1984. Some 25 years later, the hotel's designer, octogenerian French tastemaker Andrée Putman, returned to officiate over a revamp that has softened its stark monochrome appearance. Unfussy bedrooms, cast in a calming palette of silver, grey, cream and white, are hung with original Robert Mapplethorpe prints; window seats piled with linen cushions encourage quiet reflection. The bathrooms, with classic black and white tiles, offer products from NYC's Malin + Goetz. The guests' living room, stocked with coffee and tea, is equally understated.
237 Madison Avenue, between 37th & 38th Streets, New York, NY 10016 (1-212 686 0300, www.morgans hotel.com). Subway S, 4, 5, 6, 7 to 42nd Street-Grand Central. Rooms 113.

The New York Palace

Modernity literally meets tradition here: a sleek 55-storey tower cantilevers over the landmark 1884 Villard Houses – the connected, courtyard-facing brownstones, commissioned by railroad tycoon and financier Henry Villard, were designed by McKim, Mead and White to look like a single Italian Renaissance mansion. In autumn 2013, the New York Palace officially unveiled the results of a $140 million rolling renovation that introduced six new bars and eateries and updated all the guest rooms. Rain showerheads, custom-made rosewood headboards and hand-picked art now enhance many quarters. Accommodation ranges from understated luxury in the original building, where many west-facing rooms overlook St Patrick's Cathedral, to a more contemporary, residential style in the Towers. Occupying the hotel's top 14 floors, these premium rooms and suites have a separate check-in and exclusive perks such as a private bar. The Palace is now home to James Beard Award-winning chef Michel Richard's first NYC restaurant, which stretches over several opulent rooms of Villard's old residence. The top toque also helms a casual café and patisserie, Pomme Palais.
455 Madison Avenue, between 50th & 51st Streets, New York, NY 10022 (1-212 888 7000, www.newyorkpalace. com). Subway E, M to Fifth Avenue-53rd Street. Rooms 893.

Library Hotel

This bookish boutique hotel is organised on the principles of the Dewey decimal system – each of its ten floors is allocated a category, such as Literature, the Arts, and General Knowledge, and each elegantly understated guest room contains a collection of books and artwork pertaining to a subject within that category. The popular Love room (filed under Philosophy) has a king-size bed, an ivy-clad balcony overlooking the New York Public Library and reading matter ranging from Ovid's *The Art of Love* to Dr Ruth Westheimer's *The Art of Arousal* (the veteran sexpert is honorary curator of the room's book collection). Nightly receptions dish out wine and cheese, while upstairs in the rooftop bar, libations are inspired by Ernest Hemingway and Harper Lee.
299 Madison Avenue, at 41st Street, New York, NY 10017 (1-212 983 4500, www.libraryhotel.com). Subway S, 4, 5, 6, 7 to 42nd Street-Grand Central; 7 to Fifth Avenue. Rooms 60.

Pod 39

The city's second Pod occupies a 1918 residential hotel for single men – you can hang out by the fire or play ping-pong in the redesigned gents' sitting room. As the name suggests, rooms are snug, but not oppressively so; some have queen-size beds, others stainless-steel bunk beds with individual TVs and bedside shelves inspired by plane storage lockers. But you should probably know your roommate well since the utilitarian, subway-tiled bathrooms are partitioned off with sliding frosted-glass doors. April Bloomfield and Ken Friedman are behind on-site eaterie Salvation Taco (*see p60*), which also supplies the margaritas at the seasonal rooftop bar.
145 E 39th Street, between Lexington & Third Avenues, New York, NY 10016 (1-212 865 5700, www.thepod hotel.com). Subway S, 4, 5, 6, 7 to 42nd Street-Grand Central. Rooms 366.

Upper West Side

Hotel Belleclaire

This landmark Upper West Side hotel, a short walk from Central Park and the Museum of Natural History, debuted a complete renovation in early 2013, in time for its 100th birthday. The grand panelled lobby, which retains its original skylight and mosaic-tiled floor, now has a stylish coffee bar furnished with café tables and crushed-velvet chaise-style sofas.

TOP TIP!
Bunking with the band
The Wythe Hotel (*see p120*) literally rocks, hosting Billyburg's many touring bands in quarters that sleep four to six. Look out for familiar faces in the bar.

Guest quarters feature wooden floors and comfort-centric details such as padded headboards, Frette linens and iHome iPod docks. Snacks from gourmet grocer Dean & Deluca (complimentary in the premium rooms) and bath products courtesy of iconic East Village chemist CO Bigelow are further perks. Parents, in particular, will appreciate the refrigerators in every room and DVD players in the suites. Also family-friendly is the 'media lounge' housing two arcade stations loaded with thousands of games, in addition to three free-to-use iMacs.
250 W 77th Street, at Broadway, New York, NY 10024 (1-212 362 7700, www.hotelbelleclaire.com). Subway 1 to 79th Street. Rooms 240.

NYLO New York City
The name is short for New York Loft, but the Texas-incubated hotel group launched by former W honcho Michael Mueller didn't have an NYC property until 2013, when it overhauled and rebranded the On the Ave Hotel. The airy guest quarters have stacked-plywood furnishings, original art and 'brick' wallpaper that playfully references the loft-living archetype. The functional style doesn't skimp on comfort, though: beds have a cushy, custom-made pillow-top mattress, and in-room amenities include free Wi-Fi and a Keurig coffeemaker to brew your free Wolfgang Puck joe. Deluxe rooms on the top three floors open on to terraces, some with views of the Hudson River or Central Park. The bar serves NYC-made drinks and snacks, and the uptown arm of acclaimed contemporary Chinese restaurant RedFarm is another strong pull.
2178 Broadway, at 77th Street, New York, NY 10024 (1-212 362 1100, www.nylohotels.com/nyc). Subway 1 to 79th Street. Rooms 285.

BUDGET

Broadway Hotel & Hostel
For those who have outgrown the no-frills backpacker experience but haven't quite graduated to a full-service hotel, the hybrid Broadway Hotel & Hostel, which has been given a 'boutique-style' makeover, fills the gap. On the ground floor, exposed brick, leather sofas and three large flatscreen TVs give the sprawling communal spaces a slick, urban veneer, but they still follow the traditional youth-hostel blueprint: TV room, shared kitchen, plus a computer area with eight credit card-operated terminals (if you have your own gadget, Wi-Fi is free). You won't find six-bed set-ups here, though: the cheapest option, the small, basic 'dormitory-style' rooms, jazzed up with mass-produced art and ceiling fans, accommodate two in bunk beds. The good-value 'semi-private' rooms offer a queen bed or two doubles/twins, with luxuries like down comforters and flatscreen TVs, but you'll have to use the (well-scrubbed) shared bathrooms. There are also en suite quarters. The Broadway provides free linens and towels and daily housekeeping service.

THE NEW 57
A midtown hotel boom is glamming up Carnegie Hall's staid strip.

Viceroy New York

When boutique hotels began springing up downtown in the 1990s and early noughties, cool-hunting visitors eschewed midtown for newly affluent neighbourhoods like Soho and Tribeca. But a cluster of sophisticated new properties on or around 57th Street signals a return to classic hotel luxury. Designed by Roman and Williams, **Viceroy New York** (*see p118*) has a cool midcentury vibe. In the snug standard quarters, custom-made iroko-wood cabinets flanking the bed evoke a first-class cabin back when ocean liners were glamorous. You'll find an Illy espresso maker tucked behind one of the tambour doors, while on the nightstand is a Beats by Dr Dre Beatbox Portable sound system that blows away standard iPod docks. The on-site American eaterie, Kingside, is helmed by Landmarc chef Marc Murphy.

The **Quin** (*see p118*) has an evocative past and some impressive perks. Less than a block from Carnegie Hall, the former Hotel Buckingham opened in 1929 and put up a colourful cast of divas and virtuosos. In the hotel's new incarnation, comforts and conveniences are to the fore. An automated system turns on the lights and raises the blinds as you open the door, and the cushy Dux by Duxiana bed is an insomniac's dream. Further treats include exclusive Fresh products in the roomy marble-tiled showers. **WestHouse** (*see p118*) aims to evoke an intimate townhouse atmosphere. The 1920s-inspired decor feels like a hotel to us, but rooms do feature residential-style touches like marble-topped desk-cum-vanity tables. Perhaps the most impressive perk is the concept of a blanket 'residents' fee' ($30 per day) that entitles you to Wi-Fi, breakfast, snacks, coffee and, best of all, unlimited drinks in the 'den' off the lobby or the 23rd-floor guests-only terrace.

230 W 101 Street, at Broadway, New York, NY 10024 (1-212 865 7710, www.broadwayhotelnyc.com). Subway 1, 2, 3 to 96th Street. Rooms 100.

HOSTELS

Hostelling International New York
This budget lodging is actually the city's only 'real' hostel (a non-profit accommodation that belongs to the International Youth Hostel Federation). The handsome gabled, Gothic-inspired brick and stone building – the largest hostel in America – spans the length of an entire city block. Most of the accommodation is in four- to 12-bed dorms, which are spare but clean and air-conditioned with immaculate shared bathrooms. There is also a handful of private rooms that sleep up to four with en-suite facilities and standard hotel amenities including a 32-inch plasma

TV, fridge and toiletries (but no in-room phone). You can get to know your fellow travellers in the on-site café, the large shared kitchen, and the backyard and patio. Linen and towels are free of charge, as is the property-wide Wi-Fi.
891 Amsterdam Avenue, at 103rd Street, New York, NY 10025 (1-212 932 2300, www.hinewyork.org). Subway 1 to 103rd Street. Rooms 672 beds in dorms; 5 private rooms.

Upper East Side

DELUXE

The Pierre
The 1930 landmark overlooking Central Park became part of the posh Indian Taj Hotels, Resorts and Palaces in 2005, setting in motion a $100-million overhaul – but it retains delightfully

old-fashioned elements such as elevator operators and original fireplaces in some suites. In contrast to the glitzy public spaces, including the mural-clad Rotunda and the Grand Ballroom, the classic rooms are understated, dressed in a neutral colour palette and immaculate upholstery, with modern gadgets including Bose radio/iPod docks. The sumptuous Turkish marble bathrooms are generously stocked with Molton Brown bath products. The Asian influence is reflected in silk bedspreads from Bangalore and contemporary Indian art.
2 E 61st Street, at Fifth Avenue, New York, NY 10065 (1-212 838 8000, www.tajhotels.com/thepierre). Subway N, Q, R to Fifth Avenue-59th Street. Rooms 189.

The Surrey
Occupying an elegant 1920s building given a $60 million overhaul, the Surrey pitches at both traditionalists and the trend-driven. The coolly elegant limestone and marble lobby showcases museum-quality contemporary art – by the likes of Chuck Close, Jenny Holzer and William Kentridge – and rooms are dressed in a refined palette of cream, grey and beige, with luxurious white marble bathrooms. But the centrepiece is undoubtedly the incredibly comfortable Dux by Duxiana bed, swathed in sumptuous Sferra linens. The hotel is flanked by top chef Daniel Boulud's Café Boulud and his chic cocktail destination, Bar Pleiades; there's also a luxurious spa.
20 E 76th Street, between Fifth & Madison Avenues, New York, NY 10021 (1-212 288 3700, www.thesurreyhotel.com). Subway 6 to 77th Street. Rooms 189.

MODERATE

Hotel Wales
Purpose-built as a hotel in the early 1900s, the ten-storey Wales is a comfortable, convenient choice close to Museum Mile and the posh shops of Madison Avenue. Standard double rooms are small, but high ceilings, large windows and an unfussy contemporary-classic style prevents them from seeming cramped; about half of the accommodation consists of suites. Guest quarters have been spruced up with designer wallpaper, sleek modern bathrooms and HD TVs. Higher-floor rooms on the east side have Central Park views, but all guests can enjoy them on the large roof terrace.
1295 Madison Avenue, at 92nd Street, New York, NY 10128 (1-212 876 6000, www.hotelwalesnyc.com). Subway 4, 5, 6 to 86th Street; 6 to 96th Street. Rooms 89.

Harlem

MODERATE

Aloft Harlem
Starwood Hotels' fast-expanding Aloft brand pitches to a young, design-conscious traveller whose budget might not stretch to a room at one of the company's W properties.

Hotels

Launched in December 2010, Aloft Harlem was the first hotel to open in the area since the early 1960s. The public spaces combine high-tech amenities (a pair of iMacs, in addition to free hotel-wide Wi-Fi) with colourful, contemporary decor (a scrolling news ticker above the elevators, a pool table in the lobby-lounge). Despite 275sq ft dimensions, standard quarters are outfitted with king-size beds and 42in flatscreen TVs, while bathrooms feature oversize rainfall showerheads and products created by W collaborator Bliss Spa. *2296 Frederick Douglass Boulevard (Eighth Avenue), between 123rd & 124th Streets, New York, NY 10027 (1-212 749 4000, www.alofthotels. com). Subway A, B, C, D, 2, 3 to 125th Street. Rooms 124.*

BUDGET

Harlem Flophouse

The dark-wood interior, moody lighting and lilting jazz make musician Rene Calvo's Harlem inn feel more like a 1930s speakeasy than a 21st-century B&B. The airy suites, named after Harlem Renaissance figures such as Chester Himes and Cozy Cole, have restored tin ceilings, a quirky mix of junk-store furnishings and period knick-knacks, and working sinks in antique cabinets. There are two suites per floor; each pair shares a bathroom. *242 W 123rd Street, between Adam Clayton Powell Jr Boulevard (Seventh Avenue) & Frederick Douglass Boulevard (Eighth Avenue), New York, NY 10027 (1-917 720 3707, www. harlemflophouse.com). Subway A, B, C, D to 125th Street. Rooms 4.*

Brooklyn

EXPENSIVE

King & Grove Williamsburg

Small boutique-hotel chain King & Grove, which operates an ironically retro retreat in Montauk, Long Island, brings resort style to Brooklyn. The place comes into its own in summer when the 40-foot saltwater pool opens to guests (and fee-paying locals) on the secluded back patio. The ninth-floor roof bar, furnished with cushion-strewn banquettes, comfy canvas sofas and rustic log stools, takes in an expansive panorama that includes McCarren Park across the street, the East River and Manhattan skyline. Guest rooms evoke midcentury minimalism with bamboo flooring, taupe leather platform beds, Frette linens and charcoal-grey accents. The Carrara-marble-tiled bathrooms are supplied with toiletries from NYC's Malin + Goetz. The hotel restaurant, the Elm, is helmed by Michelin-starred chef Paul Liebrandt. *160 North 12th Street, between Bedford Avenue & Berry Street, Williamsburg, Brooklyn, NY 11249 (1-718 218 7500, www.kingandgrove.com). Subway L to Bedford Avenue. Rooms 64. Other location 29 East 29th Street, between Madison & Park Avenues, Flatiron District (1-212 689 1900).*

MODERATE

Hotel Le Bleu

The Manhattanisation of Park Slope hit new heights in late 2007, when Andres Escobar's steel and glass hotel popped up on industrial Fourth Avenue. Couples may find the open shower design a plus point; more conventional draws include 42in plasma TVs with Bose system DVD/CD players, goose-down comforters, iPod docking stations and free Wi-Fi in every room. *370 Fourth Avenue, between 3rd & 5th Streets, Park Slope, Brooklyn, NY 11215 (1-718 625 1500, www.hotellebleu.com). Subway F, R to Fourth Avenue-9th Street; R to Union Street. Rooms 48.*

Nu Hotel

Conveniently placed for shops and restaurants, Nu Hotel has bundled quirky niceties into a classy, eco-friendly package. Rooms are decked out with wood flooring, organic linens and recycled teak furniture, 42in flatscreen TVs and Bluetooth-enabled iHome sound systems for wireless tunes. The standard accommodation is comfortably sized, but Friends Suites have bunk beds, and the lofty Urban Suites are outfitted with hammocks and a padded-leather sleeping alcove. Cyclists can borrow one of the hotel's loaner bikes to pedal around Brooklyn, and iPads are available for guest use.

The lobby bar offers a tapas menu by *Iron Chef* regular Jehangir Mehta. *85 Smith Street, between Atlantic Avenue & State Street, Boerum Hill, Brooklyn, NY 11201 (1-718 852 8585, www.nuhotelbrooklyn.com). Subway A, C, F to Jay Street-Borough Hall; F, G to Bergen Street; 2, 3, 4, 5 to Borough Hall. Rooms 93.*

HOSTELS

New York Loft Hostel

Set in an arty enclave, this budget lodging fuses the traditional youth hostel set-up (dorm-style rooms with single beds and lockers, communal lounging areas) with a fashionable loft aesthetic.

In the former clothing warehouse, linen curtains billow in front of huge windows, and there's plenty of industrial-chic exposed brick and piping. Above the big shared kitchen is a mezzanine equipped with a large flatscreen TV. The spacious patio is the site of free summer barbecues. There's no curfew; an electronic room-key card opens the front door after hours. *249 Varet Street, at Bogart Street, Bushwick, Brooklyn, New York, NY 11206 (1-718 366 1351, www.nyloft hostel.com). Subway L to Morgan Avenue. Rooms 100 beds in dorms; 31 private rooms.*

RECOMMENDED
Wythe Hotel

A 1901 cooperage near the waterfront topped with a three-storey glass-and-aluminium addition, the Wythe perfectly captures the neighbourhood's elusive hip factor. Since the launch team included Andrew Tarlow, the restaurateur behind popular local eateries Diner and Marlow & Sons, it's not surprising that the ground floor restaurant, Reynard, was an instant hit. In many of the guest rooms, floor-to-ceiling windows offer a panorama of the Manhattan skyline. Heated concrete floors, exposed brick, reclaimed-timber beds and witty custom wallpaper create a rustic-industrial vibe, offset by fully plugged-in technology: a cable by the bed turns your iPhone into a surround-sound music system. For non-couple travelling companions, compact bunk rooms are equipped with individual TVs, and some even have cute terraces. 80 Wythe Avenue, at North 11th Street, Williamsburg, Brooklyn, NY 11249 (1-718 460 8000, www.wythehotel.com). Subway L to Bedford Avenue. Rooms 72.

Queens

MODERATE

Ravel

Converted from a motel, Ravel has a vaguely 1960s feel, reflected in the lobby's cream leatherette seating and silver-bubble ceiling light. An 8,000sq ft rooftop restaurant-bar has dazzling views of midtown and hosts film screenings, DJ nights and other events. Rooms dwarf those of similarly priced hotels in Manhattan, and most (many with private balconies) face the river – although a Con-Edison facility directly below is less than picturesque. *8-08 Queens Plaza South, at Vernon Boulevard, Long Island City Queens, NY 11101 (1-718 289 6101, www. ravelhotel.com). Subway E, M, R to Queens Plaza; F to 21st Street-Queensbridge; N, Q, 7 to Queensboro Plaza. Rooms 63.*

> **TOP TIP!**
> **Home from home**
> For a budget option with a personal touch, consider a B&B. City Sonnet (1-212 614 3034, www.city sonnet.com) can set you up with a room from $135 a night.

Z NYC Hotel

The Z shares a gritty industrial side street with tool suppliers and flooring wholesalers, but the Queensboro Bridge-side setting and largely low-rise neighbours facilitate its most stunning feature: knock-your-socks-off Manhattan views through floor-to-ceiling windows. Offbeat details in the rooms, such as lightbulbs encased in mason jars dangling over the bed and black flip-flops instead of the standard white slippers, enliven the stock boutique luxury of the accommodation. The sprawling roof bar offers 360-degree panoramas. *11-01 43rd Avenue, at 11th Street, Long Island City, Queens, NY 11101 (1-212 319 7000, www. zhotelny.com). Subway E, M to Court Square-23rd Street; F to 21st Street-Queensbridge; N, Q, 7 to Queensboro Plaza. Rooms 100.*

The Bronx

MODERATE

Opera House Hotel

The Bronx Opera House once showcased the Marx Brothers and Harry Houdini. Now a hotel, the striking 1913 structure is still a draw for theatre lovers – it's a mere 20-minute subway ride from the Great White Way, yet prices are a fraction of what you'd pay for similar digs in midtown. Ranging from about 275 to 450sq ft, rooms feature either one king-size or two queen beds. The decor isn't trendy, but comparable to an upscale chain hotel; all quarters are equipped with a refrigerator, microwave, flatscreen TV, iHome iPod dock and free Wi-Fi. *436 E 149th Street, between Bergen & Brook Avenues, Bronx, NY 10455 (1-718 407 2800, www.operahouse hotel.com). Subway 2, 5 to Third Avenue-149th Street. Rooms 60.*

Hotels

Directory

Everything you need to know

Directory

Getting Around

Arriving & leaving

BY AIR

John F Kennedy International Airport
The **subway** (*see right*) is the cheapest option from JFK. The **AirTrain** ($5, www.airtrainjfk.com) links to the A train at Howard Beach or the E, J and Z trains at Sutphin Boulevard-Archer Avenue ($2.50-$2.75). **NYC Airporter** buses (1-718 777 5111, www.nycairporter.com; one way $16, round trip $29) connect JFK and Manhattan, with stops near Grand Central Terminal, Penn Station and Port Authority Bus Terminal. Buses run every 30mins from 5am to 11.30pm daily. **SuperShuttle** (1-800 258 3826, www.supershuttle. com) vans offer door-to-door service between NYC and the major airports.

A **yellow cab** to Manhattan will charge a flat $52.50 fare, plus toll (usually $5) and tip (15 per cent is the norm). The fare to JFK from Manhattan is not a set rate, but is usually roughly the same (*see p123*). *1-718 244 4444, www.panynj.gov/airports/jfk.html.*

La Guardia Airport
Seasoned New Yorkers take the **M60 bus** ($2.50) to 106th Street at Broadway. The ride takes 40-60mins, depending on traffic, and buses run 24hrs daily. The route crosses Manhattan at 125th Street in Harlem. Get off at Lexington Avenue for the 4, 5 and 6 trains; at Malcolm X Boulevard (Lenox Avenue) for the 2 and 3; or at St Nicholas Avenue for the A, B, C and D trains.

Less time-consuming options include **NYC Airporter** buses (*see above*; one way $13, round trip $23). **Taxis** and **car services** charge about $30, plus toll and tip. *1-718 533 3400, www.panynj.gov/airports/laguardia.html.*

Newark Liberty International Airport
The best bet is the $12.50, half-hour trip via **New Jersey Transit** to or from Penn Station. The airport's monorail, **AirTrain Newark** (www.airtrainnewark.com), links to the New Jersey Transit and Amtrak train systems.

Bus services operated by **Coach USA** (1-877 894 9155, www.coach usa.com) run to Manhattan, stopping at Bryant Park in midtown, and inside the Port Authority Bus Terminal (one way $16, round trip $28); buses leave every 15-30mins. A **car** or **taxi** will run at $60-$75, plus toll and tip. *1-973 961 6000, www.panynj.gov/airports/newark-liberty.html.*

BY BUS

Most out-of-town buses come and go from the Port Authority Bus Terminal. **Greyhound** (1-800 231 2222, www.greyhound.com) runs long-distance travel to US destinations. The company's **BoltBus** (1-877 265 8287, www.boltbus.com), booked online, serves several East Coast cities. **New Jersey Transit** (1-973 275 5555, www.njtransit.com) runs services to most of New Jersey and parts of New York State. Finally, **Peter Pan** (1-800 343 9999, www.peterpanbus.com) runs extensive services to cities across the North-east; its tickets are also valid on Greyhound buses.

Port Authority Bus Terminal
625 Eighth Avenue, between 40th & 42nd Streets, Garment District (1-212 564 8484, www.panynj.gov/bus-terminals/port-authority-bus-terminal.html). Subway A, C, E to 42nd Street-Port Authority.

BY RAIL

America's national rail service is run by **Amtrak** (1-800 872 7245, www.amtrak.com). Nationwide routes are slow and infrequent (yet full of character), but there are some good fast services linking the eastern seaboard cities. (For commuter rail services, *see right* **Public transport: Rail**).

Grand Central Terminal
Grand Central is home to Metro-North, which runs trains to more than 100 stations in New York State and Connecticut.
42nd to 44th Streets, between Vanderbilt & Lexington Avenues, Midtown East. Subway S, 4, 5, 6, 7 to 42nd Street-Grand Central.

Penn Station
Amtrak, Long Island Rail Road and New Jersey Transit trains depart from this terminal.
31st to 33rd Streets, between Seventh & Eighth Avenues, Garment District. Subway A, C, E, 1, 2, 3 to 34th Street-Penn Station.

Public transport

Changes to schedules can occur at short notice, especially at weekends – check the MTA's website before travelling and pay attention to the posters on subway station walls and announcements on trains and subway platforms.

Metropolitan Transportation Authority (MTA)
The MTA runs the subway and bus lines, as well as services to points outside Manhattan. News of service interruptions and MTA maps are on its website. Be warned: backpacks, handbags and large containers may be subject to random searches.
511 local, 1-877 690 5116 outside New York State, 1-212 878 7000 international, www.mta.info.

FARES & TICKETS

Although you can pay with exact change (no dollar bills) on buses, to enter the subway system you'll need either a single-ride ticket ($2.75, available from station vending machines only) or a **MetroCard**. You can buy MetroCards from booths or vending machines in the stations, from the Official NYC Information Center (*see p125*), from the New York Transit Museum in Brooklyn (*see p42*) or Grand Central Terminal (*see left*), and from many hotels.

The standard base fare across the subway and bus network on a MetroCard is $2.50. Free transfers between the subway and buses are available only with a MetroCard (for bus-to-bus transfers on cash fares, *see right*). Up to four people can use a pay-per-ride MetroCard, sold in denominations from $5 to $80. If you put $5 or more on the card, you'll receive a five per cent bonus – or 25 cents for every $5 – thus reducing the cost of each ride. However, if you're planning to use the subway or buses often, an Unlimited Ride MetroCard is great value. These cards are offered in two denominations, available at station vending machines but not at booths: a seven-day pass ($30) and a 30-day pass ($112). Both are good for unlimited rides within those periods, but you can't share a card with your travelling companions.

SUBWAY

Cleaner and safer than it has been for decades, the city's subway system is one of the world's largest and cheapest. (For information on MetroCards and fares, *see above*.) Trains run around the clock. If you are travelling late at night, board the train from the designated off-peak waiting area, usually near the middle of the platform; this is more secure than the ends of the platform, which are often less populated in the wee hours.

Stations are most often named after the street on which they're located. Entrances are marked with a green and white globe (open 24 hours) or a red and white globe (limited hours). Many stations have separate entrances for the uptown and downtown platforms – look before you pay. Trains are identified by letters or numbers, colour-coded according to the line on which they run. Local trains stop at every station on the line; express trains stop at major stations only.

The New York City subway map is reproduced on p128 of this guide; you can also ask MTA staff in service booths for a free copy, or refer to enlarged maps displayed in each subway station.

CITY BUSES

White and blue MTA buses are usually the best way to travel crosstown and a pleasant way to travel up- or downtown, as long as you're not in a hurry. They have a digital destination sign on the front, along with a route number preceded by a letter (M for Manhattan, B for Brooklyn, Bx for the Bronx, Q for Queens and S for Staten Island). Maps are posted on most buses and at all subway stops; they're also available from the Official NYC Information Center (*see p125*). All local buses are equipped with wheelchair lifts.

The fare is payable with a MetroCard (*see left*) or exact change ($2.50 in coins only; no pennies or dollar bills). MetroCards allow for an automatic transfer from bus to bus, and between bus and subway. If you pay cash, and you're travelling uptown or downtown and want to go crosstown (or vice versa), ask the driver for a transfer when you get on – you'll be given a ticket for use on the second leg of your journey, valid for two hours. MTA's express buses usually head to the outer boroughs for a $6 fare.

RAIL

The following commuter trains serve New York's hinterland.

Long Island Rail Road
The LIRR provides rail services from Manhattan's Penn Station, Brooklyn and Queens to towns throughout Long Island.
511 local, 1-718 217 5477 outside New York State, www.mta.info/lirr.

Metro-North Railroad
Commuter trains serve towns north of Manhattan and leave from Grand Central Terminal.
511 local, 1-212 532 4900 outside New York State, www.mta.info/mnr.

New Jersey Transit

Service from Penn Station reaches most of New Jersey, some points in New York State and Philadelphia. *1-973 275 5555, www.njtransit.com.*

PATH Trains

PATH (Port Authority Trans-Hudson) trains run from six stations in Manhattan to various New Jersey destinations, including Hoboken, Jersey City and Newark. The 24-hour service costs $2.50. *1-800 234 7284, www.panynj.gov/path.*

BOAT

NY Waterway (1-800 533 3779, www.nywaterway.com) runs a water-transport service that connects Manhattan to Queens, Brooklyn and some New Jersey cities. The East River Ferry runs between Midtown East at 34th Street and downtown Manhattan at Pier 11, via Long Island City in Queens and Greenpoint, Williamsburg and Dumbo in Brooklyn (from $4 one way, $12 day pass). On the West Side of the island, NY Waterway's Hudson River ferries link Pier 79 on 39th Street and Brookfield Place in lower Manhattan to destinations in New Jersey, including Hoboken and Jersey City ($7-$21.50 one-way). Visit the website for routes and schedules.

In addition to its hop-on hop-off service and tours, **New York Water Taxi** (*see right*) offers a popular shuttle service connecting Pier 11 in Manhattan and IKEA in Red Hook, Brooklyn (2-8pm Mon-Fri; 11.20am-9.20pm Sat, Sun). The $5 fare is waived on weekends and for children under 12.

Taxis

If the centre light atop the taxi is lit, the cab is available and should stop if you flag it down. Get in before telling the driver where you're going. (New Yorkers generally give cross-streets rather than addresses.) By law, taxis cannot refuse to take you anywhere inside the five boroughs or to New York airports. Green Boro Taxis serving the outer boroughs can now be hailed on the street in the Bronx, Queens (excluding airports), Brooklyn, Staten Island and Manhattan north of West 110th and East 96th Streets. Use only yellow or green medallion (licensed) cabs.

Taxis will carry up to four passengers for the same price: $2.50 plus 50¢ per fifth of a mile or per minute idling, with an extra 50¢ charge (a new state tax), another 50¢ from 8pm to 6am and a $1 surcharge during rush hour (4-8pm Mon-Fri). The average fare for a three-mile ride is $14, but this will vary depending on the time and traffic.

If you have a problem, take down the medallion and driver's numbers, posted on the partition. Always ask for a receipt – there's a meter number on it. To complain or to trace lost property, call the Taxi &

Limousine Commission (1-212 227 0700, 8.30am-5pm Mon-Fri) or visit www.nyc.gov/taxi. Tip 15-20 per cent, as in a restaurant. All taxis now accept major credit cards.

CAR SERVICES

Car services are regulated by the Taxi & Limousine Commission. Unlike cabs, drivers can make only pre-arranged pickups. Don't try to hail one, and be wary of those that offer you a ride. These companies will pick you up anywhere in the city for a set fare.

Carmel *1-212 666 6666.*
Dial 7 *1-212 777 7777.*
GroundLink *1-877 227 7260.*

Driving

CAR HIRE

You need a credit card to rent a car in the US, and usually must be at least 25 years old. Car hire is cheaper in the city's outskirts and further afield than in Manhattan. NYC companies add 19.875 per cent in taxes. If you just want a car for a few hours, **Zipcar** (US: 1-866 494 7227, www.zipcar.com; UK: 0333 240 9000, www.zipcar.co.uk) is cost-effective.

Alamo
US: 1-877 222 9075, www.alamo.com. UK: 0871 384 1086, www.alamo.co.uk.

Avis
US: 1-800 230 4898, www.avis.com. UK: 0844 581 0147, www.avis.co.uk.

Budget
US: 1-800 527 0700, www.budget.com. UK: 0844 581 2231, www.budget.co.uk.

Enterprise
US: 1-800 261 7331, www.enterprise. com. UK: 0800 800 227, www.enterprise.co.uk.

Hertz
US: 1-800 654 3131, www.hertz.com. UK: 0843 309 3099, www.hertz.co.uk.

PARKING

Make sure you read parking signs and never park within 15 feet of a fire hydrant (to avoid a $115 ticket and/or having your car towed). Parking is off-limits on most streets for at least a few hours daily. The Department of Transportation provides information on daily changes to regulations (dial 311). If precautions fail, call 1-212 971 0771 for Manhattan towing and impoundment information; go to www.nyc.gov for phone numbers in other boroughs.

Cycling

While biking on NYC's streets is only recommended for experienced cyclists, the new **Citi Bike** system (www.citibikenyc.com, 1-855 245 3311) gives you temporary access to

bikes at 600 stations in Manhattan and Brooklyn. Visitors can purchase a 24-hour ($9.95) or three-day ($25) Access Pass at a station kiosk with a credit or debit card. You'll then receive a 'ride code' that will allow you to undock and ride for 30 minutes at a stretch. A longer trip will incur an extra fee.

The evolving Manhattan Waterfront Greenway, a 32-mile route that circumnavigates the island of Manhattan, is a fantastic asset: you can ride, uninterrupted, along the Hudson River from Battery Park up to the George Washington Bridge, at 178th Street. The free **NYC Cycling Map**, covering cycle lanes in all five boroughs, is available from the Department of City Planning Bookstore (22 Reade Street, between Broadway & Elk Street, Civic Center, 1-212 720 3667, open noon-4pm Mon, 10am-1pm Tue-Fri), or you can download it from www.nyc.gov/planning. **Bike and Roll** (1-212 260 0400, www.bikeandroll.com/newyork) is the city's biggest cycle-hire company, with 11 outposts. Rates (incl helmet) start at $10 per hour.

Walking

One of the best ways to take in NYC is on foot. Most of the streets are laid out in a grid pattern and are relatively easy to navigate.

Tours

BIKE TOURS

Bike the Big Apple
Licensed guides lead cyclists through historic and newly hip 'hoods: tours include Harlem (the 'Sensational Park and Soul' tour), Chinatown ('From High Finance to Hidden Chinatown') and a twilight ride across the Brooklyn Bridge. *1-877 865 0078, www.bikethebig apple.com. Tickets (incl bicycle & helmet rental) $80-$99.*

BOAT TOURS

Circle Line Cruises
The Circle Line's famed three-hour guided circumnavigation of Manhattan Island ($38; $25-$33 reductions) is a fantastic way to get your bearings and see many of the city's sights. The company also has a roster of themed tours. The separately run **Circle Line Downtown** (Pier 16, South Street Seaport, 1-212 742 1969, www.circlelinedowntown.com) has a more intimate vessel, the Zephyr, for tours of lower Manhattan (Apr-Dec, $30, $19 reductions). The two companies' rival speedboats – Circle Line's Beast (May-Sept, $27, $21 reductions) and Circle Line Downtown's Shark (May-Sept, $28, $19 reductions) – offer fun, adrenalin-inducing and splashy 30-minute rides. *Pier 83, 42nd Street, at the Hudson River, Hell's Kitchen (1-212 563 3200, www.circleline42.com). Subway A,*

C, E to 42nd Street-Port Authority. Tickets $27-$38; $21-$33 reductions.

New York Water Taxi
New York water taxis are also bright yellow, but unlike cabs, they run on a set schedule. You can hop on and off with a day pass ($28, $16 reductions), enjoying neighbourhood attractions along the way. *1-212 742 1969, www.nywater taxi.com. Tickets $28-$35; $16-$25 reductions.*

BUS TOURS

Gray Line
Gray Line offers more than 20 tours, from a two-hour ride (with 40-plus hop-on, hop-off stops) to the guided 'Classic New York' tour, which includes lunch, admission to Top of the Rock or the Empire State Building, and a boat ride to Ellis Island and the Statue of Liberty. *777 Eighth Avenue, at 48th Street, Theater District (1-212 445 0848, www.newyorksightseeing.com). Subway A, C, E to 42nd Street-Port Authority; C, E to 50th Street; N, Q, R to 49th Street. Tickets $39-$120.*

WALKING TOURS

Big Onion Walking Tours
New York was known as the Big Onion before it became the Big Apple. The tour guides will explain why, and they should know – all guides hold advanced degrees in history (or a related field). Among the offerings is the 'Official Gangs of New York' walk and a weekly 'Multi-Ethnic Eating Tour' that explores the history of the Lower East Side, Chinatown and Little Italy with a little cuisine sampling along the way. *1-888 606 9255, www.bigonion.com. Tickets $18-$40; $15-$28 reductions.*

Boroughs of the Dead
Horror writer Andrea Janes, author of *Boroughs of the Dead: New York City Ghost Stories*, explores the dark side of various neighbourhoods, and offers a spine-tingling tour of Brooklyn's Green-Wood Cemetery. *1-212 209 3370, www.boroughs ofthedead.com. Tickets $20-$25.*

City Running Tours
Guided four- to 26-mile city jogs. *1-877 415 0058, www.cityrunning tours.com. Tickets from $35 group tour; $75 individual tour.*

Municipal Art Society Tours
Walking tours led by architects, art historians and others reflect the society's focus on contemporary architecture, urban planning and historic preservation. *1-212 935 3960, www.mas.org/ tours. Tickets $20.*

Urban Oyster
Food-centric expeditions such as 'Brewed in Brooklyn' ($65), which illuminates the borough's suds-making legacy, and a 'Tenement, Tales and Taste' tour ($65) of the Lower East Side. *1-347 618-8687, www.urbanoyster. com. Tickets $60-$85 (incl food & drink).*

Resources A-Z

Addresses

Addresses follow the standard US format. The room, apartment or suite number usually appears after the street address, followed on the next line by the name of the city and the zip code.

Age restrictions

Buying/drinking alcohol 21.
Driving 16.
Sex 17.
Smoking 18.

Customs

US Customs allows foreigners to bring in $100 worth of gifts (the limit is $800 for returning Americans) without paying duty. One carton of 200 cigarettes (or 100 cigars) and one litre of liquor (spirits) are allowed. Plants, meat and fresh produce of any kind cannot be brought into the country. You will have to fill out a form if you carry more than $10,000 in currency. You will be handed a white form on your inbound flight to fill in, confirming that you haven't exceeded any of these allowances.

If you need to bring prescription drugs into the US, make sure the container is clearly marked, and bring your doctor's statement or a prescription. Marijuana, cocaine and most opiate derivatives, along with a number of other drugs and chemicals, are not permitted: the possession is punishable by a stiff fine and/or imprisonment. Check in with the US Customs and Border Protection Service (www.cbp.gov) before you arrive if you're unsure.

HM Revenue & Customs allows returning visitors to the UK to bring £390 worth of 'gifts, souvenirs and other goods' into the country duty-free, along with the usual duty-free goods.

Disabled

Under New York City law, facilities constructed after 1987 must provide complete access for the disabled – restrooms, entrances and exits included. In 1990, the Americans with Disabilities Act made the same requirement federal law. Many older buildings have added disabled-access features. There has been widespread compliance with the law, but call ahead to check facilities.

For information on accessible cultural institutions, contact the Mayor's Office for People with Disabilities (*see above right*). All Broadway theatres are equipped with devices for the hearing-impaired; call **Sound Associates** (1-888 772 7686, www.sound associates.com) for more information. For the visually impaired, **HAI** (1-212 284 4100, www.hainyc.org) offers live audio descriptions of selected theatre performances.

Lighthouse International

In addition to running a store that sells handy items for the vision-impaired, Lighthouse provides helpful information for blind people (residents and visitors). *111 E 59th Street, between Park & Lexington Avenues, Upper East Side (1-212 821 9200, 1-212 821 9384 store, www.lighthouse.org). Subway N, R to Lexington Avenue-59th Street; 4, 5, 6 to 59th Street. Open 9am-5pm Mon-Fri. Store 10am-5.30pm Mon-Fri.*

Mayor's Office for People with Disabilities

This city office provides a broad range of services for the disabled. *2nd Floor, 100 Gold Street, between Frankfort & Spruce Streets, Financial District (1-212 788 2830). Subway J, Z to Chambers Street; 4, 5, 6 to Brooklyn Bridge-City Hall. Open 9am-5pm Mon-Fri.*

New York Society for the Deaf

Information and a range of services for the deaf and hearing-impaired. *315 Hudson Street, between Vandam & Spring Streets, Soho (1-212 366 0066, www.fegs.org). Subway C, E to Spring Street; 1 to Houston Street. Open 8.30am-7pm Mon-Thur; 8.30am-5pm Fri.*

Society for Accessible Travel & Hospitality

This non-profit group educates the public about travel facilities for people with disabilities, and promotes travel for the disabled. Membership ($49/yr; $29 reductions) includes access to an information service and a quarterly newsletter. *1-212 447 7284, www.sath.org.*

Embassies & Consulates

Check the phone book or look online for details of the embassies and consulates of additional countries.

Australia *1-212 351 6500.*
Canada *1-212 596 1628.*
Great Britain *1-212 745 0200.*
Ireland *1-212 319 2555.*
New Zealand *1-212 832 4038.*

Internet

Cycle Café

A bike-rental shop and internet café rolled into one. *250 W 49th Street, between Broadway & Eighth Avenue, Theater District (1-212 380 1204, www.cycle-cafe.com).*

Subway C, E, 1 to 50th Street; N, Q, R to 49th Street. Open 8am-midnight daily. Cost from $3.15/15mins.

FedEx Office

Outposts of this ubiquitous and very efficient computer and copy centre are peppered throughout the city; many are open 24 hours a day. *1-800 463 3339, www.fedex.com.*

New York Public Library

Branches of the NYPL are great places to get online for free, offering both Wi-Fi and computers for public use. (Ask for an out-of-state card, for which you need proof of residence, or a guest pass.) The **Science, Industry & Business Library** (188 Madison Avenue, at 34th Street, Midtown East), part of the Public Library system, has about 70 computers. All libraries have a computer limit of 45 minutes per day. *1-212 592 7000, www.nypl.org.*

NYCWireless

This group has established dozens of hotspots in the city for free Wi-Fi access. (For example, most parks below 59th Street are covered.) Visit the website for information and a map. *www.nycwireless.net.*

Starbucks

Many branches offer free Wi-Fi; the website has a search facility. *www.starbucks.com.*

Left Luggage

There are luggage-storage facilities at arrivals halls in **JFK Airport** (Terminal 1: 7am-11pm, $4-$16 per bag per day; call 1-718 751 2947); (Terminal 4: 24hrs, $4-$16 per bag per day; call 1-718 751 4020). At **Penn Station**, Amtrak offers checked baggage services for a small fee for some of its ticketed passengers. Due to heightened security, luggage storage is not available at the Port Authority Bus Terminal, Grand Central, or LaGuardia or Newark airports.

One Midtown alternative is to leave bags with the private firm, located between Penn Station and Port Authority, listed below. Some hotels may allow you to leave suitcases with the front desk before check-in or after check-out; if so, be sure to tip the concierge.

Schwartz Travel Services

2nd Floor, 355 W 36th Street, between Eighth & Ninth Avenues (1-212 290 2626, www.schwartztravel.com). Open 8am-11pm daily. Rates $7-$10 per bag per day. No credit cards. Other location 4th Floor, 34 W 46th Street, between Fifth & Sixth Avenues (same phone).

Lost Property

For lost credit cards or travellers' cheques, see p125.

Grand Central Terminal

You can call 24 hrs a day to file a claim if you've left something on a Metro-North train. *Lower level, near Track 100 (1-212 532 4900). Open 7am-6pm Mon-Fri.*
JFK Airport *1-718 244 4225, or contact your airline.*
La Guardia Airport *1-718 533 3988, or contact your airline.*
Newark Liberty International Airport *1-973 961 6243, or contact your airline.*
Penn Station: Amtrak *1-212 630 7389. Open 6am-2.30pm daily.*
Penn Station: Long Island Rail Road *1-718 217 5477. Open 24hrs.*
Penn Station: New Jersey Transit *1-973 275 5555. Open 6am-10pm Mon-Fri; 8am-8pm Sat; 9am-8pm Sun.*

Subway & Buses

Visit or call if you've left something on a subway train or a bus. *New York City Metropolitan Transit Authority, 34th Street-Penn Station, near the A train platform, Garment District (call 511). Open 8am-3.30pm Mon, Tue, Fri; 11am-6.30pm Wed, Thur.*
Taxis Call the all-purpose city-services number, 311, to track down items left in a cab. *www.nyc.gov/taxi.*

Money

Over the past few years, much of American currency has undergone a subtle facelift, partly to deter increasingly adept counterfeiters; all denominations except the $1 bill have recently been updated by the US Treasury. (However, 'old' money still remains in circulation.) Coins include copper pennies (1¢) and silver-coloured nickels (5¢), dimes (10¢) and quarters (25¢). Half-dollar coins (50¢) and the gold-coloured dollar coins are less common.

All paper money is the same size, so make sure you fork over the right bill. It comes in denominations of $1, $2, $5, $10, $20, $50 and $100 (and higher, but you'll never see those bills). The $2 bills are quite rare. Try to keep some low notes on you because getting change may be a problem with anything bigger than a $20 bill.

ATMs

The city is full of ATMs – in bank branches, delis and many small shops. Most accept Visa, MasterCard and major bank cards. Some UK banks charge up to £4 per transaction plus a variable payment to cover themselves against exchange rate fluctuations. Most ATM cards now double as debit cards, if they bear Maestro or Cirrus logos.

BANKS & BUREAUX DE CHANGE

Banks are generally open from 9am to 6pm Monday to Friday, though some stay open longer and/or on Saturdays. You need photo ID, such as a passport, to cash travellers' cheques. Many banks will not exchange foreign currency; many bureaux de change, limited to tourist-trap areas, close at around 6pm or 7pm. In emergencies, most large hotels offer 24-hour exchange facilities, but the rates won't be great.

CREDIT CARDS & TRAVELLERS' CHQUES
Credit cards are essential for renting cars and booking hotels, and handy for buying tickets over the phone and the internet. The five major cards accepted in the US are American Express, Diners Club, Discover, MasterCard and Visa.

MasterCard and Visa are the most popular; American Express is also widely accepted. Thanks to a 2004 deal between MasterCard and Diners Club, all businesses that accept the former can now in theory accept the latter, though in practice many business are unaware of this and may not comply.

If your cards or travellers' cheques are lost or stolen, call the following numbers:

American Express
1-800 528 2122, 1-800 221 7282 travellers' cheques.
Diners Club *1-800 234 6377.*
Discover *1-800 347 2683.*
Mastercard/Maestro
1-800 826 2181, 1-800 223 9920 travellers' cheques.
Visa/Cirrus
1-800 336 8472, 1-800 336 8472 travellers' cheques.

TAX
Sales tax is 8.875 per cent in New York City, and is applicable to restaurant bills, services and the purchase of just about anything, except most store-bought foods, clothing and shoes under $110.

In the US, sales tax is almost never included in the price of the item, but added on to the final bill at the till. There is no tax refund option for foreign visitors.

WIRE SERVICES
Funds can be wired from home through the following companies:

Moneygram *1-800 666 3947, www.moneygram.com.*
Western Union *1-800 325 6000, www.westernunion.com.*

Postal Services

Stamps are available at all US post offices, from drugstore vending machines and at most newsstands. It costs 49¢ to send a 1oz letter within the US. Each additional ounce costs 21¢. Postcards mailed within the US cost 34¢. Airmailed letters or postcards to Canada and Mexico cost 85¢ for the first ounce. The Global Forever Stamp ($1.15) can be used to send a postcard or 1oz letter anywhere in the world.

For faster Express Mail, you must fill out a form, either at a post office or by arranging a pick-up; 24-hour delivery to major US cities is guaranteed. International delivery takes two to three days, with no guarantee. Call 1-800 275 8777 for more information.

James A Farley Post Office
In addition to operating a counter service, NYC's general post office has automated self-service machines for buying stamps and posting packages around the clock.
421 Eighth Avenue, between 31st & 33rd Streets, Garment District (1-212 330 3296, 1-800 275 8777 24hr information, www.usps.com). Subway A, C, E to 34th Street-Penn Station. Open 24 hrs daily. Counter service 7am-10pm Mon-Fri; 9am-9pm Sat; 11am-7pm Sun.

General Delivery
US residents without local addresses and foreign visitors can receive their post here; it should be addressed to the recipient, General Delivery, 390 Ninth Avenue, New York, NY 10001. You will need to show a passport or ID card when picking up letters.
390 Ninth Avenue, between 31st & 33rd Streets, Garment District (1-212 330 3099). Subway A, C, E to 34th Street-Penn Station. Open 10am-1pm Mon-Fri; 10am-noon Sat.

Telephones

DIALLING & CODES
As a rule, you must dial 1 + the area code before a number, even if the place you are calling is in the same area code. The area codes for Manhattan are 212 and 646; Brooklyn, Queens, Staten Island and the Bronx are 718 and 347; 917 is now reserved mostly for mobile phones and pagers. Long Island area codes are 516 and 631; codes for New Jersey are 201, 551, 609, 732, 848, 856, 862, 908 and 973. Numbers preceded by 800, 877 and 888 are free of charge when dialled from within the US.

In an emergency, dial 911. All calls are free (including those from pay and mobile phones).

For the operator, dial 0. If you're not used to US phones, then note that the ringing tone is long; the engaged tone, or 'busy signal', consists of much shorter, higher pitched beeps.

Collect calls are also known as reverse-charge calls. To make one, dial 0 followed by the number, or dial AT&T's 1-800 225 5288, Sprint's 1-800 663 3463, or the aptly named 1-800-Collect's 1-800 265 5328.

For directory assistance, dial 411 or 1 + area code + 555 1212. Doing so may cost nothing, depending on the pay phone you are using; carrier fees may apply. Long-distance directory assistance may also incur long-distance charges. For a directory of toll-free numbers, dial 1-800 555 1212.

For international calls, dial 011 + country code (Australia 61; New Zealand 64; UK 44), then the number (omitting any initial zero).

MOBILE PHONES
Most US mobile phones will work in NYC, but since the US doesn't have a standard national network, visitors should check with their provider that their phone will work here, and whether they need to unlock a roaming option. Visitors from other countries will need a tri-band handset and a roaming agreement, and may find charges so high that rental or purchase of a US phone (or SIM card) will make better economic sense. Phones can be hired from Jojo Talk (www.jojotalk.com).

If you carry a mobile phone, make sure you turn it off in museums and restaurants, and at plays, movies and concerts. New Yorkers are quick to show their annoyance at an ill-timed ring. Some establishments now even post signs designating a cellular-free zone.

PUBLIC PHONES
Functioning public pay phones are becoming increasingly hard to find. Phones take any combination of silver coins: local calls usually cost 50¢ for three minutes. To call long-distance or to make an international call from a pay phone, you need to go through a long-distance company. Most of the pay phones in New York automatically use AT&T, but phones in and around transportation hubs usually contract other long-distance carriers, and charges can be outrageous. MCI and Sprint are respected brand names.

Make the call by either dialling 0 for an operator or dialling direct, which is cheaper. To find out how much it will cost, dial the number, and a computerised voice will tell you how much money to deposit. You can pay for calls with your credit card. The best way to make long-distance calls is with a phone card, available from any post office branch, many newsagents and delis, or from chain stores such as Duane Reade and Rite Aid.

Time

New York is on Eastern Standard Time, which extends from the Atlantic coast to the eastern shore of Lake Michigan and south to the Gulf of Mexico. This is five hours behind Greenwich Mean Time. Clocks are set forward one hour in early March for Daylight Saving Time (Eastern Daylight Time) and back one hour at the beginning of November. Going from east to west, Eastern Time is one hour ahead of Central Time, two hours ahead of Mountain Time and three hours ahead of Pacific Time.

In the United States, the date is written as month, day and year; so 6/9/14 is 9 June 2014. Forms that foreigners may need to fill in, however, are often the other way round.

Tipping

In restaurants, it's customary to tip at least 15 per cent, and since NYC tax is 8.875 per cent, a quick way to calculate the tip is to double the tax. In many restaurants, when you are with a group of six or more, the tip will be included in the bill. For tipping on taxi fares, *see p123*.

Tourist Information

Official NYC Information Center
The city's official (private, non-profit) visitors' information centre recently got a high-tech renovation, complete with interactive map tables that allow visitors to navigate the city's attractions, hotels and restaurants, and send your itineraries to your email address or mobile device. The centre also doles out maps, leaflets, coupons and advice; and sells MetroCards and tickets to attractions such as Top of the Rock, the Statue of Liberty and the Empire State Building, potentially saving you time waiting in line. For other locations and information kiosks around the city, go to www.nycgo.com/articles/official-nyc-information-centers.
810 Seventh Avenue, between 52nd & 53rd Streets, Theater District (1-212 484 1222, www.nycgo.com). Subway B, D, E to Seventh Avenue. Open 8.30am-6pm Mon-Fri; 9am-5pm Sat, Sun. Other locations throughout the city.

Brooklyn Tourism & Visitors Center
A wealth of information on attractions, sights and events in the borough, plus local-interest books and gifts.
Brooklyn Borough Hall, 209 Joralemon Street, between Court & Adams Streets (1-718 802 3846, www.visitbrooklyn.org). Subway A, C, F to Jay Street-Borough Hall; R to Court Street; 2, 3, 4, 5, to Borough Hall. Open 10am-6pm Mon-Fri.

Websites

www.timeout.com/newyork
The *Time Out New York* website covers all the city has to offer, from upcoming museum exhibitions, shows and events to the latest shop openings, plus thousands of restaurant and bar reviews written by our critics.
www.clubplanet.com
Follow the city's nocturnal scene and buy tickets to big events.
www.forgotten-ny.com
Discover old New York here.

www.hopstop.com
Works out door-to-door directions on public transportation.
www.manhattanusersguide.com
An insiders' guide to what's going on around town.
www.mta.info
Subway and bus service news.
www.nyc.gov
City Hall's official New York City website has lots of useful links.
www.nycgo.com
The official New York City tourism organisation provides information on sights, attractions, hotels, restaurants, shops and more.
www.nytimes.com
'All the News That's Fit to Print' from the *New York Times* (limited access for non-subscribers).

Emergencies

In an emergency only, dial **911** for an ambulance, the police or the fire department, or call the operator (dial 0).

Health

Public health care is virtually nonexistent in the US, and private health care is very expensive. Make sure you have comprehensive medical insurance before you leave. For HIV testing and HIV/AIDS counselling, *see right*.

For HIV testing and HIV/AIDS counselling, *see right*.

ACCIDENT & EMERGENCY

You will be billed for any emergency treatment. Call your travel insurance company before seeking treatment to find out which hospitals accept your insurance. The following hospitals have emergency rooms:

New York Presbyterian/ Lower Manhattan Hospital
170 William Street, between Beeckman & Spruce Streets (1-212 312 5000). Subway 1 to Chambers Street; 2, 3 to Fulton Street; 4, 5, 6 to Brooklyn Bridge-City Hall.

Mount Sinai Hospital
Madison Avenue, at 100th Street, Upper East Side (1-212 241 6500). Subway 6 to 103rd Street.

New York-Presbyterian Hospital/Weill Cornell Medical Center
525 E 68th Street, at York Avenue, Upper East Side (1-212 746 5454). Subway 6 to 68th Street.

Mount Sinai Roosevelt Hospital
1000 Tenth Avenue, at 59th Street, Upper West Side (1-212 523 4000). Subway A, B, C, D, 1 to 59th Street-Columbus Circle.

CLINICS

Walk-in clinics offer treatment for minor ailments. Most clinics will require immediate payment for treatments and consultations,

though some will send their bill directly to your insurance company if you're a US resident. You will have to file a claim to recover the cost of any prescription medication that is required.

Beth Israel Medical Group
Primary-care facilities offering by-appointment and walk-in services. *55 E 34th Street, between Madison & Park Avenues, Murray Hill (1-212 252 6000, www.wehealny.org/ services/bimg). Subway 6 to 33rd Street. Open walk-in 8am-5pm Mon-Fri; 9am-2pm Sat, Sun; also by appt. Cost from $125. Other location 309 W 23rd Street, at Eighth Avenue, Chelsea (1-212 256 7000).*

NY Hotel Urgent Medical Services
This clinic can provide everything from a simple prescription to urgent medical care. House calls are available. *Suite 1D, 952 Fifth Avenue, between 76th & 77th Streets, Upper East Side (1-212 737 1212, www.travelmd.com). Subway 6 to 77th Street. Open 24hrs by appt only. Cost from $200.*

DENTISTS

New York County Dental Society
Can provide local referrals. An emergency line at the number below runs outside office hours; alternatively, use the search facility on the society's website. *1-212 573 8500, www.nycdental society.org. Open 9am-5pm Mon-Fri.*

OPTICIANS

Morgenthal Frederics
The house-designed, handmade frames displayed in Morgenthal Frederics' Soho shop (which has a stylish interior courtesy of David Rockwell) exude quality and subtly nostalgic style. Frames start at around $325 for plastic, but the buffalo horn and gold ranges are more expensive. *399 W Broadway, at Spring Street, Soho (1-212 966 0099,*

www.morgenthalfrederics.com). Subway C, E to Spring Street. Open 11am-8pm Mon-Fri (10am-7pm in autumn & winter); 11am-7pm Sat; noon-6pm Sun. Other locations throughout the city.

PHARMACIES

The fact that there's a **Duane Reade** pharmacy on almost every corner of Manhattan is lamented among chain-deriding locals; however, it is convenient if you need an aspirin pronto. Several branches, including the one at 250 W 57th Street, at Broadway (1-212 265 2101, www.duanereade.com), are open 24 hours. Competitor **Rite Aid** (with one of several 24-hour branches at 301 W 50th Street, at Eighth Avenue, 1-212 247 8384, www.riteaid.com) is also widespread. For New York's oldest apothecary, **CO Bigelow**, *see p77*.

STDs, HIV & AIDS

For the National STD & AIDS Hotline, *see right* **Helplines**.

NYC Department of Health Chelsea Health Center
Call 311 or visit www.nyc.gov for additional free clinics. *303 Ninth Avenue, at 28th Street, Chelsea (no phone). Subway C, E to 23rd Street. Open walk-in 8.30am-3pm Tue-Sat.*

Gay Men's Health Crisis
GMHC was the world's first organisation dedicated to helping people with AIDS, and offers testing, counselling and other services on a walk-in and appointment basis, regardless of sexual orientation. The Testing Center is now located within the new Center for HIV Prevention (224 W 29th Street, between Seventh & Eighth Avenues, Chelsea, 1-212 367 1100). Check the website for separate walk-in and appointment-only hours.

446 W 33rd Street, at Tenth Avenue, Hell's Kitchen (1-212 367 1000, 1-800 243 7692 HIV/AIDS helpline, www.gmhc.org). Subway A, C, E, 1, 2, 3 to 34th Street-Penn Station. Open Centre 10am-5pm Mon-Fri. Hotline 2-6pm Mon, Fri; 10am-2pm Wed; recorded information at other times.

CONTRACEPTION & ABORTION

Planned Parenthood of New York City
The best-known network of family-planning clinics in the US. Counselling and treatment are available for a full range of needs, including abortion, contraception, HIV testing and treatment of STDs.
Margaret Sanger Center, 26 Bleecker Street, at Mott Street, Greenwich Village (1-212 965 7000, 1-800 230 7526, www.ppnyc.org). Subway B, D, F, M to Broadway-Lafayette Street; N, R to Prince Street; 6 to Bleecker Street. Open 8am-4.30pm Mon, Tue; 8am-6.30pm Wed-Fri; 7.30am-4pm Sat. Other location 44 Court Street, between Joralemon & Remsen Streets, Brooklyn Heights, Brooklyn (1-212 965 7000).

HELPLINES

All numbers are open 24 hours unless otherwise stated.

Addictions Hotline
1-800 522 5353.
Alcoholics Anonymous
1-212 647 1680. Open 9am-2am daily.
Cocaine Anonymous
1-212 262 2463.
National STD & AIDS Hotline
1-800 232 4636.
Pills Anonymous
1-212 874 0700 recorded information.
Samaritans
Counselling for suicide prevention. *1-212 673 3000.*
Special Victims Liaison Unit of the NYPD Rape Hotline
1-212 267 7273.

Safety & Security

New York's crime rate, particularly for violent crime, has waned during the past two decades. Most crime occurs late at night and in low-income neighbourhoods. Don't arrive in NYC thinking your safety is at risk wherever you go; it is unlikely that you will ever be bothered.

Still, a bit of common sense won't hurt. Don't flaunt your money and valuables, keep phones and other electronic gadgets out of sight, and try not to look obviously lost. Avoid deserted and poorly lit streets; walk facing oncoming traffic so no one can drive up alongside you undetected, and close to or on the street; muggers prefer to hang back in doorways and shadows. If you are threatened, hand over your valuables at once, then dial 911.

Be extra alert to pickpockets and street hustlers – especially in crowded, tourist-heavy areas like Times Square.

Directory

Index

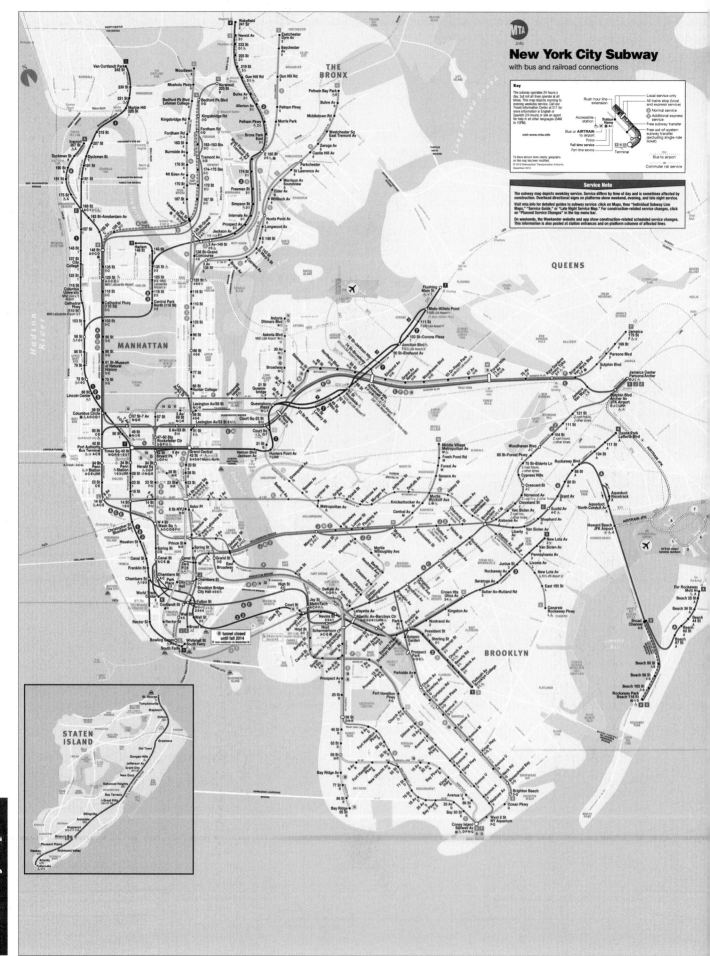

New York City Subway with bus and railroad connections

Subway Map